1 BORN GREAT ?
  (while at it or come
  natural)

2 effect of education

3 effect of parents

4 effect of environment

5 outstanding quality

6 greatest shortcoming

7 turning pt in life

8 would he be successful today?

9 would he be successful
  in another area.

10 any resemblance to me.

.00
23
TT

ADVENTURES IN GOOD

(FOR GRADES 7-12)

TEACHER'S MAN

ADVENTURES

IN

POETRY

An Introduction and a Collection

EDWIN C. CUSTER

Harcourt Brace Jovanovich, Inc.

New York   Chicago   San Francisco   Atlanta   Dallas

EDWIN C. CUSTER, presently a member of the Department of English of Kent School, Kent, Connecticut, was formerly Instructor of English at The Hill School, Pottstown, Pennsylvania. He has also taught at Mercersburg Academy in Pennsylvania and at Thomas Jefferson School, St. Louis, Missouri.

This book is dedicated to Edward Tuck Hall, Headmaster of The Hill School.

Grateful acknowledgment is due to William W. Patterson for his thorough and helpful criticism of the manuscript of this book.

ACKNOWLEDGMENTS

Brandt & Brandt: "The Shrine of Gettysburg," "Jake Diefer Leaves His Native Pennsylvania" from *John Brown's Body.* Holt, Rinehart & Winston, Inc. Copyright 1927, 1928 by Stephen Vincent Benét. Copyright renewed 1955, 1956 by Rosemary Carr Benét. "Concert Party" from *Picture Show.* E. P. Dutton & Company, Inc. Copyright 1920, 1948 by Siegfried Sassoon. Reprinted by permission of Brandt & Brandt. *The Clarendon Press, Oxford:* "London Snow," "Nightingales," from *The Shorter Poems by Robert Bridges.* Reprinted by permission of The Clarendon Press. *Dodd, Mead & Company,* and *William Heinemann, Ltd.:* "Modern Beauty" Reprinted by permission of Dodd, Mead & Company from *Poems* by Arthur Symons, and by permission of William Heinemann, Ltd., from *The Poems of Arthur Symons. Doubleday & Company, Inc., A. P. Watt & Son, Macmillan Company of Canada, Ltd.:* "If" from *Rewards and Fairies* by Rudyard Kipling. "The Ballad of East and West," "Danny Deever," from *Departmental Ditties and Ballads and Barrack-Room Ballads* by Rudyard Kipling. Reprinted by permission of Mrs. George Bambridge, Doubleday and Company, Inc., A. P. Watt & Son, and Macmillan Company of Canada, Ltd. *Norma Millay Ellis:* "Wild Swan," "I shall go back again to the bleak shore" from *Collected Poems,* Harper & Row, Publishers. Copyright 1921–1923–1948–1951 by Edna St. Vincent Millay and Norma Millay Ellis. Permission of Norma Millay Ellis. *Charles Goodwin:* "Soundings" Reprinted from *Experiment* Magazine by permission of Charles Goodwin: "Lyric" by Charles

ISBN 0-15-345000-2

Goodwin. *Harcourt, Brace & World, Inc.:* "in Just—," "Sonnet," (a wind has blown) Copyright 1923, 1951 by E. E. Cummings. Reprinted from *Poems 1923–1954* by E. E. Cummings by permission of Harcourt, Brace & World, Inc. "Jazz Fantasia," "Wind Song" from *Smoke and Steel* by Carl Sandburg, copyright 1920 by Harcourt, Brace & World, Inc.; renewed 1948 by Carl Sandburg. Reprinted by permission of the publishers. "A Black November Turkey" Copyright 1953 by *The New Yorker* Magazine, Inc. Reprinted from *Things of This World* by Richard Wilbur by permission of Harcourt, Brace & World, Inc. "The Holy Innocents" from *Lord Weary's Castle*, copyright 1944, 1946 by Robert Lowell. "Confession Overheard in a Subway" from *Afternoon of a Pawnbroker and Other Poems*, copyright 1943 by Kenneth Fearing. Reprinted by permission of Harcourt, Brace & World, Inc. *Harcourt, Brace & World, Inc.,* and *Faber and Faber, Ltd.:* "The Love Song of J. Alfred Prufrock," "The Hollow Men," "Journey of the Magi," from *Collected Poems of T. S. Eliot*, copyright 1936 by Harcourt, Brace & World, Inc., and reprinted with their permission. From *Collected Poems 1909–1935* by T. S. Eliot published by Faber & Faber, Ltd., and reprinted with their permission. *Harper & Row, Publishers:* "Warning," "The Sword" from *Spell Against Death* by Harold Lewis Cook. Copyright 1933 by Harold Lewis Cook. Reprinted by permission of Harper & Row, Publishers. *Raymond P. Holden:* "Christmas Eve, 1959" by Raymond P. Holden. Reprinted by permission of the author. *Holt, Rinehart & Winston, Inc.:* "The Pasture," "Stopping by Woods on a Snowy Evening," "Neither Out Far nor In Deep," "The Death of the Hired Man," "Acquainted with the Night," "A Leaf-Treader," "Provide, Provide," "Departmental," "Bereft," from *Complete Poems of Robert Frost*. Copyright 1923, 1928, 1930, 1939 by Holt, Rinehart & Winston, Inc. Copyright 1936 by Robert Frost. Copyright renewed 1951, © 1956 by Robert Frost. "Fog" from *Chicago Poems* by Carl Sandburg. Copyright 1916 by Holt, Rinehart & Winston, Inc. Copyright renewed 1944 by Carl Sandburg. "Grass" from *Cornhuskers* by Carl Sandburg. Copyright 1918 by Holt, Rinehart & Winston, Inc. Copyright renewed 1946 by Carl Sandburg. All poems reprinted by permission of Holt, Rinehart & Winston, Inc. *Holt, Rinehart & Winston, Inc.,* and *The Society of Authors:* "Eight O'Clock" from *Complete Poems* by A. E. Housman. Copyright 1922 by Holt, Rinehart & Winston, Inc. Copyright renewed 1950 by Barclays Bank, Ltd. "The Carpenter's Son," "Farewell to barn and stack and tree," "To an Athlete Dying Young," "White in the moon the long road lies," from "A Shropshire Lad"—Authorized Edition—from *Complete Poems* by A. E. Housman. © 1959 by Holt, Rinehart & Winston, Inc. All poems reprinted by permission of Holt, Rinehart & Winston, Inc. Permission has also been granted by The Society of Authors as the literary representative of the Estate of the late A. E. Housman and Messrs. Jonathan Cape, Ltd., publishers of A. E. Housman's *Collected Poems. Houghton Mifflin Company:* "Little Exercise" from *Poems: North and South* by Elizabeth Bishop; "Ars Poetica," "The End of the World" from *Collected Poems* by Archibald MacLeish; "Meeting House Hill" by Amy Lowell. All poems reprinted by permission of Houghton Mifflin Company. *Alfred A. Knopf, Inc.:* "War Is Kind," "I Saw a Man," "The Wayfarer" from *The Collected Poems of Stephen Crane.* Copyright 1930 by Alfred A. Knopf, Inc. "Piazza Piece," "Janet Waking," from *Selected Poems* by John Crowe Ransom. Copyright 1927, 1945 by Alfred A. Knopf, Inc. "Madman's Song" from *Collected Poems of Elinor Wylie.* Copyright 1932 by Alfred A. Knopf, Inc. "Gallant Château" copyright 1935, 1936, 1954 by Wallace Stevens, "Bouquet of Belle Scavoir," "Of Modern Poetry," copyright 1954 by Wallace Stevens. All poems reprinted from *The Collected Poems of Wallace Stevens* by permission of Alfred A. Knopf, Inc. *J. B. Lippincott Company* and *Hugh Noyes:* "The Highwayman" from *Collected Poems,* Volume I, by Alfred Noyes. Copyright 1913, 1941 by Alfred Noyes. Published by J. B. Lippincott Company. *Little, Brown & Company:* "If I should die," "The mountain sat upon the plain," "Elysium is as far," "A route of evanescence," "My life closed twice," "These are the days when birds come back" ("Indian Summer"), "There's a certain slant of light," "I taste a liquor never brewed," and "I like to see it lap the miles," from *Poems by Emily Dickinson,* edited by Martha Dickinson Bianchi and Alfred Leete Hampson. "After great pain" from *Poems by Emily Dickinson.* Copyright 1929 by Martha Dickinson Bianchi. © 1957 by Mary L. Hampson. Reprinted by permission of Little, Brown & Company. *Liveright Publishing Corporation:* "North Labrador," "Fear," "Postscript," "At Melville's Tomb," from *The Collected Poems of Hart Crane.* By permission of *Liveright,* Publishers, N.Y. © R–1961, by Liveright Publishing Corp. *The Macmillan Company:* "Karma," "New England," reprinted with permission of the publisher from *Collected Poems* by Edwin Arlington Robinson. Copyright 1925 by The Macmillan Company, Copyright 1952 by Ruth Nivison and Barbara R. Holt. "Mr. Flood's Party" Reprinted with permission of The Macmillan Company from *Collected Poems* by Edwin Arlington Robinson. Copyright 1921 by Edwin Arlington Robinson. Copyright 1949 by Ruth Nivison. "The Leaden-Eyed" reprinted with the permission of the publisher from *Collected Poems* by Vachel Lindsay. Copyright 1914 by The Macmillan Company. Copyright 1942 by Elizabeth C. Lindsay. "Sea Fever," "West Wind," reprinted with the permission of the publisher from *Poems* by John Mase-

vi   *Acknowledgments*

Modern Library, Inc. Reprinted from *The Selected Poetry of Robinson Jeffers.* "Voyage West" copyright 1941 by Archibald MacLeish. Reprinted from *Actfive and Other Poems* by Archibald MacLeish. "Auto Wreck" (*Person, Place and Thing*) copyright 1941 by Karl Shapiro. Reprinted from *Poems 1940–1953* by Karl Shapiro. All three poems reprinted by permission of Random House, Inc. *Random House, Inc.* and *Faber & Faber, Ltd.:* "The Unknown Citizen," "Musée des Beaux Arts," "In Memory of W. B. Yeats" (*Another Time*), copyright 1940 by W. H. Auden. Reprinted from *The Collected Poems of W. H. Auden* by permission of Random House, Inc. Reprinted from *Collected Poems* by permission of Faber & Faber, Ltd. "The Express" copyright 1934 and renewed 1961 by Stephen Spender. Reprinted from *Collected Poems 1928–1953* by Stephen Spender by permission of Random House, Inc. Reprinted from *Collected Poems* by permission of Faber & Faber, Ltd. "The Mask" copyright 1942 by Stephen Spender. Reprinted from *Ruins and Visions* by Stephen Spender by permission of Random House, Inc. Reprinted from *Collected Poems* by Stephen Spender by permission of Faber & Faber, Ltd. *Charles Scribner's Sons:* "Silence" (Copyright 1927 Charles Scribner's Sons; renewal copyright 1955) is reprinted with the permission of Charles Scribner's Sons from *Poems Old and New* (1956) by John Hall Wheelock. "Cliff Klingenhagen," "The Clerks," "George Crabbe" from *The Children of the Night* by Edwin Arlington Robinson (Charles Scribner's Sons). *Martin Secker & Warburg, Limited:* "To a Poet a Thousand Years Hence" from *Collected Poems* by James Elroy Flecker. Reprinted by permission of Martin Secker & Warburg, Limited. *The Society of Authors:* "The Listeners" from *Collected Poems* by Walter de la Mare. Reprinted by permission of the Literary Trustees of Walter de la Mare and The Society of Authors as their representative. *Mrs. Edward Thomas:* "The New House" by Edward Thomas. Reprinted with the permission of Mrs. Edward Thomas. *Peter Viereck:* "Kilroy" Reprinted from Peter Viereck's book *Terror & Decorum,* winner of the 1949 Pulitzer prize for poetry, published by Charles Scribner's Sons, New York. Copyright owned by author.

CONTENTS

xvi

xx

PREFACE

To many people poetry is the last thing any normal human being would want to have anything to do with. Some think of it as a sing-song language that rambles on about pretty flowers or duty or beauty or something else equally tiresome. Others think of it as something immensely beyond their reach, something to be kept on a dusty shelf and spoken of as great or profound but scarcely to be understood or enjoyed—except by a few geniuses or quacks. Still others think of poetry as an elaborate, roundabout way of saying something very simple and obvious: "If that is what the poet meant, then why didn't he say it that way?"

Here are two lines which "say" approximately the same thing:

> The empty desert stretches as far as we can see

> The lone and level sands stretch far away

The purpose of this book is to help you toward an awareness of the difference between these two lines. Here are some more examples. Can you see any difference between these lines?

> The yellow fog that brushes against the window-panes

> The yellow fog that rubs its back upon the window-panes

or these?

> And each slow dusk a drawing-down of blinds

> And every evening the blinds are drawn down

or these?

> [life] is a tale
> Told by an idiot, full of sound and fury,
> Signifying nothing

> Life is noisy and meaningless

or these?

> when the ground is full of wonderful puddles
>
> when the world is puddle-wonderful

Because good poetry is not always easy to understand, the process of discovering what it is all about must be a gradual one. It involves reading many poems and thinking about them. This process need not be a painful one. If you are willing to admit that your present tastes and opinions are not necessarily going to be with you forever, you will probably find an increasing pleasure in poetry. Bear in mind that man has enjoyed hearing or reading poetry since the beginning of recorded history.

In this book Part One, "An Introduction to Poetry," is a discussion of some of the important elements and characteristics of poetry. Part Two, "A Collection of British and American Poems," is a representative selection of the best poetry that has been written in English from the fifteenth century to our own day. Some of the poems in this book are simple, some are difficult. Even the simplest will show you that a good poem is a complex organization of sound, mood, idea, and implication. You will see that poetry deals with all attitudes, ideas, and things—from a spider to the most abstract philosophical conception. Poetry takes all human experience for its province and in so doing enlarges our vision and our understanding.

AN INTRODUCTION TO POETRY

paring experience to a lamp. He is using a specific *image* to suggest an abstract idea.

You will note too that the image of the lamp evokes an emotional response. Had Patrick Henry said merely that experience is the only guide he knows, the statement would have been abstract and flat. The words *lamp* and *feet* bring this idea into sharper focus. They suggest more than they say. For instance, at night a lamp prevents one from stumbling; it can light the twisting path to one's destination. The image suggests, or *connotes,* many other things too; and that is why Patrick Henry used it—to reinforce and make rich and dramatic his *idea* about experience and conduct.

Here is another example:

> Uncultivated minds are not full of wild flowers. Villainous weeds grow in them, and they are the haunt of toads.
>
> —*Logan Pearsall Smith*

Here author is attempting to communicate a certain attitude by using specific image. Had he said merely that uncultivated minds are innocent and natural, but evil and ugly, he would have sacrificed effect. "Villainous weeds" and "the haunt of toads" suggest much more than "evil" and "ugly."

The rative use of vivid and connotative language is essentially the of poetry; but as you have seen, it can also appear in pro difference is one of degree.

As r of fact, the only language that completely avoids figure which is the language of mathematics or of chemistry. There is in "$3xy + 2z$" or in "H_2O." But the minute you say "water" of "H_2O," an element of poetry gets in. In different situ word *water* can suggest many things. Notice the difference tions of *water* in the following quotations:

> Go get some water
> wash this filthy witness from your hands.
> —*Shakespeare*

> Water, water, everywhere,
> Nor any drop to drink.
> —*Coleridge*

Poetry is very difficult to define; no single statement can describe it completely. The best anyone can do is to make a series of statements that point the way to an understanding of the nature of poetry and then to offer some poems that will illustrate the statements. Even though we may not be able to define poetry, we can learn to recognize it and to respond to it in its various forms.

Before we begin, however, we must be clear about what poetry is *not*. People who care little for poetry (and even some who claim to like it) tend to hold three highly questionable beliefs about its nature: (1) poetry is a way of saying something "poetic"; (2) poetry is a means of communicating information; (3) poetry is a vague language. Let's examine these ideas one by one:

1. Is poetry a way of saying something "poetic"?

There is no such thing as a "poetic" or an "unpoetic" subject. The poetry is created by the way the poet treats his subject. Some of the finest poetry is about ordinary or even sordid events, dull or even dismal scenes. The description of a beautiful scene or emotion does not in itself make a beautiful poem. It would take anyone about two minutes to write something like this:

A Moonlit Night

> The golden moon shines beautifully on the water,
> And O! how I wish you were here!
> Most lovely of women, most charming daughter
> Of Love—my own, my dear!

Isn't that ridiculous! And yet the subject is pretty enough, is it not? Now look at the following poem:

A Deep Sworn Vow

WILLIAM BUTLER YEATS
1865–1939

Others because you did not keep
That deep-sworn vow have been friends of mine;
Yet always when I look death in the face,
When I clamber to the heights of sleep,
Or when I grow excited with wine,   5
Suddenly I meet your face.

The picture here isn't half as charming, and the tone is not romantic; yet this is a powerful and dramatic poem. The difference between it and the first poem is one of the subjects of this book.

2. *Is poetry a means of communicating information?*

Anyone can understand the value of an article describing the causes and effects of the War Between the States or explaining what to do if your car breaks down. We could not get along without the communication of this kind of knowledge. Poetry is another kind of communication, and it gives us another kind of knowledge. It gives us knowledge only in the sense that it describes, comments on, and makes meaningful various aspects of experience. Having read a good poem—"A Deep Sworn Vow," for instance—you will have gained a new insight into experience; but you will not necessarily profit immediately from this insight. A poem could be written about the breakdown of a car, but you would not read it in order to learn what to do in that emergency; you would read it for other reasons.

For what other reasons? Perhaps the problem will become clearer if we compare a poem to a painting or a musical composition or a statue. The "function" of a painting or a symphony is easier to understand because we can see that neither is concerned with communicating information or with usefulness. But because poetry uses words and words are most often used to communicate information, we tend to confuse its purpose with the purpose of, say, the newspaper article, whose aim is to communicate information; or with the advertisement, whose aim is to lead the reader to purchase some product. A great deal of the misunderstanding about poetry arises from the idea that poetry should be practical or useful—that it is a prettified way of communicating information or encouraging a certain kind of behavior.

Poetry exists for itself, not for what it can do. And it does not deal primarily with information, but rather with ideas, attitudes, and emotions.

3. *Is poetry a vague language?*

Poetry deals with ideas and attitudes and emotions rather with information, and it does so through *imagery*. An image representation in words of any sense experience—for instance vivid description of a sound or a smell or a texture. Most common images are pictures to be visualized. As you will see, the imagery makes the abstract or the general become concrete and vivid. Here is a fairly general and abstract statement: is a period of physical decay." Now here are two lines from

> An aged man is but a paltry thing,
> A tattered coat upon a stick . . .
> —*Yeats*

The ideas expressed in each statement are approximate but the image of the scarecrow is concrete and vi *suggests* the idea and suggests it in the most precise

Having glanced at a few of the basic misconcepti we are ready to reach some positive conclusions Poetry is a method of expression made vivid and use of imagery and figures of speech. Because language, it suggests more than it says; and bec titudes rather than with information, it achie tensity greater than that of most prose.

Of course, many of these statements are t prose.

> I have but one lamp by which my fe
> that is the lamp of experience.

Here you see that the author is express figure of speech called *metaphor*, a form

> Great waves looked over others coming in,
> And thought of doing something to the shore
> That water never did to land before.
> > —*Frost*

Or take the word *night*. It can mean many things: the time from dusk to dawn; intellectual, moral, or spiritual darkness; a period of affliction; the period after life; and so on. Notice the use of *night* in the two following quotations. In both it means literally, or *denotes*, the period between dusk and dawn, but in each case it *connotes* a different attitude toward night.

> I arise from dreams of thee
> In the first sweet sleep of night.
> > —*Shelley*

> > Come, thick night,
> And pall thee in the dunnest smoke of Hell.
> > —*Shakespeare*

Without reading any more of either of these poems, we can easily see that *night* in the first is quite different from *night* in the second. As we shall see in almost every poem we read, words derive their significance from the way the poet uses them and from their relationship to the words that surround them.

As soon as you put words together, you are in a sense creating poetry because your words have connotations as well as denotations, that is, suggestions or overtones as well as literal meanings. As you have seen, poetry in general uses words with greater precision than does prose. The poet uses a particular word rather than another that denotes the same thing because his word connotes something more.

Poetry deals with the *quality* of things, with the sheer sensation of being alive. It records experiences so intense that they can be expressed in no other way. Poetry achieves its intensity in many ways: through simplicity and restraint and understatement as well as through vividness and precision of description.

We can now make three positive statements about poetry:

1. It creates its total effect through imagery and figures of speech.
2. It is a language of suggestion as well as statement, of connotation as well as denotation.

3. It is a language of intense awareness and *therefore* of heightened emotion.

To these we might add a fourth statement:

4. It communicates its total effect through *form* or *structure*.

The form helps to create the meaning. A poem is not a *means* of expressing an idea; it *is* the idea. If the meaning is implied in the imagery, you remove the meaning when you remove the imagery. Even a rather ordinary idea can be turned into something fresh and vivid and dramatic if it is suggested through images ordered and arranged into a formal structure.

Ozymandias*

PERCY BYSSHE SHELLEY
1792–1822

I met a traveler from an antique land
Who said: Two vast and trunkless legs of stone
Stand in the desert. Near them, on the sand,
Half sunk, a shattered visage lies, whose frown,
And wrinkled lip, and sneer of cold command,   5
Tell that its sculptor well those passions read
Which yet survive, stamped on these lifeless things,
The hand that mocked them, and the heart that fed; °
And on the pedestal these words appear:
"My name is Ozymandias, king of kings: 10
Look on my works, ye Mighty, and despair!"
Nothing beside remains. Round the decay
Of that colossal wreck, boundless and bare
The lone and level sands stretch far away.

* **Ozymandias** (ŏz′ĭ·măn′dĭ·ăs): a version of one of the names of Rameses II (1324?–1258? B.C.), a famous Egyptian king. 7–8. **Which . . . fed:** the passions of the king, as shown on the statue's face, have survived both the hand of the sculptor, who imitated ("mocked") them, and the heart of the king, which caused ("fed") them. (Notice the small circle after the word *fed*. This sign is used throughout this book to call your attention to each word or phrase that is explained in a footnote. The number in the footnote refers to the line of the poem.)

A paraphrase of this poem might say something like this: *Even the glory of mighty kings and empires fades away; pretensions are empty in death.* Without using Shelley's imagery, that is about as near as we can come to what he has said. And that isn't very near. The prose statement is direct and dull: direct because it leaves nothing to the imagination, suggests nothing beyond what it says; and dull because it has been said so often that it has become trite.

How has Shelley taken a common idea and made it seem fresh and interesting? He has used an image to *suggest* his idea. Nowhere does he *say* that power is transitory and vain. The idea is implied by the image he evokes of the broken statue. Into the vivid and specific image we read the abstract and general idea.

Notice how casually Shelley introduces the theme:

> I met a traveler from an antique land
> Who said . . .

By beginning in this manner, Shelley suggests that what is to follow is not his idea: he is merely reporting what he has heard from a chance acquaintance. The opening is deliberately casual. The importance of what follows is dramatized by its contrast with the offhand tone of the introduction.

In the desert the traveler has seen a broken statue. Only the legs are still standing. The head is half buried in the sand beside them, and the body is nowhere to be seen. The expression on the face is sneering and haughty, as befits a man of great power and fame. The traveler reads the inscription:

> "My name is Ozymandias, king of kings:
> Look on my works, ye Mighty, and despair!"

Apparently Ozymandias at the height of his power ordered a statue of himself to be carved. It stood, proudly, in the midst of his glorious empire. "'Look on my works, ye Mighty,'" says Ozymandias, "'and despair!'" Now, all that is left of the "king of kings" are a head and two legs of stone in the sand. The once mocking king is himself mocked by his own statue—a statue that has become a symbol, not of power and glory, but of the transitory nature of power and glory. The two stone legs in the middle of the desert make vivid the idea that earthly power must crumble and is therefore vain. What is left of the great empire which surrounded the statue? After the pompous inscription, the stark simplicity of the last line comes with ironic shock.

The lone and level sands stretch far away.

Poetry is an economical language because it uses no unessential words or details. Our analysis of "Ozymandias" uses more words than the poem does but doesn't begin to say as much. Without the use of imagery we have to express our thoughts abstractly. Imagery conveys meaning more quickly and more vividly.

"Ozymandias" illustrates various elements of the poetic method. The following chapters will deal more thoroughly with the elements of poetry. Bear in mind constantly that a poem owes its total effect to all of its elements—imagery, sound, connotation, tone, and rhythm —working together and reinforcing each other. That is what makes poetry so subtle, complex, and effective—and sometimes difficult.

CHAPTER II *Shades of Meaning*

Poetry is a language of suggestion as well as statement, of connotation as well as denotation. In other words, some poems have meaning on one level only, but some suggest meanings on two levels, and some reveal many shades of meaning.

If

RUDYARD KIPLING
1865–1936

If you can keep your head when all about you
    Are losing theirs and blaming it on you;
If you can trust yourself when all men doubt you,
    But make allowance for their doubting too:
If you can wait and not be tired by waiting,   5
    Or being lied about, don't deal in lies,
Or being hated, don't give way to hating,
    And yet don't look too good, nor talk too wise;

If you can dream—and not make dreams your master;
    If you can think—and not make thought your aim,   10
If you can meet with Triumph and Disaster
    And treat those two impostors just the same:
If you can bear to hear the truth you've spoken
    Twisted by knaves to make a trap for fools,
Or watch the things you gave your life to, broken,   15
    And stoop and build 'em up with worn-out tools;

If you can make one heap of all your winnings
    And risk it on one turn of pitch-and-toss,
And lose, and start again at your beginnings
    And never breathe a word about your loss: 20
If you can force your heart and nerve and sinew
    To serve your turn long after they are gone,
And so hold on when there is nothing in you
    Except the will which says to them: "Hold on!"

If you can talk with crowds and keep your virtue,   25
    Or walk with kings—nor lose the common touch,
If neither foes nor loving friends can hurt you,
    If all men count with you, but none too much:
If you can fill the unforgiving minute
    With sixty seconds' worth of distance run,   30
Yours is the earth and everything that's in it,
    And—which is more—you'll be a man, my son!

In *The Name and Nature of Poetry*, the poet A. E. Housman made
a statement that should become more and more meaningful to you.
"Poetry," he said, "is not the thing said, but the way of saying it."
And yet many people admire a poem *solely* because it says things
that are noble and true.

Few people would disagree with what Kipling says in "If." The
poem is a collection of fine ideas shrewdly conceived and smoothly
expressed. As a sermon "If" is splendid, but as a poem it exists on
only one level.

We can see this lack of depth clearly by comparing "If" with
"Ozymandias." You recall that Shelley's poem was a picture of the
impermanence and therefore the vanity of power and fame. Shelley
implied this meaning by presenting a picture of a broken statue in
the middle of a desert. The irony of the situation and the vividness
of the picture give the poem its dramatic power.

"If" is not a picture of anything. Kipling's words state very clearly
what he wants to say, but they suggest nothing beyond their literal
meaning. They say no more than a prose statement could say. Be-

cause "If" is a collection of direct statements and because there is no vital use of imagery, the lines have little power.

We have used the word *collection* on purpose. The various ideas in the verse occur in no particular order. Except for the last two lines, which contain the "point," they could be arranged in any other order. One idea does not grow from another and proceed naturally and inevitably toward a climax or development of some sort.

We can never remove the meaning of a poem from the poem itself. We have seen how the meaning is dependent on the imagery *by which it is created.* Remove the imagery and you lose the meaning. Moreover, the meaning may be valid only within the context of the poem. A famous poem by John Keats ("Ode on a Grecian Urn," page 139) ends with the astonishing lines

> Beauty is truth, truth beauty—that is all
> Ye know on earth, and all ye need to know.

If we consider this statement by itself, it becomes ridiculous. After all, there is a great deal more that we need to know. And beauty (whatever that is) isn't always truth (whatever that is), and truth certainly isn't always beauty. But within the poem itself the statement is meaningful because it proceeds naturally from all that has occurred in the poem before we reach these concluding lines.

With "If" the situation is reversed. We accept what the poet has to say, not because of the way he has said it, but in spite of the way he has said it. If we like the poem, we like it because we agree with what it says, not because it has presented an idea in a fresh and vivid light.

There is no reason why we shouldn't like such poems as "If" for what they are; but there is every reason why we should learn to go beyond them, to climb to a new level of understanding and experience. A poem which merely tells us that something is sad or true or ironic is much less powerful than a poem which lets us make the discovery for ourselves. This effect is what we refer to when we speak of the "power of suggestion." A poem which states everything and suggests nothing is a poem on only one level.

Now let us look at a poem that goes a step beyond the level of "If":

Karma*

EDWIN ARLINGTON ROBINSON
1869–1935

Christmas was in the air and all was well
With him, but for a few confusing flaws
In divers° of God's images. Because
A friend of his would neither buy nor sell,
Was he to answer for the ax that fell?   5
He pondered; and the reason for it was,
Partly, a slowly freezing Santa Claus
Upon the corner, with his beard and bell.

Acknowledging an improvident surprise,
He magnified a fancy° that he wished   10
The friend whom he had wrecked were here again.
Not sure of that, he found a compromise;
And from the fullness of his heart he fished
A dime for Jesus who had died for man.

* **Karma:** here, fate or destiny, in the sense that the consequences of a man's actions determine his future existence. (The term is from Hindu and Buddhist philosophy.) 3. **divers:** several. 10. **fancy:** whim, fanciful thought.

"Karma" differs from "If" not only because it is a more difficult poem to understand at once but also because it is based on an image. A poet uses images for their vividness and, more important, for their associations. "Karma" has two levels of experience: the first level concerns the speaker's regret over the way he has treated a friend, and the second level concerns the image of Santa Claus and the various associations it suggests.

Questions

1. Is the man in the poem completely honest with himself? What do the first few lines, especially line 5, tell you about the man?
2. Look up *irony* in the glossary. Does "Karma" employ irony? How? (Consider especially the last two lines.)
3. What do you think Robinson means by "He magnified a fancy"?

The following two poems may appear somewhat easier than "Karma."

The Pasture

ROBERT FROST
1874–1963

I'm going out to clean the pasture spring;
I'll only stop to rake the leaves away
(And wait to watch the water clear, I may):
I shan't be gone long.—You come too.

I'm going out to fetch the little calf   5
That's standing by the mother. It's so young,
It totters when she licks it with her tongue.
I shan't be gone long.—You come too.

Questions

1. What details in this little poem suggest the speaker's attitude toward his chores? What is his attitude?
2. What is this poem really about: the raking of leaves and the fetching of a calf? a farmer about to do some chores? or what?
3. During the first reading which poem, "Karma" or "The Pasture," is apparently the more difficult? Why?
4. On further reading which poem reveals more shades of meaning? Explain.

Stopping by Woods on a Snowy Evening

ROBERT FROST
1874–1963

Whose woods these are I think I know.
His house is in the village though;
He will not see me stopping here
To watch his woods fill up with snow.

My little horse must think it queer 5
To stop without a farmhouse near
Between the woods and frozen lake
The darkest evening of the year.

He gives his harness bells a shake
To ask if there is some mistake. 10
The only other sound's the sweep
Of easy wind and downy flake.

The woods are lovely, dark and deep.
But I have promises to keep,
And miles to go before I sleep, 15
And miles to go before I sleep.

Many of Frost's poems appear to be extremely simple. Certainly "Stopping by Woods on a Snowy Evening" presents no apparent difficulties to immediate understanding. A man on his way somewhere stops to watch snow falling into some woods. After a short pause he reluctantly moves on, realizing that he has a long way to go and that he has "promises to keep." Although we need not go beyond this simple level, the poem invites us to discover other shades of meaning. Perhaps "invites" is too weak a word. It "urges" us. How does it do so?

Even the first stanza suggests that a purely *literal* reading, one that ignores the connotations of the poem, does not go far enough. Notice that the speaker doesn't mention where he is going or where he is coming from but that he does mention that the owner of the woods lives in the village. Why this particular choice of detail? It is perhaps too early to guess, but the choice itself is significant.

The second stanza introduces the horse, who in the third stanza becomes impatient with his master for stopping. Now we have by implication three characters: the speaker, who wants to look at the woods; the owner of the woods, who lives in the village; and the horse, who wants to move on. What do we feel is the owner's attitude toward the woods? the horse's? Can you see how various shades of meaning are beginning to develop?

Notice that the speaker has not yet said why he has stopped. It is only in the last stanza that we are told his reason: "The woods are lovely, dark and deep." But the speaker is about to move on; the lines are a sigh of regret, a sigh followed by

> But I have promises to keep,
> And miles to go before I sleep,
> And miles to go before I sleep.

Surely by now the reader, if he is at all aware of what has been going on in the poem, will read into the "promises" and the "miles" more than their literal meaning. They have become *ambiguous*. Ambiguity (two or more possible meanings) is a weakness in most prose, but it frequently lends richness to poetry because it creates a level of meaning deeper than the meaning that appears on the surface.

The literal meaning remains, of course. No matter how many levels or shades of meaning a poem may have, the literal level must always remain as a basis for the suggested meanings. "Stopping by Woods on a Snowy Evening" begins as a simple little story. Basically it remains a simple little story, but by the time the end is reached the poem has suggested meanings far beyond the narrative. It begins with the specific and ends with the general—a method common in poetry. But the shades of meaning, or the implications, or the overtones—or whatever you choose to call them—are not pasted onto the end; they are part of the fabric of the entire poem; they develop as it proceeds. Unlike "If," "Stopping by Woods on a Snowy Evening" does not give us a series of ideas; it gives us an experience. The poem does the acting; we must do the thinking.

Why is it significant that the speaker's errand is not mentioned? Why does the speaker bother to tell us that the owner of the woods lives in the village? What does the contrast between the horse's attitude and the speaker's attitude suggest? What about the owner's attitude toward the woods? How does this poem go beyond the level of "If" and even of "Karma"? Would it be stretching imagery too far to say that "Stopping by Woods on a Snowy Evening" might be about death?

There is, perhaps, no specific answer to this last question. We may read the poem literally or we may read into it a wistful longing for a surrender of some kind, perhaps to death. Between these two ex-

tremes lie other possibilities. The poem creates a mystery, and it is
partly the excitement of mystery that gives the poem its power.

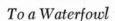

To a Waterfowl

WILLIAM CULLEN BRYANT
1794–1878

Whither, midst falling dew,
While glow the heavens with the last steps of day,
Far, through their rosy depths, dost thou pursue
    Thy solitary way?

Vainly the fowler's eye   5
Might mark thy distant flight to do thee wrong,
As, darkly seen against the crimson sky,
    Thy figure floats along.

Seek'st thou the plashy brink
Of weedy lake, or marge of river wide,   10
Or where the rocking billows rise and sink
    On the chafed ocean side?

There is a Power whose care
Teaches thy way along that pathless coast—
The desert and illimitable° air—   15
    Lone wandering, but not lost.

All day thy wings have fanned,
At that far height, the cold thin atmosphere,
Yet stoop not, weary, to the welcome land,
    Though the dark night is near.   20

And soon that toil shall end;
Soon shalt thou find a summer home, and rest,
And scream among thy fellows; reeds shall bend
    Soon, o'er thy sheltered nest.

15. **illimitable** (ĭl·lĭm′ĭt·á·b'l): immeasurable, boundless.

Thou'rt gone, the abyss of heaven   25
Hath swallowed up thy form; yet, on my heart
Deeply has sunk the lesson thou hast given,
    And shall not soon depart.

He who, from zone to zone,
Guides through the boundless sky thy certain flight,   30
In the long way that I must tread alone,
    Will lead my steps aright.

Questions

1. Like "Stopping by Woods on a Snowy Evening," "To a Waterfowl"
   begins with the specific and ends with the general. How is the last
   stanza prepared for?
2. Does Bryant draw a "moral lesson"? If so, is it merely added at the
   end, or is it implied in the action of the poem?

Nearing Again the Legendary Isle

C. DAY LEWIS

1904–

Nearing again the legendary isle°
Where Sirens sang and mariners were skinned,
We wonder now what was there to beguile
That such stout fellows left their bones behind.

Those chorus girls are surely past their prime,   5
Voices grow shrill and paint is wearing thin,
Lips that sealed up the sense from gnawing time
Now beg the favor with a graveyard grin.

1. **legendary isle:** The island of Calypso, described in Book XII of Homer's
Odyssey. The Sirens, by their melodious singing, lure sailors to destruction on
the dangerous rocks of the island. Odysseus, the hero of Homer's poem, averts
the Sirens' threat by plugging his men's ears and by having himself bound to
his ship's mast.

We have no flesh to spare and they can't bite,
Hunger and sweat have stripped us to the bone;   10
A skeleton crew we toil upon the tide
And mock the theme song meant to lure us on:

No need to stop the ears, avert the eyes
From purple rhetoric of evening skies.

Questions

1. Contrast the Sirens of Homer with the Sirens of C. Day Lewis (*see* footnote). How do they differ? How do Lewis' sailors differ from Homer's?
2. In what way is Lewis' poem a comment on the modern world?
3. Of what might Lewis' Sirens be symbolic? his sailors?

For Further Study

Among the poems in Part Two of this book, the following provide good examples of the way the poetic method develops various levels of meaning:

Robert Herrick, "Delight in Disorder," page 215
Andrew Marvell, "The Garden," page 243
John Keats, "La Belle Dame sans Merci," page 343
Thomas Hardy, "The Darkling Thrush," page 435
Theodore Spencer, "The Circus, or One View of It," page 535

It is customary to divide poetry into three categories—narrative, lyric, and dramatic—each with characteristics of its own. Like most convenient classifications, these can be very misleading. In a sense, almost any poem is narrative, lyric, and dramatic at the same time. After we have examined these three categories of poetry, we shall be better able to see how they tend to merge and sometimes to become indistinguishable.

A narrative is a story. Thus narrative poetry is poetry whose primary function is to tell a story. But that isn't the whole purpose of the poem; if it were, there would be no reason for telling the story in poetic form. As you have seen in your study of "Ozymandias," a prose statement can relate the events of a story in a fairly complete fashion, but it cannot go as far as a poem in suggestiveness or in emotional effect. The effectiveness of a narrative poem lies not in the events that it relates, but in the selection and arrangement of the events.

Here is a *ballad* (*see* Glossary), perhaps the most common kind of narrative poem. On the surface the poem seems to be very simple, but when you examine it closely, you will discover that its narrative method is a very subtle one.

Lord Randal

ANONYMOUS
15th Century

"O where hae ye been, Lord Randal, my son?
O where hae ye been, my handsome young man?"
"I hae been to the wild wood; mother, make my bed soon,
For I'm weary wi' hunting, and fain wald lie down."

"Where gat ye your dinner, Lord Randal, my son?   5
Where gat ye your dinner, my handsome young man?"
"I dined wi' my true love; mother, make my bed soon,
For I'm weary wi' hunting, and fain wald lie down,"

"What gat ye to your dinner, Lord Randal, my son?
What gat ye to your dinner, my handsome young man?"   10
"I gat eels boiled in broo;° mother, make my bed soon,
For I'm weary wi' hunting, and fain wald lie down."

"What became of your bloodhounds, Lord Randal, my son?
What became of your bloodhounds, my handsome young man?"
"O they swelled and they died; mother, make my bed soon,   15
For I'm weary wi' hunting, and fain wald lie down."

"O I fear ye are poisoned, Lord Randal, my son!
O I fear ye are poisoned, my handsome young man!"
"O yes! I am poisoned; mother, make my bed soon,
For I'm sick at the heart, and I fain wald lie down."   20

11. **broo:** broth.

As you can see, this is a murder story. An account of it in the local
newspaper might run something like this:

> Amelia, Lady Randal, widow of Lord Francis Randal,
> Twelfth Earl of Glentworth, has reported the death of her
> son, Lord Thomas Randal. He returned late Friday night
> from the house of his fiancée, Miss Pamela Wetherby-
> Parks, daughter of Col. Sir Hubert and Lady Wetherby-
> Parks, where he had been dining. He complained that he
> was tired from hunting all day and seemed to want to
> retire at once. Lady Randal, made suspicious by the ab-
> sence of her son's prize bloodhounds, questioned him at
> length about his activities. On learning that his dogs had
> swelled up and died, she suspected foul play. She finally
> forced him to admit that Miss Wetherby-Parks had poi-
> soned him. No motive for the crime has yet been ascer-
> tained.

This account contains all the facts—it has even added some. But it does not say as much as the poem does.

You may complain that we have cheated by lifting the events out of their proper historical period. Here then is a less whimsical statement of the poem: Lord Randal's mother gradually learns that her son has been poisoned by his true love. Attempting to hide this fact from his mother, Lord Randal merely says that hunting has tired him and that he would like to go to bed. His mother is suspicious, particularly since he has come home without his dogs. She questions him closely and finally forces him to admit the truth.

You can easily see that "Lord Randal" carries much more emotional impact than this summary would suggest. The rhythm and sound of the poem and the arrangement of the few facts combine to suggest an attitude and a mood that are absent from the prose account. If we seem to overemphasize the point that poetry suggests more than it says, we do so because this is a very important idea and one which is easy to overlook.

You may also object that by giving a dull, factual statement of the contents of the poem, we are not doing justice to the powers of prose. You might argue that the material of the poem could be made into a very effective short story. Of course it could. But the story would have to make use of a great many more details than the poem does; and the more the details are *suggested* rather than *stated*, the closer the story would approach the language of poetry. "Lord Randal" is an effective ballad because the details have been carefully selected and because the poem suggests much more than it states.

At this point you may want to ask about the "power of suggestion." Why is suggestion more powerful than direct statement?

When an idea or emotion or attitude is suggested rather than stated, something has to take place in the mind of the reader; he must imaginatively discover the idea for himself; and it is this mental activity, this imaginative discovery, that gives the idea its power. All good literature leaves a great deal to the imagination.

Although the facts of Lord Randal's tragedy are perhaps interesting in themselves, the two prose accounts above are dull because they are purely factual. They leave little to the imagination.

The form of the poem has much to do with its total effect. The story is framed in a series of five questions and answers, each of which is followed by a *refrain,* a phrase that is repeated regularly throughout the poem. The narrative is presented entirely through dialogue. We know only what Lord Randal chooses to tell us. That isn't very much, but it is enough. The poem takes a single dramatic moment in the life of Lord Randal and by giving us a few hints of what happened, creates a moving story.

The method is much more selective than that of a prose story. Why was Lord Randal poisoned? If this were a detective story, one would want to know the motive. In the poem it doesn't matter: we are concerned with the simple fact that Lord Randal *has* been poisoned and with his reaction to this fact. What was the relationship between his mother and his true love? The poem doesn't tell us specifically, although his mother's quick suspicions seem to hint that she mistrusted the girl. We are given just enough information to provide a glimpse into the lives of three people, and in this glimpse we see the tragic and ironic implications of the story more clearly than we would in a more detailed account. This glimpse of the personal relations of the mother, the son, and the girl stimulates our imagination (and *therefore* our emotions) more powerfully than any purely factual account could.

One of the most dramatic devices of the poem is the refrain. With each repetition it acquires more meaning. The action described in the first stanza seems innocent enough, but thereafter we become increasingly suspicious that all is not as it seems, and each repetition of the refrain becomes more sinister. Finally we realize what we had begun to suspect—that not merely fatigue but approaching death makes Lord Randal weary.

Why was Lord Randal so reluctant to tell his mother the truth? The last line gives us a hint. We have come to expect the refrain

"For I'm weary wi' hunting, and fain wald lie down"

but now we have

"For I'm sick at the heart, and I fain wald lie down"

Whenever we encounter something unexpected, we are forced into paying special attention. And the last line is the climax of the poem. Lord Randal is "sick at the heart," he is weary of life because of the way his true love has treated him. He couldn't bear to admit to his mother that what he believed in had failed him. The term *true love* has become ironical. The tragedy is not that he has been poisoned but that he has been betrayed.

So we see how, even in a simple narrative, the way the facts are organized—in other words, the form—plays an important part in the meaning of the poem.

Let us glance briefly at another ballad, this time a modern one.

Farewell to Barn and Stack and Tree

A. E. HOUSMAN
1859–1936

"Farewell to barn and stack and tree,
    Farewell to Severn° shore.
Terence, look your last at me,
    For I come home no more.

"The sun burns on the half-mown hill,   5
    By now the blood is dried;
And Maurice amongst the hay lies still
    And my knife is in his side.

"My mother thinks us long away;
    'Tis time the field were mown.   10
She had two sons at rising day,
    Tonight she'll be alone.

"And here's a bloody hand to shake,
    And oh, man, here's good-by;
We'll sweat no more on scythe and rake,   15
    My bloody hands and I.

"I wish you strength to bring you pride,
    And a love to keep you clean,
And I wish you luck, come Lammastide,°
    At racing on the green.   20

2. **Severn:** a river in east central England.   19. **Lammastide:** August 1; the date of a traditional harvest festival.

"Long for me the rick° will wait,
    And long will wait the fold,°
And long will stand the empty plate,
    And dinner will be cold."

21. **rick**: a stack of grain or hay in a field, usually protected with thatching. 22. **fold**: a pen for sheep.

In narrative poetry the story is more prominent than in other kinds of poetry. But even in narrative poetry the poet is interested primarily in selecting and arranging the events and details so as to communicate his own feeling about them and thus determine or at least influence the reader's reaction. Because the poet seems to let the story tell itself with no comment from him, the way he presents the facts and chooses the details is extremely important.

Notice the form of Housman's poem. The form is a common one, a series of four-line stanzas. It is often used for love poems, but it is not ordinarily a form in which poets present tragic or pathetic tales because a series of short stanzas usually fails to create a sustained effect. (Although, as we have seen, "Lord Randal" does use this form to present its tragic story.)

Housman, like the unknown author of "Lord Randal," chose the ballad form for a murder story. Apparently the murder was completely unpremeditated and unnecessary; and from the tone of the murderer's words, we gather that he immediately repented of the act. The speaker is telling his friend that he has just killed his brother and therefore cannot go home to his mother. The restraint of the murderer's confession is reinforced by the formality of the strict verse form, and the effect is one of stark simplicity. If the speaker had said, "Oh! oh! I've done a terrible thing! I've murdered my brother! What am I going to do? What is poor Mother going to do? What will she think of me? I can't bear to go home!" the dramatic effect would have been lost. All of this is obviously in the back of his mind anyway, and the fact that he keeps it to himself makes his situation all the more pathetic. In poetry, not saying something is often more effective than saying it. The unadorned objective speech suggests not indifference on the part of the speaker but rather a horror and despair too deep for elaborate expression. The contrast between the casual tone and the bloody event heightens the dramatic effect.

The speaker's words are full of implications. "For I come home no more." Why? He cannot return to face his mother with his guilt. Even if she did not suspect the truth, he could not go on in the old life after what he has done. The old life and the old pleasures would be a lie; and now that he has lost them forever, they have more meaning than ever before. The last line of the third stanza, "Tonight she'll be alone," implies that the mother is a widow. Why is this a significant detail?

In the fifth stanza the speaker, having shaken hands with his friend, wishes him

> . . . strength to bring you pride
> And a love to keep you clean

implying that he himself has not had and will never have a pure and simple love and that never again will he enjoy the innocent pastime of "racing on the green."

The two pictures in the last stanza are very important. In describing the rick and the fold waiting for the two young men who will never come, the poet suggests that the farm will probably fall into ruin and decay. The last stanza also implies the mother's grief. The speaker might have stated directly that his mother was going to be grief-stricken. Instead, Housman has let the image of the table suggest this: he has given us a concrete, specific picture rather than an abstract statement of grief. The table set for three functions exactly as does the broken statue in "Ozymandias." Imagery stimulates the imagination and therefore evokes a response which mere statement cannot evoke. We suspect that when the mother learns what has happened, she will not clear the table at once but will probably sit silently and motionlessly in the room for a long time, unable to understand all that has happened.

And dinner will be cold.

The two poems which we have just studied are alike in many ways. "Lord Randal" is an authentic folk ballad; "Farewell to Barn and Stack and Tree" is a modern poem modeled on the ballad structure and the ballad style. Both of these poems could just as well have been put in the chapter on dramatic poetry: each presents a dramatic scene in the life of its speaker and by a series of comments implies a story that is not actually presented.

Now let us look at a poem that tells a story directly from beginning to end.

The Destruction of Sennacherib*

GEORGE GORDON, LORD BYRON
1788–1824

The Assyrian came down like the wolf on the fold,
And his cohorts° were gleaming in purple and gold;
And the sheen of their spears was like stars on the sea,
When the blue wave rolls nightly on deep Galilee.

Like the leaves of the forest when summer is green,   5
That host with their banners at sunset were seen:
Like the leaves of the forest when autumn hath blown,
That host on the morrow lay withered and strown.

For the Angel of Death spread his wings on the blast,
And breathed in the face of the foe as he passed;   10
And the eyes of the sleepers waxed deadly and chill,
And their hearts but once heaved, and forever grew still!

And there lay the steed with his nostril all wide,
But through it there rolled not the breath of his pride:
And the foam of his gasping lay white on the turf,   15
And cold as the spray of the rock-beating surf.

And there lay the rider distorted and pale,
With the dew on his brow, and the rust on his mail;
And the tents were all silent, the banners alone,
The lances unlifted, the trumpet unblown.   20

---

* **Sennacherib** (sĕ·năk′ĕr·ĭb): king of Assyria (705–681 B.C.), who besieged Jerusalem in 701 B.C. 2. **cohorts:** legions of warriors.

And the widows of Ashur° are loud in their wail,
And the idols are broke in the temple of Baal;°
And the might of the Gentile, unsmote by the sword,
Hath melted like snow in the glance of the Lord!

21. **Ashur:** The ancient Assyrian god of war. 22. **Baal:** Another Assyrian god.

You can easily see that this poem is different from the two previous ones. In the first place the speaker is the poet himself, not a character whom he has created. He does not take part in the events of the story, but merely describes something that happened long ago. It is therefore a much less personal poem. We do not as readily identify ourselves with Sennacherib and his people as we do with Lord Randal or the young man in Housman's poem who killed his brother. Because these two men do the talking themselves, they draw us into their lives. Byron's is a much less moving poem. But Byron was not trying to move us; he was trying to excite us with the sheer force and magnitude of the event. Byron's is also a more direct poem: it begins at the beginning and describes the events that lead to the conclusion.

Before we discuss some of the devices that Byron has used to make the ancient Hebrew story vivid, here is the Biblical passage that describes the same event.

And it came to pass that night, that the angel of the Lord went out, and smote in the camp of the Assyrians an hundred fourscore and five thousand: and when they arose early in the morning, behold, they were all dead corpses.

—II Kings 19:35
(King James Version)

Byron has not given us a more complete account than the Bible has; but he has, by using various devices, given us a more vivid description. What poetic techniques has he used to achieve this vividness and sense of excitement?

Probably the first thing you noticed about the poem is its rhythm.

The rhythm is *anapestic*. That is, in each line every third syllable is accented or stressed:

With the DEW on his BROW, and the RUST on his MAIL.

Anapestic rhythm, because it contains more light than heavy beats, gives the effect of speed: on the RUN, on the RUN, on the RUN, on the RUN. This kind of rhythm would be out of character in a sad or contemplative poem, but it is admirably suited to poems describing fast-moving action. In "The Destruction of Sennacherib" the galloping anapests quicken our awareness of the action and the excitement of the poem. The rhythm compels the poem onward to its fatal climax and compels the reader with it. This sense of warlike rush is entirely lacking in the Biblical account.

Notice the vividness that a few carefully selected details give to the scene of death in the forth and fifth stanzas: " . . . the steed with his nostrils all wide . . . the foam of his gasping lay white on the turf . . . With the dew on his brow, and the rust on his mail." These are images, little flashes of realistic detail that give the poem strength and vigor.

"The Destruction of Sennacherib" contains a series of vivid *similes*. A simile is a comparison of one thing to another through the use of "like" or "as": *the old man was like an oak tree*. Although Byron's poem is not entirely dependent on these similes, it is strengthened by them:

> Like the leaves of the forest when summer is green,
> That host with their banners at sunset were seen:
> Like the leaves of the forest when autumn hath blown,
> That host on the morrow lay withered and strown.

This is a double simile, comparing the army to both living and dead leaves. The figures of speech reinforce the picture of sudden destruction.

Of course, the poet must be very careful that the comparisons he makes are legitimate ones. "The Destruction of Sennacherib" is not an altogether successful poem because the first stanza makes use of a simile that is somewhat misleading: "The Assyrian came down like a wolf on the fold." This comparison implies stealth, but the other elements in the poem contradict the idea of stealth. We are given a vivid description of an army approaching, "gleaming in purple and gold." Because the army is made visible to our eyes—"And the sheen of their spears was like stars on the sea"—we wonder how it can creep up so stealthily on the Hebrews. Why don't they see it too? Does this approach take place at night? The comparison of the sheen of the spears to starlight on the sea would seem to suggest that it does. But no matter how bright a moonlit or starlit night it may be, the purple of the cohorts would certainly not be visible, as Byron suggests it is. (In the second stanza we discover that it is not night, but dusk, and that the Hebrews did see the army, or at least the warriors "were seen.")

Another element which contradicts the impression of stealth is the rhythm. Certainly the army is not galloping if it is approaching stealthily, yet the anapestic rhythm suggests speed.

Very well then, perhaps the army is charging upon the city, as the galloping rhythm suggests. A wolf might well rush upon a fold; but he would not then lie down and go to sleep before he had killed any of the sheep, as the Assyrians apparently did. Because Byron has used a simile whose implications obscure rather than clarify what he is describing, the poem is weakened.

Now we come to a curious discovery. We have said that anapestic rhythm is suitable for a poem describing action and that in this poem the meter quickens our awareness of the action and excitement. But when we examine the poem carefully, we discover that there is no action except the approach of the army, stealthy or otherwise. After they arrive, the Assyrians go to sleep and are destroyed during the night by the Angel of Death. The results of the destruction wrought by the Angel of Death are shown in detail, but the process itself is not described (apparently it is swift and effortless). Certainly, no real action is involved. You have seen how in "Lord Randal" and "Farewell to Barn and Stack and Tree" form contributes to meaning and total effect. Can the same be said of "The Destruction of Sennacherib," or does the form, especially the rhythm, tend to contradict the narrative and weaken the effect?

The three poems that we have examined in this chapter are all fairly clear examples of narrative poetry. Some of the poems that follow contain less narrative. In one or two of them scarcely any explicit story exists at all; the story is implied by the description of a situation. With such poems the lines between narrative and lyric and dramatic become very thin or even disappear. As we shall see, almost all poems have stories behind them, whether expressed or implied. We call poetry *narrative* if the story is a prominent element, but we must be careful not to insist too much on classifications.

The Lady of Shalott

ALFRED, LORD TENNYSON
1809–1892

PART ONE

On either side the river lie
Long fields of barley and of rye,
That clothe the wold° and meet the sky;
And thro' the field the road runs by
      To many-towered Camelot;°   5
And up and down the people go,
Gazing where the lilies blow
Round an island there below,
      The island of Shalott.

Willows whiten, aspens quiver,   10
Little breezes dusk and shiver
Thro' the wave that runs for ever
By the island in the river
      Flowing down to Camelot.
Four gray walls, and four gray towers,   15
Overlook a space of flowers,
And the silent isle imbowers
      The Lady of Shalott.

3. **wold:** a treeless stretch of high ground. 5. **Camelot:** the legendary site of the court of King Arthur and his Knights of the Round Table.

By the margin, willow-veiled,
Slide the heavy barges trailed   20
By slow horses; and unhailed
The shallop° flitteth silken-sailed
      Skimming down to Camelot:
But who hath seen her wave her hand?
Or at the casement seen her stand?   25
Or is she known in all the land,
      The Lady of Shalott?

Only reapers, reaping early
In among the bearded barley,
Hear a song that echoes cheerly   30
From the river winding clearly,
      Down to towered Camelot;
And by the moon the reaper weary,
Piling sheaves in uplands airy,
Listening, whispers " 'Tis the fairy   35
      Lady of Shalott."

PART TWO

There she weaves by night and day
A magic web with colors gay.
She has heard a whisper say,
A curse is on her if she stay   40
      To look down to Camelot.
She knows not what the curse may be,
And so she weaveth steadily,
And little other care hath she,
      The Lady of Shalott.   45

And moving thro' a mirror clear
That hangs before her all the year,
Shadows of the world appear.
There she sees the highway near
      Winding down to Camelot;   50

22. shallop: a light open boat.

There the river eddy whirls,
And there the surly village-churls,
And the red cloaks of market girls,
      Pass onward from Shalott.

Sometimes a troop of damsels glad,   55
An abbot on an ambling pad,°
Sometimes a curly shepherd lad,
Or long-haired page in crimson clad,
      Goes by to towered Camelot;
And sometimes thro' the mirror blue   60
The knights came riding two and two:
She hath no loyal knight and true,
      The Lady of Shalott.

But in her web she still delights
To weave the mirror's magic sights,   65
For often thro' the silent nights
A funeral, with plumes and lights
      And music, went to Camelot;
Or when the moon was overhead,
Came two young lovers lately wed: 70
"I am half-sick of shadows," said
      The Lady of Shalott.

PART THREE

A bow-shot from her bower eaves,
He rode between the barley sheaves,
The sun came dazzling thro' the leaves,   75
And flamed upon the brazen greaves°
      Of bold Sir Lancelot.
A redcross knight for ever kneeled
To a lady in his shield,
That sparkled on the yellow field,   80
      Beside remote Shalott.

56. **pad:** a gentle horse. 76. **greaves:** armor for the legs.

y is it significant that the lady lives on an island?

at does the lady mean when she says, "I am half-sick of shadows"?

int to some examples of realistic detail. What do they contribute to
e poem?

What effect does the rhythm have on the mood of the poem?

In what way is "The Lady of Shalott" like "Lord Randal"? How do
the poems differ?

In Time of "The Breaking of Nations"

THOMAS HARDY
1840–1928

Only a man harrowing clods
  In a slow silent walk,
With an old horse that stumbles and nods
  Half asleep as they stalk.

Only thin smoke without flame   5
  From the heaps of couch grass:
Yet this will go onward the same
  Though Dynasties pass.

Yonder a maid and her wight°
  Come whispering by;   10
War's annals will fade into night
  Ere their story die.

9. wight: an archaic word for *man*.

Questions

1. How much story is actually stated in this poem? How much is implied?
2. Like "Ozymandias," this poem has an abstract theme presented
   through specific images. Can you state the theme in a few words? How
   do the images imply it?
. What does *this* mean in line 7?

The Poem as Narrative

The gemmy bridle glittered free,
Like to some branch of stars we see
Hung in the golden Galaxy.
The bridle bells rang merrily   85
    As he rode down to Camelot:
And from his blazoned baldric° slung
A mighty silver bugle hung,
And as he rode his armor rung,
    Beside remote Shalott.   90

All in the blue unclouded weather
Thick jeweled shone the saddle leather,
The helmet and the helmet feather
Burned like one burning flame together,
    As he rode down to Camelot;   95
As often thro' the purple night,
Below the starry clusters bright,
Some bearded meteor, trailing light,
    Moves over still Shalott.

His broad clear brow in sunlight glowed;   100
On burnished hooves his war horse trode;
From underneath his helmet flowed
His coal-black curls as on he rode,
    As he rode down to Camelot.
From the bank and from the river   105
He flashed into the crystal mirror,
"Tirra lirra," by the river
    Sang Sir Lancelot.

She left the web, she left the loom,
She made three paces thro' the room,   110
She saw the water lily bloom,
She saw the helmet and the plume,
    She looked down to Camelot.

87. blazoned baldric: an ornamental belt worn diagonally across the chest
and decorated with a coat of arms—that is, blazoned.

Out flew the web and floated wide;
The mirror cracked from side to side;   115
"The curse is come upon me," cried
      The Lady of Shalott.

PART FOUR

In the stormy east wind straining,
The pale yellow woods were waning,
The broad stream in his banks complaining,   120
Heavily the low sky raining
      Over towered Camelot;
Down she came and found a boat
Beneath a willow left afloat,
And round about the prow she wrote   125
      The Lady of Shalott.

And down the river's dim expanse—
Like some bold seer° in a trance,
Seeing all his own mischance—
With a glassy countenance   130
      Did she look to Camelot.
And at the closing of the day
She loosed the chain, and down she lay;
The broad stream bore her far away,
      The Lady of Shalott.   135

Lying, robed in snowy white
That loosely flew to left and right—
The leaves upon her falling light—
Thro' the noises of the night
      She floated down to Camelot;   140
And as the boat head wound along
The willowy hills and fields among,
They heard her singing her last song,
      The Lady of Shalott.

128. **seer** (sē′ẽr): one who forsees events; a prophet.

Heard a carol, mournful, holy
Chanted loudly, chanted l[...]
Till her blood was frozen s[...]
And her eyes were darkened [...]
      Turned to towered C[...]
For ere she reached upon the tide
The first house by the water side,
Singing in her song she died,
      The Lady of Shalott.

Under tower and balcony,
By garden wall and gallery,
A gleaming shape she floated by,
Dead-pale between the houses high,
      Silent into Camelot.
Out upon the wharfs they came,
Knight and burgher,° lord and dame,
And round the prow they read her name,
      The Lady of Shalott.

Who is this? and what is here?
And in the lighted palace near
Died the sound of royal cheer;
And they crossed themselves for fear,
      All the knights at Camelot:
But Lancelot mused a little space;
He said, "She has a lovely face;
God in his mercy lend her grace,
      The Lady of Shalott."

160. **burgher:** a citizen of a town.

Questions

1. Describe the story briefly. How much of the story is sugge[...]
   much is stated directly?
2. What specific thing does the Lady of Shalott do to br[...]
   upon herself, and why does she do it?

The Listeners

WALTER DE LA MARE
1873–1956

"Is there anybody there?" said the Traveler,
    Knocking on the moonlit door;
And his horse in the silence champed the grasses
    Of the forest's ferny floor.
And a bird flew up out of the turret,   5
    Above the Traveler's head:
And he smote upon the door again a second time;
    "Is there anybody there?" he said.
But no one descended to the Traveler;
    No head from the leaf-fringed sill   10
Leaned over and looked into his gray eyes,
    Where he stood perplexed and still.
But only a host of phantom listeners
    That dwelt in the lone house then
Stood listening in the quiet of the moonlight   15
    To that voice from the world of men:
Stood thronging the faint moonbeams on the dark stair
    That goes down to the empty hall,
Hearkening in an air stirred and shaken
    By the lonely Traveler's call.   20
And he felt in his heart their strangeness,
    Their stillness answering his cry,
While his horse moved, cropping the dark turf,
    'Neath the starred and leafy sky;
For he suddenly smote on the door, even   25
    Louder, and lifted his head:
"Tell them I came, and no one answered,
    That I kept my word," he said.
Never the least stir made the listeners,
    Though every word he spake   30
Fell echoing through the shadowiness of the still house
    From the one man left awake:

Aye, they heard his foot upon the stirrup,
    And the sound of iron on stone,
And how the silence surged softly backward,   35
    When the plunging hoofs were gone.

Questions

1. Here is only the shadow of a story. What is this story that is suggested
   but not revealed? Which lines clearly suggest happenings that precede
   the action of the poem?
2. Can you point out some devices that contribute to the musical effect?
   to the mood?
3. What are some of the realistic details that keep the story from being
   completely shadowy and unreal?

from *John Brown's Body*

STEPHEN VINCENT BENÉT
1898–1943

This is the eighth section of Book II of Benét's *John Brown's
Body*, a book-length poem set during the War Between the
States. In these lines Jake Diefer is leaving for service in the
Northern army.

Jake Diefer, the barrel-chested Pennsylvanian,
Hand like a ham and arms that could wrestle a bull,
A roast of a man, all solid meat and good fat,
A slow-thought-chewing Clydesdale horse of a man,
Roused out of his wife's arms. The dawn outside   5
Was ruddy as his big cheeks. He yawned and stretched
Gigantically, hawking and clearing his throat.
His wife, hair tousled around her like tousled corn,
Stared at him with sleep-blind eyes.
                              "Jake, it ain't come morning,
Already yet?"
        He nodded and started to dress.   10

She burrowed deeper into the bed for a minute
And then threw off the covers.
                              They didn't say much
Then, or at breakfast. Eating was something serious.
But he looked around the big kitchen once or twice
In a puzzled way, as if trying hard to remember it.   15
She too, when she was busy with the first batch
Of pancakes, burnt one or two, because she was staring
At the "SALT" on the salt box, for no particular reason.
The boy ate with them and didn't say a word,
Being too sleepy.
                              Afterwards, when the team   20
Was hitched up and waiting, with the boy on the seat,
Holding the reins till Jake was ready to take them,
Jake didn't take them at once.
                              The sun was up now,
The spilt-milk-mist of first morning lay on the farm,
Jake looked at it all with those same mildly puzzled eyes,   25
The red barn, the fat rich fields just done with the winter,
Just beginning the work of another year.
The boy would have to do the rest of the planting.

He blew on his hands and stared at his wife dumbly.
He cleared his throat.
                              "Well, good-by, Minnie," he said,   30
"Don't you hire any feller for harvest without you write me,
And if any more of those lightning rodders come around,
We don't want no more dum lightning rods."
                              He tried
To think if there was anything else, but there wasn't.
She suddenly threw her big, red arms around his neck,   35
He kissed her with clumsy force.
                              Then he got on the wagon
And clucked to the horses as she started to cry.

Questions

1. What are some of the realistic, commonplace details that make this
   such a vivid description?

2. The Diefers go through the motions of getting up and having breakfast as if it were an ordinary morning. What is there in their actions which suggests tension, suggests that they are trying desperately to pretend that everything is all right?
3. What are some reasons, one mentioned and several not mentioned, why they talk so little?
4. The situation itself is a sad one. Does Benét insist on its pathos or does he let the situation speak for itself?

For Further Study

The following poems in Part Two of this book are good examples of poetry that is primarily narrative in nature:

"Sir Patrick Spens," page 150

"The Wife of Usher's Well," page 151

Samuel Taylor Coleridge, "The Rime of the Ancient Mariner," page 302

Robert Frost, "The Death of the Hired Man," page 496

CHAPTER **IV** *The Poem as Lyric*

Lyric poetry is so called because in ancient days such poetry was frequently sung while the singer accompanied himself on a *lyre,* a stringed instrument somewhat like a small harp.

There are many different kinds of lyric poems with many different characteristics. In general a lyric poem does not primarily tell a story. A lyric poem may be merely a description of a landscape or of a person, it may create a mood, or it may have philosophical implications. It may be many other things as well, as we shall see as we go along. Most lyric poetry is *subjective* (personal) rather than *objective* (impersonal). That is, it communicates its author's moods, attitudes, and ideas.

The following poem is an apparently simple one, but it clearly demonstrates the subtlety and power of lyric poetry. "North Labrador" is a description of a landscape, and in the process of description a mood is created and communicated.

North Labrador

HART CRANE
1899–1932

A land of leaning ice
Hugged by plaster-gray arches of sky,
Flings itself silently
Into eternity.

"Has no one come here to win you,   5
Or left you with the faintest blush
Upon your glittering breasts?
Have you no memories, O Darkly Bright?"

Cold-hushed, there is only the shifting of moments
That journey toward no Spring—   10
No birth, no death, no time nor sun
In answer.

Although this is a description, you will note that there is almost
no indication of how the land looks. We are told that there is some
"leaning ice," over which the sky is "plaster-gray." That is all. The
poem is not meant to be a substitute for a photograph of the scene.
We are told not how the land looks, but how the poet feels about it.
Another observer of the scene might describe it in an entirely different way. Crane has given us a very particular impression of the
scene, and through this impression he has communicated an emotional experience to the reader.

What is Crane's impression, and how does he communicate it?

The first stanza is the simplest. It contains the only physical description in the poem. We have seen that poetry uses words econom-
ically and that each word is therefore very important. Five of the
words in the first stanza are particularly important to the total effect
of the poem: *hugged, arches, flings, silently,* and *eternity. Hugged*
suggests that the sky seems close to the land, that it is almost a part
of the land, indistinguishable from it. *Arches* carries this idea further: one sees nothing beyond the land but the arch of the sky enclosing it, shutting it off from the rest of the world. One of the most
impressive and awe-inspiring qualities of the scene is its silence. It
is completely silent because it is lifeless. The poet uses the word
eternity to suggest the timelessness of the land: timeless because unchanging, and unchanging because no life will change its contours
and no seasons will change its appearance.

Thus in four short lines Crane suggests pictorially that the landscape is silent, dead, timeless. *Flings* suggests action; yet it is the
very lack of action, the changelessness, that is awesomely impressive. This *paradox* (an apparent contradiction that contains some
truth) emphasizes the void, both of time and of space, in which
North Labrador exists. The speed implied by *flings* is in contrast to
the immobility of the land; and yet it is flinging itself because it is
part of the earth, which is quite literally speeding through the uni-

verse. The blurring of time and space in the poem is deliberate: it helps to imply the mysterious, unreal quality of the land's existence. And all of this creates an overwhelming sense of loneliness.

In the second stanza Crane uses a figure of speech common in poetry—*personification*, a kind of metaphor in which objects or ideas are given human attributes. The first stanza was a statement about what sort of land North Labrador is. Now all of a sudden as the poet addresses the land, we discover that he is picturing it as a woman. He also uses another device, often found in oratory—the rhetorical question:

> "Has no one come here to win you . . .
> Have you no memories . . . ?"

The poet questions the land—or as it has now become, the woman—not because he expects her to supply him with information but because he wants to pose the question in the reader's mind. Rhetorical questions suggest their own answers. By asking the questions, the poet communicates to the reader his amazement. If he had said, "No one has come here to win you . . . You have no memories," we would feel no sense of amazement. The questions are a dramatic device for suggesting more than the corresponding statements could.

"Darkly Bright" is a paradox that lends richness of meaning on two levels. If you observe a glacier or an iceberg or, indeed, an ice cube, you will notice that from some angles it glitters with a metallic brightness, whereas from other angles it appears inky black. But "darkly" also has a deeper meaning. Darkness implies mystery. The land is bright because it is icy, dark because it is mysterious, and mysterious because it is silent. Whatever secrets it has it does not share. Perhaps it has no secrets, since it has no past and no memories; this possibility too is mysterious. The land, the woman, is a dark puzzle, awe-inspiring in her silences.

In the last stanza Crane returns to the more straightforward method of the opening stanza. Again he comments on the timelessness of the scene. There is no real awareness of the progress of time, only a "shifting of moments" that leads nowhere, "toward no Spring —No birth, no death. . . ." Why is the word *shifting* exactly the right word, and how does it, like *flings*, connote more than one level of meaning?

The middle stanza is thus framed by two stanzas of highly subjective description. The emotional effect of the last stanza is greater than that of the first, because now the woman image lends it greater poignancy. It is human loneliness and isolation that Crane is picturing, not just the starkness of a landscape. One of the more common types of personification (often called *pathetic fallacy*) is that in which inanimate objects or aspects of nature are endowed with human emotions. The sea can be called angry for instance, or as in this poem, a landscape can be pictured as lonely. Literally, of course, the landscape itself is not lonely; but by looking at the landscape, we are made to experience loneliness. By thinking of the land as a woman, Crane makes the loneliness more moving because it is human loneliness. Poetry deals for the most part not with things themselves, but with man's reaction to things: the fear, joy, despair that things inspire in the human consciousness.

The total effect of "North Labrador" is the result of several elements: of the connotations of its words; of the sound of its words; and perhaps most important of all, of the paradox implied by the image of the woman. The paradox has to do with life and death. It is only through thinking of the landscape as a living human being that we fully comprehend its deadness. Because the land is given a living consciousness of its own, its deathlike isolation and timelessness are infinitely greater than they would be if it were merely a question of hills and glaciers.

At first sight Crane's seems to be a simple poem. But as you have seen, it is really a highly complex organization. The words are simple, the final impression is simple; but the method of creating that impression is not simple.

Acquainted with the Night

ROBERT FROST
1874–1963

I have been one acquainted with the night.
I have walked out in rain—and back in rain.
I have outwalked the furthest city light.

I have looked down the saddest city lane.
I have passed by the watchman on his beat   5
And dropped my eyes, unwilling to explain.

I have stood still and stopped the sound of feet
When far away an interrupted cry
Came over houses from another street,

But not to call me back or say good-by;   10
And further still at an unearthly height,
One luminary clock against the sky

Proclaimed the time was neither wrong nor right.
I have been one acquainted with the night.

The speaker of this poem is in much the same plight as is the land
in "North Labrador." Frost's method, however, is different from
Crane's. Frost's speaker is commenting on his own loneliness. Frost
does not use a metaphor to dramatize the loneliness; instead, he
gives us a series of images, the accumulated effect of which makes
the situation particularly vivid.

Notice that the poem begins and ends with the same line. When
we encounter it again at the end, we find that it means much more
than it seemed to the first time. "I have been one acquainted with
the night." Obviously the speaker means that he is familiar with the
night because he is often out in it. But *night* has meaning on another
level as well, and the gradual process by which we learn all that
the word means is one of the things that makes the poem intensely
dramatic.

"I have walked out in rain—and back in rain." For some reason the
speaker goes for nocturnal walks, even in the rain. Already we begin
to suspect what the poem is going to be about. What does the
second half of the line, "—and back in rain," suggest? What is the
effect of the dash?

In the next line we learn that his walks are in the city. Many people like to walk in the country and observe the beauties of nature;
others like to watch the busy life of crowded city streets. But this
man walks at night, when the only sounds are his own footsteps, an

occasional cry in the distance, and the steady, monotonous beat of the rain. The rain, of course, is an important element in the mood. What kind of rain is it? a sweet-smelling spring rain? a torrential downpour? or what? Does the speaker anywhere *say* what kind of rain it is? Does the poem *suggest* what kind it is?

The incident of the watchman is very significant. Why does the speaker avoid speaking to him? What is the speaker "unwilling to explain"?

On his nocturnal walks the speaker occasionally hears a cry from another street. It may be a cry of anguish or joy, but it has nothing to do with his life. No one ever calls to him. Notice that the third stanza ends in the middle of a sentence. Since this sort of break has not occurred before in the poem, the effect is an emphasis on the second half of the sentence, the half that begins the fourth stanza: "But not to call me back or say good-by."

The clock says again what the cry, the watchman, and the rain say. Why is the time "neither wrong nor right"? The clock is "at an unearthly height," alone against the dark sky. Often an illuminated clock at night seems to be higher than it really is because in the surrounding darkness it has no relation to anything else. The unearthliness of its height is a further detail of the unreality of the whole scene. The speaker is walking through life like a person in a dream.

"I have been one acquainted with the night." What are some of the implications of *night*?

Is the speaker the poet himself? Is there any way of knowing whether he is?

The poem is complete in itself even though it leaves many possible questions unanswered. Why isn't the man home asleep? What does he do in the day? Why is he so lonely? Why is his life so lacking in any purpose? We don't know. It doesn't matter. Frost has told us all that we need to know. This brief poem is simply a comment on the sadness of a particularly human experience.

The poem that follows is a comment on another aspect of experience. It is more abstract than any poem discussed so far in this chapter, but notice that the abstract theme is presented through a specific situation.

When I Heard the Learn'd Astronomer

WALT WHITMAN

1819–1892

When I heard the learn'd astronomer,
When the proofs, the figures, were ranged in columns, be-
    fore me,
When I was shown the charts and diagrams, to add, di-
    vide, and measure them,
When I sitting heard the astronomer where he lectured
    with much applause in the lecture room,
How soon unaccountable I became tired and sick,   5
Till rising and gliding out I wandered off by myself,
In the mystical moist night air, and from time to time,
Looked up in perfect silence at the stars.

When Whitman's poetry first appeared in 1855, most readers, ac-
customed to poetry with regular rhythm and rhyme schemes, were
repelled by what seemed to them to be sloppy prose passed off as
poetry. But this poem isn't as simple as it looks. Although it seems
to be a matter-of-fact account of an attitude toward an astronomy
lecture, it has much wider implications. And the total effect of the
poem derives from several subtle rhythmic devices. Whitman has
dispensed with a consistent pattern of rhythm, but that does not
mean that the poem has no rhythm at all. On the contrary, Whitman is one of the most rhythmical of poets.

The speaker says that he once attended an astronomy lecture, became bored, and left early. He went outdoors and looked at the
stars by himself. Although he does not *say* that he found this approach to the stars more satisfying (he *says* only that in the lecture
room he became tired and sick), the various sound devices imply
this.

Notice the length of the lines, particularly of lines 2, 3, and 4, in
which Whitman talks about the lecture. Notice how beginning with
line 5, in which the poet turns to an expression of emotion, the line
length decreases: the last line is shorter than all the others except
the first. Notice also that the first four lines all begin with *when*.

If you were to analyze these first four lines, you would find that their rhythm is less smooth than that of the last four lines and that they contain a larger proportion of heavy beats (that is, accented syllables).

This arrangement is not accidental. Both line length and rhythm are used deliberately to indicate the speaker's attitude toward his subject.

How do they do this? First let us consider the length of the lines.

> When the proofs, the figures, were ranged in columns
> before me,
> When I was shown the charts and diagrams, to add,
> divide, and measure them,
> When I sitting heard the astronomer where he lectured
> with much applause in the lecture room,

The lines seem to go on and on just as the professor's voice goes on and on, droning out detail after detail. The room seems stuffy; our attention wanders; and we experience a sense of relief when we come to the shorter lines. That is exactly the impression Whitman wished to convey: he is relieved when he goes out into the fresh air. Similarly the hammering repetition of *when* becomes tiresome, and we are relieved to come upon line 5.

The shift in the second half of the poem to a larger proportion of light beats has the same effect. The lines seem to go more smoothly because heavy beats tend to slow down the speed, light beats to quicken it. The first lines are interrupted by frequent commas; the last lines are relatively free of punctuation.

In the phrase "In the mystical moist night air" Whitman uses two effective devices. The repetition of the *m* sound tends here to give a flowing, musical effect. This device, the repetition of beginning consonant sounds, is called *alliteration*. The other device is that of putting three heavy beats in a row—"moist night air." None of these sounds can be slurred over, as we slur the last two syllables of "mystical," for instance. The reader is forced at this point to slow down and read the words carefully. The series of heavy accents occurring after a number of lighter ones gives emphasis.

One word more about rhythm before we examine the implications of the poem. We can see that there is no regular rhythmical pattern in the poem as a whole; but if we analyze the last line, we will find that it follows a system: almost all of the even numbered syllables are accented. ("Looked" would probably be read as an accented syllable; otherwise the line is completely regular.) This kind of rhythm—perhaps the most common in English poetry—is known as *iambic:* each foot contains two syllables, an unaccented followed by an accented. A regular line will somehow seem more musical if it occurs after a series of irregular lines. And in this case the regular iambic beat of the last line gives an effect of smoothness and striking simplicity. It is an important line, the climax of the poem, and its rhythm sets it apart from the preceding lines.

In "Acquainted with the Night" we have seen how the images suggest a great deal more about a man's life than the poet tells us. In "When I Heard the Learn'd Astronomer" Whitman uses the rhythmic devices mentioned above to reinforce what his words say and to make them more suggestive and meaningful.

So much for technical matters. What is the "point" of the poem? Does it mean what it says or does it have "hidden meaning"? Actually there is no such thing as a "hidden meaning" in poetry. We have seen that a poem usually suggests more than it says. Only when the reader is not trained to catch the suggestions of a poem, does he complain of "hidden meaning." The meaning of a poem is the poem itself, not something concealed beneath or behind the words.

"When I Heard the Learn'd Astronomer" contrasts two kinds of experience: the scientific and the spiritual. Whitman uses the astronomy lecture as a kind of parable of man's search for truth, of man's attempt to understand his place in the universe around him.

Not only do astronomers know what the stars are, but they are able to compute the distances between them, their sizes, weights, etc. This is the world of the first half of the poem. Using charts and diagrams and various scientific instruments, the astronomer explains many facts about the stars. No doubt they are useful facts.

But it is with another kind of truth that the second half of the poem deals. Man's search for this kind of truth is the theme of all religion, all myth, all art, all poetry. Man learns this kind of truth sometimes through experience, sometimes by intuition, sometimes simply by inner conviction—and sometimes not at all. It is for spiritual truth that the speaker is searching when he leaves the lecture and goes out by himself into the night to look at the stars. He has an experience which the people in the room are missing: he is looking at the stars themselves, not at charts; he is discovering not that this star is so many light-years from that star but that the stars are beautiful, mysterious, and awe-inspiring. In effect the speaker is saying to the lecturer: All right, you have told me many facts about the stars, but you have not and cannot tell me what is of far greater importance—that the stars are beautiful and mysterious, that they are beautiful *because* they are mysterious. Whitman is implying that when man becomes too concerned with factual knowledge, he is in danger of losing his capacity for awe; and when he is no longer able to be moved by the majesty of the star-filled sky, he has lost something supremely important.

The implications of Whitman's poem are based upon a paradox: the larger mysteries of life remain unsolved, and it is in the realization of our profound ignorance that we approach truth and wisdom.

> I wandered off by myself,
> In the mystical moist night air, and from time to time,
> Looked up in perfect silence at the stars.

Nightingales

ROBERT BRIDGES

1844–1930

Beautiful must be the mountains whence ye come,
And bright in the fruitful valleys the streams wherefrom
    Ye learn your song:
Where are those starry woods? O might I wander there,
    Among the flowers, which in that heavenly air   5
    Bloom the year long!

Nay, barren are those mountains and spent the streams:
Our song is the voice of desire, that haunts our dreams,
     A throe of the heart,
Whose pining visions dim, forbidden hopes profound,   10
   No dying cadence° nor long sigh can sound,
     For all our art.

Alone, aloud in the raptured ear of men
We pour our dark nocturnal secret; and then,
     As night is withdrawn   15
From these sweet springing meads° and bursting boughs of May,
   Dream, while the innumerable choir of day
     Welcome the dawn.

11. **cadence** (kā'dĕns): here, the closing strain of a piece of music.
16. **meads:** meadows.

Questions

1. Who is speaking in the first stanza? in the second and third?
2. What does the speaker in the first stanza assume about the land in which the nightingales learned their song? Why? Is his assumption correct? What does his assumption imply about his own world?
3. Does the song of the nightingales express their emotions completely? Quote the lines which give the answer. What is the nightingale's "dark nocturnal secret"?
4. How does the nightingale's song differ from that of "the innumerable choir of day"?

Dover Beach

MATTHEW ARNOLD
1822–1888

The sea is calm tonight,
The tide is full, the moon lies fair
Upon the straits; on the French coast the light
Gleams and is gone; the cliffs of England stand,

Glimmering and vast, out in the tranquil bay. 5
Come to the window, sweet is the night air!

Only, from the long line of spray
Where the sea meets the moon-blanched land,
Listen! you hear the grating roar
Of pebbles which the waves draw back, and fling, 10
At their return, up the high strand,
Begin, and cease, and then again begin,
With tremulous cadence slow, and bring
The eternal note of sadness in.

Sophocles° long ago 15
Heard it on the Aegean,° and it brought
Into his mind the turbid° ebb and flow
Of human misery; we
Find also in the sound a thought,
Hearing it by this distant northern sea. 20

The Sea of Faith
Was once, too, at the full, and round earth's shore
Lay like the folds of a bright girdle furled.
But now I only hear
Its melancholy, long, withdrawing roar, 25
Retreating, to the breath
Of the night wind, down the vast edges drear
And naked shingles° of the world.

Ah, love, let us be true
To one another! for the world, which seems 30
To lie before us like a land of dreams,
So various, so beautiful, so new,
Hath really neither joy, nor love, nor light,
Nor certitude, nor peace, nor help for pain;
And we are here as on a darkling plain 35
Swept with confused alarms of struggle and flight,
Where ignorant armies clash by night.

15. **Sophocles:** a Greek tragic dramatist of the fifth century B.C. 16. **Aegean**
(Sea): an arm of the Mediterranean Sea between Asia Minor and Greece.
17. **turbid:** muddled, confused. 28. **shingles:** pebbly shores.

Questions

1. At what point does the poem cease to be purely descriptive?
2. Arnold specifically mentions two seas. What are they? The speaker finds a difference between them. What is it?
3. What is the theme of the poem? What is the importance of the first stanza to the theme?
4. According to the speaker, what one thing of value is left in the world?
5. What have armies to do with the speaker and the moonlit sea? Why are they "ignorant" armies?

Sonnet 73

WILLIAM SHAKESPEARE
1564–1616

That time of year thou mayst in me behold
When yellow leaves, or none, or few, do hang
Upon those boughs which shake against the cold,
Bare ruined choirs, where late the sweet birds sang.
In me thou see'st the twilight of such day   5
As after sunset fadeth in the west,
Which by and by black night doth take away,
Death's second self, that seals up all in rest.
In me thou see'st the glowing of such fire
That on the ashes of his youth doth lie,   10
As the deathbed whereon it must expire,
Consumed with that which it was nourished by.
     This thou perceivest, which makes thy love more strong,
     To love that well which thou must leave ere long.

Questions

1. This is a Shakespearean sonnet, a fourteen-line poem containing three *quatrains* (four line stanzas) and a concluding *couplet* (two rhyming lines). It is a poem about old age. Is it about anything else?

2. Each quatrain states the same idea through different imagery. What are the three images?

3. The concluding couplet presents a commentary on the preceding quatrains. What is the commentary?

For Further Study

The following poems in Part Two of this book provide examples of some of the typical characteristics of lyric poetry:

CHAPTER **V** *The Poem as Drama*

We might say that narrative poetry relates a series of actions, that lyric poetry expresses personal emotions and attitudes, and that dramatic poetry analyzes character. Like most generalizations, this is true to only a very limited extent. As the poems at the end of the preceding chapters have shown you, definite lines cannot always be drawn between the categories.

So-called dramatic poems often present an action or a situation as seen through the eyes of a character created by the poet; often the poem is presented as the words of the character rather than of the poet himself—in which case the ideas and attitudes may or may not be the poet's own. One of the best-known kinds of dramatic poetry is the *dramatic monologue,* a type developed largely by the nineteenth-century English poet, Robert Browning. In the dramatic monologue the poet presents a character—who may be historical, mythical, or purely fictitious—at a crucial point in his life: he may be faced with an important decision; he may be commenting on a new discovery; he may be looking back upon his life with the insight gained from experience. Because the character interprets his situation in the light of his experience of life, we are able to learn a great deal about him and hence about human nature in general. The main interest in such poems is the character and personality of the speaker and the drama of the situation. In the dramatic monologue the speaker usually addresses his words to a second character or group of characters.

All the poems that we have studied so far we have called either narrative or lyric. Before we go on to read a dramatic poem, let us briefly examine some of the previous poems to see if they could be called dramatic as well. In a sense all poetry is dramatic, because all poetry implies a speaker and involves his reaction to some aspect of experience. Even when the poem is a purely descriptive one such as "North Labrador," it involves a special interpretation of the things described, and this interpretation is the result of a dramatic organization. We call "North Labrador" a lyric poem because the main interest is the landscape rather than the speaker; but to a small degree at least, we learn something about the speaker as well.

And all good poetry is dramatic because, like the drama, it presents its themes vividly and specifically through action or situation. It would be difficult to find a good poem which has no dramatic element at all. We can call "Lord Randal" (page 21) a narrative poem because it relates, or rather, suggests a series of events. It could equally well be called a dramatic poem. It takes a crucial moment in the life of Lord Randal and, through his conversation with his mother, dramatizes his reaction to his plight. Because we learn a little bit about his mother too, the poem is almost like a miniature play or the last scene of a tragedy. It also has a lyrical quality: it expresses a mood of despair and defeat.

Because "Acquainted with the Night" (page 46) is a comment on loneliness, we call it a lyric. In a way, though, it is a narrative: it relates what the speaker does and sees, and it suggests what he thinks. It could also be called a dramatic poem because Frost is examining through action the mood of another man, analyzing his emotions, and showing his reactions to life.

Certainly "When I Heard the Learn'd Astronomer" is highly dramatic. It describes in concrete terms a moment of heightened consciousness and awareness of nature's beauty.

So you see that few poems can be labeled as exclusively narrative, lyric, or dramatic. If the emphasis of a poem is on a story, the poem may conveniently be called narrative; if the emphasis is on the expression of an emotion or idea, the poem may conveniently be called lyric; and if the emphasis is on a reaction to a situation, the poem may conveniently be called dramatic.

In view of the difficulty of assigning a poem to a particular category, perhaps you wonder why we make the effort at all. Classifying poems merely for the sake of having classifications would be pointless. The value of labeling a poem lyric, narrative, or dramatic is that such a distinction provides a starting point for interpretation and often helps prevent misunderstandings at the outset.

Petit, the Poet

EDGAR LEE MASTERS
1869–1950

Seeds in a dry pod, tick, tick, tick,
Tick, tick, tick, like mites in a quarrel—
Faint iambics that the full breeze wakens—
But the pine tree makes a symphony thereof.
Triolets, villanelles, rondels, rondeaus.   5
Ballades by the score with the same old thought;
The snows and the roses of yesterday are vanished;
And what is love but a rose that fades? °
Life all around me here in the village:
Tragedy, comedy, valor, and truth,   10
Courage, constancy, heroism, failure—
All in the loom, and, oh, what patterns!
Woodlands, meadows, streams, and rivers—
Blind to all of it all my life long.
Triolets, villanelles, rondels, rondeaus,   15
Seeds in a dry pod, tick, tick, tick,
Tick, tick, tick, what little iambics,
While Homer and Whitman roared in the pines!

7–8. **The snows . . . fades:** these lines translate freely some famous lines from fifteenth- and sixteenth-century French poems.

This poem is from *Spoon River Anthology,* a collection of poems in which Masters created a variety of characters, each of whom speaks from his grave and comments on his life. Some have overcome suffering and lived nobly; some have frittered away their lives in trivial pursuits.

Petit, contemplating his life from the perspective of the grave, realizes that he has been a failure. The title of the poem tells us that Petit was a poet, and it implies that he was an insignificant poet. (*Petit* is a French word meaning *little.* From it we get the English word *petty*). Petit has spent his time writing petty poetry, and his poems have gone with him to the grave. His poetry has been as meaningless as the petty sound of seeds in a dry pod.

Petit tells us about the poetry that he has written and then about the poetry that he hasn't written. He has written triolets, villanelles, rondels, rondeaus. These are all technically complex verse forms. Poems in these forms are often clever and shallow, polished miniatures, too fragile for any profound or sustained emotion. Petit has written scores of such poems about how love is like a flower that withers and dies or like snow that soon melts. This theme itself is trite, though a gifted poet could reinterpret it with freshness and vigor. Petit implies that his interpretations have not been fresh and vigorous but as tired and faded as the roses of which he writes.

And all his life he has been surrounded by noble themes for poetry. He hasn't had the imagination to see that the ordinary village life, which on the surface appears to be humdrum, is really intensely dramatic. The lives of the villagers are full of "tragedy, comedy, valor, truth, courage, constancy, heroism, failure." The mere enumeration of these nouns emphasizes the enormity of what Petit has missed. He hasn't been sensitive enough to see the poetry in the daily struggles, sorrows, and delights of ordinary people. Nor has he noticed the lyric beauty of the "woodlands, meadows, streams, and rivers." Instead, he has written trite and stilted little poems.

Here is another poem, more dramatic than "Petit, the Poet" because it reveals a character in action rather than in contemplation.

My Last Duchess

ROBERT BROWNING
1812–1889

Scene: Ferrara

That's my last Duchess painted on the wall,
Looking as if she were alive. I call
That piece a wonder, now: Frà Pandolf's° hands
Worked busily a day, and there she stands.

3. Frà Pandolf: a fictitious painter and monk of the Italian Renaissance. "Frà" means "Brother."

Will't please you sit and look at her? I said   5
"Frà Pandolf" by design, for never read
Strangers like you that pictured countenance,
The depth and passion of its earnest glance,
But to myself they turned (since none puts by
The curtain I have drawn for you, but I)   10
And seemed as they would ask me, if they durst,
How such a glance came there; so, not the first
Are you to turn and ask thus. Sir, 'twas not
Her husband's presence only, called that spot
Of joy into the Duchess' cheek: perhaps   15
Frà Pandolf chanced to say, "Her mantle laps
Over my Lady's wrist too much," or "Paint
Must never hope to reproduce the faint
Half-flush that dies along her throat"; such stuff
Was courtesy, she thought, and cause enough   20
For calling up that spot of joy. She had
A heart—how shall I say?—too soon made glad,
Too easily impressed; she liked whate'er
She looked on, and her looks went everywhere.
Sir, 'twas all one! My favor at her breast,   25
The dropping of the daylight in the West,
The bough of cherries some officious fool
Broke in the orchard for her, the white mule
She rode with round the terrace—all and each
Would draw from her alike the approving speech,   30
Or blush, at least. She thanked men—good; but thanked
Somehow—I know not how—as if she ranked
My gift of a nine-hundred-years-old name
With anybody's gift. Who'd stoop to blame
This sort of trifling? Even had you skill   35
In speech (which I have not) to make your will
Quite clear to such an one, and say, "Just this
Or that in you disgusts me; here you miss,
Or there exceed the mark"—and if she let
Herself be lessoned so, nor plainly set   40
Her wits to yours, forsooth, and made excuse
—E'en then would be some stooping, and I choose

Never to stoop. Oh, sir, she smiled, no doubt,
Whene'er I passed her; but who passed without
Much the same smile? This grew; I gave commands;   45
Then all smiles stopped together. There she stands
As if alive. Wil't please you rise? We'll meet
The company below, then. I repeat,
The Count your master's known munificence°
Is ample warrant that no just pretence   50
Of mine for dowry will be disallowed;
Though his fair daughter's self, as I avowed
At starting, is my object. Nay, we'll go
Together down, sir! Notice Neptune, though,
Taming a sea horse, thought a rarity,   55
Which Claus of Innsbruck° cast in bronze for me!

49. **munificence** (mū·nĭf′ĭ·sĕns): great generosity.   56. **Claus of Innsbruck:**
a fictitious sculptor.

"My Last Duchess" is unlike "Petit, the Poet" in several ways.
First, the speaker is addressing a listener, not just thinking aloud.
Second, we see the speaker at a highly dramatic moment in his life,
not at some period after his death. Third, there is a real story involved. Finally, by implication, the poem is a study of an entire
culture—that of the Italian Renaissance.

The story is told indirectly. From a line here and a phrase there,
the reader must construct it for himself. It is briefly this: the Duke
of Ferrara, a widower, is chatting amiably with a representative, or
emissary, from another noble family and making final arrangements
to marry the daughter of that family.

Let us look at the poem carefully and see how we can construct
this story from the hints which the Duke gives.

"My Last Duchess" is, of course, a dramatic monologue, similar
in many respects to a scene from a play. The Duke has already
completed his business with the emissary before the action begins
and is now making a few remarks before dismissing him. As the
curtain goes up, the Duke is showing him a painting of his previous
wife. He comments at some length on the artistry of the painting.

He likes it, not because it is a memorial to his dead wife, but because it is a "wonder" and because the painter has skillfully captured his wife's characteristic expression. Apparently the emissary has commented on the lady's expression, "The depth and passion of its earnest glance," as do all people who see the portrait. (Notice that the portrait is kept behind a curtain which the Duke allows no one but himself to draw aside.) The Duke goes on to explain what "called that spot / Of joy into the Duchess' cheek." Almost anything and anyone pleased her. The Duke was annoyed. His pride was wounded. He felt that as the wife of a great nobleman she should be conscious of her position, haughty and dignified, less amiable to her social inferiors,

> as if she ranked
> My gift of a nine-hundred-years-old name
> With anybody's gift.

In his aristocratic pride the Duke felt that his wife had stooped too low and that for him to call her attention to the fact would itself be to stoop,

> . . . and I choose
> Never to stoop.

He was jealous that his wife should smile at everyone just as she smiled at him. So,

> I gave commands;
> Then all smiles stopped together.

After giving this rather surprising information and with scarcely a pause, the Duke invites the emissary to "meet the company below." He hints that he expects a large dowry to come with his new wife. As they start down the stairs, the emissary instinctively draws back to allow his superior to precede him, but the Duke with infinite politeness suggests that they go down together.

The curtain goes down on a particularly dramatic and ironic note. Having just revealed that he has caused the death of his wife and may even have murdered her, the Duke casually points out a figure of Neptune taming a sea horse, "Which Claus of Innsbruck cast in bronze for me!"

So much for the story. What have we learned about the culture and morality of Renaissance Italy? We may take the Duke of Ferrara to be a typical representative of his period. The way he behaves and thinks is perhaps indicative of the way the Italian nobility of the fifteenth and sixteenth centuries behaved and thought. The nobility of that period was proud, brutal, ruthless, and artistic. The Duke got rid of his wife simply because her attitude didn't please him. Afterward, he was obviously not filled with remorse at what he had done. He calmly began to make arrangements to marry a new duchess.

The Duke was above the law and had therefore not committed a crime as far as society was concerned. What police there were in those centuries had little jurisdiction over the nobility; their function was simply to maintain order among the rabble. A powerful nobleman like the Duke of Ferrara would have his own police force or maybe even a small army to protect him against any hostile neighbors.

The most important thing about the life of a nobleman was his family honor. Anything likely to endanger that honor had to be destroyed. We cannot picture the Duke of Ferrara, even from the little glimpse we have had of him, as being the sort of man who would spend anguished hours trying to decide whether or not to commit murder. And once having acted, he would suffer no pangs of conscience.

We must not forget that the Duke is talking to someone. How does this man react to the strange things that he hears? There is no evidence that he is the slightest bit surprised. He is, after all, merely a rather high-ranking servant. The job of such an official was to bow and agree; there could be no question of judging the Duke's conduct. Why does the Duke tell the story at all? Possibly it was already common knowledge that he had done away with his wife, but he certainly does not tell the story in order to justify himself. Nor does he tell it in a boastful manner, as a bully boasts of his questionable achievements. The Duke tells the story casually, as though it were of little importance. But by so doing he has very subtly made it quite plain to the representative of his future father-in-law how he expects his new wife to conduct herself as the Duchess of Ferrara.

The statue of Neptune taming a sea horse, obviously only one object in the duke's large collection of *objets d'art,* is indicative of the Duke's love of art, as is his attitude toward the portrait of his last Duchess. One of the most important aspects of Renaissance civilization was its intense artistic awareness. In the arts of painting and sculpture, it was the most brilliant period that Western civilization has known.

Of course, "My Last Duchess" is not a history lesson. Browning assumed that his readers would be familiar enough with Renaissance Italy to understand his poem. It is simply a dramatic study of, and comment on, aristocratic Renaissance character.

One of the most dramatic things about the poem is its casual tone. You will note that it is written in couplets (pairs of rhyming lines). Compare the effect of Browning's lines with the following lines from a poem in the same meter and rhyme.

from *An Essay on Man*

ALEXANDER POPE
1688–1744

Know then thyself, presume not God to scan;
The proper study of mankind is man.
Placed on this isthmus of a middle state,
A being darkly wise, and rudely great:
With too much knowledge for the skeptic side,
With too much weakness for the stoic's pride,
He hangs between; in doubt to act, or rest,
In doubt to deem himself a God, or beast.

You can see at once that Pope's lines are much more formal: you are very much aware of the meter and rhyme. How has Browning achieved a more conversational effect?

First of all, although the meter is iambic pentameter (five feet to a line, each foot containing an unaccented syllable followed by an accented), "My Last Duchess" contains very few regular lines. Within the iambic pattern Browning has freely introduced many variations: accents occur in places that would ordinarily take an unaccented syllable if the rhythm were strictly iambic, and some lines contain only three or four accents rather than the usual five. Thus the rhythm approaches that of ordinary conversational speech.

Second, there are far more *run-on* lines than *end-stopped* lines. A run-on line is a line whose ending does not coincide with a distinct pause.

> Though his fair daughter's self, as I avowed
> At starting, is my object. Nay we'll go
> Together down, sir! Notice Neptune, though,
> Taming a sea horse, . . .

At the end of an end-stopped line there is a pause.

> Know then thyself, presume not God to scan,
> The proper study of mankind is man.

The run-on lines make for a looser and more conversational structure; and further, they reduce the importance of the rhymes. In the Pope poem we pause at the end of each line, and the rhymes are therefore very noticeable. But Browning forces us to hurry over his rhymes so that we are scarcely aware of them at all. In his later dramatic monologues Browning dispensed with rhythm altogether and wrote in blank verse—unrhymed iambic pentameter (the verse form, incidentally, of Shakespeare's plays).

Third, the language of the Duke is itself informal. He uses contractions—"That's my last Duchess"—as anyone does in speech but rarely in formal writing. Sometimes he seems to be thinking before he speaks, searching for the right phrase: "A heart—how shall I say?— too soon made glad."

By all of these methods Browning has achieved a high degree of realism. The Duke speaks informally, even colloquially. The terrible revelations that he is making seem more appalling when made in this casual way than they would if stiffly declaimed in formal diction and regular meter. And the casualness of the tone reflects the casualness of the Duke's attitude toward what he has done.

> Notice Neptune, though,
> Taming a sea horse . . .

Why is a statue of Neptune "taming a sea horse" particularly appropriate to Browning's story?

Eight O'Clock

A. E. HOUSMAN
1859–1936

He stood, and heard the steeple
  Sprinkle the quarters on the morning town.
One, two, three, four, to market place and people
  It tossed them down.

Strapped, noosed, nighing his hour,   5
  He stood and counted them and cursed his luck;
And then the clock collected in the tower
  Its strength, and struck.

Here is a little drama of a different kind. Like most so-called dramatic poems, it is fairly objective: the poet is looking at a situation through the eyes of another man. In Browning's poem the Duke of Ferrara's words imply a view of life which was not Browning's. "Eight O'Clock" is too short a poem to imply a view of life or even to be much of a character study. What makes it dramatic is that although the criminal does not speak and although he is referred to as "he," Housman has forced the reader to look at the fatal clock through the condemned man's eyes. The clock is the man's enemy: when it strikes, he dies.

In the first stanza the condemned man hears the clock "Sprinkle the quarters on the morning town." To the townspeople the striking of the clock heralds all the color and excitement of the beginning of a new day in the market place. The clock "sprinkles" and "tosses" its tones gaily to the people outside the world of the criminal's experience. What about "Sprinkle the quarters"? Does that phrase have any connotation other than the quarter hours?

The message that the clock has for the criminal is in ironic contrast. Perhaps he reflects bitterly on what might have been. For him the clock *strikes*. The word *struck* is particularly appropriate. Although we often speak of a clock as having *struck,* a person can also be struck by a blow.

> And then the clock collected in the tower
> Its strength, and struck.

The last two lines contain an example of personification; the clock, like a man about to deliver a blow, "collected . . . / Its strength, and struck." Why do you think Housman chose to use this figure of speech?

We call a poem *dramatic* if its theme is presented primarily through speech and action rather than as pure meditation. But, as we saw in the beginning of this chapter, all poetry is in the broadest sense dramatic because all poetry implies a speaker and involves his reaction to some aspect of experience. Furthermore, the word *dramatic* implies the power of deeply stirring the imagination and emotions.

The following lines are from Shakespeare's *Macbeth.* Although it is part of a play, this *soliloquy* may be considered separately as a dramatic poem in its own right. Unlike a dramatic monologue, which is usually addressed to a listener, a soliloquy is represented as being the thought of the speaker and is not addressed to another person.

Macbeth is the most famous warrior in Scotland. Although he is essentially an honest man, he has allowed himself to be persuaded to murder the King in order that he himself may be king and his wife queen. The moment he has committed the deed he realizes that he will never again be at peace with the world or with himself. He cannot turn back. He becomes King, but the Scottish nobles turn against him. His position becomes desperate, and in an almost insane frenzy he causes the assassination of the wife and children of Macduff, a nobleman who has fled to England. Macduff returns to lead an army of Scottish and English against Macbeth. Macbeth now realizes that by killing a fellow man he has killed his own soul and that he has sacrificed "that which should accompany old age, / As honor, love, obedience, troops of friends." As the attack begins, Macbeth is informed that his wife is dead. He has lost his last support.

from *Macbeth, Act V, scene v*

1564–1616

She should have died hereafter;
There would have been a time for such a word.
Tomorrow, and tomorrow, and tomorrow,
Creeps in this petty pace from day to day,
To the last syllable of recorded time;   5
And all our yesterdays have lighted fools
The way to dusty death. Out, out, brief candle!
Life's but a walking shadow, a poor player
That struts and frets his hour upon the stage,
And then is heard no more: it is a tale   10
Told by an idiot, full of sound and fury,
Signifying nothing.

Questions

1. What is the candle (line 7)? Lines 8–12 contain three metaphors. What are they? How are all three related?
2. The dramatic power of these lines comes partly from the paradox which they imply. Does Macbeth really mean that life is a "tale . . . signifying nothing"? Can you see how he might believe just the opposite?

The following poems are less obviously dramatic than the previous ones. They could equally well have been included in the chapter on

The Poem as Drama   69

lyric poetry. Why is it fitting, however, that they should provide the conclusion to this chapter?

The Woodspurge

DANTE GABRIEL ROSSETTI
1828–1882

The wind flapped loose, the wind was still,
Shaken out dead from tree and hill:
I had walked on at the wind's will—
I sat now, for the wind was still.

Between my knees my forehead was—   5
My lips, drawn in, said not Alas!
My hair was over in the grass,
My naked ears heard the day pass.

My eyes, wide open, had the run
Of some ten weeds to fix upon;   10
Among those few, out of the sun,
The woodspurge flowered, three cups in one.

From perfect grief there need not be
Wisdom or even memory:
One thing then learnt remains to me—   15
The woodspurge has a cup of three.

Questions

1. The poem describes a particularly crucial moment in the life of the speaker. Explain. Would you call the poem restrained? sentimental?
2. What has the speaker learned about the nature of grief?
3. What might Rossetti mean by "perfect grief"?
4. What is ironic about the last two lines?

Taking Leave of a Friend
(after Rihaku) *

EZRA POUND

1885–

Blue mountains to the north of the walls,
White river winding about them;
Here we must make separation
And go out through a thousand miles of dead grass.
Mind like a floating white cloud,   5
Sunset like the parting of old acquaintances
Who bow over their clasped hands at a distance.
Our horses neigh to each other
    as we are departing.

* after Rihaku: with this phrase Pound indicates that his poem is modeled
on a poem by the eighth-century Chinese poet Rihaku, better known as Li Po.

Questions

1. How has Pound dramatized this simple situation?
2. Although the poem is in free verse, Pound has used some subtle rhythmic devices. What is the effect of the length of line 4 and of the pre-
   dominance of accented syllables?
3. What concrete details make the picture vivid?

For Further Study

All poetry is essentially dramatic, but the following poems in Part
Two of this book offer particularly clear examples of the dramatic
method:

A poem is a description of an experience and also an expression of an attitude toward that experience. A poet reveals his attitude by the way in which he organizes his poem. In conversation we can express our attitudes by our tone of voice. We say, "That's a bright idea" one way to mean that it *is* a bright idea and quite another way to mean that it is really a stupid idea. A poet must reveal his attitude through his choice of words, imagery, rhythm, figures of speech, and so on. He does not reveal it by saying, "Now this is a very sad poem; you are meant to be moved by it." Instead he reveals his attitude through a series of hints. This subtle method of revealing attitude, or creating tone, is one reason why all good poetry is essentially dramatic and one reason why untrained readers sometimes complain of "hidden meanings."

Rose Aylmer

WALTER SAVAGE LANDOR
1775–1865

Ah, what avails the sceptered race,°
  Ah, what the form divine!
What every virtue, every grace!
  Rose Aylmer, all were thine.

Rose Aylmer, whom these wakeful eyes   5
  May weep, but never see,
A night of memories and of sighs
  I consecrate to thee.

1. **sceptered race:** the ruling class. (A scepter is a staff carried by a ruler as a symbol of authority.)

Landor's poem is frequently said to be an expression of profound personal sorrow and loss. That may be, but a careful and imaginative reading will show that its tone is not one of personal grief. Whatever the final effect is, all the details seem to express merely a rather wistful regret that a beautiful lady is dead.

The structure is highly balanced. In the first stanza several elements contribute to establish a formal, elevated, and rather impersonal tone. Notice the regularity of the meter, the pause at the end of each line, the repetition in the first two lines, and the fact that these lines are a series of rhetorical questions. This is scarcely the way a bereaved lover would be likely to speak to his dead love. Rhetorical questions are formal in their effect: they occur commonly in public speeches and are generally asked to provide rather than to obtain information.

The only metrical irregularity in the first stanza occurs in the first foot of each line. Each line begins with a heavy accent. The repetition of the irregularity throughout the stanza establishes a kind of pattern of its own. The words *Ah* and *What* are emphasized by their heavy accent, and this emphasis helps to establish the questioning attitude of the stanza.

The second stanza is structurally different in that lines 1 and 3 are run-on lines and line 2 has a pause in the middle. Although the structure is less formal, the connotations of the words help to maintain the attitude of polite formality. The stanza begins with a repetition of the lady's full name. If the poet were addressing his dead love personally and passionately, he would probably not address her quite as formally. At first glance it seems that the next line expresses heartfelt grief: not only may his eyes weep, but they are wakeful eyes. But notice that he says his eyes *may* weep, not that they *will* weep. The rest of the poem implies that they will not weep, at least not for very long nor very profusely. There are two particularly important words in the stanza: *night,* and *consecrate.* The poet is going to spend one *night*—not the rest of his life or even every night for a week—remembering and sighing.

Consecrate is the most important word in the stanza. It means "to dedicate or devote to some particular purpose," and it connotes sacred purposes. It implies, therefore, a degree of impersonal formality. The poet is *planning* to set aside a particular night for the purpose of mourning the lady's death. The following night presumably he will think about something else.

So much for the details of "Rose Aylmer." What about the poem's final effect? Although the details create a formal and polite tone, we could quite reasonably maintain that "Rose Aylmer" *does* express a profound and personal loss. The restrained and formal tone then becomes a kind of understatement, and the "night of memories" is not to be taken literally. The poet deliberately uses the word *consecrate* to indicate that the memory of the lady has an almost religious sacredness. By making the mourning into a sacred rite, formal and awe-inspiring, the poet accomplishes two things: he enhances the importance of the lady, and he avoids the sentimental self-pity that "I mournfully give to thee," for instance, would suggest. The poet's grief is restrained and refined by philosophy and spiritual strength.

The tone is not one of grief; but the final effect may, if you want to interpret it that way, *be* one of grief. The poem belongs to us, and the choice is ours. Are there any other possible interpretations? Would we be justified in reading the poem as an example of irony? Could it even be argued that the poem is satirical? Reconsider the tone of the first two lines.

A Lament
(PUKE)

PERCY BYSSHE SHELLEY
1792–1822

O world! O life! O time!
On whose last steps I climb,
   Trembling at that where I had stood before;
When will return the glory of your prime?
   No more—Oh, never more!   5

Out of the day and night
A joy has taken flight
   Fresh spring, and summer, and winter hoar,
Move my faint heart with grief, but with delight
   No more—Oh, never more!   10

Here is a poem whose tone *is* one of grief—if not quite real grief, at least imagined grief. And yet when we examine it carefully and compare it to "Rose Aylmer," we shall find "A Lament" to be a much less moving poem.

At the beginning of this book we came to four conclusions about poetry:

1. It creates its total effect through imagery and figures of speech.
2. It is a language of suggestion as well as of statement.
3. It is a language of intense awareness and *therefore* of heightened emotion.
4. It communicates its total effect through form or structure.

Obviously a great deal more could be said about the language of poetry. But as we examine more and more poems, we shall find that these four statements are generally true. Usually, when each of these statements cannot be applied to a particular poem, the poem is not entirely successful.

None of these statements can be made about "A Lament," except possibly the last. In the first place, "A Lament" states everything, suggests nothing. In the first stanza Shelley says that the world, life, and time have lost forever their glory. In the second stanza he says that day, night, spring, summer, and winter move him with grief rather than delight, as they used to. That is all. And that isn't enough. Why is the speaker "trembling"? Why is his "faint heart" moved with grief? He suggests no reasons; he simply states that this is so. To be convincing, a mood must grow out of a specific situation, as it does in "Acquainted with the Night" (page 46). In that poem, although the speaker does not tell us why he is lonely, neither does he *tell* us that he is lonely at all. He simply draws a picture of a situation which communicates a mood of loneliness. And "The Woodspurge" (page 70) is both an analysis of grief and a *picture* of it, not simply an abstract statement. In Shelley's poem there is no situation at all, specific or otherwise, to communicate grief. The poet merely plunks his tears in front of us and says, "Here you are—now cry." We are justified in wondering why we should cry.

Compare this poem also with "Farewell to Barn and Stack and Tree" (page 25). In Housman's poem the emotion—a very real grief—develops naturally from the tragic situation and is suggested by a series of specific images. Housman doesn't say a word about grief, but compare the vagueness of "When will return the glory of your prime?" with the sharpness of "And dinner will be cold." "A Lament" is an exhibition of unexplained grief, a mere display of emotion which is not shown to have resulted from a cause; hence its tone is one of *sentimentality*. Do not confuse sentimentality with *sentiment*. A man of sentiment is said to be *sensitive:* capable of being moved to joy or grief or awe or disgust by the proper situation. Sentimentality, on the other hand, is an excess of emotion, a display of more emotion than is called for by the situation. A sentimental person's emotions are likely to burst forth on the slightest provocation—or on no provocation at all, as in "A Lament." "A Lament" may be the result of a sincere and profound emotion, but Shelley cannot make us feel that emotion simply by saying that *he* feels it. The statement is too flimsy: it has no backbone on which to hang a flesh and blood emotion. In "Rose Aylmer" Landor's tone of wistful regret results naturally from the theme and from the structure of the poem; and in "Farewell to Barn and Stack and Tree," Housman's implied grief is justified by the tragic event.

Mr. Flood's Party

EDWIN ARLINGTON ROBINSON
1869–1935

Old Eben Flood, climbing alone one night
Over the hill between the town below
And the forsaken upland hermitage
That held as much as he should ever know
On earth again of home, paused warily.   5
The road was his with not a native near;
And Eben, having leisure, said aloud,
For no man else in Tilbury Town to hear:

"Well, Mr. Flood, we have the harvest moon
Again, and we may not have many more;   10
The bird is on the wing, the poet says,
And you and I have said it here before.

Drink to the bird." He raised up to the light
The jug that he had gone so far to fill,
And answered huskily: "Well, Mr. Flood,   15
Since you propose it, I believe I will."

Alone, as if enduring to the end
A valiant armor of scarred hopes outworn,
He stood there in the middle of the road
Like Roland's ghost winding° a silent horn.   20
Below him, in the town among the trees,
Where friends of other days had honored him,
A phantom salutation of the dead
Rang thinly till old Eben's eyes were dim.

Then, as a mother lays her sleeping child   25
Down tenderly, fearing it may awake,
He set the jug down slowly at his feet
With trembling care, knowing that most things break;
And only when assured that on firm earth
It stood, as the uncertain lives of men   30
Assuredly did not, he paced away,
And with his hand extended paused again:

"Well, Mr. Flood, we have not met like this
In a long time; and many a change has come
To both of us, I fear, since last it was   35
We had a drop together. Welcome home!"
Convivially returning with himself,
Again he raised the jug up to the light;
And with an acquiescent quaver said:
"Well, Mr. Flood, if you insist, I might.   40

"Only a very little, Mr. Flood—
For auld lang syne. No more, sir; that will do."
So, for the time, apparently it did,
And Eben evidently thought so too;

20. **winding** (wīnd'ĭng): blowing.

For soon amid the silver loneliness   45
Of night he lifted up his voice and sang,
Secure, with only two moons listening,
Until the whole harmonious landscape rang—

"For auld lang syne." The weary throat gave out,
The last word wavered; and the song being done,   50
He raised again the jug regretfully
And shook his head, and was again alone.
There was not much that was ahead of him,
And there was nothing in the town below—
Where strangers would have shut the many doors   55
That many friends had opened long ago.

Here is a poem whose tone is fairly complex. The subject is an old man in the act of getting slightly drunk. A poet might describe such a man in a variety of ways: as disgraceful, comic, ridiculous, tragic, or merely pathetic. Any one of these viewpoints could be made legitimate. But any one of them to the exclusion of all the other possible viewpoints would run into the danger of oversimplifying an experience—the major fault of "A Lament." Good poetry looks at life from many angles, sometimes several at once; and they do not necessarily contradict each other. The phenomenon of Eben's solitary party is sufficiently complex to necessitate a complex approach. Since Robinson has chosen to regard old Eben Flood from several angles, the complexity of approach results in a richness and strength that a simpler treatment might have lacked.

The first stanza of "Mr. Flood's Party" sketches the situation which the succeeding stanzas will develop. An old man is walking home alone at night. There is an element of pathos: he is alone, he is walking away from the town to his

> foresaken upland hermitage
> That held as much as he should ever know
> On earth again of home . . .

We do not yet know why the old man lives in a "forsaken hermitage," but the fact itself is rather touching.

The second stanza introduces several new elements. Perhaps the most important is the comic element. Not only is the man talking to himself (which is almost always amusing), but he is answering himself as though he were two persons, and he is doing it with a formal politeness and even a playful kind of gallantry. Eben is shown to be a man of gentlemanly manners and apparently some education: "The bird is on the wing" is a quotation from the "Rubáiyát of Omar Khayyám" (see page 362).

In the third stanza we begin to have an inkling of the sadness of Mr. Flood's futile existence. The word *alone* occurs several times in the poem. Eben has outlived his friends. He mourns the good old days and has taken to drink as an escape from the loneliness of the present.

In this stanza we have an important simile:

> He stood there in the middle of the road
> Like Roland's ghost winding a silent horn.

The lines have meaning on at least two levels. A man lifting a jug to his lips might look in silhouette much like a man blowing a horn. That is the literal meaning. But this is *Roland,* a specific man who blew his horn on a specific occasion. The legendary French hero, Roland, was one of Charlemagne's most famous warriors. He possessed a horn with which he was supposed always to be able to summon Charlemagne's aid. At Roncevaux in the Pyrenees (near the present border of France and Spain) in 778, his forces were beset by a vastly superior foe. When Roland saw that the fight was hopeless, he blew his horn. But help came too late, and he perished.

How does Eben's jug resemble Roland's horn in more than mere appearance? Robinson is suggesting here that just as Roland blew his horn when he needed help, so Eben, too, needs help. Robinson is further suggesting that just as Roland's horn failed to bring him help when he most needed it, so Eben's jug ultimately fails him. Although he can momentarily lose himself in " auld lang syne," he cannot permanently escape the loneliness of his old age.

The fourth stanza has another significant simile:

> Then, as a mother lays her sleeping child
> Down tenderly, fearing it may awake,
> He set the jug down slowly at his feet . . .

The suggestion that Eben feels for his jug the same loving care that a mother feels for her child is a continuation of the rather poignant humor as well as a powerful means of indicating the poverty of his existence. The jug is all that Eben has left in the world.

Besides the jug-child figure of speech the fourth stanza contains one of the central ideas of the poem, expressed with deliberate casualness. Eben sets the jug down "With trembling care, knowing that most things break." Eben has learned from bitter experience that "most things break": his lonely life is an illustration of that. He has nothing left but an "upland hermitage," a kind of pathetic-comic dignity, and a jug. He certainly isn't going to risk breaking the jug, his sleeping child, his Roland's horn. Although in the lines

> And only when assured that on firm earth
> It stood, as the uncertain lives of men
> Assuredly do not . . .

Robinson is looking at life through Eben's eyes, we may safely assume that he is using Eben's eyes as a vehicle for commenting on life—that the poem is a specific and dramatic way of commenting on an aspect of human experience. The poem is about a man called Eben Flood, but the idea that most things break and that men's lives are uncertain need not be restricted to his experience.

The fifth stanza, containing more of Eben's conversation with himself, carries the comedy and the pathos one step further. By now it has become apparent that by talking this way Eben is trying to fool himself into believing that he is back in the old days convivially having a drink with an old friend—or if not trying to fool himself, at least reliving in his imagination those long-dead days.

The sixth stanza has further complexities of tone. The word *apparently* is important because it indicates that Robinson is telling his story in a casual way. We feel that he is at least partly amused by it but that his amusement does not prevent him from feeling its darker implications.

By now Eben is drunk, but Robinson suggests it only in passing: "Secure, with only two moons listening . . ." At the end of his song

> He raised again the jug regretfully
> And shook his head and was again alone.

Already, before he has even reached his solitary home, the jug "that he had gone so far to fill" is empty, and he is "again alone."

So you see, the tone of "Mr. Flood's Party" is strengthened by irony and understatement. Because a lonely old man drinking himself into momentary forgetfulness is a rather complex subject, a poem which did not grapple with its complexities would be an over-simplification. Eben is comic and pathetic for obvious reasons. And on a higher level he is tragic because he is a symbol of loneliness, a man who has learned that "most things break."

The tone of "Mr. Flood's Party" is one of amused irony and compassion. Unlike Shelley in "A Lament," Robinson does not insist on an emotion. Rather, by his somewhat wistful and whimsical method he seems to be presenting his story objectively. But if we are alive to the various hints that he has given us, we are made to feel both the tragedy and the comedy of old Eben. Robinson's ironic under-statements stimulate our imagination.

Channel Firing

THOMAS HARDY
1840–1928

That night your great guns, unawares,
Shook all our coffins as we lay,
And broke the chancel° window squares,
We thought it was the Judgment Day

And sat upright. While drearisome   5
Arose the howl of wakened hounds:
The mouse let fall the altar crumb,
The worms drew back into the mounds,

3. **chancel**: the part of a church between the nave and the altar, originally occupied by the choir.

The glebe cow° drooled. Till God called, "No;
It's gunnery practice out at sea   10
Just as before you went below;
The world is as it used to be:

"All nations striving strong to make
Red war yet redder. Mad as hatters
They do no more for Christés sake   15
Than you who are helpless in such matters.

"That this is not the judgment hour
For some of them's a blessed thing,
For if it were they'd have to scour
Hell's floor for so much threatening . . .   20

"Ha, ha. It will be warmer when
I blow the trumpet (if indeed
I ever do; for you are men,
And rest eternal sorely need)."

So down we lay again. "I wonder,   25
Will the world ever saner be,"
Said one, "then when He sent us under
In our indifferent century!"

And many a skeleton shook his head.
"Instead of preaching forty year,"   30
My neighbor Parson Thirdly said,
"I wish I had stuck to pipes and beer."

Again the guns disturbed the hour,
Roaring their readiness to avenge,
As far inland as Stourton Tower,°   35
And Camelot,° and starlit Stonehenge.°

9. **glebe cow:** a cow belonging to the parish church or grazing on church
land.   35. **Stourton Tower:** a monument built in 1772 to commemorate the site
where King Alfred (849–899) first opened war on the Danes, who were eventually driven completely out of England.   36. **Camelot:** see page 32. **Stonehenge:** an ancient temple in southern England made of upright stones in a
series of concentric circles, probably built for the worship of a sun god.

Questions

1. Who is speaking in the first two stanzas? What is the setting of the poem?
2. The situation is weird, but what is the tone of the poem? Are we meant to be frightened by the tone?
3. "The glebe cow drooled." What effect does this little detail have on the tone? Notice the many run-on lines, two of them broken by stanza divisions. How does this characteristic affect the tone? Can you point out other details which have a similar effect?
4. Is the theme of the poem serious? Can you point out any instances of humor in the poem? If the theme is serious, is the humor out of place?
5. What happens to the tone in the last stanza? Camelot, Stourton Tower, and Stonehenge are rich in connotations in English history. What bearing does this have on the theme?

from *John Brown's Body*

STEPHEN VINCENT BENÉT
1898–1943

The Shrine of Gettysburg

You took a carriage to that battlefield.
Now, I suppose, you take a motor bus,
But then, it was a carriage—and you ate
Fried chicken out of wrappings of waxed paper,
While the slow guide buzzed on about the war   5
And the enormous, curdled summer clouds
Piled up like giant cream puffs in the blue.
The carriage smelt of axle grease and leather
And the old horse nodded a sleepy head
Adorned with a straw hat. His ears stuck through it.   10
It was the middle of hay fever summer
And it was hot. And you could stand and look
All the way down from Cemetery Ridge,
Much as it was, except for monuments
And startling groups of monumental men   15
Bursting in bronze and marble from the ground,
And all the curious names upon the gravestones. . . .

So peaceable it was, so calm and hot,
So tidy and great-skied.

                      No men had fought
There but enormous, monumental men   20
Who bled neat streams of uncorrupting bronze,
Even at the Round Tops, even by Pickett's boulder,
Where the bronze, open book could still be read
By visitors and sparrows and the wind:
And the wind came, the wind moved in the grass,   25
Saying . . . while the long light . . . and all so calm . . .

              "Pickett came
              And the South came
              And the end came,
              And the grass comes   30
              And the wind blows
              On the bronze book
              On the bronze men
              On the grown grass,
              And the wind says   35
              'Long ago
              Long
              Ago.'"

Then it was time to buy a paperweight
With flags upon it in decalcomania°   40
And hope you wouldn't break it, driving home.

    40. **decalcomania:** a picture or design transferred from specially prepared
paper to china, glass, etc.

Questions

1. What is the function of the many seemingly trivial details: the fried
   chicken wrapped in wax paper, the summer clouds, the smell of the
   carriage?
2. What does "the slow guide buzzed on about the war" indicate about
   the guide? About his audience? The readers of the bronze book are
   "visitors and sparrows and the wind." What does this further detail
   suggest about the visitors?

3. What are some connotations of the words *monumental* and *startling* in line 15 and of *curious* in line 17?
4. Why does Benét say "No men had fought / There but enormous monumental men / Who bled neat streams of uncorrupting bronze"?
5. Why are the last three lines so important to the tone? What *is* the tone? If the tone is at least partly ironic, how is the irony created?

The End of the World

ARCHIBALD MACLEISH
1892–

Quite unexpectedly as Vasserot
The armless ambidextrian° was lighting
A match between his great and second toe
And Ralph the lion was engaged in biting
The neck of Madame Sossman while the drum   5
Pointed, and Teeny was about to cough
In waltz time swinging Jocko by the thumb—
Quite unexpectedly the top blew off:

And there, there overhead, there, there, hung over
Those thousands of white faces, those dazed eyes,   10
There in the starless dark, the poise, the hover,
There with vast wings across the canceled skies,
There in the sudden blackness, the black pall
Of nothing, nothing, nothing—nothing at all.

2. **ambidextrian** (ăm′bĭ·dĕks′trĭ·ăn): literally, one capable of using both hands with equal skill.

Questions

1. With what is the imagery of this poem concerned?
2. What various activities do the first eight lines describe? What happens in the end?
3. What view of the world does the imagery suggest?

Indian Summer

EMILY DICKINSON
1830–1886

These are the days when birds come back,
A very few, a bird or two,
To take a backward look.

These are the days when skies put on
The old, old sophistries° of June,—   5
A blue and gold mistake.

Oh, fraud that cannot cheat the bee,
Almost thy plausibility
Induces my belief,

Till ranks of seeds their witness bear,   10
And softly through the altered air
Hurries a timid leaf!

Oh, sacrament of summer days,
Oh, last communion in the haze,
Permit a child to join,   15

Thy sacred emblems to partake,
Thy consecrated bread to break,
Taste thine immortal wine!

5. sophistries: false, deceptive methods of reasoning.

Questions

1. What is the tone of this poem? Does the tone seem to change during the poem? If so, at what point? Does it really change? Explain.
2. What effect have the words *sophistries, mistake, fraud,* and *cheat* on the tone?
3. What new imagery occurs in the last two stanzas, and what effect does it have?

The Leaden-eyed

VACHEL LINDSAY
1879–1931

Let not young souls be smothered out before
They do quaint deeds and fully flaunt their pride.
It is the world's one crime its babes grow dull,
Its poor are ox-like, limp, and leaden-eyed.
Not that they starve, but starve so dreamlessly;   5
Not that they sow, but that they seldom reap;
Not that they serve, but have no gods to serve;
Not that they die, but that they die like sheep.

At Galway Races

WILLIAM BUTLER YEATS
1865–1939

There where the course is,
Delight makes all of the one mind,
The riders upon the galloping horses,
The crowd that closes in behind:
We, too, had good attendance once,   5
Hearers and hearteners of the work;
Aye, horsemen for companions,
Before the merchant and the clerk
Breathed on the world with timid breath.
Sing on: somewhere at some new moon,   10
We'll learn that sleeping is not death,
Hearing the whole earth change its tune,
Its flesh being wild, and it again
Crying aloud as the racecourse is,
And we find hearteners among men   15
That ride upon horses.

Questions

1. What "smothers" the "young souls" of Lindsay's poem?
2. The theme of "The Leaden-eyed" is stated most directly in which line?
3. In what way is the theme of Yeats's poem similar to that of Lindsay's?
4. Which poem makes the more vigorous use of imagery? Explain.
5. Are the two poems similar in attitude toward their theme? Explain.
6. How does Yeats feel toward "the merchant and the clerk"? Why? How do you suppose Lindsay feels about the merchant and the clerk? Why?

For Further Study

Among the poems in Part Two of this book, the following reveal clearly the importance of tone in creating the total effect of a poem:

Christopher Marlowe, "The Passionate Shepherd to His Love," page 182

Sir Walter Raleigh, "The Nymph's Reply to the Shepherd," page 183

Thomas Gray, "Elegy Written in a Country Churchyard," page 273

Lord Byron, "So, We'll Go No More A-Roving," page 332

Siegfried Sassoon, "Concert Party," page 464

E. E. Cummings, "in Just-," page 527

CHAPTER VII   *Imagery*

The total effect of a poem is the result of many elements: the literal meaning of the words, the connotations of the words, the sounds of the words, the rhythm of the lines, the form of the poem, the imagery. Of these elements the most important is imagery. The other elements help to shape the meaning; the image *is* the meaning. Without it the poem would not be.

Imagery is a broad term applied to the representation in words of any sense experience. In almost all cases, imagery involves the use of figures of speech. Figures of speech are, of course, not restricted to poetry; prose uses figures, sometimes for decoration, sometimes for illustration, and sometimes for vividness. In good poetry figures are never merely decorative or even illustrative; they are essential to the total meaning.

Figurative language is, in most cases, a language of comparison. Since poetry frequently deals with abstract themes in concrete terms, the comparison is often that of an abstraction with an object. We've already discussed most of the more common figures of speech in connection with specific poems, but let's pause for a moment to review them:

SIMILE

A stated comparison, usually introduced by *like* or *as*, is called a simile.

> He ran like the wind.

> This city now doth, like a garment, wear
> The beauty of the morning . . .
> > —*Wordsworth*

> . . . as the waves make toward the pebbled shore,
> **So** do our minutes hasten to their end.
> > —*Shakespeare*

METAPHOR

A *metaphor* is a comparison; one thing is said to be another:

> Life's but a walking shadow, a poor player
> That struts and frets his hour upon the stage . . .
> —*Shakespeare*

Metaphor also involves speaking of one thing in terms of another:

> The ship plows the sea.

Literally a ship does not *plow* the sea; but figuratively the comparison is effective because the wake of a ship resembles furrows made by a plow in a field.

SYMBOL

A *symbol* is a thing which stands for something else; often an object which stands for an idea. The cross, for instance, is a symbol of the Christian religion, the flag a symbol of a country. These are common symbols whose meanings are fixed; that is, the object always suggests the same idea. Poetry often creates its own symbols: the broken statue in "Ozymandias" is, within the poem, a symbol of the impermanence of human power. Shelley has *made* it that.

As you can see, a symbol is a kind of metaphor. A metaphor emphasizes the comparison of two things. A symbol does not emphasize the comparison; it is a kind of metaphor without the first term. In "Ozymandias" Shelley does not say that power is a broken statue; he simply describes the statue and lets the image imply power. A symbol usually has more overtones of meaning than a metaphor because its meaning is not necessarily fixed to one thing or idea; it often suggests several.

The differences between simile, metaphor, and symbol are perhaps rather subtle. Let us sum up by putting it this way:

> simile: *a* is like *b*
> metaphor: *a* is *b*
> symbol: the poet talks about *b*, letting *b* stand for *a*
>   (and perhaps *c, d, e*, etc.)

Personification is the giving of human powers or characteristics to inanimate objects or ideas.

> And then the clock collected in the tower
> Its strength, and struck.
>
> *—Housman*

> When Duty whispers low, "Thou must,"
> The youth replies, "I can."
>
> *—Emerson*

As you can see, personification is a kind of metaphor; in Housman's lines the clock is looked upon as a person; in Emerson's lines Duty becomes a speaking human being.

Fog

CARL SANDBURG
1878–

> The fog comes
> on little cat feet.
> It sits looking
> over harbor and city
> on silent haunches   5
> and then moves on.

This poem is a metaphor because in it Sandburg talks about fog as though it were a cat. The metaphor is easy to follow. Sandburg tells us in the second line that the fog comes on "little cat feet." Thereafter all the details are feline. The fog comes in quietly, sits for a while on "silent haunches" calmly surveying the harbor and city, and silently withdraws. By using the cat image Sandburg suggests some qualities of the fog without having to mention them. He suggests that the fog is, like a cat, rather impersonal, aloof, and elusive. (The fog is like a *cat,* not a kitten. There is a vast difference.)

This is a slight but effective poem because every detail is right. Try rewriting it, using a dog as the image. It wouldn't work. The entire poem is two sentences long. It is simply a tiny but perceptive observation on an aspect of the physical world—a very interesting and neat little comparison.

War Is Kind

STEPHEN CRANE

1871–1900

Do not weep, maiden, for war is kind.
Because your lover threw wild hands toward the sky
And the affrighted steed ran on alone,
Do not weep.
War is kind.   5

Hoarse, booming drums of the regiment,
Little souls who thirst for fight—
These men were born to drill and die.
The unexplained glory flies above them;
Great is the battle god, great—and his kingdom   10
A field where a thousand corpses lie.

Do not weep, babe, for war is kind.
Because your father tumbled in the yellow trenches,
Raged at his breast, gulped, and died,
Do not weep.   15
War is kind.

Swift-blazing flag of the regiment,
Eagle with crest of red and gold,
These men were born to drill and die.
Point for them the virtue of slaughter,   20
Make plain to them the excellence of killing,
And a field where a thousand corpses lie.

Mother whose heart hung humble as a button
On the bright splendid shroud of your son,
Do not weep.   25
War is kind.

In this poem Crane states that war is kind and then proceeds to
draw some pictures of its cruelty. Had the poem been called "War
Is Cruel," the effect would have been lost. The tone is one of bitter
irony:

Point for them the virtue of slaughter,
Make plain to them the excellence of killing.

The structure is interesting. It consists of three stanzas of specific
pictures, each addressed to a different person. Alternating with these
stanzas are two stanzas of general evocation of the spirit of war.
The poem is in free verse—that is, it has no regular metrical scheme
and, although one repeated rhyme does occur, there is no rhyme
scheme.

What makes the poem noteworthy is the sharpness of the imagery
in stanzas 1, 3, and 5. There are many ways of describing the horrors of war. Crane might have said something like this:

Because your lover was one of six thousand men
Who suffered agonies and died,
Do not weep.

These lines are too vague to be effective. The reader may be ap-
palled that so many men were killed, but he doesn't have a precise
picture of what happened. Crane describes pictorially the death of
one man and lets the sudden and vivid glimpse of war suggest all
the rest.

Because your lover threw wild hands toward the sky
And the affrighted steed ran on alone,
Do not weep.

The last image, that of the mother standing over the coffin of her
son, is equally moving. Crane merely draws a very simple picture
and lets it do the work of evoking an emotion from us. Here is a
more difficult poem.

Soundings

1924–

Silent, they take their soundings
As though they did not understand
That having once departed the land
There would be need for sleep.

There is no longer separation   5
Of foam riders from the foam.
And who is far from home?
Half pity and half envy them.

As though they did not understand
It little matters that the waves disclose   10
No blind and derelict repose
With secrets they cannot share.

The whitened marvelous bone compels
Them all day long beneath the sea
To search, and searching, be. Silently   15
They go about their soundings.

    The theme of this poem is abstract: the poet is talking about people who are searching for something; perhaps the meaning of life. These men are pictured concretely as taking soundings: measuring the depth of the sea. The sea is perhaps a symbol of life; the men are measuring the depth of life. Because they are engaged in a serious business, they are silent. The speaker is commenting on their activities.

    In the first stanza he says that these searchers will soon be in need of sleep. He implies that anyone who occupies himself with such a difficult task will wear himself out.

    The second stanza begins to reveal the complexity of the speaker's attitude.

There is no longer separation
Of foam riders from the foam.

He says that these people who are searching for the meaning of life
have themselves become a part of life. His attitude toward them is
mixed: "Half pity and half envy them."
In the third stanza the speaker says that the search is futile:

It little matters that the waves disclose
No blind and derelict repose
With secrets they cannot share.

But we see how, even as he states this attitude, he is questioning it.
He half envies the searchers. They are compelled "to search, and
searching, be," and it is only by attempting to discover what life is
all about that one really lives. The speaker's attitude has changed
during the course of the poem.

The poem ends with almost the same line that began it, but notice
how the statement about soundings has acquired symbolic meaning.
There is an important difference between the first and last lines.
The substitution of "They go about their soundings" for "They take
their soundings" is significant because it implies that the searchers
are still at their job and will continue to be at it all their lives—that
the search is their life.

Tears, Idle Tears

ALFRED, LORD TENNYSON
1809–1892

Tears, idle tears, I know not what they mean,
Tears from the depth of some divine despair
Rise in the heart, and gather to the eyes,
In looking on the happy autumn fields,
And thinking of the days that are no more.   5

Fresh as the first beam glittering on a sail,
That brings our friends up from the underworld,
Sad as the last which reddens over one
That sinks with all we love below the verge;
So sad, so fresh, the days that are no more.   10

Ah, sad and strange as in dark summer dawns
The earliest pipe of half-awakened birds
To dying ears, when unto dying eyes
The casement slowly grows a glimmering square;
So sad, so strange, the days that are no more.   15

Dear as remembered kisses after death,
And sweet as those by hopeless fancy feigned
On lips that are for others; deep as love,
Deep as first love, and wild with all regret;
O Death in Life, the days that are no more!   20

Questions

1. If the tears are tears which "from the depths of some divine despair /
   Rise in the heart," why does Tennyson call them "idle"? Does *idle*
   mean *meaningless* or something quite different?
2. Try changing line 4 to "In looking on the happy summer fields." What
   difference does this make? Why then does Tennyson call his autumn
   fields "happy"?
3. The speaker is re-creating the past in his mind. Why is the first word
   of stanza 2 "fresh"?
4. *Underworld* in stanza 2 has two levels of meaning. What are they?
   Does this ambiguity make the lines unclear or does it make them
   richer in meaning?
5. In the first two stanzas Tennyson has called the days that are no more
   "sad" and "fresh." In stanza 3 he calls them "strange." Why do they
   seem strange? In stanza 4 Tennyson has used successively the adjectives *dear, sweet, deep,* and *wild.* In what sense is each of these appropriate to the past as re-created in the speaker's mind?

Break, Break, Break

ALFRED, LORD TENNYSON

1809–1892

Break, break, break,
   On thy cold gray stones, O Sea!
And I would that my tongue could utter
   The thoughts that arise in me.

   O, well for the fisherman's boy,   5
   That he shouts with his sister at play!
O, well for the sailor lad,
   That he sings in his boat on the bay!

And the stately ships go on
   To their haven under the hill;   10
But O for the touch of a vanished hand,
   And the sound of a voice that is still!

Break, break, break,
   At the foot of thy crags, O Sea!
But the tender grace of a day that is dead   15
   Will never come back to me.

Questions

1. "Break, Break, Break" and "Tears, Idle Tears" have very much the same theme. In what important ways does the treatment of this theme in the two poems differ?
2. Which is the easier poem? Why?
3. Which poem achieves the greater intensity of emotion? In which poem does the past seem more real? Why? In which poem does Tennyson make a more vigorous use of imagery?
4. In "Tears, Idle Tears" memory comes to possess a kind of life of its own. What happens to memory in "Break, Break, Break"?

Voyage West

ARCHIBALD MACLEISH
1892–

There was a time for discoveries—
For the headlands looming above in the
First light and the surf and the
Crying of gulls: for the curve of the
Coast north into secrecy.   5

That time is past.
The last lands have been peopled.
The oceans are known now.

Señora: once the maps have all been made
A man were better dead than find new continents.   10

A man would better never have been born
Than find upon the open ocean flowers
Drifted from islands where there are no islands,

Or midnight, out of sight of any land,
Smell on the altering air the odor of rosemary.   15

No fortune passes that misfortune—

To lift along the evening of the sky,
Certain as sun and sea, a new-found land
Steep from an ocean where no landfall can be.

Questions

1. This poem seems to be about lands and oceans and discoveries, but its theme is really a much more abstract one. MacLeish presents his theme through imagery having to do altogether with exploration. Why does he do this? How is MacLeish's treatment of an abstract theme similar to the method of Charles Goodwin's "Soundings" (page 94)?
2. What kind of discoveries and "new continents" is MacLeish really talk-

ing about? Why would a man be "better dead than find new continents"?

3. How can a voyager discover a "new-found land . . . where no landfall can be"? Why is it that "no fortune passes that misfortune"?

The Sword

HAROLD LEWIS COOK
1897–

Here lies the flesh that tortured me.
    Stand here and gaze upon this ground.
Through this thin, flowered grass you see
    The skeleton beneath the mound:

The blue eyes that could never weep,   5
    The soft mouth that could never sleep,
Nerveless now, and deep, deep—
    Trapped, and bound.

The heart is still that never yet
    Sucked upon the core of pain,   10
And still the hand that could forget
    How touch may cool a burning brain.

Stand still, and gaze. Then tell me why
    From flesh long dead leaps up so high
This two-edged sword on which I die   15
    Again, again.

Questions

1. What was the relationship of the speaker to the dead person? How did she treat him?
2. How *did* he feel about her? How *does* he feel about her now?
3. What is the sword? Why is it "two-edged"?

For Further Study

A reading of the following poems in Part Two of this book will provide further practice in understanding and interpreting imagery:

VIII *Fabric*

In previous chapters we have sometimes spoken of the rhythmic effects in specific poems. Now let's look at this topic and some others, in more general terms.

Fabric (sometimes called *texture*, sometimes *melody*) has to do with sound. Rhythm and meter form part of the fabric of a poem, and so do such devices as *cacophony, euphony, onomatopoeia, alliteration, assonance,* and *consonance.* Fabric has to do also with the position of the pause (or the *caesura*) within a line and whether the lines are *end-stopped* or *run-on.* The character of the rhyme is also part of the fabric. There are *masculine rhyme, feminine rhyme, unaccented rhyme,* and various kinds of *imperfect rhyme.*

Don't be alarmed. If some of these terms seem difficult, the things they name are simple—and most of them occur every day in your speech.

RHYTHM

English is necessarily a rhythmical language because it is an accented language: in any word of more than one syllable there is an accent on one of the syllables, that is, one syllable is spoken with greater emphasis than the others. An accent (or beat) is indicated like this: ′ A syllable that is not accented is indicated like this: ˘

Let us scan, or indicate the beats of, some words: *sĭng-ĭng, ŏc-cúr, prĕ-fér, préf-ĕr-ĕnce, rĕ-ór-găn-ĭze.* Now let us scan a sentence: *Ónce ŭp-ón ă tíme thĕre wăs ă béau-tĭ-fŭl, rích prín-cĕss.* Rhythm is simply the rise and fall of accented and unaccented syllables (light and heavy beats). It is not confined to poetry: all prose has rhythm to a greater or lesser degree.

Meter is the systematic arrangement of light and heavy beats into more or less regular patterns. Most poetry is metrical as well as rhythmical.

Any line with a metrical scheme can be divided into units called *feet*. This process of analysis is called *scansion*. In poetry written in English, a *foot* is a combination of one heavy beat and one or two light beats. Here are four kinds of feet:

iamb—a light and a heavy beat: be̬ló̵w

trochee—a heavy and a light beat: óf̵fe̬r

anapest—two light beats and a heavy beat: u̬nde̬rné̵ath

dactyl—a heavy and two light beats: whí̵msi̬ca̬l

These names apply to the *kinds* of feet that make up a line of poetry. The *number* of feet determines the length of the line.

> monometer—one foot
> dimeter—two feet
> trimeter—three feet
> tetrameter—four feet
> pentameter—five feet
> hexameter—six feet
> heptameter—seven feet
> octameter—eight feet

Here are some examples:

A̬fár / the̬ me̵l / a̬nchó / ly̵ thún / de̬r moáned.[1]
                                              —Shelley

This line is in iambic pentameter (five iambs). Note that the foot divisions frequently cut across the word divisions. *Melancholy* forms part of three feet; and the last foot contains a word and a half.

1. Scansion is sometimes arbitrary—a reader's characteristics of pronunciation will determine how he scans a line. This line could equally well be scanned like this:

A̵fa̬r / the̬ me̵l /a̬ncho̵ / ly̵ thún / de̬r moáned.

Furthermore, the foot divisions are meaningful only as an aid to identifying the meter; they do not indicate pauses.

Once úp / on a / mídníght / dréary, / while Ĭ / pón-
deréd / wéak and / wéary . . .   —Poe

This is trochaic octameter (eight trochees).

The Ãssýr / ian came dówn / like a wólf / on the fóld . . .
                                                —Byron

This is anapestic tetrameter (four anapests).

Lóve agáin, / sóng agáin, / nést agáin, / yóung agáin.
                                                —Tennyson

This is dactylic tetrameter (four dactyls).

The iambic meter is probably the commonest in English poetry.
The rhythm of an iambic line is closest to the rhythm of ordinary
speech:

   To him who in the love of Nature holds communion with
   her visible forms, she speaks a various language. For his
   gayer hours, she has a voice of gladness and a smile and
   eloquence of beauty . . .

Unless you recognize this as being a rearrangement of lines from a
poem called "Thanatopsis," by William Cullen Bryant, you were
probably not aware that they are iambic. When you hear a good
actor recite lines from one of Shakespeare's plays, you are not constantly aware that he is speaking poetry written in iambic pentameter.

For some reason trochaic meter tends to have a more sing-song
quality than iambic:

   And he wooed her with caresses, wooed her with his
   smile of sunshine, with his flattering words he wooed her,
   with his sighing and his singing . . .

Even if you do not know that these are lines from Longfellow's
"Hiawatha" arranged into prose form, you realize that the rhythm
is not that of normal prose. You are constantly aware of the strong
trochaic beat.

The rhythm of anapestic and dactylic feet is likely to be even
farther removed from prose rhythm. For this reason such meters

are not suitable for very long poems, as they tend to become monotonous. They are special meters for special effects.

So far we have examined lines whose meter is fairly regular. In any poem not all the lines are completely regular. The effectiveness of a metrical scheme is influenced by its irregularities, by the variations within it. There are two main types of metrical irregularity. The first consists of the substitution of one kind of foot where another is expected:

Ĭt wăs mán / y̆ ănd mán / y̆ ă yéar / ă gó

Ĭn ă kíng / dŏm bý / thĕ séa . . .

—Poe

Here you see that the meter is anapestic but that there are occasional iambic feet. The main reason for this is that the English language cannot easily be forced into strict anapestic meter without distorting the accents of words. A poet writing in anapests often makes use of iambs for the sake of smoothness and naturalness. An iamb is related to an anapest because each begins with a light beat. Similarly, a trochee is related to a dactyl, and a poet writing in dactylic meter often substitutes trochees:

Hálf ă léague, / hálf ă léague, /

Hálf ă léague / ónwărd . . .

—Tennyson

Another type of variation related to this is the *feminine ending*. In this variation the line ends with a light beat left over:

Thĕ skíes / thĕy wĕre ásh / ĕn ănd só / bĕr . . .

—Poe

This type of irregularity, the feminine ending, occurs most frequently in poems whose meter is anapestic or dactylic.

The second type of variation is much more subtle. It consists of the substitution of a heavy for a light beat, or vice versa, for a special effect:

Thĕ lóne / ănd lév / ĕl sánds / strétch fár / ă wáy.

—Shelley

Note that the fourth foot contains two heavy beats, the effect of which is to slow the line down—and thus to emphasize the monotonous emptiness of the desert. The foot containing two heavy beats is called a *spondee;* it occurs only as an irregularity because a poem could not be composed in only heavy beats.

Often a poet substitutes one type of foot for another in order to slow or quicken the speed, to give emphasis or to slur over some words:

Múch hăve / Ĭ tráv / elĕd ĭn / the reálms / ŏf góld . . .

—Keats

Here is a trochaic substitution: an iambic line begins with a trochee. The heavy beat coming at the beginning gives impact to the word *Much.* Notice that the third foot contains two light beats. This is called a *pyrrhic* foot. Like a spondaic foot, it occurs only as an irregularity.

The poet's choice of what kind of meter to use, or whether to have meter at all, is not arbitrary. The nature of the poem—its theme, its tone, and so on—will influence his choice. We have seen how Whitman deliberately increased the proportion of light beats in the second half of "When I Heard the Learn'd Astronomer" (page 49) in order to achieve a particular emotional effect.

Most good poetry, with or without a metrical scheme, is musical; but a too rigid use of meter gives a sing-song effect, which, unless the poet wants to lull the reader into semiconsciousness, *may* ruin the poem. And because the rhythm of a line of poetry or even a sentence of prose is determined by the words themselves—some syllables being naturally accented and others not—the poet using an unvarying meter must either distort the word order so that the accents will fit his predetermined pattern, or he must ignore the natural rhythm of his words.

"When I Heard the Learn'd Astronomer" is written in free verse. We have seen how Whitman manipulates his rhythm in such a way that it reinforces the sense. The same thing may be done in a poem which has a metrical scheme. Notice how, in the following lines of iambic pentameter, metrical variations within the iambic pattern dramatize the sense of the words. This is a stanza from Shelley's lament on the early death of the poet John Keats.

from *Adonais*

PERCY BYSSHE SHELLEY

1792–1822

All he had loved, and molded into thought
From shape, and hue, and odor, and sweet sound,
Lamented Adonais.° Morning sought
Her eastern watchtower, and her hair unbound,
Wet with the tears which should adorn the ground,   5
Dimmed the aërial° eyes that kindle day;
Afar the melancholy thunder moaned,
Pale Ocean in unquiet slumber lay,
And the wild winds flew round, sobbing in their dismay.

3. Adonais (á·dŏn·ā'ĭs) or Adonis: in Greek mythology, a beautiful youth
who was loved by Aphrodite and who was killed while still young. 6. aërial
(ā·ēr'ĭ·ăl): inhabiting the air or sky.

The first line starts with a trochaic substitution. The opening
heavy beat emphasizes the importance of *All*. In lines 2 and 3, the
succession of qualities—*shape, hue, odor,* and *sound*—builds up to
the *Lamented Adonais.* The succession is slowed down by the heavy
accent on *sweet*, which makes the last foot of the second line a
spondee. *Lamented Adonais* is further emphasized by the fact that
the sentence ends in the middle of a line. Because lines 2, 3, and 4
each begin with a regular iambic foot, the trochaic substitutions
at the beginning of lines 5 and 6 add emphasis to the important
words *wet* and *dimmed*. In line 7 the meter returns to a regular, or
nearly regular, iambic rhythm; in its return it is more effective than
it would have been had the preceding lines been regular, and the
shift in rhythm gives very subtly an effect of distance. The flow
of rhythm in line 8 is broken by the opening spondee emphasizing
Pale and by the placing together of the sounds *in-* and *un-*, which
cannot be slurred over. Thus the restlessness of the ocean is reflected in the rhythm. The last line speaks of the wild winds, and
very windlike, it begins with two short, quick beats. After the pause

in the middle of the line, *sobbing* bursts out on a heavy beat. The line is very irregular:

Aňd the / wíld winds / fléw round, / sóbbing / iň théir / dismáy.

The *wild* and the *sob-* of "sobbing" and *flew*, all important ideas, are emphasized by their coming where a light beat would ordinarily occur. The extra foot in the last line is a characteristic of this stanza form, which was created by the sixteenth-century poet, Edmund Spenser. Shelley has skillfully taken advantage of the form to produce a strong closing to the stanza.

So you see that meter is not a helter-skelter sort of thing; the poet does not let the beats fall where they may. He manipulates the rhythm to reinforce the spirit of the words.

RHYME

Masculine rhyme is the commonest kind of rhyme. It is rhyme which occurs on the last syllables of the word: "day–away." *Feminine rhyme* occurs before the last syllables. The rhyming syllables are followed by identical unaccented syllables: "station–conversation (*double rhyme*); "unthinkable–undrinkable" (*triple rhyme*). Triple rhyme often occurs in light verse: "hen-pecked you all—intellectual"; "he has 'em—enthusiasm." Masculine and feminine rhyme ordinarily occur at the ends of lines:

> One thing then learnt remains to *me*,
> The woodspurge has a cup of *three*.
> > —Rossetti

Internal rhyme is sometimes used:

> I bring fresh *showers* to the thirsting *flowers*.
> > —Shelley

Initial or *beginning rhyme* occurs occasionally:

> *Vainly* might Plato's brain revolve it;
> *Plainly* the heart of a child might solve it.
> > —Lanier

Weak rhyme is rhyme which occurs on unaccented syllables: "dullest—nest"; "meadow—blow."

Imperfect rhyme involves sound *correspondences* of various types, rather than identical sounds. *Alliteration* is the repetition of beginning sounds: *weary, way-worn wanderer. Assonance* is the similarity of vowel sounds within words: *feel—need—beam; crown—loud —powder. Consonance* is the similarity of consonant sounds: *road— red; steady—study;* ba*ld—*co*ld.* These types of imperfect rhyme occur internally more often than as end rhymes.

In indicating the rhyme *scheme* of a stanza or an entire poem (for rhymes at the ends of lines) we use letters. Lines labeled with the same letter end in the same sound:

Only a man harrowing clods	A
In a slow silent walk,	B
With an old horse that stumbles and nods	A
Half asleep as they stalk	B

—Hardy

The rhyme scheme of the stanza from "Adonais" is A-B-A-B-B-C-B-C-C.

SOME OTHER DEVICES

Onomatopoeia: the imitation in a word, or series of words, of the sound the word or words designate: *bang, hiss, whisper,* etc. The effect of onomatopoeia is to reinforce the meaning of words through their sounds. The following line is a good example of onomatopoeia, alliteration, assonance, consonance, and internal rhyme:

The silken sad uncertain rustling of each purple curtain . . .

—Poe

The line is onomatopoeic because the hissing sound made by the *s*'s and soft *c* is imitative of the sound the curtain makes. Why is the line also alliterative, assonant, and consonant?

Cacophony: any combination of consonants which, because it is difficult to pronounce smoothly, slows the rhythm:

He clasps the crag with crooked hands
—Tennyson

Euphony: any combination of sounds which speeds up the rhythm because of ease of pronunciation:

Flies o'er the unbending corn, and skims along the main
—Pope

End-stopped lines: lines whose endings coincide with a natural speech pause:

The curfew tolls the knell of parting day,
The lowing herd wind slowly o'er the lea,
The plowman homeward plods his weary way,
And leaves the world to darkness and to me.
—Thomas Gray

Run-on lines: lines whose endings do not coincide with natural pauses:

To him who in the love of Nature holds
Communion with her visible forms, she speaks
A various language; for his gayer hours
She has a voice of gladness, and a smile
And eloquence of beauty; and she glides   5
Into his darker musings, with a mild
And healing sympathy . . .
—Bryant

Caesura: the main pause within a line. In the second line of the passage above the caesura occurs after *forms.* Lesser pauses are called *secondary pauses.* Obviously the number of pauses, their location, and their emphasis are important influences on the speed of a line.

We have already seen something of the importance of fabric in the discussion of "When I Heard The Learn'd Astronomer." We saw how Whitman used various sound devices (slow rhythm, cacophony, and many pauses) to convey the impression of tiresomeness and boredom in the first half of the poem, and other devices (swift rhythm, euphony, and fewer pauses) to convey in the second half of the poem the feeling of serenity.

Notice how the impression created in the following little poem is enhanced by careful manipulation of sound effects.

The Eagle

ALFRED, LORD TENNYSON

1809–1892

He clasps the crag with crooked hands;
Close to the sun in lonely lands,
Ringed with the azure° world, he stands.

The wrinkled sea beneath him crawls;
He watches from his mountain walls,   5
And like a thunderbolt he falls.

3. azure (ăzh'ēr): blue.

In the first line we have alliteration, assonance, consonance, and cacophony. It is impossible to read the line smoothly; the care that we must take to pronounce the words emphasizes them. The harsh consonants (*clasps, crag, crooked*) reinforce the idea of the strength of the eagle and the barrenness of the rocky landscape that is the eagle's home.

Tennyson uses two important devices in the second line. Again there is assonance: *close, lonely*; and alliteration: *lonely lands*; but the effect this time is euphonious. The *l*'s and *n*'s are softer, easier to pronounce than *clasps* and *crag*. The second device is a metrical one. The first line is regular iambic tetrameter. The second line starts with a trochaic substitution, so that there are two light beats in a row: *to the;* and the effect of the first half of the line is one of greater speed. With *lonely lands* the tempo slows down again, adding emphasis to the idea of loneliness.

Notice the caesura in line 3. This is the first caesura in the poem and the pause emphasizes *he stands,* throwing our attention to the majestic eagle surveying the landscape.

The last line contains the heavily accented word *thúnderbŏlt.* (A three-syllable word with two syllables accented is rare in English.) The *bolt* of *thunderbolt* seems to jump out at us from the rest of the line, just as the eagle suddenly plummets to the sea.

A classic illustration of fabric occurs in the following poem, in which Alexander Pope talks about the craftsmanship of poetry:

from *An Essay on Criticism*

ALEXANDER POPE

1688–1744

True ease in writing comes from art, not chance,
As those move easiest who have learned to dance.
'Tis not enough no harshness gives offense,
The sound must seem an echo to the sense.
Soft is the strain when zephyr gently blows,   5
And the smooth stream in smoother numbers flows;
But when loud surges lash the sounding shore,
The hoarse, rough verse should like the torrent roar:
When Ajax° strives some rock's vast weight to throw,
The line too labors, and the words move slow;   10
Not so, when swift Camilla° scours the plain,
Flies o'er the unbending corn,° and skims along the main.

9. **Ajax:** a Greek warrior noted for his strength and bravery. 11. **Camilla:** in Virgil's *Aeneid*, a princess described as so fleet of foot that she could run over a wheat field without bending the blades and over the ocean without wetting her feet. 12. **corn:** used in a general sense to indicate the principal grain of a region; here, wheat.

Beginning with line 5 the sound is indeed an echo of the sense. In lines 5 and 6 the *s*'s and soft consonants, the alliteration, and the placing together of the two light beats (line 5 begins with a trochaic substitution, line 6 with an irregular foot of two light beats) produce a smooth, euphonious effect. In line 7 heavy beats are substituted for light, and the consonants are harder and rougher. Notice the slow heaviness of line 10:

> The line too labors, and the words move slow

And the last line skims along with the fleetness which the poet is describing.

Although you may not immediately be aware of these devices when you read a poem, you could easily see the difference if they were removed. Compare the last line:

Flies o'er the unbending corn, and skims along the main.

with this version of the line:

Flies o'er the upright corn and plows along the main.

Poetry is a figurative language, a language of suggestion, a language of intense awareness, a language which communicates its meaning through a more or less formal structure. It seems almost unnecessary to add that poetry is also a musical language. We would be hard-pressed to find a poem—even though it had no rhyme and no regular meter—that had no music in it. Some poems derive their effect almost entirely from their music—or, as we have called it in this chapter, their fabric. The following poem makes less use of metaphor and symbol than do such poems as "Stopping by Woods on a Snowy Evening" and "Soundings." It is a straightforward narrative told, not as "Lord Randal" is told—in a series of dramatic hints —but in a direct way. It is a simple story and not altogether an original one. If you have enjoyed some of the preceding poems, difficult poems like "North Labrador" and "My Last Duchess," you may find "The Highwayman" rather childish. But the chances are that you will enjoy it nevertheless, for the story is an exciting one—as is any well-told story of passionate love, valiant fighting, heroism, and death. And what raises the story above the childish level is the musical quality of the language. The poem is made more exciting by the swing of the rhythm and the repetition of rich vowel sounds.

The Highwayman

ALFRED NOYES
1880–1958

PART ONE

The wind was a torrent of darkness and among the gusty trees,
The moon was a ghostly galleon tossed upon cloudy seas,
The road was a ribbon of moonlight over the purple moor,
And the highwayman came riding—
  Riding—riding—   5
The highwayman came riding, up to the old inn door.

He'd a French cocked hat on his forehead, a bunch of lace at his chin,
A coat of the claret° velvet, and breeches of brown doeskin;
They fitted with never a wrinkle; his boots were up to the thigh!
And he rode with a jeweled twinkle,   10
      His pistol butts a-twinkle,
His rapier hilt a-twinkle, under the jeweled sky.

Over the cobbles he clattered and clashed in the dark inn yard,
And he tapped with his whip on the shutters, but all was locked and
      barred:
He whistled a tune to the window, and who should be waiting there
But the landlord's black-eyed daughter,   16
      Bess, the landlord's daughter,
Plaiting a dark red love knot into her long black hair.

And dark in the dark old inn yard a stable wicket creaked
Where Tim the ostler° listened; his face was white and peaked;   20
His eyes were hollows of madness, his hair like moldly hay,
But he loved the landlord's daughter,
      The landlord's red-lipped daughter,
Dumb as a dog he listened, and he heard the robber say—

"One kiss, my bonny sweetheart, I'm after a prize tonight,   25
But I shall be back with the yellow gold before the morning light;
Yet, if they press me sharply, and harry me through the day,
Then look for me by moonlight,
      Watch for me by moonlight,
I'll come to thee by moonlight, though hell should bar the way."   30

He rose upright in the stirrups; he scarce could reach her hand,
But she loosened her hair i' the casement! His face burned like a
      brand
As the black cascade of perfume came tumbling over his breast;
And he kissed its waves in the moonlight,
      (Oh, sweet black waves in the moonlight!)   35
Then he tugged at his rein in the moonlight, and galloped away to
      the West.

8. **claret:** the color of claret wine, a deep red.   20. **ostler:** a stableman.

He did not come in the dawning; he did not come at noon;
And out o' the tawny sunset, before the rise o' the moon,
When the road was a gipsy's ribbon, looping the purple moor,
A red-coat troop came marching—   40
    Marching—marching—
King George's men came marching, up to the old inn door.

They said no word to the landlord, they drank his ale instead,
But they gagged his daughter and bound her to the foot of her narrow bed;
Two of them knelt at her casement, with muskets at their side!   45
There was death at every window;
    And hell at one dark window;
For Bess could see, through her casement, the road that *he* would ride.

They had tied her up to attention, with many a sniggering jest;
They had bound a musket beside her, with the barrel beneath her breast!   50
"Now keep good watch!" and they kissed her. She heard the dead man say—
Look for me by moonlight;
    Watch for me by moonlight;
I'll come to thee by moonlight, though hell should bar the way!

She twisted her hands behind her; but all the knots held good!   55
She writhed her hands till her fingers were wet with sweat or blood!
They stretched and strained in the darkness, and the hours crawled by like years,
Till now, on the stroke of midnight,
    Cold, on the stroke of midnight,
The tip of one finger touched it! The trigger at least was hers!   60

The tip of one finger touched it; she strove no more for the rest!
Up, she stood up to attention, with the barrel beneath her breast,
She would not risk their hearing: she would not strive again;

For the road lay bare in the moonlight;
    Blank and bare in the moonlight;   65
And the blood of her veins in the moonlight throbbed to her love's
    refrain.

Tlot-tlot; tlot-tlot! Had they heard it? The horse-hoofs ringing clear;
Tlot-tlot, tlot-tlot, in the distance? Were they deaf that they did not
    hear?
Down the ribbon of moonlight, over the brow of the hill,
The highwayman came riding,   70
        Riding, riding!
The red coats looked to their priming! She stood up, straight and
    still!

Tlot-tlot, in the frosty silence! *Tlot-tlot,* in the echoing night!
Nearer he came and nearer! Her face was like a light!
Her eyes grew wide for a moment; she drew one last deep breath,
Then her finger moved in the moonlight,   76
        Her musket shattered the moonlight,
Shattered her breast in the moonlight and warned him—with her
    death.

He turned; he spurred to the westward; he did not know who stood
Bowed, with her head o'er the musket, drenched with her own red
        blood!   80
Not till the dawn he heard it, his face grew gray to hear
How Bess, the landlord's daughter,
        The landlord's black-eyed daughter,
Had watched for her love in the moonlight, and died in the darkness
    there.

Back he spurred like a madman, shrieking a curse to the sky,   85
With the white road smoking behind him, and his rapier brandished
        high!
Blood red were his spurs in the golden moon; wine red was his velvet
    coat,

When they shot him down on the highway,
    Down like a dog on the highway,
And he lay in his blood on the highway, with a bunch of lace at his
    throat.   90

         ✿   ✿   ✿

And still of a winter's night, they say, when the wind is in the trees,
When the moon is a ghostly galleon tossed upon cloudy seas,
When the road is a ribbon of moonlight over the purple moor,
A highwayman comes riding—
    Riding—riding—   95
A highwayman comes riding, up to the old inn door.

Over the cobbles he clatters and clangs in the dark inn yard;
And he taps with his whip on the shutters, but all is locked and
    barred;
He whistles a tune to the window, and who should be waiting there
    But the landlord's black-eyed daughter,   100
        Bess, the landlord's daughter,
Plaiting a dark red love knot into her long black hair.

Had this narrative been told in prose, the sense of tension, hurry,
and excitement which the anapestic meter and the long lines give
would have been lacking. The meter is appropriate, not only for the
description of the highwayman on horseback, but also for the scenes
within the inn, where the atmosphere is one of tension and sudden
death.

The poem makes constant use of alliteration, consonance, and assonance.

> The moon was a ghostly galleon tossed upon cloudy seas,
> The road was a ribbon of moonlight over the purple
>   moor . . .

> Over the cobbles he clattered and clashed . . .

> He whistled a tune to the window, and who should be
>   waiting there . . .

The two most important ingredients of the poem are the moonlight and the love. The metaphor "The moon was a ghostly galleon" makes the atmosphere one of secrecy, mystery, and beauty; and the love is so passionate that each is prepared to die for the other. Toward the end of each stanza occurs what amounts to a little refrain. The constant repetition helps us to feel the effect.

> But the landlord's black-eyed daughter,
> Bess, the landlord's daughter, . . .

> Then look for me by moonlight,
> Watch for me by moonlight . . .

All of these things—the constant alliteration, the repetition of words and phrases, the feeling of urgency suggested by the deliberately insistent rhythm—combine to make the poem exciting. The story itself is trite, but these devices make its telling intense and memorable; they help us to "see more clearly [and] feel more deeply." The poem "enters [our] stock of memories and remains there." [1]

1. Stephen Vincent Benét. Foreword to *John Brown's Body*.

The Main-Deep

JAMES STEPHENS
1882–1950

The long rólling,
Steady-póuring,
Deep-trenchéd,
Green billow:

The wide-topped,   5
Unbróken,
Green glacid,°
Slow-sliding.

7. glacid: here, smooth and glossy.

Cold-flushing,
On—on—on—   10
Chill-rushing,
Hush-hushing,

Hush—hushing. . . .

Questions

1. The poet is obviously not attempting to give a full description of the
   sea. How has he selected and arranged his details so as to give a particular view?
2. How does Stephens suggest the feeling of movement? What is the
   wave doing in the last two lines?
3. Can you find some instances of alliteration? Of onomatopoeia? Of any
   of the other devices discussed in this chapter?

Bereft

ROBERT FROST
1874–1963

Where had I heard this wind before
Change like this to a deeper roar?
What would it take my standing there for,
Holding open a restive door,
Looking down hill to a frothy shore?   5
Summer was past and day was past.
Somber clouds on the West were massed.
Out in the porch's sagging floor
Leaves got up in a coil and hissed,
Blindly struck at my knee and missed,   10
Something sinister in the tone
Told me my secret must be known:
Word I was in the house alone
Somehow must have gotten abroad;
Word I was in my life alone;   15
Word I had no one left but God.

Questions

1. What situation does this poem describe? What is its mood?
2. What is the metrical scheme? What effect does it have on the mood?
3. Lines 6 and 7 are each one short sentence. What effect does this have?
4. What sort of arrangement of rhyme is there? What does the rhyme contribute to the total effect? At what point does the rhyme become most irregular? Why?

The Bells

EDGAR ALLAN POE
1809–1849

I

Hear the sledges with the bells,
    Silver bells!
What a world of merriment their melody foretells!
    How they tinkle, tinkle, tinkle,
      In the icy air of night!   5
    While the stars, that oversprinkle
    All the heavens, seem to twinkle
      With a crystalline delight;
    Keeping time, time, time,
    In a sort of runic° rhyme,   10
To the tintinnabulation° that so musically wells
    From the bells, bells, bells, bells,
      Bells, bells, bells—
  From the jingling and the tinkling of the bells.

II

    Hear the mellow wedding bells,   15
      Golden bells!
What a world of happiness their harmony foretells!
    Through the balmy air of night
    How they ring out their delight!

---

10. **runic:** here, magical, strange. (*Runes* were letters in an ancient Germanic alphabet.)   11. **tintinnabulation:** jingling of bells.

From the molten-golden notes,   20
And all in tune,
What a liquid ditty floats
To the turtledove that listens, while she gloats
On the moon!
Oh, from out the sounding cells,   25
What a gush of euphony voluminously wells!
How it swells!
How it dwells
On the future! how it tells
Of the rapture that impels   30
To the swinging and the ringing
Of the bells, bells, bells,
Of the bells, bells, bells, bells,
Bells, bells, bells—
To the rhyming and the chiming of the bells!   35

III

Hear the loud alarum bells,
Brazen bells!
What a tale of terror, now, their turbulency tells!
In the startled ear of night
How they scream out their affright!   40
Too much horrified to speak,
They can only shriek, shriek,
Out of tune,
In a clamorous appealing to the mercy of the fire,
In a mad expostulation with the deaf and frantic fire,   45
Leaping higher, higher, higher,
With a desperate desire,
And a resolute endeavor
Now—now to sit or never,
By the side of the pale-faced moon.   50
Oh, the bells, bells, bells!
What a tale their terror tells
Of despair!
How they clang, and clash, and roar!
What a horror they outpour   55

On the bosom of the palpitating air!
   Yet the ear, it fully knows,
     By the twanging
     And the clanging,
   How the danger ebbs and flows;   60
   Yet the ear distinctly tells,
     In the jangling
     And the wrangling,
   How the danger sinks and swells—
By the sinking or the swelling in the anger of the bells,   65
     Of the bells,
   Of the bells, bells, bells, bells,
     Bells, bells, bells—
In the clamor and the clangor of the bells!

IV

   Hear the tolling of the bells,   70
     Iron bells!
What a world of solemn thought their monody° compels!
     In the silence of the night
     How we shiver with affright
   At the melancholy menace of their tone!   75
     For every sound that floats
     From the rust within their throats
       Is a groan.
     And the people—ah, the people,
     They that dwell up in the steeple,   80
       All alone,
     And who tolling, tolling, tolling
      In that muffled monotone,
     Feel a glory in so rolling
      On the human heart a stone—   85
   They are neither man nor woman,
   They are neither brute nor human,
     They are ghouls:
   And their king it is who tolls;

72. **monody:** a type of music sung by one voice; in ancient times a monody was sung as a funeral song.

And he rolls, rolls, rolls,   90
 Rolls
  A paean° from the bells;
And his merry bosom swells
 With the paean of the bells,
And he dances, and he yells: 95
 Keeping time, time, time,
In a sort of runic rhyme,
  To the paean of the bells,
   Of the bells:
 Keeping time, time, time,   100
 In a sort of runic rhyme,
  To the throbbing of the bells,
 Of the bells, bells, bells—
  To the sobbing of the bells;
 Keeping time, time, time,   105
  As he knells, knells, knells,
 In a happy runic rhyme,
  To the rolling of the bells,
 Of the bells, bells, bells:
  To the tolling of the bells, 110
 Of the bells, bells, bells, bells,
  Bells, bells, bells—
To the moaning and the groaning of the bells.

92. **paean:** a song of praise or joy.

Questions

1. "The Bells" is primarily a study in sound. To achieve his effects, Poe makes liberal use of many of the devices mentioned in this chapter. Each of the four stanzas is meant to evoke a different mood. Each has a different kind of bell for its symbol. What kind of bell is described in each stanza, and what mood is each meant to evoke?
2. What devices does Poe use to achieve his effects? Quote specific lines from each stanza to illustrate the devices.
3. Are there any metrical variations other than the varying length of the lines? Do these variations (if any) serve a purpose, or are they due merely to the accidental accents of the words? Does the meter change as the mood changes, or is it the same throughout?

Sea-Fever

JOHN MASEFIELD
1878–

I must down to the seas again, to the lonely sea and the sky,
And all I ask is a tall ship and a star to steer her by,
And the wheel's kick and the wind's song and the white sail's shaking
And a gray mist on the sea's face and a gray dawn breaking.

I must down to the seas again, for the call of the running tide   5
Is a wild call and a clear call that may not be denied;
And all I ask is a windy day with the white clouds flying,
And the flung spray and the blown spume,° and the sea gulls crying.

I must down to the seas again to the vagrant gypsy life.
To the gull's way and the whale's way where the wind's like a
    whetted knife;   10
And all I ask is a merry yarn from a laughing fellow rover,
And quiet sleep and a sweet dream when the long trick's° over.

    8. spume: foam.   12. trick: turn of duty at the helm; here, figuratively, life.

Questions

1. What is the character of the meter? Is it swift, slow, light, heavy, or what? Is it fairly regular or are there frequent irregularities? If there are irregularities, do they seem arbitrary or do they add something to the music of the verse? What do they add?
2. Is the meter appropriate to the subject?
3. What kind of rhyme occurs in the second couplet of each stanza? What does this rhyme add to the poem?
4. What device has Masefield used in line 10? Can you find instances of it in other lines? Can you find examples of assonance?
5. Is "Sea-Fever" a musical poem or merely a sing-song poem? Would you call it a more musical poem than "The Bells"? Why, or why not?

Lyric

CHARLES GOODWIN

1924–

Lightning licks the surfaces
The old uncertainties remain.
Thunder past the farthest hill
Mumbles half-truths and is still.
There is no rain.   5

Somewhere sea gulls cry and soar,
Tomorrow, yesterday, today.
Somewhere breakers reach the shore
Somewhere distantly implore.
They turn away.   10

Sorrow like the rotting pear
Falls and leaves the branches bare
Falls and leaves the autumn air
No memories. Yet I swear
I do not care.   15

Questions

1. What seems to be the theme of this poem as announced in the first
   stanza? How is this theme developed in the second stanza? What new
   element is introduced in the third stanza?
2. How does the fabric of the poem help to create its mood? For instance,
   what about the rhyme scheme of the first stanza? What happens to it
   in the second stanza? in the third? What effect do these changes have
   on the mood?
3. What about the meter? How does the meter of the last stanza differ
   from that of the first two stanzas? What effect has this variation? Why
   is the second line of the last stanza not indented?
4. What effect has the caesura in line 14?

Silence

JOHN HALL WHEELOCK
1886–

There is a mystery too deep for words:
The silence of the dead comes nearer to it,
Being wisest in the end. What word shall hold
The sorrow sitting at the heart of things,
The majesty and patience of the truth!   5
Silence will serve; it is an older tongue:
The empty room, the moonlight on the wall,
Speak for the unreturning traveler.

Questions

1. What is the character of the meter: swift, slow, heavy, light, formal,
   conversational, sing-song, or what? How is this character achieved? Is
   it appropriate to the theme?
2. What is the effect of the caesuras in lines 3 and 6?
3. What is the effect of the opening trochaic substitutions in lines 6 and 8?
4. What is the effect of the absence of rhyme?

High Flight

JOHN GILLESPIE MAGEE, JR.
1922–1941

Oh, I have slipped the surly bonds of earth,
And danced the skies on laughter-silvered wings;
Sunward I've climbed and joined the tumbling mirth
Of sun-spilt clouds—and done a hundred things
You have not dreamed of—wheeled and soared and swung   5
High in the sunlit silence. Hovering there
I've chased the shouting wind along and flung
My eager craft through footless halls of air.
Up, up the long delirious burning blue
I've topped the windswept heights with easy grace,   10

Where never lark, or even eagle, flew;
And, while with silent, lifting mind I've trod
The high untrespassed sanctity of space,
Put out my hand, and touched the face of God.

Questions

1. In this sonnet what is the effect of the metrical variations in lines
6 and 9? Of the caesuras in lines 4, 5, and 14?
2. Of what kind of experience is this poem a description? What is its
tone?

For Further Study

Among the poems in Part Two of this book, the following offer
good examples of the way the fabric of a poem contributes to its
effect:

Ben Jonson, "Slow, Slow, Fresh Fount," page 198
John Milton, "The Departure from Eden," page 237
John Dryden, "Alexander's Feast," page 250
Alfred, Lord Tennyson, "The Lotos-Eaters," page 351
Algernon Charles Swinburne, "A Forsaken Garden," page 387
Gerard Manley Hopkins, "Spring and Fall: To a Young Child,"
page 439
William Butler Yeats, "After Long Silence," page 452

CHAPTER IX *Imagination and Truth*

"Poetry," said Carl Sandburg, "is the synthesis of hyacinths and biscuits." In other words, poetry combines the ideal, the romantic, and the beautiful with the usual, the everyday, and the seemingly unromantic. (Notice that Sandburg's statement is more poetic than the explanation of it because it suggests in a specific picture everything that the explanation says in a string of adjectives.)

Sometimes poetry reveals the everyday qualities of an unusual situation, sometimes the mysterious and romantic qualities of an ordinary situation.

The Solitary Reaper

WILLIAM WORDSWORTH
1770–1850

Behold her, single in the field,
Yon solitary highland lass!
Reaping and singing by herself;
Stop here, or gently pass!
Alone she cuts and binds the grain,   5
And sings a melancholy strain;
O listen! for the vale profound
Is overflowing with the sound.

No nightingale did ever chaunt
More welcome notes to weary bands   10
Of travelers in some shady haunt,
Among Arabian sands:
A voice so thrilling ne'er was heard
In spring time from the cuckoo bird,

Breaking the silence of the seas   15
Among the farthest Hebrides.°

Will no one tell me what she sings?
Perhaps the plaintive numbers flow
For old, unhappy, far-off things,
And battles long ago: 20
Or is it some more humble lay,
Familiar matter of today?
Some natural sorrow, loss, or pain,
That has been, and may be again?

Whate'er the theme, the maiden sang   25
As if her song could have no ending;
I saw her singing at her work,
And o'er the sickle bending;
I listened, motionless and still;
And, as I mounted up the hill   30
The music in my heart I bore,
Long after it was heard no more.

16. **Hebrides:** a group of islands off the west coast of Scotland.

   This poem illustrates on a fairly simple level the lure of the mysterious. While walking in the highlands of Scotland, the speaker
has come upon a girl reaping and singing alone. Enchanted by her
song, he has stopped to listen. She is apparently singing in Gaelic,
for the speaker cannot understand her words. The sadness of her
mood stirs his imagination, and he speculates on the subject of the
song. It doesn't really matter what the song is about; it is the experience of hearing it that is meaningful. This experience is so real
and so powerful that after the speaker has passed the lone singer
and gone on his way, he continues to hear the song in his mind and
to be moved by it. In describing an ordinary kind of event Wordsworth has given us a sudden glimpse into the profound mystery of
life.

The scientist searches for his kind of truth with his reason, the poet with his imagination. The poet's truth is not a logical truth. He is not interested in the general rule, but in the particular experience. His truth is the experience itself, and it is true because he has made it true. He is intensely aware of the mysteries of life and fascinated by them, but unlike the scientist, he is not necessarily concerned with solving them.

Perhaps this concept is difficult to understand at once. It will become clearer as you read more poems. In this regard, let us reconsider briefly "The Highwayman."

In "The Highwayman" we are beguiled into sympathizing with a criminal and hating the officers of the law. The power of Noyes' verse moves us momentarily into taking the criminal's point of view. Why do we sympathize with the highwayman? We are made to identify ourselves with him because the story is presented from his point of view. We do not see him indulging in his questionable trade; there is only one allusion to it, and that has a romantic flavor: "One kiss, my bonny sweetheart, I'm after a prize tonight . . ." Furthermore, we see him only as a lover, and "all the world loves a lover." He is also a hero who fights valiantly to avenge his sweetheart's heroic death. The lovers' enemies are made mean and ungentlemanly. Tim, the ostler, whose eyes are "hollows of madness," spies on the lovers and "squeals" on them; and the Redcoats treat Bess with rudeness and brutality.

Thus the poet has tricked us into cheering for the wrong side—by making it seem for a moment to be the right side, the true side. Indeed, in the world of the poem it *is* the true side. Noyes retains our allegiance to the end by giving his hero a splendid death. Then, in order not to make the ending too unhappy for us, he uses a device frequently found in stories and poems with similar circumstances: he suggests that the ghosts of the lovers return to re-enact their love scene. He does not insist that this really does happen. He presents it as something "they say" happens. By presenting it as a kind of legend rather than as fact, he takes care of his more literal-minded readers.

Thus has Noyes made a rather sordid story into something moving and heroic. He has made us feel the "truth" of the passionate love and the gallant deeds.

The poet Edwin Arlington Robinson once said that poetry is "a language that tells us, through a more or less emotional reaction, something that cannot be said."

To a Poet a Thousand Years Hence

JAMES ELROY FLECKER
1884–1915

I who am dead a thousand years,
    And wrote this sweet archaic song,
Send you my words for messengers
    The way I shall not pass along.

I care not if you bridge the seas,   5
    Or ride secure the cruel sky,
Or build consummate palaces
    Of metal or of masonry.

But have you wine and music still,
    And statues and a bright-eyed love,   10
And foolish thoughts of good and ill,
    And prayers to them who sit above?

How shall we conquer? Like a wind
    That falls at eve our fancies blow,
And old Maeonides° the blind   15
    Said it three thousand years ago.

O friend unseen, unborn, unknown,
    Student of our sweet English tongue,
Read out my words at night, alone:
    I was a poet, I was young.   20

15. **Maeonides** (mē·o′nĭ·dēz): Homer, reputedly the author of the *Iliad* and the *Odyssey*.

Since I can never see your face,
And never shake you by the hand,
I send my soul through time and space
To greet you. You will understand.

This poem "tells" us something that "cannot be said." The word *tells* means in this context, of course, *suggests* or *causes the reader to perceive*. It tells us that the things in life that really matter, the things that are timeless and changeless, are the things of the spirit: not the skyscrapers and airplanes, the speed and the power, but the "wine and music," the "statues and a bright-eyed love," the "foolish thoughts" and the "prayers to them who sit above." These are the things that elevate the spirit and bring joy and meaning into life.

The poem communicates this idea to us, not as a person might state a fact to which a listener might well say, "Oh? Indeed?"; rather, the poem communicates it to us as an active experience. The experience is one that any thoughtful person might have: it is simply the insight into human values, into what is important and lasting and what is not. It is an insight that cannot be taught. One must experience it for himself.

Read out my words at night, alone:
I was a poet, I was young.

The poet a thousand years hence, looking back on our civilization, may be bewildered by some of our customs; but if he is a poet, the spark which kindles his imagination and spirit will respond to the spark which kindles ours, just as we can still respond to the creative spark of the Greeks and the men of the Middle Ages and the Renaissance.

Flecker is suggesting that if man's spiritual life does not die, the man of the future will understand our emotions and aspirations, though perhaps not our automobiles and our hats.

I send my soul through time and space
To greet you. You will understand.

To an Athlete Dying Young

A. E. HOUSMAN
1859–1936

The time you won your town the race
We chaired° you through the market place;
Man and boy stood cheering by,
And home we brought you shoulder-high.

Today, the road all runners come,   5
Shoulder-high we bring you home,
And set you at your threshold down,
Townsman of a stiller town.

Smart lad, to slip betimes° away
From fields where glory does not stay,   10
And early though the laurel° grows
It withers quicker than the rose.

Eyes the shady night has shut
Cannot see the record cut,
And silence sounds no worse than cheers   15
After earth has stopped the ears:

Now you will not swell the rout
Of lads that wore their honors out,
Runners whom renown outran
And the name died before the man.   20

So set, before its echoes fade,
The fleet foot on the sill of shade,
And hold to the low lintel° up
The still-defended challenge cup.

2. **chaired**: carried publicly in triumph on a chair.   9. **betimes**: early.
11. **laurel**: A wreath of laurel was worn by the victors in the ancient Olympic
games.   23. **lintel**: a horizontal span over a doorway.

And round that early laureled head
Will flock to gaze the strengthless dead,
And find unwithered on its curls
The garland briefer than a girl's.

"To an Athlete Dying Young" illustrates the validity of Housman's statement, "Poetry is not the thing said, but the way of saying it." The situation is one which in less skillful hands might have become sentimental. Death is a sad thing, especially the death of a promising youth. This poem escapes sentimentality for several reasons.

The most obvious reason is that Housman congratulates rather than mourns the youth. All the imagery suggests that the death was a victory, not a defeat. The lad's funeral is presented as a last race, which he has won. In an earlier race the victor had been carried home in triumph "shoulder-high." Now the "shoulder-high" has a new meaning—this is the manner in which a coffin is carried—but the implications are the same: the runner is again victorious. The imagery of the funeral as a race is carried out in detail. The "sill of shade" on which the runner has set his "fleet foot" is the edge of the grave. Because the runner has beaten his competitors in the race to the grave, he can hold up forever the "still-defended challenge cup." The entire theme of the poem is a paradox because one does not usually think of early death as a desirable thing. The sixth stanza contains a specific paradox. We think of a corpse as being inert. But here the dead youth has a "fleet foot" and is able to hold aloft the challenge cup. The lad's foot is fleet because the imagery has made it so: the lad is running his last race, winning his greatest victory. The adjective *still-defended* is especially rich because it has meaning on two levels. It means, of course, defended still: not surrendered even now; and it also means defended in the stillness of death. The stillness will never be broken. The laurel will never wither.

Of course the athlete's early death really is a sad thing, yet we feel the sadness precisely because Housman does not present the occasion as sad. The irony of the poet's congratulations, the richness of the paradoxes, and the precision and originality of the imagery ask of us a certain mental activity; and in this activity we discover for ourselves the pathos of the lad's death.

We are made to *feel* the truth of the poem; and because we feel it so strongly, it is a truth we remember long after we have forgotten thousands of facts that we have simply been told.

"Truth," then, has little to do with whether the bare idea of a poem is factually accurate; the poem is "true" if it succeeds in making the world that it has created convincing and vivid and alive.

------••◁◇▷••------

Madman's Song

ELINOR WYLIE
1886–1928

Better to see your cheek grown hollow,
Better to see your temple worn,
Than to forget to follow, follow,
After the sound of a silver horn.

Better to bind your brow with willow   5
And follow, follow until you die,
Than to sleep with your head on a golden pillow,
Nor lift it up when the hunt goes by.

Better to see your cheek grown sallow
And your hair grow gray, so soon, so soon,   10
Than to forget to hallo, hallo,
After the milk-white hounds of the moon.

Questions

1. What does the poem imply will happen to you if you do follow the "milk-white hounds of the moon"? If you ignore the hounds and the horn and the hunt, what then?
2. Is the title meant to be ironic?
3. What do you think the hunt imagery symbolizes? A rereading of "Voyage West" (page 98) may affect your answer. Are the attitudes expressed in these two poems similar or different?

Elysium Is as Far

EMILY DICKINSON
1830–1886

Elysium° is as far as to
The very nearest room,
If in that room a friend await
Felicity or doom.

What fortitude the soul contains,   5
That it can so endure
The accent of a coming foot,
The opening of a door.

1. **Elysium** (ê·lĭzh'ĭ·ŭm): in Greek mythology, the place where the good dwell after death; hence, a place of ideal happiness.

Questions

1. Keeping in mind the traditional meaning of "Elysium," explain the first stanza. What does the second stanza suggest?
2. In what sense is this a poem about a mystery?

The Man with the Hoe

EDWIN MARKHAM
1852–1940

Written after Seeing Millet's World-famous Painting
of a Brutalized Toiler in the Deep Abyss of Labor

God made man in His own image; in the image of God made He him.

—GENESIS

Bowed by the weight of centuries he leans
Upon his hoe and gazes on the ground,
The emptiness of ages in his face,
And on his back the burden of the world.
Who made him dead to rapture and despair,   5
A thing that grieves not and that never hopes,
Stolid and stunned, a brother to the ox?

Who loosened and let down this brutal jaw?
Whose was the hand that slanted back this brow?
Whose breath blew out the light within this brain?   10
Is this the thing the Lord God made and gave
To have dominion over sea and land;
To trace the stars and search the heavens for power;
To feel the passion of eternity?
Is this the dream He dreamed who shaped the suns   15
And marked their ways upon the ancient deep?
Down all the caverns of hell to their last gulf
There is no shape more terrible than this—
More tongued with cries against the world's blind greed—
More filled with signs and portents° for the soul—   20
More packed with danger to the universe.

What gulfs between him and the seraphim!°
Slave of the wheel of labor, what to him
Are Plato and the swing of Pleiades?°
What the long reaches of the peaks of song,   25
The rift of dawn, the reddening of the rose?
Through this dread shape the suffering ages look;
Time's tragedy is in that aching stoop;
Through this dread shape humanity betrayed,
Plundered, profaned, and disinherited,   30
Cries protest to the Powers that made the world,
A protest that is also prophecy.
O masters, lords and rulers in all lands,
Is this the handiwork you give to God,
This monstrous thing distorted and soul-quenched?   35
How will you ever straighten up this shape;
Touch it again with immortality;
Give back the upward looking and the light;
Rebuild in it the music and the dream;
Make right the immemorial infamies,   40
Perfidious wrongs, immedicable° woes?

20. **portents** (pŏr′tĕnts): forewarnings. 22. **seraphim** (sĕr′á·fĭm): the highest order of angels. 24. **Pleiades** (plē′yá·dēz): a group of stars near the constellation Orion. 41. **immedicable** (ĭm·mĕd′ĭ·ká·b'l): incurable.

O masters, lords and rulers in all lands,
How will the future reckon with this man?
How answer his brute question in that hour
When whirlwinds of rebellion shake all shores?   45
How will it be with kingdoms and with kings—
With those who shaped him to the thing he is—
When this dumb Terror shall rise to judge the world,
After the silence of the centuries?

Questions

1. Markham communicates his ideas largely through direct statement.
   Can you point to at least four passages that are abstract, direct statements?
2. Beginning with line 42 "The Man with the Hoe" is primarily a series
   of prophetic rhetorical questions. Does the accuracy or inaccuracy of
   the prophecies affect the value of the poem? Why, or why not?

The Oxen

THOMAS HARDY
1840–1928

Christmas Eve, and twelve of the clock,
    "Now they are all on their knees,"
An elder said as we sat in a flock
    By the embers in hearthside ease.

We pictured the meek mild creatures where   5
    They dwelt in their strawy pen,
Nor did it occur to one of us there
    To doubt they were kneeling then.

So fair a fancy few would weave
    In these years! Yet, I feel,   10
If someone said on Christmas Eve,
    "Come; see the oxen kneel

"In the lonely barton° by yonder coomb°
  Our childhood used to know,"
I should go with him in the gloom,   15
  Hoping it might be so.

13. **barton:** farmyard. **coomb:** a narrow valley.

Questions

1. The theme of "The Oxen" is based on what old belief?
2. What happens in the last two lines of the second stanza and the first two lines of the third? How has the speaker's belief changed with the years? How does he feel about the change?
3. How does the theme of "The Oxen" compare to the theme of "Dover Beach" (page 53)?

Christmas Eve, 1959

RAYMOND HOLDEN
1894–

Deep on this roof a ponderous air is piled
And round its masses the unreconciled,
Clenched fire of plunging fury burns, and yet
The roof tree holds, and the rose-misty jet
Of hearth smoke, tendril-frail and light,   5
Climbs without hindrance cold's uncreviced height.
Night holds its breath. The snow, with mouse-foot fall
That, were it not to end, would slay us all,
Seals motion, shortens breath, stills sound, and stops
Short, though it need not, of our chimney-tops.   10

This respite is our refuge, like that poise
Which the momentous universe employs
To print itself upon the recipient sense
And place small man on terms with the immense:

An Archimedes'° point on which to stand   15
With reason's lever in the body's hand
And hold the ponderous beast of space at bay
For long enough to learn the time of day.

It is a winter evening. We are here,
Marking with fire the season of the year,   20
Aware of evil's possible portent,
Of that ungovernable government
Which keeps, between reality and wraith,°
The checks of hope, the balances of faith;
Aware of death, aware of life, aware   25
Of love, a violence in a cage of care,
That could destroy, but will not, those consents
Which give cohesion to man's elements.

15. **Archimedes** (är'kĭ·mē'dēz): a Greek mathematician of the third century B.C. He claimed that if he had a place to stand and to rest his lever, he could move the world. 23. **wraith** (rāth): an apparition.

Questions

1. What is the significance of "The roof tree holds" in line 4? Why in line 7 does night hold "its breath"?
2. What is the theme of this poem? In which line is the theme most explicitly expressed?

Ode on a Grecian Urn

JOHN KEATS
1795–1821

Thou still unravished bride of quietness,
    Thou foster child of silence and slow time,
Sylvan° historian, who canst thus express
    A flowery tale more sweetly than our rime:
What leaf-fringed legend haunts about thy shape   5

3. **Sylvan:** pertaining to the forest.

Of deities or mortals, or of both,
    In Tempe° or the dales of Arcady?°
What men or gods are these? What maidens loth?
What mad pursuit? What struggle to escape?
    What pipes and timbrels?° What wild ecstasy?   10

Heard melodies are sweet, but those unheard
    Are sweeter; therefore, ye soft pipes, play on;
Not to the sensual ear, but, more endeared,
    Pipe to the spirit ditties of no tone:
Fair youth, beneath the trees, thou canst not leave   15
    Thy song, nor ever can those trees be bare;
        Bold Lover, never, never canst thou kiss,
Though winning near the goal—yet, do not grieve;
    She cannot fade, though thou hast not thy bliss,
    For ever wilt thou love, and she be fair!   20

Ah, happy, happy boughs! that cannot shed
    Your leaves, nor ever bid the Spring adieu;
And, happy melodist, unwearied,
    For ever piping songs for ever new;
More happy love! more happy, happy love!   25
    For ever warm and still to be enjoyed,
        For ever panting and for ever young;
All breathing human passion far above,
    That leaves a heart high-sorrowful and cloyed,°
    A burning forehead, and a parching tongue.   30

Who are these coming to the sacrifice?
    To what green altar, O mysterious priest,
Lead'st thou that heifer lowing at the skies,
    And all her silken flanks with garlands dressed?
What little town by river or sea-shore,   35
    Or mountain-built with peaceful citadel,
        Is emptied of its folk, this pious morn?

7. **Tempe:** a beautiful valley in Greece. **Arcady** (or **Arcadia**): in ancient
Greece, a region noted for its beauty and for the contentment of those who
dwelt there. 10. **timbrels:** small drums or tambourines. 29. **cloyed:** over-
satisfied, satiated.

And, little town, thy streets for evermore
Will silent be; and not a soul to tell
Why thou art desolate, can e'er return.   40

Attic° shape! Fair attitude! with brede°
Of marble men and maidens overwrought,
With forest branches and the trodden weed;
Thou, silent form, dost tease us out of thought
As doth eternity: Cold Pastoral!°   45
When old age shall this generation waste,
Thou shalt remain, in midst of other woe
Than ours, a friend to man, to whom thou say'st,
"Beauty is truth, truth beauty—that is all
Ye know on earth, and all ye need to know."   50

41. **Attic:** pertaining to Attica, a region of ancient Greece. **brede:** embroidery; here, probably the decorative band running around the urn. 45. **Cold Pastoral:** Pastoral poetry, a popular verse form among the ancient Greeks, deals with the simple lives of shepherds in rural settings; here, Keats compares the urn to such a poem.

Questions

1. Whom or what does Keats address in the first stanza? in each of the succeeding stanzas?
2. Stanzas 2, 3, and 4 each present a series of scenes: various people are shown. What do all of these people have in common?
3. In what sense is the urn a "historian"?

Now we come to the central problem of the poem: the apparent absurdity of the ending. Taken from its context, the statement about truth and beauty is either meaningless or silly. We have seen that the "meaning" of a poem cannot be removed from the poem, because that meaning is the result of the imagery, the symbols, the sound, and all the other elements that combine to create it. In order to determine whether the statement of the last two lines was arbitrarily (and therefore meaninglessly) applied to the poem or whether it is an idea that properly belongs to the world of the marble urn, let us look again at the poem rather closely.

4. In stanza 2, Keats says to the lover who is about to kiss, "do not grieve." Why should he grieve? Why shouldn't he?

5. What does the last half of stanza 3 imply about the real world? about the world of the marble urn?
6. You will note that the scenes on the urn are scenes of intense vitality and warmth, most of them even of "wild ecstasy." Why is this paradoxical? The paradox of the poem is summed up finally in "Cold Pastoral!" Explain.
7. What does Keats mean when he says in the last stanza that the urn "dost tease us out of thought / As doth eternity"? Why does eternity tease us out of thought? Why does the urn?
8. The urn and the scenes are apparently very beautiful. On what is this beauty based? Does this beauty have anything in common with truth? (Glance again at questions 3 and 7.)
9. Notice that the statement about truth and beauty is made by the urn itself. In what sense is this statement a commentary on its own nature or on the nature of all artistic expression?
10. Does this final statement develop from the poem, or is it a "moral" tacked onto the end?

For Further Study

The following poems in Part Two of this book are all related, in various ways, to the questions about imagination and truth that have been raised in this chapter:

Robert Greene, "Doron's Description of Samela," page 174
Robert Herrick, "Corinna's Going A-Maying," page 216
John Suckling, "The Constant Lover," page 224
Alexander Pope, From *The Dunciad*, page 265
Robert Burns, "My Luve," page 289
William Wordsworth, "The World Is Too Much with Us," page 299
Dylan Thomas, "Do Not Go Gentle into That Good Night," page 487
Marianne Moore, "Poetry," page 518
W. H. Auden, "The Unknown Citizen," page 538
Peter Viereck, "Kilroy," page 547

Conclusion to Part One

Now that we have read several chapters on the nature of poetry and studied many poems, have we arrived any closer to a definition of poetry? As a matter of fact, we are now further than ever from a definition, because we can see how vast is the range of poetry and how various are its modes of expression. Any definition is going to be too narrow. How could any statement completely describe, for instance, Sandburg's "Fog," Frost's "Stopping by Woods on a Snowy Evening," Keats's "Ode on a Grecian Urn," Whitman's "When I Heard the Learn'd Astronomer," Browning's "My Last Duchess," and Dickinson's "Indian Summer"? The mere listing of these titles shows us what a variety of things poetry can do and how different one poem can be from another.

Let us hope, however, that we are nearer to an awareness of what kind of thing poetry is. No one can define life, but he who has lived intensely and has had a wide range of experience knows more about life than he who has never opened his eyes.

This book began with four generalizations about poetry:

1. It creates its total effect through imagery and figures of speech.
2. It is a language of suggestion as well as statement.
3. It is a language of intense awareness and *therefore* of heightened emotion.
4. It communicates its meaning through form or structure.

By now these statements should be meaningful to you. As you read the poems in Part Two of this book and react to them, you will learn much more—but these ideas are basic.

Let us examine the third idea again very briefly—the idea of intense awareness.

A poem engages our whole attention, whether it is simply a description of a wave, like "The Main-Deep," or a philosophical observation about modern life, like "Nearing Again the Legendary

Isle." The imaginative insights into experience that a good poem gives us cannot help but sharpen our own perceptions and increase our awareness of life's possibilities and significance. A good poem is *exciting*. It is an active experience, just as active as climbing a mountain or handling a sailboat in a stiff wind. All three kinds of experience demand heightened awareness; and awareness is exciting.

Little Exercise

ELIZABETH BISHOP

1911–

Think of the storm roaming the sky uneasily
like a dog looking for a place to sleep in,
listen to it growling.

Think how they must look now, the mangrove keys
lying out there unresponsive to the lightning   5
in dark, course-fibred families,

where occasionally a heron may undo his head,
shake up his feathers, make an uncertain comment
when the surrounding water shines.

Think of the boulevard and the little palm trees   10
all stuck in rows, suddenly revealed
as fistfuls of limp fish-skeletons.

It is raining there. The boulevard
and its broken sidewalks with weeds in every crack,
are relieved to be wet, the sea to be freshened.   15

Now the storm goes away again in a series
of small, badly lit battle scenes,
each in "Another part of the field."

Think of someone sleeping in the bottom of a row boat
tied to a mangrove root or the pile of a bridge;   20
think of him as uninjured, barely disturbed.

The insights, the perceptions, the pictures, and the music of the
lines—all these combine to create the complex, subtle, and intense
experience that is a poem. Poetry has been called "the chemistry of
words." More than anyone else, poets explore the possibilities of
language. By making new combinations of words, by using ordinary
words in a fresh way, poetry reveals the power and splendor of
language. When you can respond to such lines as

> For old, unhappy, far-off things,
> And battles long ago . . .
> —Wordsworth

and

> But such a tide as moving seems asleep,
> Too full for sound and foam . . .
> —Tennyson

and

> O for a beaker full of the warm South!
> Full of the true, the blushful Hippocrene,
> With beaded bubbles winking at the brim,
> And purple-stainèd mouth . . .
> —Keats

you will possess a source of pleasure that "age cannot wither . . .
nor custom stale."

2

A
COLLECTION
OF BRITISH
AND AMERICAN
POEMS

*From the Fifteenth Century
to the Present Day*

EARLY BALLADS AND TUDOR POETRY

Some of the English and Scottish folk ballads must have developed from very old originals, but the majority seem to have originated during the fourteenth and fifteenth centuries. It was not until the late eighteenth century that any attempt was made to collect and publish the ballads. The typical folk ballad is simple in form, brief, and dramatic in effect. The apparent simplicity is often the result of remarkable technical skill (see "Lord Randal," page 21).

The Tudor period in English poetry takes its title from the name of the royal family that began its reign in 1485, the year that Henry Tudor overthrew Richard III and became Henry VII. The year 1485 is often considered the end of the medieval period in England. This year could also be said to mark the beginning of Modern English poetry, as opposed to poetry in Middle English, the language of Chaucer. One of the earliest of the Tudor poets, John Skelton, personifies the change. His language, though it may sometimes seem strange to a present-day reader, is nevertheless clearly Modern English. In tone and spirit, however, Skelton's poetry is in the medieval tradition.

In 1557 Richard Tottel published an anthology of poetry called *Songs and Sonnets*. Popularly known as *Tottel's Miscellany*, the book was much imitated throughout the sixteenth century. It is important not only because it was the first anthology of its kind, but also because it contained the first sonnets in English (by Sir Thomas Wyatt) and the first significant use of blank verse (by Henry Howard, Earl of Surrey). Both verse forms were to come to full flower in the next period of English poetry, the Elizabethan Age.

EARLY BALLADS

Sir Patrick Spens

The king sits in Dumferling toune,
　　Drinking the blude-reid wine:
"O whar will I get guid sailor,
　　To sail this schip of mine?"

Up and spak an eldern knicht,　　　　　　5
　　Sat at the kings richt kne:
"Sir Patrick Spens is the best sailor,
　　That sails upon the se."

The king has written a braid° letter,
　　And signed it wi his hand,　　　　　　10
And sent it to Sir Patrick Spens,
　　Was walking on the sand.

The first line that Sir Patrick red,
　　A loud lauch lauched he;
The next line that Sir Patrick red,　　　　15
　　The teir blinded his ee.

"O wha is this has don this deid,
　　This ill deid don to me,
To send me out this time o' the yeir,
　　To sail upon the se!　　　　　　　　20

"Mak haste, mak haste, my mirry men all,
　　Our guid schip sails the morne."
"O say na sae, my master deir,
　　For I feir a deadlie storme.

9. **braid:** broad; explicit.

Late, late yestreen I saw the new moone, 25
   Wi the auld moone in hir arme,
And I feir, I feir, my deir master,
   That we will cum to harme."

O our Scots nobles wer richt laith°
   To weet their cork-heild schoone;° 30
Bot lang owre a' the play wer playd,
   Their hats they swam aboone.°

O lang, lang may their ladies sit,
   Wi their fans into their hand,
Or eir° they se Sir Patrick Spens 35
   Cum sailing to the land.

O lang, lang may the ladies stand,
   Wi thair gold kems° in their hair,
Waiting for thair ain deir lords,
   For they'll se thame na mair. 40

Haf owre,° haf owre to Aberdour,
   It's fiftie fadom deip,
And thair lies guid Sir Patrick Spens,
   Wi the Scots lords at his feit.

29. **richt laith:** right loath; very reluctant.   30. **cork-heild schoone:** cork-
heeled shoes.   32. **aboone:** above.   35. **Or eir:** or ere, before.   38. **kems:**
combs.   41. **Haf owre:** half over, halfway.

The Wife of Usher's Well

There lived a wife at Usher's Well,
   And a wealthy wife was she;
She had three stout and stalwart sons,
   And sent them o'er the sea.

They hadna been a week from her,   5
    A week but barely ane,
Whan word came to the carline° wife
    That her three sons were gane.

They hadna been a week from her,
    A week but barely three,   10
Whan word came to the carline wife
    That her sons she'd never see.

"I wish the wind may never cease,
    Nor fashes° in the flood,
Till my three sons come hame to me,   15
    In earthly flesh and blood."

It fell about the Martinmas,
    When nights are lang and mirk,°
The carline wife's three sons came hame,
    And their hats were o the birk.°   20

It neither grew in syke° nor ditch,
    Nor yet in ony sheugh;°
But at the gates o Paradise,
    That birk grew fair eneugh.°

"Blow up the fire, my maidens,   25
    Bring water from the well;
For a' my house shall feast this night,
    Since my three sons are well."

And she has made to them a bed,
    She's made it large and wide,   30
And she's taen her mantle her about,
    Sat down at the bedside.

---

7. **carline**: old.   14. **fashes**: troubles.   18. **mirk**: dark.   20. **birk**: birch.
21. **syke**: trench.   22. **sheugh** (shŭk): furrow.   24. **eneugh** (ĕ·nōōk′): enough.

Up then crew the red, red cock,
  And up and crew the gray;
The eldest to the youngest said,   35
  " 'T is time we were away."

The cock he hadna crawd but once,
  And clapped his wings at a',
When the youngest to the eldest said,
  "Brother, we must awa.   40

"The cock doth craw, the day doth daw,
  The channerin° worm doth chide;
Gin° we be mist out o' our place,
  A sair° pain we maun° bide.

"Fare ye weel, my mother dear!   45
  Fareweel to barn and byre!°
And fare ye weel, the bonny lass
  That kindles my mother's fire!"

42. **channerin**: devouring.   43. **Gin**: if.   44. **sair**: sore.   **maun**: must.
46. **byre**: a cowhouse.

White Was the Sheet

White was the sheet that she spread for her lover,
White was the sheet and embroidered the cover.
But whiter the sheet and the canopy grander,
When he lay down to sleep where the hill-foxes wander.

Questions

Sir Patrick Spens

1. At what point in the poem are we *told* that Sir Patrick's ship has
sunk? How are we told? What is the earliest *hint* that the ship may
sink?
2. What is the effect of such details as the "blude-reid wine" in Stanza 1
and the mention of the "fans" in Stanza 9?

3. Would you describe the poem as narrative, dramatic, or a combination of both? Explain.

The Wife of Usher's Well

1. What are some of the details that help keep the story from being completely shadowy and unreal?
2. This poem could easily have become a "horror story." What are some of the things that prevent it from becoming that?

White Was the Sheet

How would you describe the tone of this brief poem? Explain your answer.

JOHN SKELTON

1460?–1529

Skelton apparently attended Cambridge University, where it is said he was an outstanding student. After completing his studies, Skelton served for a time in the household of Henry VII as a tutor to the next Henry, and he seems to have kept up his connection with the court for a number of years. Toward the end of his life, however, his satirical writings offended the powerful Cardinal Wolsey, and Skelton was forced to leave the court and take sanctuary in Westminster Abbey. Skelton is known as a humorous, robust satirist, but lyrics like "To Mistress Margaret Hussey" show a gentler, more eloquent side. The form that Skelton used for much of his poetry, a succession of short lines rhyming in no set pattern, has come to be known as "Skeltonic meter."

To Mistress Margaret Hussey

Merry Margaret,
As midsummer flower,
Gentle° as falcon,
Or hawk of the tower;
With solace and gladness,   5

3. **Gentle:** here, noble.

Much mirth and no madness,
All good and no badness;
 So joyously,
 So maidenly,
 So womanly   10
Her demeaning,
In everything
Far, far passing
That I can indite,
Or suffice to write,   15
Of merry Margaret,
As midsummer flower,
Gentle as falcon
Or hawk of the tower;
As patient and as still,   20
And as full of good-will,
As fair Isiphil,°
Coliander,°
Sweet pomander,°
Good Cassander;°   25
Steadfast of thought,
Well made, well wrought;
Far may be sought
Ere you can find
So courteous, so kind   30
As merry Margaret,
This midsummer flower,
Gentle as falcon,
Or hawk of the tower.

22. **Isiphil:** Hypsipyle, a beautiful woman of classical legends.   23. **Colian-der:** an aromatic herb.   24. **pomander:** a bag containing perfumes, worn about the neck.   25. **Cassander:** Cassandra—in Greek legend, the daughter of the King of Troy. She was noted for her ability to foretell the future and also for her beauty and virtue.

Questions

1. What is meant by "Gentle as falcon / Or hawk of the tower"?
2. Point out the refrain of the poem. What is its effect?

SIR THOMAS WYATT

1503?–1542

Wyatt attended Cambridge University and soon after completing his studies entered the service of Henry VIII. He went on diplomatic missions to France and Italy before he was twenty-five, and in later years became a member of the King's Privy Council, a member of Parliament, Ambassador to Spain, and Commander of the Fleet. His early trip to Italy was especially important to English poetry: it was there that Wyatt was first introduced to the sonnet form, which had been developed in that country during the thirteenth and fourteenth centuries. Wyatt imported the form to England, and it has remained popular to this day. During his lifetime, Wyatt's poetry was often overshadowed by the work of his friend, the Earl of Surrey, but Wyatt's reputation has grown considerably in the past forty or fifty years. He is now considered the equal of many of the finest poets in English.

My Galley Chargèd with Forgetfulness

My galley° chargèd° with forgetfulness
Through sharp seas, in winter nights, doth pass
'Tween rock and rock; and eke° my foe,° alas,
That is my lord, steereth with cruelness;
And every oar a thought in readiness,   5
As though that death were light in such a case.
An endless wind doth tear the sail apace,
Of forcèd sighs and trusty fearfulness;
A rain of tears, a cloud of dark disdain,
Have done the wearied cords great hinderance;   10
Wreathèd with error and with ignorance,
The stars be hid that led me to this pain;
Drowned is reason, that should be my comfort,
And I remain despairing of the port.

1. **galley:** a large ship. **chargèd:** loaded, filled.   3. **eke:** also. **foe:** that is, his love (as is "my lord" in l. 4).

A Renouncing of Love

Farewell, love, and all thy laws for ever,
Thy baited hooks shall tangle me no more;
Senec° and Plato call me from thy lore
To perfect wealth, my wit° for to endeavor;°
In blindè error when I did persèver,   5
Thy sharp repulse that pricketh aye so sore
Taught me in trifles that I set no store,
But 'scape forth thence, since liberty is lever.°
Therefore, farewell! Go trouble younger hearts,
And in me claim no more authority;   10
With idle youth go use thy property,
And thereon spend thy many brittle darts.
For hitherto though I have lost my time,
Me list° no longer rotten boughs to climb.

3. **Senec:** Seneca, a Roman playwright and philosopher (4? B.C.–A.D. 65).
4. **wit:** mind. **endeavor:** employ. 8. **lever:** preferable. 14. **Me list:** I choose;
I desire.

They Flee from Me

They flee from me, that sometime did me seek,
With naked foot stalking within my chamber.
Once have I seen them gentle, tame, and meek,
That now are wild, and do not once remember
That sometime they have put themselves in danger   5
To take bread at my hand; and now they range,
Busily seeking in continual change.
    Thanked be fortune it hath been otherwise,
Twenty times better; but once especial,°
In thin array, after° a pleasant guise,°   10
When her loose gown did from her shoulders fall,
And she me caught in her arms long and small,
And therewithal so sweetly did me kiss
And softly said, "Dear heart, how like you this?"

9. **especial:** particularly. 10. **after . . . guise:** probably, in a pleasing
style (of clothing).

It was no dream, for I lay broad awaking.   15
But all is turned now, through my gentleness,
Into a bitter fashion of forsaking;
And I have leave to go, of her goodèness,
And she also to use newfangleness.°
But since that I so kindèly am served,   20
How like you this? what hath she now deserved?

19. use newfangleness: seek novelty (compare line 7).

Questions

1. "My Galley Chargèd with Forgetfulness" is a sonnet made up of one
   elaborate metaphor. What is the metaphor; that is, what things are
   being compared? Are there any details in the poem that do not relate
   directly to this metaphor?
2. Is there any change of tone in "A Renouncing of Love"? If so, how
   does the imagery contribute to the change?
3. "They Flee from Me" contains many metrical irregularities. Point out
   some examples. What effect do these irregularities have on the poem?
4. How would you describe the tone of "They Flee from Me"? How does
   line 14 affect the tone? What about the effect of the last four lines?
   How would the tone be affected if the poem ended at line 17?

HENRY HOWARD, EARL OF SURREY

1517?–1547

Henry Howard, Earl of Surrey, was a descendent of two kings of
England and a member of the court of Henry VIII. Surrey was
noted for his intolerable pride, and during his brief life he offended
many noblemen. When Henry VIII was in his last illness, Surrey
was accused of planning to claim the throne after the King's death.
He was convicted of treason and beheaded at the age of thirty, but
before his death he had translated the first two books of Virgil's
Aeneid into blank verse, a new style that he was the first to use
consistently. Surrey also developed a variation of the Italian sonnet,
consisting of three quatrains and a couplet, which later became
known as the Shakespearean sonnet. Although he lacked the orig-

inality and emotional depth of Wyatt, Surrey was capable of excellent poetry, and he remained a strong influence throughout the sixteenth century.

Complaint of a Lover Rebuked

Love that liveth and reigneth in my thought,
That built his seat within my captive breast,
Clad in the arms wherein with me he fought,
Oft in my face he doth his banner rest.
She that me taught to love and suffer pain,   5
My doubtful hope and eke° my hot desire
With shamefast cloak to shadow and refrain,
Her smiling grace converteth straight to ire;
And coward love then to the heart apace
Taketh his flight, whereas he lurks and plains°   10
His purpose lost, and dare not show his face.
For my lord's guilt thus faultless bide I pains;
Yet from my lord shall not my foot remove—
Sweet is his death that takes his end by love.

6. **eke:** also.   10. **plains:** complains, bemoans.

Description of Spring

The soote° season that bud and bloom forth brings
With green hath clad the hill and eke the vale,
The nightingale with feathers new she sings,
The turtle° to her mate hath told her tale.
Summer is come, for every spray now springs,   5
The hart hath hung his old head on the pale,°
The buck in brake his winter coat he flings,
The fishes float with new repairèd scale,
The adder all her slough° away she slings,

1. **soote:** sweet. 4. **turtle:** turtledove. 6. **hath . . . pale:** has shed his horns. 9. **slough** (slŭf): the outer skin periodically shed by a snake.

The swift swallow pursueth the flyès smale,　　　　10
The busy bee her honey now she mings°—
Winter is worn, that was the flowers' bale:°
And thus I see, among these pleasant things
Each care decays—and yet my sorrow springs.

11. **mings:** mixes.　12. **bale:** woe.

Questions

1. Explain the imagery of the first four lines of "Complaint of a Lover Rebuked." What is the meaning of the couplet of this sonnet?
2. Compare the rhyme schemes of the two sonnets. What is the effect of the unusual rhyme scheme of "Description of Spring"?
3. "Description of Spring" ends with a pun. What is it, and what is its effect?

THE ELIZABETHAN AGE

The Renaissance is generally considered to have begun in continental Europe during the fourteenth century. In Italy and France particularly, this period was marked by two major changes: first, the basic structure of society changed as the older feudal pattern gave way to the beginnings of nationalism; second, a knowledge of Greek and Roman civilization became the basis of much higher education. The Renaissance had other effects as well: trade and exploration flourished, as did all the known sciences. England responded to some of these changes early in the fifteenth century, but it was not until the late 1500's that English literature felt the full impact of the Renaissance.

During the period from approximately 1580 to 1625, England experienced the greatest outpouring of poetry in its history. The Elizabethan Age is famous for its great poetic drama—in addition to Shakespeare, Jonson, and Marlowe, there were many other talented dramatists working during these years—but all forms of poetry flourished, particularly the sonnet and the song. Queen Elizabeth I died in 1603, but the remarkable poetic activity continued well into the reign of her successor, James I. Elizabeth's name is generally given to the entire period.

SIR WALTER RALEIGH

1552?–1618

Raleigh is typical in many ways of the Elizabethan Age. He is also a fine example of the ideal of that period, the so-called "universal" (or "well-rounded") man. He was a skilled poet, but was even more famous as a soldier, sailor, courtier, statesman, and explorer. Raleigh was a favorite of Queen Elizabeth. Shortly after the accession of James I, however, he came into conflict with the king and was imprisoned for some thirteen years. He was eventually released but two years later was beheaded for treason. Many of Raleigh's poems have been lost but those that remain are notable for their vigor and clarity. (See page 183 for Raleigh's "Reply" to Marlowe.)

The Silent Lover

I

Passions are likened best to floods and streams:
    The shallow murmur, but the deep are dumb;
So, when affection yields discourse, it seems
    The bottom is but shallow whence they come.
They that are rich in words, in words discover°   5
That they are poor in that which makes a lover.

II

Wrong not, sweet empress of my heart,
    The merit of true passion,
With thinking that he feels no smart,°
    That° sues° for no compassion.   10

Silence in love betrays more woe
    Than words, though ne'er so witty:
A beggar that is dumb, you know,
    May challenge double pity.

Then wrong not, dearest to my heart,   15
    My true, though secret passion;
He smarteth most that hides his smart,
    And sues for no compassion.

5. discover: reveal.   9. smart: sharp pain.   10. That: who. sues: pleads.

Questions

1. What is the figure of speech in Part I? Explain it in detail.
2. What is the relationship between Part I and Part II?

EDMUND SPENSER

1552?–1599

Edmund Spenser was born in London and educated at Cambridge, where he acquired a circle of influential friends. After receiving his Master's degree, he became secretary to the Earl of Leicester and a close friend of the Earl's nephew, Sir Philip Sidney. In 1580 Spenser became secretary to the Lord Deputy of Ireland. Except for an occasional visit to England, he remained in Ireland until the Irish rebellion of 1598, during which his home was destroyed. Broken in health, he returned to London, where he died the following year.

Spenser's most ambitious and most famous work, *The Faerie Queene*, is an elaborate combination of medieval romantic adventure with religious and political allegory. Spenser died after having completed only six of the twelve books he had planned for the poem.

Like many of his contemporaries, Spenser wrote a sonnet sequence. His *Amoretti*, containing eighty-seven sonnets, records his courtship of Elizabeth Boyle, whom he later married. One of his two famous marriage hymns, "Epithalamion," was written to celebrate his own marriage. The other, "Prothalamion," honored the double marriage of the Ladies Elizabeth and Katherine Somerset.

Spenser has never appealed to as wide a range of readers as have most of the other major English poets. His work contains a rich but sometimes confusing mixture of medieval, Renaissance, Christian, and classical influences. However, the music and imagery of his verse have rarely been equaled in English poetry. He is often called "the poet's poet."

from *Amoretti* *

Sonnet 75

One day I wrote her name upon the strand,
But came the waves and washèd it away;
Again I wrote it with a second hand,

* **Amoretti:** literally, "little love poems" (Italian).

But came the tide, and made my pains his prey;
Vain man, said she, that dost in vain assay   5
A mortal thing so to immortalize!
For I myself shall like to this decay,
And eke° my name be wipèd out likewise.
Not so (quod I), let baser things devise
To die in dust, but you shall live by fame: 10
My verse your virtues rare shall eternize,°
And in the heavens write your glorious name;
Where, whenas death shall all the world subdue,
Our love shall live, and later life renew.

8. **eke:** also.   11. **eternize:** make eternal.

Sonnet 79

Men call you fair, and you do credit it,°
For that your self ye daily such do see;
But the true fair, that is the gentle wit˅
And virtuous mind, is much more praised of me.
For all the rest, how ever fair it be,   5
Shall turn to nought and lose that glorious hue:
But only that° is permanent and free
From frail corruption, that doth flesh ensue.°
That is true beauty; that doth argue you
To be divine and born of heavenly seed,   10
Derived from that fair spirit from whom all true
And perfect beauty did at first proceed.
He only fair, and what he fair hath made;
All other fair, like flowers, untimely fade.

1. **credit it:** bring honor to it (the word "fair"). 3. **wit:** reason, judgment.
7. **that:** what. 8. **ensue:** come after, survive. The sense of ll. 7–8 is, Only
what is permanent and indestructible—the gentle wit and virtuous mind—will
remain after the flesh dies.

Prothalamion *

Calm was the day, and through the trembling air
Sweet-breathing Zephyrus° did softly play,
A gentle spirit, that lightly did delay
Hot Titan's° beams, which then did glister fair;
When I (whom sullen care,   5
Through discontent of my long fruitless stay
In Princes' Court, and expectations vain
Of idle hopes, which still do fly away,
Like empty shadows, did afflict my brain)
Walked forth to ease my pain   10
Along the shore of silver streaming Thames,
Whose rutty° bank, the which his river hems,
Was painted all with variable flowers,
And all the meads adorned with dainty gems
Fit to deck maiden's bowers,   15
And crown their paramours°
Against° the bridal day, which is not long:°
    Sweet Thames! run softly, till I end my song.

There, in a meadow, by the river's side,
A flock of nymphs I chanced to espy,   20
All lovely daughters of the flood° thereby,
With goodly greenish locks, all loose untied,
As° each had been a bride;
And each one had a little wicker basket,
Made of fine twigs, entrailèd curiously,°   25
In which they gathered flowers to fill their flasket,°
And with fine fingers cropped full feateously°
The tender stalks on high.
Of every sort, which in that meadow grew,

* Prothalamion (prō'thá·lā'mĭ·ŏn): marriage song.   2. Zephyrus: the West
Wind.   4. Titan's: the sun's.   12. rutty: rooty.   16. paramours: lovers.
17. Against: in anticipation of. long: far away.   21. flood: river.   23. As:
as if (the Elizabethan custom was for the bride to wear her hair loose).
25. entrailèd curiously: entwined carefully.   26. flasket: basket.   27. feat-
eously (fēt'ē·ŭs·lĭ): skillfully.

They gathered some: the violet, pallid blue,   30
The little daisy, that at evening closes,
The virgin lily, and the primrose true,
With store of vermeil° roses,
To deck their bridegrooms' posies
Against the bridal day, which was not long: 35
    Sweet Thames! run softly, till I end my song.

With that I saw two swans° of goodly hue
Come softly swimming down along the Lee;°
Two fairer birds I yet did never see;
The snow, which doth the top of Pindus° strew,   40
Did never whiter shew;°
Nor Jove himself, when he a swan would be,
For love of Leda,° whiter did appear;
Yet Leda was (they say) as white as he,
Yet not so white as these, nor nothing near;   45
So purely white they were,
That even the gentle stream, the which them bare,
Seemed foul to them, and bade his billows spare
To wet their silken feathers, lest they might
Soil their fair plumes with water not so fair,   50
And mar their beauties bright,
That shone as heaven's light,
Against their bridal day, which was not long:
    Sweet Thames! run softly, till I end my song.

Eftsoons° the nymphs, which now had flowers their fill,   55
Ran all in haste to see that silver brood,
As they came floating on the crystal flood;
Whom when they saw, they stood amazèd still,
Their wond'ring eyes to fill;
Them seemed they never saw a sight so fair,   60

---

33. **vermeil** (vûr'mĭl): bright red. 37. **swans:** i.e., the two brides. 38. **Lee:** probably a river flowing into the Thames. 40. **Pindus:** a mountain in Thessaly (eastern Greece). 41. **shew:** show (the older spelling has been retained to indicate the pronunciation). 43. **Leda:** a human woman loved by Jove, who visited her in the shape of a swan. 55. **Eftsoons:** at once.

Of fowls, so lovely, that they sure did deem
Them heavenly borne, or to be that same pair
Which through the sky draw Venus' silver team;°
For sure they did not seem
To be begot of any earthly seed,   65
But rather angels, or of angels' breed;
Yet were they bred of summer's-heat,° they say,
In sweetest season, when each flower and weed
The earth did fresh array;
So fresh they seemed as day,   70
Even as their bridal day, which was not long:
    Sweet Thames! run softly, till I end my song.

Then forth they all out of their baskets drew
Great store of flowers, the honor of the field,
That to the sense did fragrant odors yield,   75
All which upon those goodly birds they threw
And all the waves did strew,
That like old Peneus'° waters they did seem,
When down along by pleasant Tempe's shore,
Scattered with flowers, through Thessaly they stream,   80
That they appear, through lilies' plenteous store,
Like a bride's chamber floor.
Two of those nymphs, meanwhile, two garlands bound
Of freshest flowers which in that mead they found,
The which presenting all in trim array,   85
Their snowy foreheads therewithal they crowned,
Whilst one did sing this lay,
Prepared against that day,
Against that bridal day, which was not long:
    Sweet Thames! run softly, till I end my song.   90

"Ye gentle birds! the world's fair ornament,
And heaven's glory, whom this happy hour

---

63. **Venus' silver team:** Spenser pictures the Roman goddess of love as being
drawn through the sky by two Thames' swans. 67. **summer's-heat:** a pun on
Somerset, the family name of the two brides. 78. **Peneus** (pē·nyŏs'); a
river in Thessaly which flowed through **Tempe** (l. 79), a valley in Greece
renowned in ancient times as a place of ideal happiness.

Doth lead into your lovers' blissful bower,
Joy may you have, and gentle hearts content
Of your loves' couplement;°   95
And let fair Venus, that is queen of love,
With her heart-quelling son° upon you smile,
Whose smile, they say, hath virtue to remove
All love's dislike, and friendship's faulty guile
For ever to assoil.°   100
Let endless peace your steadfast hearts accord,
That fruitful issue may to you afford,
Which may your foes confound,
And make your joys redound
Upon your bridal day, which is not long: 105
    Sweet Thames! run softly, till I end my song."

So ended she; and all the rest around
To her redoubled that her undersong,°
Which said their bridal day should not be long;
And gentle Echo° from the neighbor ground   110
Their accents did resound.
So forth those joyous birds did pass along,
Adown the Lee, that to them murmured low,
As he would speak, but that he lacked a tongue,
Yet did by signs his glad affection show,   115
Making his stream run slow.
And all the fowl which in his flood did dwell
Gan° flock about these twain, that did excel
The rest, as far as Cynthia° doth shend°
The lesser stars. So they, enrangèd° well,   120
Did on those two attend,
And their best service lend
Against their wedding day, which was not long:
    Sweet Thames! run softly, till I end my song.

95. **couplement:** union.   97. **son:** Cupid.   100. **assoil:** absolve.   108. **re-doubled . . . undersong:** repeated the refrain.   110. **Echo:** in Greek mythology, a nymph of the woods and hills who was punished for chattering by being deprived of all speech except to repeat the words of others.   118. **Gan:** began to.   119. **Cynthia:** the moon goddess.   **shend:** outshine.   120. **enrangèd:** arranged.

At length they all to merry London came,   125
To merry London, my° most kindly nurse,
That to me gave this life's first native source,
Though from another place I take my name,°
An house of ancient fame:
There when they came, whereas those bricky towers°   130
The which on Thames' broad aged back do ride,
Where now the studious lawyers have their bowers,
There whilom° wont° the Templar Knights to bide,
Till they decayed through pride:
Next whereunto there stands a stately place,   135
Where oft I gainèd gifts and goodly grace
Of that great lord,° which therein wont to dwell,
Whose want° too well now feels my friendless case;
But ah! here fits not well
Old woes, but joys, to tell   140
Against the bridal day, which is not long:
    Sweet Thames! run softly, till I end my song.

Yet therein now doth lodge a noble peer,°
Great England's glory, and the world's wide wonder,
Whose dreadful name late through all Spain did thunder   145
And Hercules' two pillars° standing near
Did make to quake and fear:
Fair branch of honor, flower of chivalry!
That fillest England with thy triumphs' fame,
Joy have thou of thy noble victory,   150
And endless happiness of thine own name
That promiseth the same;
That through thy prowess, and victorious arms,

---

126. **my:** Spenser's.   128. **place . . . name:** Spenser's family may have
come originally from northern England.   130. **towers:** the Middle, or Inner,
Temple, occupied by law students (l. 132) after the original occupants, the
Knights Templar (l. 133), were disbanded. The Templars were a religious
and military organization founded during the Crusades.   133. **whilom:** formerly. **wont:** used.   137. **lord:** the Earl of Leicester, Spenser's former patron.
138. **want:** absence.   143. **peer:** the Earl of Essex, who had just returned from
a successful naval campaign against Spain.   146. **Hercules' two pillars:** the
old name for the Straits of Gibralter.

Thy country may be freed from foreign arms,
And great Eliza's° glorious name may ring   155
Through all the world, filled with thy wide alarms,°
Which some brave muse may sing
To ages following,
Upon the bridal day, which is not long:
    Sweet Thames! run softly, till I end my song.   160

From those high towers this noble lord issùing,
Like radiant Hesper,° when his golden hair
In th'ocean billows he hath bathèd fair,
Descended to the river's open viewing,
With a great train ensuing.   165
Above the rest were goodly to be seen
Two gentle knights of lovely face and feature,
Beseeming well the bower of any queen,
With gifts of wit, and ornaments of nature,
Fit for so goodly stature,   170
That like the twins of Jove° they seemed in sight,
Which deck the baldric° of the heavens bright;
They two, forth pacing to the river's side,
Received those two fair brides, their loves' delight;
Which, at th'appointed tide,   175
Each one did make his bride
Against their bridal day, which is not long:
    Sweet Thames! run softly, till I end my song.

155. **Eliza's:** Queen Elizabeth. 156. **alarms:** calls to arms. 162. **Hesper:**
the evening star. 171. **twins of Jove:** Castor and Pollux, the offspring of
Jove and Leda (l. 43), and the twin stars that form the constellation Gemini.
172. **baldric:** a richly ornamented belt.

Questions

FROM *Amoretti*

1. What is the theme of Sonnet 75?
2. What two types of "fairness" does Sonnet 79 describe? Why is one
   preferred to the other? To whom does "he" refer in line 13?

Prothalamion

1. What is the significance of the refrain? What are some of its most important effects?
2. The tradition in which Spenser wrote was a mixture of classical (that is, pagan) philosophy and Christian theology. What are some of the classical elements in this marriage hymn? the Christian elements?
3. This is presumably a poem to celebrate the double marriage of two prominent women, yet there are many elements in it that have no apparent connection with the marriages. Particularly noticeable are the autobiographical details that Spenser introduces. What is the effect of these details? Do they merely distract us from the real subject of the poem? Or do they add something valuable? Explain your answer.
4. In addition to the autobiographical details, Spenser introduces other things that are not directly related to the marriages, such as the mention of some public events and prominent Elizabethan figures. What is the effect of these details?

SIR PHILIP SIDNEY

1554–1586

Like Sir Walter Raleigh, Sidney was renowned as a "universal" man —a poet, soldier, courtier, diplomat, and scholar. He attended both Oxford and Cambridge, and at eighteen was sent to France as an assistant to the English ambassador. A few years later he returned to Europe as ambassador to the Emperor of Germany. Sidney was famous for the nobility and gentleness of his character, and when he died after being wounded during a battle in the Netherlands, all of England and a considerable share of Europe joined in mourning. Sidney did not publish any of his writings during his lifetime, but after his death two of his works became extremely influential. His sequence of one hundred and eight sonnets, *Astrophel and Stella,* published in 1591, helped start an outburst of Elizabethan sonnet cycles that lasted for twenty years. The sonnet cycle attracted the energies of the finest poets of the time, including Spenser and Shakespeare. Sidney's other major work, the *Defense of Poesy,* marked the beginning of English literary criticism.

from *Astrophel and Stella* *

Sonnet 1

Loving in truth, and fain° in verse my love to show,
That she, dear she, might take some pleasure of my pain,
Pleasure might cause her read, reading might make her know,
Knowledge might pity win, and pity grace obtain—
I sought fit words to paint the blackest face of woe;   5
Studying inventions fine,° her wits to entertain,
Oft turning others' leaves to see if thence would flow
Some fresh and fruitful showers upon my sunburned brain.
But words came halting forth, wanting invention's stay;°
Invention, nature's child, fled stepdame study's blows,   10
And others' feet still seemed but strangers in my way.°
Thus, great with child to speak, and helpless in my throes,
Biting my truant° pen, beating myself for spite,
Fool, said my muse to me, look in thy heart and write.

* **Astrophel and Stella:** the names of the lovers the sonnet sequence cele-
brates. Literally, *Astrophel,* from the Greek, means "star-lover"; *Stella,* from
the Latin, means "star." **1. fain:** desirous. **6. inventions fine:** fine poetic devices other poets have used. *Invention* (see also ll. 9–10) refers to the creative
power of the mind, or to the products of that power. **9. stay:** support.
11. others' feet . . . way: the methods of other poets seemed out of place in
this work. **13. truant:** wayward.

Sonnet 5

It is most true that eyes are formed to serve
The inward light,° and that the heavenly part°
Ought to be king, from whose rules who do swerve,
Rebels to nature, strive for their own smart.°
It is most true what we call Cupid's dart   5
An image is which for ourselves we carve,

2. inward light: the light of the soul, which shines through the eyes. **heavenly part:** the soul. **3–4. from . . . smart:** Those who disobey the soul's
rules rebel against nature and cause themselves pain.

And fools, adore in temple of our heart
Till that good god make church and churchman starve.
True, that true beauty virtue is indeed,
Whereof this beauty can be but a shade,   10
Which elements with mortal mixture breed.
True, that on earth we are but pilgrims made,
And should in soul up to our country move;
True, and yet true that I must Stella love.

Sonnet 31

With how sad steps, O moon, thou climb'st the skies,
How silently, and with how wan a face!
What, may it be that even in heav'nly place
That busy archer° his sharp arrows tries?
Sure, if that long-with-love-acquainted eyes   5
Can judge of love, thou feel'st a lover's case;
I read it in thy looks: thy languished grace,
To me, that feel the like, thy state descries.°
Then, ev'n of° fellowship, O moon, tell me,
Is constant love deemed there but want of wit?°   10
Are beauties there as proud as here they be?
Do they above love to be loved, and yet
Those lovers scorn whom that love doth possess?
Do they call virtue there ungratefulness?

4. busy archer: Cupid.   8. descries: reveals.   9. ev'n of: equal in.
10. want of wit: madness.

Questions

1. In Sonnet 1, what has prevented the speaker from expressing his love?
   What is his solution to the problem? Note that this sonnet is written
   in twelve-syllable lines (hexameters) rather than the more traditional ten-syllable (pentameters). What is the effect of this variation?
2. What is the paradox on which Sonnet 5 is based? Compare this poem
   to Spenser's Sonnet 79 (p. 164).

3. In Sonnet 31, why does the moon have "long-with-love-acquainted eyes"? What is the tone of this poem? How is the tone affected by the many direct questions asked throughout the sonnet?

ELIZABETHAN LYRICS

The six poets included in this section are merely a few among the many excellent minor poets of the Elizabethan period. ROBERT GREENE (1560?–1592) is known as a pamphleteer, a playwright, and a writer of *romances* (prose works something like novels, except that the events they portrayed were highly fanciful and their language was affected and extravagant). Many fine lyrics are scattered throughout his romances and plays. GEORGE PEELE (1558?–?1597) was a popular playwright, but the brief songs he wrote for his plays are now far better known than the plays themselves. SAMUEL DANIEL (c. 1562–1619) is known for his sonnet sequence, *Delia,* and for his critical essay, *Defense of Rhyme.* MICHAEL DRAYTON (1563–1631), who wrote odes, plays, legends, ballads, and patriotic poems, is best known for a sonnet sequence entitled *Idea.* Most of THOMAS NASHE'S (1567–1601) best songs occur in his play *Summer's Last Will and Testament.* THOMAS CAMPION (1567–1620) was both a poet and musician, and his clear, simple songs are among the finest of the period.

Doron's Description of Samela

ROBERT GREENE

Like to Diana° in her summer weed,
Girt with a crimson robe of brightest dye,
    Goes fair Samela.
Whiter than be the flocks that straggling feed,
When washed by Arethusa° faint they lie,   5
    Is fair Samela.

1. **Diana:** the Roman goddess of the wood.   5. **Arethusa** (ăr'ê·thū'zá): in Greek mythology, a nymph who was changed into a stream.

As fair Aurora° in her morning gray,
Decked with the ruddy glister of her love,
    Is fair Samela.
Like lovely Thetis° on a calmèd day,   10
Whenas her brightness Neptune's° fancy move,
    Shines fair Samela.
Her tresses gold, her eyes like glassy streams,
Her teeth are pearl, the breasts are ivory
    Of fair Samela;   15
Her cheeks, like rose and lily, yield forth gleams,
Her brows, bright arches framed of ebony.
    Thus fair Samela
Passeth fair Venus in her bravest hue,
And Juno° in the show of majesty   20
    (For she's Samela),
Pallas° in wit. All three, if you well view,
For beauty, wit, and matchless dignity,
    Yield to Samela.

7. **Aurora:** (ô·rō′rȧ): the dawn personified.   10. **Thetis** (thē′tĭs): a sea nymph.   11. **Neptune:** the Roman god of the sea.   20. **Juno:** the highest of the Roman goddesses.   22. **Pallas:** Pallas Athena, one of the greatest of the Greek goddesses.

Sweet Are the Thoughts

ROBERT GREENE

Sweet are the thoughts that savor of content,
    The quiet mind is richer than a crown;
Sweet are the nights in careless slumber spent,
    The poor estate scorns fortune's angry frown:
Such sweet content, such minds, such sleep, such bliss,   5
Beggars enjoy, when princes oft do miss.

The homely house that harbors quiet rest,
    The cottage that affords no pride nor care,

The mean° that 'grees° with country music best,
The sweet consort° of mirth and music's fare,   10
Obscurèd life sets down a type° of bliss;
A mind content both crown and kingdom is.

9. **mean:** middle point, neither too high nor too low. **'grees:** agrees, is in harmony. 10. **consort:** concert. 11. **type:** perfect example.

His Golden Locks Time Hath to Silver Turned

GEORGE PEELE

His golden locks time hath to silver turned;
    Oh, time too swift, oh, swiftness never ceasing!
His youth 'gainst time and age hath ever spurned,
    But spurned in vain; youth waneth° by increasing.
Beauty, strength, youth, are flowers but fading seen;
Duty, faith, love, are roots, and ever green.

His helmet now shall make a hive for bees,
    And lover's sonnets turned to holy psalms,
A man-at-arms must now serve on his knees,
    And feed on prayers, which are age his° alms;   10
But though from court to cottage he depart,
His saint is sure of his unspotted heart.

And when he saddest sits in homely cell,°
    He'll teach his swains° this carol for a song:
Blest be the hearts that wish my sovereign well,   15
Cursed be the souls that think her any wrong!
Goddess, allow this aged man his right,
To be your beadsman° now, that was your knight.

4. **waneth:** diminishes, draws to an end. 10. **age his:** age's. 13. **cell:** a small room. 14. **swains:** servants. 18. **beadsman:** one who is supported by alms, and who is obliged to pray for his benefactor.

Are They Shadows That We See?

Are they shadows that we see?
And can shadows pleasure give?
Pleasures only shadows be,
Cast by bodies we conceive,
And are made the things we deem°   5
In those figures which they seem.
But these pleasures vanish fast,
Which by shadows are expressed,
  Pleasures are not, if they last;
  In their passing is their best.   10
Glory is most bright and gay
In a flash, and so away.

Feed apace then, greedy eyes,
On the wonder you behold.
  Take it sudden as it flies,   15
  Though you take it not to hold;
  When your eyes have done their part,
Thought must length° it in the heart.

5. deem: think. 18. length: lengthen.

from *Delia*

SAMUEL DANIEL

Care-Charmer Sleep

Care-charmer sleep, son of the sable° night,
Brother to death, in silent darkness born,
Relieve my languish and restore the light;
With dark forgetting of my care, return.

1. sable: black.

Elizabethan Lyrics 177

And let the day be time enough to mourn   5
The shipwreck of my ill-adventured youth;
Let waking eyes suffice to wail their scorn
Without the torment of the night's untruth.
Cease, dreams, th' images of day-desires,
To model forth the passions of the morrow;   10
Never let rising sun approve° you liars,
To add more grief to aggravate my sorrow.
Still let me sleep, embracing clouds in vain,
And never wake to feel the day's disdain.

11. approve: prove.

from *Idea*

MICHAEL DRAYTON

Since There's No Help, Come Let Us Kiss and Part

Since there's no help, come let us kiss and part—
Nay I have done, you get no more of me;
And I am glad, yea, glad with all my heart,
That thus so cleanly I myself can free.
Shake hands for ever, cancel all our vows,   5
And when we meet at any time again,
Be it not seen in either of our brows
That we one jot of former love retain!
Now at the last gasp of Love's° latest breath,
When his pulse failing, Passion speechless lies,   10
When Faith is kneeling by his bed of death,
And Innocence is closing up his eyes,
—Now if thou would'st, when all have given him over,
From death to life thou might'st him yet recover!

9. Love's: The capitalization here, and those in the following lines ("Passion," "Faith," and "Innocence"), indicate that Drayton is personifying these abstract nouns.

Adieu, Farewell Earth's Bliss

THOMAS NASHE

Adieu, farewell earth's bliss,
This world uncertain is;
Fond° are life's lustful joys,
Death proves them all but toys,
None from his darts can fly.   5
I am sick, I must die.
          Lord, have mercy on us!

Rich men, trust not in wealth,
Gold cannot buy you health;
Physic° himself must fade,   10
All things to end are made.
The plague full swift goes by;
I am sick, I must die.
          Lord, have mercy on us!

Beauty is but a flower   15
Which wrinkles will devour:
Brightness falls from the air,
Queens have died young and fair,
Dust hath closed Helen's° eye.
I am sick, I must die.   20
          Lord, have mercy on us!

Strength stoops unto the grave,
Worms feed on Hector° brave,
Swords may not fight with fate.
Earth still holds ope her gate;   25
Come! Come! the bells do cry.

3. **Fond:** foolish. 10. **Physic:** medical science. 19. **Helen:** in Homer's
Iliad, Helen is the beautiful wife of the Spartan, Menelaus. She runs away with
Paris of Troy and this event begins the Trojan War. 23. **Hector:** in the *Iliad,*
Hector is the greatest of the Trojan heroes.

I am sick, I must die.
    Lord, have mercy on us!

Wit with his wantonness
Tasteth death's bitterness;   30
Hell's executioner
Hath no ears for to hear
What vain art can reply.
I am sick, I must die.
    Lord, have mercy on us!   35

Haste, therefore, each degree,
To welcome destiny.
Heaven is our heritage,
Earth but a player's stage;
Mount we unto the sky.   40
I am sick, I must die.
    Lord, have mercy on us!

When to Her Lute Corinna Sings

THOMAS CAMPION

When to her lute Corinna sings,
Her voice revives the leaden strings,
And doth in highest notes appear
As any challenged echo clear;
But when she doth of mourning speak,   5
Ev'n with her sigh the strings do break.

And as her lute doth live or die,
Led by her passion, so must I:
For when of pleasure she doth sing,
My thoughts enjoy a sudden spring,   10
But if she doth of sorrow speak,
Ev'n from my heart the strings do break.

Thou Art Not Fair

THOMAS CAMPION

Thou art not fair for all thy red and white,
   For all those rosy ornaments in thee;
Thou art not sweet, though made of mere delight,
   Nor fair nor sweet, unless you pity me.
I will not soothe thy fancies; thou shalt prove°   5
That beauty is no beauty without love.

Yet love not me, nor seek thou to allure
   My thoughts with beauty, were it more divine;
Thy smiles and kisses I cannot endure,
   I'll not be wrapped up in those arms of thine.   10
Now show it, if thou be a woman right—
Embrace, and kiss, and love me in despite.

5. **prove:** learn from experience.

Questions

1. "Doron's Description of Samela" is an example of hyperbole, that is, deliberate exaggeration or overstatement for a special effect. Are the many comparisons meant to be taken literally? If not, is the poem insincere? What is its tone?
2. In "His Golden Locks . . ." who are "His saint" in line 12 and the "Goddess" in line 17? What is the meaning of the metaphor in the last line?
3. In "Are They Shadows . . ." what attitude toward pleasures is expressed? What is the meaning of lines 9–12, and lines 17–18?
4. In "Care-Charmer Sleep" why does the speaker want sleep to come? What kind of sleep does he desire?
5. In "Since There's No Help . . ." is there a change in tone anywhere in the poem? If so, where? Explain. How do the personifications in lines 9–12 influence the final effect of the sonnet?
6. In "Adieu, Farewell Earth's Bliss" each of the first five stanzas says much the same thing through different imagery. Explain.
7. How are the two stanzas related in "When to Her Lute Corinna Sings"? Compare lines 6 and 12. What is the effect of the last two lines of "Thou Art Not Fair"?

CHRISTOPHER MARLOWE

1564-1593

The Elizabethan Age was a period of many distinguished dramatists, among whom stand out three giants—Shakespeare, Jonson, and Marlowe. Marlowe's work was the first to appear, and his achievement helped pave the way for the others.

Marlowe was the son of a Canterbury shoemaker. After receiving his Master's degree from Cambridge, he began associating in London with a group of writers known as the "university wits," which included the playwrights Nashe, Peele, and Greene. From this point on, little is known of Marlowe's life. He may have gone with Sir Philip Sidney to the wars in the Netherlands. He may possibly have been an actor for a short time. His death came just as he was beginning to reach the height of his poetic powers. At the age of twenty-nine, he was stabbed to death in a brawl.

Marlowe's reputation rests today primarily on five plays: *Tamburlaine the Great* (two separate plays under the same title), *Doctor Faustus, The Jew of Malta,* and *Edward II.* A number of other plays are also believed to be at least partly his.

Marlowe's nondramatic poetry includes "Hero and Leander," a long love poem based on a classical myth, and "The Passionate Shepherd to His Love." "The Passionate Shepherd" was so popular that it caused many imitations, sequels, and "replies," the most famous of which is included here. (Most scholars think that "The Nymph's Reply" is by Sir Walter Raleigh.)

The Passionate Shepherd to His Love

Come live with me and be my love,
And we will all the pleasures prove
That hills and valleys, dales and fields,
Or woods or steepy mountain yields.

And we will sit upon the rocks   5
And see the shepherds feed their flocks

By shallow rivers, to whose falls
Melodious birds sing madrigals.°

And I will make thee beds of roses
And a thousand fragrant posies;   10
A cap of flowers, and a kirtle°
Embroidered all with leaves of myrtle;

A gown made of the finest wool
Which from our pretty lambs we pull;
Fair-linèd slippers for the cold,   15
With buckles of the purest gold;

A belt of straw and ivy buds
With coral clasps and amber studs—
And if these pleasures may thee move,
Come live with me and be my love.   20

The shepherd swains° shall dance and sing
For thy delight each May morning—
If these delights thy mind may move,
Then live with me and be my love.

8. madrigals: lyrics adapted to a musical setting.   11. kirtle: gown.
21. swains: young gallants.

The Nymph's Reply to the Shepherd

(attributed to RALEIGH)

If all the world and love were young,
And truth in every shepherd's tongue,
These pretty pleasures might me move,
To live with thee and be thy love.

But time drives flocks from field to fold,   5
When rivers rage, and rocks grow cold;
And Philomel° becometh dumb;
The rest complains of cares to come.

7. Philomel (fĭl'ô-mĕl): the nightingale.

Christopher Marlowe   183

The flowers do fade, and wanton° fields
To wayward winter reckoning yields;   10
A honey tongue, a heart of gall,°
Is fancy's spring, but sorrow's fall.

Thy gowns, thy shoes, thy beds of roses,
Thy cap, thy kirtle, and thy posies,
Soon break, soon wither, soon forgotten,   15
In folly ripe, in reason rotten.

Thy belt of straw and ivy buds,
Thy coral clasps and amber studs,
All these in me no means can move,
To come to thee and be thy love.   20

But could youth last, and love still breed,
Had joys no date,° nor age no need,
Then these delights my mind might move,
To live with thee and be thy love.

9. wanton: merry, gay.   11. gall: bitterness.   22. date: end.

from *Doctor Faustus*

A crude version of the Faustus legend appeared as early as
the sixth century. By Marlowe's time the legend had come to
be connected with a real person, Dr. Johann Faust, a German magician and astrologer of the fifteenth century. Marlowe was the first to dramatize the story. Since Marlowe, the
most famous treatment has been *Faust*, a poetic drama by
the German poet Goethe. The legend has also been made
into at least three operas and into numerous novels and short
stories.

Marlowe's version of the tale has become the most accepted interpretation—the story of a young scholar obsessed
by beauty and power, who renounces God and sells his soul
to the devil in return for twenty-four years of pleasure and
supernatural knowledge and power. The following passage
occurs at the end of the play, just before Mephistopheles appears at midnight to claim Faustus' soul.

Faustus.   Ah, Faustus,
Now hast thou but one bare hour to live,
And then thou must be damned perpetually!
Stand still, you ever moving spheres° of heaven,
That time may cease, and midnight never come;   5
Fair nature's eye,° rise, rise again, and make
Perpetual day; or let this hour be but
A year, a month, a week, a natural day,
That Faustus may repent and save his soul!
O lente, lente currite, noctis equi!°   10
The stars move still, time runs, the clock will strike,
The devil will come, and Faustus must be damned.
O, I'll leap up to my God! Who pulls me down?
See, see, where Christ's blood streams in the firmament!
One drop would save my soul, half a drop: ah, my Christ!—   15
Ah, rend not my heart for naming of my Christ!
Yet will I call on him: O, spare me, Lucifer!—
Where is it now? 'Tis gone: and see, where God
Stretcheth out his arm, and bends his ireful brows!
Mountains and hills, come, come, and fall on me,   20
And hide me from the heavy wrath of God!
No, no!
Then will I headlong run into the earth:
Earth, gape! O, no, it will not harbor me!
You stars that reigned at my nativity,   25
Whose influence hath allotted death and hell,°
Now draw up Faustus, like a foggy mist,
Into the entrails of yon laboring clouds,
That, when they vomit forth into the air,
My limbs may issue from their smoky mouths,   30
So that my soul may but ascend to heaven!

---

4. **spheres:** Elizabethans believed that all the heavenly bodies were attached
to a series of crystal spheres that revolved continuously. 6. **nature's eye:**
the sun. 10. *O lente . . . equi!:* run slowly, slowly, horses of the night.
(From *Amores,* by the Roman poet Ovid.) 25–26. **stars . . . hell:** referring to
the old astrological belief that a person's fate was determined by the position
of the stars at his birth.

Ah, half the hour is past! 'twill all be past anon.
O God,
If thou wilt not have mercy on my soul,
Yet for Christ's sake, whose blood hath ransomed me,   35
Impose some end to my incessant pain;
Let Faustus live in hell a thousand years—
A hundred thousand, and at last be saved!
O, no end is limited to damned souls!
Why wert thou not a creature wanting soul?   40
Or why is this immortal that thou hast?
Ah, Pythagoras'° metempsychosis!° were that true,
This soul should fly from me, and I be changed
Unto some brutish beast! All beasts are happy,
For, when they die,   45
Their souls are soon dissolved in elements;
But mine must live still to be plagued in hell.
Cursed be the parents that engendered° me!
No, Faustus, curse thyself, curse Lucifer
That hath deprived thee of the joys of heaven.   50

[*The clock strikes twelve.*]
O, it strikes, it strikes! Now, body, turn to air,
Or Lucifer will bear thee quick to hell!

[*Thunder and Lightning.*]
O soul, be changed into little water drops,
And fall into the ocean, ne'er be found!

Enter DEVILS.

My God, my God, look not so fierce on me!   55
Adders and serpents, let me breathe a while!
Ugly hell, gape not! come not, Lucifer!
I'll burn my books!—Ah, Mephistopheles!

---

42. **Pythagoras** (pĭ·thăg'ŏ·răs): an ancient Greek philosopher. **metempsy-chosis** (mé·tĕmp'sĭ·kō'sĭs): the belief that at death one's soul passed to another body. 48. **engendered:** gave birth to.

Questions

The Passionate Shepherd AND *The Nymph's Reply*

1. What attitudes about life and love does the shepherd express in Marlowe's poem? What attitude does Raleigh's nymph express? How do the two poems differ in tone? What details contribute to the difference?
2. Which poem do you prefer? Why?

FROM *Doctor Faustus*

1. Examine line 2 and discuss the effect of its rhythm.
2. To whom are lines 40 and 41 addressed?
3. Is there any particular order to the many pleas that Faustus makes? If so, what is the order and why is it significant?
4. What is the effect of the striking clock?

WILLIAM SHAKESPEARE
1564–1616

Probably more has been written about Shakespeare than about any other writer (the Folger Shakespeare Library in Washington, D. C., has more than 100,000 books, essays, and articles), but very little is known about his life, particularly his early years. We do know that he was born in Stratford-on-Avon, the son of a merchant and minor town official who rose to the position of alderman after a few years. His mother was the daughter of a farmer of some social position. At eighteen Shakespeare was married and at nineteen he became a father. Two years later, twins—a boy and a girl—were born; the boy, Hamnet, died in childhood. Sometime around 1585, Shakespeare left Stratford for London. By 1592 he had made a name for himself as an actor (particularly for "kingly parts," according to a contemporary), and he had also written a few plays. By 1594 he had earned a reputation as a dramatist and had become a stockholder in the Lord Chamberlain's theatrical company, to which he devoted his talents as an actor and playwright until about 1611. He then retired to Stratford, where he died five years later at fifty-two.

During his years in London, Shakespeare wrote a sequence of 154 sonnets, a few longer poems, and 37 plays (he probably collaborated on many others).

It is the plays, of course, on which his fame is based today. Although he was only one among many excellent playwrights of the time, his drama reveals a range and a depth that no other writer approached. Included in the following pages are passages and songs from *The Tempest*, *The Merchant of Venice*, *As You Like It*, *Hamlet*, and *Macbeth*.

Shakespeare's other works include the long narrative "Venus and Adonis," which appeared in 1593. His sonnets, however, are his most important nondramatic poetry. Of the 154 sonnets in the sequence, the first 126 are addressed to a noble youth, probably Shakespeare's patron; numbers 127 to 152 are addressed to a mysterious "dark lady." The last two sonnets seem to be unrelated to the rest. The sonnets are not all equally good, but the best are probably the greatest short poems in the English language.

Sonnet 29

When, in disgrace with fortune and men's eyes,
I all alone beweep my outcast state,
And trouble deaf heaven with my bootless° cries,
And look upon myself, and curse my fate,
Wishing me like to one more rich in hope,   5
Featured° like him, like him with friends possessed,
Desiring this man's art° and that man's scope,°
With what I most enjoy contented least;
Yet in these thoughts myself almost despising—
Haply° I think on thee: and then my state,   10
Like to the lark at break of day arising
From sullen° earth, sings hymns at heaven's gate;
    For thy sweet love remembered such wealth brings
    That then I scorn to change my state with kings.

3. **bootless:** vain, profitless. 6. **Featured:** formed. 7. **art:** skill. **scope:** range of thought. 10. **Haply:** perhaps. 12. **sullen:** gloomy.

Sonnet 87

Farewell! thou art too dear° for my possessing,
And like enough thou knowest thy estimate:
The charter° of thy worth gives thee releasing;
My bonds° in thee are all determinate.°
For how do I hold thee but by thy granting?   5
And for that riches where is my deserving?
The cause of this fair gift in me is wanting,
And so my patent° back again is swerving.
Thyself thou gav'st, thy own worth then not knowing,
Or me, to whom thou gav'st it, else mistaking;   10
So thy great gift, upon misprision growing,°
Comes home again, on better judgment making.
    Thus have I had thee, as a dream doth flatter,°
    In sleep, a king; but waking, no such matter.

1. **dear:** expensive (with overtones of the more common meaning of the word). 3. **charter:** a written guarantee of rights and privileges, usually granted to a newly formed corporation. 4. **bonds:** a pun: 1. anything binding or joining together; 2. a legal certificate, bearing interest, issued by a corporation. **determinate:** ended. 8. **patent:** an official document conferring rights and privileges. 11. **upon . . . growing:** based on a misunderstanding. 13. **flatter:** deceive.

Sonnet 116

Let me not to the marriage of true minds
Admit impediments. Love is not love
Which alters when it alteration finds.
Or bends with the remover to remove.°
O no! it is an ever-fixed mark   5
That looks on tempests, and is never shaken;
It is the star to every wandering bark,
Whose worth's unknown, although his height be taken.°

4. **Or . . . remove:** or ceases when the other ceases to love. 7-8. **It . . . taken:** The elevation of a star can be measured ("taken"), but its true value (like that of love) can never be calculated.

Love's not Time's fool,° though rosy lips and cheeks
Within his bending sickle's compass come;°   10
Love alters not with his brief hours and weeks,
But bears it out even to the edge of doom.
If this be error and upon me proved,
I never writ, nor no man ever loved.

9. **fool:** plaything. **9–10. though . . . come:** though rosy lips and cheeks
fall prey to time, come within the range ("compass") of his sickle.

Sonnet 130

My mistress' eyes are nothing like the sun;
Coral is far more red than her lips' red;
If snow be white, why then her breasts are dun;
If hairs be wires, black wires grow on her head.
I have seen roses damasked,° red and white,   5
But no such roses see I in her cheeks;
And in some perfumes is there more delight
Than in the breath that from my mistress reeks.
I love to hear her speak, yet well I know
That music hath a far more pleasing sound;   10
I grant I never saw a goddess go;°
My mistress, when she walks, treads on the ground:
    And yet, by heaven, I think my love as rare
    As any she belied° with false compare.°

5. **damasked:** having a varied pattern. 11. **go:** walk. 14. **belied:** misrep-
resented. **compare:** comparison.

from *The Merchant of Venice*

How Sweet the Moonlight Sleeps upon this Bank

How sweet the moonlight sleeps upon this bank!
Here will we sit and let the sounds of music
Creep in our ears. Soft stillness and the night
Become the touches of sweet harmony.

Sit, Jessica. Look how the floor of heaven   5
Is thick inlaid with patens° of bright gold.
There's not the smallest orb which thou behold'st
But in his motion like an angel sings,
Still quiring° to the young-eyed cherubins;°
Such harmony is in immortal souls;   10
But whilst this muddy vesture of decay°
Doth grossly close it in, we cannot hear it.

6. patens: discs (i.e., the stars). 9. quiring: choiring. cherubins: the second rank of angels. 11. muddy vesture of decay: the body, considered as a garment ("vesture") enclosing the soul.

from *As You Like It*

All the World's a Stage

All the world's a stage,
And all the men and women merely players:
They have their exits and their entrances;
And one man in his time plays many parts,
His acts being seven ages. At first the infant,   5
Mewling and puking in the nurse's arms.
And then the whining schoolboy, with his satchel,
And shining morning face, creeping like snail
Unwillingly to school. And then the lover
Sighing like furnace, with a woeful ballad   10
Made to his mistress' eyebrow. Then a soldier,
Full of strange oaths, and bearded like the pard,°
Jealous in honor, sudden and quick in quarrel,
Seeking the bubble reputation
Even in the cannon's mouth. And then the justice,   15
In fair round belly with good capon° lined,
With eyes severe, and beard of formal cut,
Full of wise saws° and modern instances;°

12. pard: leopard. 16. capon: tender chicken. 18. saws: proverbs. instances: examples.

And so he plays his part. The sixth age shifts
Into the lean and slippered pantaloon,   20
With spectacles on nose and pouch on side,
His youthful hose (well saved) a world too wide
For his shrunk shank; and his big manly voice,
Turning again toward childish treble, pipes
And whistles in his sound. Last scene of all,   25
That ends this strange eventful history,
Is second childishness and mere oblivion,
Sans° teeth, sans eyes, sans taste, sans everything.

28. Sans: without.

Blow, Blow, Thou Winter Wind

Many of Shakespeare's finest songs appear in *As You Like It;*
the following is one of the best-known.

Blow, blow, thou winter wind!
Thou art not so unkind
As man's ingratitude;
Thy tooth is not so keen
Because thou art not seen,   5
Although thy breath be rude.
Heigh ho! sing heigh ho! unto the green holly:
Most friendship is feigning, most loving mere folly:
Then, heigh ho! the holly!
This life is most jolly.   10

Freeze, freeze, thou bitter sky,
Thou dost not bite so nigh
As benefits forgot:
Though thou the waters warp,
Thy sting is not so sharp   15
As friend remembered not.
Heigh ho! sing heigh ho! unto the green holly:
Most friendship is feigning, most loving mere folly:
Then, heigh ho! the holly!
This life is most jolly.   20

from *Hamlet*

The passage that follows is the most famous of all Shakespearean soliloquies. In it, you should notice, Hamlet speculates on the question of suicide in general, not on whether he himself should commit suicide (though clearly some personal elements enter into his thought).

To be, or not to be—that is the question:
Whether 'tis nobler in the mind° to suffer
The slings and arrows of outrageous fortune
Or to take arms against a sea° of troubles,
And, by opposing, end them.° To die, to sleep—   5
No more—and by a sleep to say we end
The heartache, and the thousand natural shocks
That flesh is heir to; 'tis a consummation°
Devoutly to be wished. To die, to sleep—
To sleep, perchance to dream: ay, there's the rub!°   10
For in that sleep of death what dreams may come
When we have shuffled off° this mortal coil,°
Must give us pause. There's the respect°
That makes calamity of so long life.
For who would bear the whips and scorns of time,   15
Th' oppressor's wrong, the proud man's contumely,°
The pangs of despised love, the law's delay,
The insolence of office,° and the spurns
That patient merit of th' unworthy takes,
When he himself might his quietus° make   20
With a bare bodkin°? Who would fardels° bear,
To grunt and sweat under a weary life,
But that the dread of something after death—

2. **in the mind:** modifies "nobler." 4. **sea:** The line may refer to the old legend that Celtic warriors would sometimes dash into the sea and strike at the waves with swords and spears. 5. **end them:** by one's own death, as a warrior would die who tried to attack the incoming waves. 8. **consummation:** completion. 10. **rub:** obstacle. 12. **shuffled off:** thrown off. **coil:** tumult of human affairs, entanglements. (The word may also refer to the body, as enclosing and entangling the soul.) 13. **respect:** consideration. 16. **contumely** (kŏn'tū·mĕ'lĭ): scorn. 18. **office:** men in office. 20. **quietus** (kwī·ē'tŭs):end, death. 21. **bodkin:** knife. **fardels:** burdens.

The undiscovered country, from whose bourn°
No traveler returns—puzzles the will,   25
And makes us rather bear those ills we have
Than fly to others that we know not of?
Thus conscience° does make cowards of us all,
And thus the native hue° of resolution
Is sicklied o'er with the pale cast of thought,   30
And enterprises of great pitch° and moment°
With this regard their currents° turn awry
And lose the name of action.

24. bourn: border.   28. conscience: reflection, consciousness.   29. native
hue: natural color, complexion.   31. pitch: height.   (In falconry, the *pitch* is
the highest point of the falcon's flight.)   moment: weight, importance.   32. currents: movements, flowings.

from *Macbeth*

At this point in the play, Duncan, the King of Scotland, has
just arrived for a brief stay at Macbeth's castle. Earlier, three
witches had prophesied that Macbeth himself would one
day be king. Urged on by his ambition, Macbeth considers
hastening the fulfillment of the prophecy by killing Duncan.

If it were done when 'tis done, then 'twere well
It were done quickly: if the assassination
Could trammel up the consequence, and catch
With his surcease success;° that but this blow
Might be the be-all and the end-all here,   5
But here, upon this bank and shoal of time,
We'd jump° the life to come. But in these cases
We still have judgment here; that we but teach
Bloody instructions, which, being taught, return
To plague the inventor: this even-handed° justice   10

2–4. if . . . success: if the killing could prevent ("trammel up") any consequences, and be final and successful with the King's death ("surcease").
7. jump: risk. So long as the murder would be successful in this life ("this
bank and shoal of time"), Macbeth would risk its consequences in the after-
life.   10. even-handed: impartial.

Commends° the ingredients of our poisoned chalice
To our own lips. He's here in double trust;
First, as I am his kinsman and his subject,
Strong both against the deed; then, as his host,
Who should against his murderer shut the door,   15
Not bear the knife myself. Besides, this Duncan
Hath borne his faculties° so meek, hath been
So clear in his great office that his virtues
Will plead like angels, trumpet-tongued, against
The deep damnation of his taking-off;°   20
And pity, like a naked newborn babe,
Striding the blast, or heaven's cherubin, horsed
Upon the sightless couriers° of the air,
Shall blow the horrid deed in every eye,
That tears shall drown the wind. I have no spur   25
To prick the sides of my intent, but only
Vaulting ambition, which o'erleaps itself
And falls on the other.°

11. **Commends:** offers. 17. **faculties:** power (of kingship). 20. **taking-off:** murder. 23. **sightless couriers:** the winds (*sightless* means "unseen"). 28. **other:** i.e., other side.

from *The Tempest*

Full Fathom Five

Full fathom five thy father lies:
  Of his bones are coral made;
Those are pearls that were his eyes;
  Nothing of him that doth fade
But doth suffer a sea-change   5
Into something rich and strange.
Sea-nymphs hourly ring his knell:
  Hark! now I hear them—
  Ding, dong, bell.

Our Revels Now Are Ended

Near the end of *The Tempest*, Prospero, a magician, summons a group of spirits to present a brief play in honor of his daughter's marriage. At the end of the interlude, Prospero dismisses the spirits and then speaks the following lines.

> Our revels now are ended. These our actors,
> As I foretold you, were all spirits, and
> Are melted into air, into thin air;
> And, like the baseless° fabric of this vision,
> The cloud-capped towers, the gorgeous palaces,   5
> The solemn temples, the great globe° itself,
> Yea, all which it inherit, shall dissolve,
> And, like this insubstantial pageant faded,
> Leave not a rack° behind. We are such stuff
> As dreams are made on,° and our little life   10
> Is rounded with a sleep.°

4. **baseless:** unreal. 6. **globe:** the earth, and also the Globe Theater, where the play was first presented. 9. **rack:** cloud. 10. **on:** of. 10–11. **life . . . sleep:** Life is a brief moment of consciousness surrounded by eternal sleep.

Questions

Sonnets

1. Notice that Sonnet 29 is one long sentence. What is the effect of this unusual punctuation? How is the poem organized?
2. In Sonnet 87, what do the various figures of speech have in common? What is the tone of the poem? Is there any irony in it? If so, how is it created?
3. How does the organization of Sonnet 116 differ from that of Shakespeare's Sonnet 73 (p. 55)? In what ways are the two poems alike?
4. Sonnet 130 is a poem that satirizes the typical Elizabethan sonnet. How does it do so? Is the poem anything more than satire? Explain.

Songs and Passages from the Plays

1. What musical and rhythmic devices contribute to the effectiveness of the passage from *The Merchant of Venice?* Notice particularly the first four lines.

2. In the "All the World's a Stage" speech, what are some of the details that help to make the various stages vivid? Compare this passage to the passage from *Macbeth* on page 69. Both begin with the same metaphor. How do they differ?
3. In "Blow, Blow Thou Winter Wind" what is the effect of the refrain? How is it related to the rest of the song?
4. The "To be or not to be" soliloquy deals with extremely general and abstract questions. What are some of the details that prevent the speech itself from being general and abstract? In lines 13 and 14, Hamlet speaks of the "respect" that makes us bear life so long rather than commit suicide. What is the "respect"?
5. Compare Macbeth's soliloquy to Hamlet's. How do Macbeth and Hamlet differ in their thoughts on the "life to come"? What arguments against the killing of Duncan does Macbeth think of?
6. In "Our Revels Now Are Ended" what is the effect of the pun in line 6? On what metaphor is this passage based? Where have you seen this metaphor before?

BEN JONSON

1572?–1637

Jonson's father, a minister, died before the birth of his son, and the boy was brought up by an uncle. After a brief period of schooling, Jonson began an apprenticeship as a bricklayer. He left this job to enlist in the army and served for a few years in the wars in the Netherlands. On his return to England, he married, and then joined a theatrical company, first as an actor and later as a director. By the time he was thirty he was well known as a playwright. Largely self-taught, he also made himself one of the most respected classical scholars of his time. So famous did he become that he was patronized by three monarchs: Elizabeth I, James I, and Charles I.

He was a forceful personality as well as a poet, scholar, and critic. In his later years he attracted a group of younger poets to him, who formed a circle they called the "sons of Ben."

Jonson became a close friend of Shakespeare, in spite of their rivalry as playwrights. His plays, particularly his tragedies, though more scholarly than Shakespeare's, are less universal in their appeal. His satiric comedies, including *Volpone, The Alchemist,* and *The*

Silent Women, show him at his best. The three plays named have all been staged in recent years. Jonson was also primarily responsible for the development of the *masque,* a short dramatic interlude featuring song, dance, and elaborate settings. Opposed to the extravagant thought and language of much Elizabethan verse, Jonson urged a return to the classical principles of restraint and clarity. His own songs and lyrics reveal the qualities he admired.

Slow, Slow, Fresh Fount

Slow, slow, fresh fount, keep time with my salt tears;
   Yet slower yet, oh faintly, gentle springs;
List to the heavy part the music bears,
   Woe weeps out her division° when she sings.
      Droops herbs and flowers,   5
      Fall grief in showers;
      Our beauties are not ours;
        Oh, I could still,
Like melting snow upon some craggy hill,
Drop, drop, drop, drop,   10
Since nature's pride is now a withered daffodil.

4. **division:** a rapid series of musical notes.

Her Triumph*

See the chariot at hand here of love,
   Wherein my lady rideth!
Each that draws is a swan or a dove,
   And well the car love guideth.
As she goes all hearts do duty   5
    Unto her beauty,
And enamoured do wish so they might
    But enjoy such a sight,

* **Triumph:** ceremonial procession.

That they still were to run by her side,
Through swords, through seas, whither she would ride.   10

Do but look on her eyes; they do light
    All that love's world compriseth!
Do but look on her hair; it is bright
    As love's star when it riseth!
Do but mark her forehead's smoother   15
    Than words that sooth her;
And from her arched brows, such a grace
    Sheds itself through the face,
As alone there triumphs to the life
All the gain, all the good of the elements' strife.   20

Have you seen but a bright lily grow
    Before rude hands have touched it?
Ha' you marked but the fall o' the snow
    Before the soil hath smutched° it?
Ha' you felt the wool of beaver,   25
    Or swan's down ever?
Or have smelt o' the bud o' the briar?
    Or the nard° in the fire?
Or have tasted the bag of the bee?
O so white! O so soft! O so sweet is she!   30

   24. smutched: blackened.   28. nard: a fragrant plant.

On Something That Walks Somewhere

At court I met it, in clothes brave enough
    To be a courtier, and looks grave enough
To seem a statesman; as I near it came,
    It made me a great face; I asked the name.
A Lord, it cried, buried in flesh and blood,   5
    And such from whom let no man hope least good,
For I will do none; and as little ill,
    For I will dare none. Good Lord, walk dead still.

Ben Jonson   199

On My First Son

Jonson's first son was born in 1596 and died in 1603 of the plague.

> Farewell, thou child of my right hand,° and joy;
> My sin was too much hope of thee, loved boy.
> Seven years thou wert lent to me, and I thee pay,
> Exacted by thy fate, on the just day.
> Oh, could I lose all father° now! For why   5
> Will man lament the state he should envý?
> To have so soon 'scaped world's and flesh's rage,
> And if no other misery, yet age!
> Rest in soft peace, and asked, say, Here doth lie
> Ben Jonson his° best piece of poetry.   10
> For whose sake henceforth all his vows be such
> As what he loves may never like° too much.

1. **right hand:** "Son of my right hand" is the literal translation of *Benjamin*, which was apparently the boy's name. 5. **lose all father:** lose all sense of fatherhood (and cease grieving). 10. **Jonson his:** Jonson's. 12. **like:** perhaps, "be similar to," "imitate." The line seems to mean, "That what he—Jonson —loves may never imitate too closely (the fate of the boy)."

Song: To Celia

> Drink to me only with thine eyes,
> And I will pledge with mine;
> Or leave a kiss but in the cup
> And I'll not look for wine.
> The thirst that from the soul doth rise   5
> Doth ask a drink divine;
> But might I of Jove's nectar sup,
> I would not change for thine.
>
> I sent thee late a rosy wreath,
> Not so much honoring thee   10
> As giving it a hope that there
> It could not withered be;

But thou thereon didst only breathe
And sent'st it back to me;
Since when it grows, and smells, I swear,   15
Not of itself but thee!

Questions

1. What are some of the musical devices used in "Slow, Slow, Fresh Fount"? What is the effect of the varying line lengths?
2. In "Her Triumph" what image is used in the first stanza? Does the poem progress to some sort of a conclusion, or could its order be rearranged with no change in the effect? What is the effect of the many questions in the last stanza?
3. What are some of the details that make "On Something That Walks Somewhere" effective as satire?
4. What is the tone of "On My First Son"? If you were told that Jonson never had a son, that the situation described in the poem was entirely imaginary, how would that affect your attitude toward the poem and your judgment of its tone?
5. Compare "To Celia" to some of the other Elizabethan songs you have read in this section; for example, Peele's, Campion's, and Shakespeare's. What do the songs seem to have in common? It has been said that no period has ever surpassed the Elizabethan in the writing of songs. What seem to you to be the most striking characteristics of the Elizabethan songs you have read?

THE SEVENTEENTH
CENTURY

The seventeenth century was a period of great social and political upheaval in England. Early in the century a group within the Anglican Church (the Puritans) began to oppose many of the current religious practices. Religious differences led to political and social disagreements, with the Puritans becoming increasingly opposed to the monarchy. In 1642 civil war broke out. Led by Oliver Cromwell, the Puritan army defeated the Royalists (those loyal to the King), and executed King Charles I in 1649. The country became a Commonwealth under Cromwell, and remained so until Cromwell's death in 1658. No Puritan leader was strong enough to take his place, and the monarchy was restored in 1660. In this book we are concerned with literature, not with political or social history, but much of the poetry of the seventeenth century was directly influenced by the historical events we have outlined, and some knowledge of those events will be helpful.

The poetry of the seventeenth century, although as diverse as that of any other period, divides itself in general into two main currents. Such poets as Herrick, Waller, Lovelace, and Suckling, known as the Cavalier poets, carried on the tradition of the Elizabethan lyric as refined by Ben Jonson. (Many of the Cavaliers were former "sons of Ben.") The other current had its source in Donne, the first of the so-called Metaphysical poets. Herbert, Crashaw, Vaughan, and Traherne, different as they are from each other, were all to some extent indebted to Donne's religious poetry, and all of them are generally described as Metaphysical poets. Andrew Marvell shared some characteristics of both the Cavaliers and Metaphysicals. Quite independent of these currents were two of the greatest English poets, John Milton and John Dryden.

JOHN DONNE

1572–1631

After attending both Oxford and Cambridge and briefly studying the law, Donne enlisted as a soldier and served with the Earl of Essex on the Continent. On his return to England he became a man-about-town in London—a favorite of the ladies, a theatergoer, and a writer of love poems. Donne gained an excellent government post with Sir Thomas Egerton, but he married Egerton's niece without her family's permission and was dismissed from his job. The next few years were extremely difficult, many of them spent in poverty with a rapidly growing family. During these years, Donne, who had been born a Catholic, was drawn more and more toward the Anglican Church. Persuaded by James I, he was ordained a clergyman in 1615. The great power of his sermons made him famous as a preacher, and in 1621 he was made Dean of St. Paul's. He died at the age of fifty-nine, shortly before he was to have been made a bishop.

Donne's poetry is of two kinds: the early passionate and sometimes cynical love poems, and the later profoundly devout religious poetry. Reacting against the elaborate prettiness into which much late Elizabethan poetry had declined, Donne created a colloquial and often deliberately harsh style to express heights of emotion, both of earthly love and of mystical devotion. His images and metaphors, often very complex, come from science, philosophy, the trades, and ordinary life, rather than from nature or classical mythology, as had been true of much poetry of the past. These qualities of Donne's style and that of his followers came to be labeled as "metaphysical" in the eighteenth century.

Donne's poetry was not published until two years after his death. For a generation or so his work was very popular and much imitated, but his reputation declined toward the end of the 1600's. Throughout much of the eighteenth and nineteenth centuries his work was almost completely ignored. In the early years of this century, however, interest in his poetry revived dramatically, and he has exerted a strong influence on much modern poetry.

Woman's Constancy

Now thou hast loved me one whole day,
Tomorrow when thou leav'st, what wilt thou say?
Wilt thou then antedate° some new-made vow?
    Or say that now
We are not just those persons which we were?   5
Or, that oaths made in reverential fear
Of love, and his wrath, any may forswear?°
Or, as true deaths true marriages untie,
So lovers' contracts, images of those,°
Bind but till sleep, death's image, them unloose?   10
    Or, your own end to justify,
For having purposed change and falsehood, you
Can have no way but falsehood to be true?°
Vain lunatic, against these 'scapes° I could
    Dispute and conquer, if I would;   15
    Which I abstain to do,
For by tomorrow, I may think so too.

    3. **antedate:** assign an earlier date than the true one.   7. **forswear:** deny.
9. **those:** i.e., true marriages.   12–13. **For . . . true:** Because you have resolved to be false, you can only be true (to your resolution) by actually *being*
false.   14. **'scapes:** escapes; here, transgressions, sins.

The Message

Send home my long strayed eyes to me,
Which, oh, too long have dwelt on thee;
Yet since there they have learned such ill,
    Such forced fashions,°
    And false passions,   5
      That they be
      Made by thee
Fit for no good sight, keep them still.

    4. **forced fashions:** insincere actions.

Send home my harmless heart again,
Which no unworthy thought could stain;   10
Which if it be taught by thine
  To make jestings
  Of protestings,
    And break both
    Word and oath,   15
Keep it, for then 'tis none of mine.

Yet send me back my heart and eyes
That I may know and see thy lies,
And may laugh and joy, when thou
  Art in anguish   20
  And dost languish
    For some one
    That will none,°
Or prove as false as thou art now.

      23. **will none:** will not (languish).

Song

  Sweetest love, I do not go
    For weariness of thee,
  Nor in hope the world can show
    A fitter love for me;
      But since that I   5
  Must die at last, 'tis best,
  To use myself in jest
    Thus by feigned deaths to die.

  Yesternight the sun went hence,
    And yet is here today;   10
  He hath no desire nor sense,
    Nor half so short a way;
      Then fear not me,
  But believe that I shall make
  Speedier journeys, since I take   15
    More wings and spurs than he.

Oh, how feeble is man's power,
  That if good fortune fall,
Cannot add another hour,
  Nor a lost hour recall!   20
    But come bad chance,
And we join to it our strength,
And we teach it art and length,
    Itself o'er us to advance.

When thou sigh'st, thou sigh'st not wind,   25
  But sigh'st my soul away;
When thou weep'st, unkindly kind,
  My life's blood doth decay.
    It cannot be
That thou lov'st me, as thou say'st,   30
If in thine my life thou waste;
    Thou art the best of me.

Let not thy divining° heart
  Forethink me any ill,
Destiny may take thy part,°   35
  And may thy fears fulfil;
    But think that we
Are but turned aside to sleep;
They who one another keep
    Alive, ne'er parted be.   40

33. **divining:** prophetic.   35. **take thy part:** adopt your viewpoint.

A Valediction:* Forbidding Mourning

As virtuous men pass mildly away,
  And whisper to their souls to go,
Whilst some of their sad friends do say,
  "The breath goes now," and some say, "No."

* **Valediction:** a farewell address.

So let us melt and make no noise,   5
   No tear-floods nor sigh-tempests move;
'Twere profanation of our joys
   To tell the laity our love.

Moving of the earth brings harms and fears;
   Men reckon what it did and meant;   10
But trepidation of the spheres,°
   Though greater far, is innocent.

Dull sublunary° lovers' love,
   Whose soul is sense,° cannot admit
Absence, because it doth remove   15
   Those things which elemented° it.

But we by a love so much refined
   That ourselves know not what it is,
Interassurèd of the mind,°
   Care less eyes, lips, and hands to miss.   20

Our two souls, therefore, which are one,
   Though I must go, endure not yet
A breach, but an expansion,
   Like gold to airy thinness beat.

If they be two, they are two so   25
   As stiff twin compasses° are two;
Thy soul, the fixed foot, makes no show
   To move, but doth if th' other do.

---

11. trepidation . . . spheres: in Donne's time it was commonly thought
that the stars were permanently attached to a series of crystal spheres; "trepidation" was the term applied to the slight, irregular movements noticed in the
stars' (and thus the spheres') courses.   13. sublunary: literally, "below the
moon"—in other words, earthly.   14. sense: (merely) sensual.   16. elemented:
formed.   19. Interassurèd . . . mind: together assured of the mind's love.
26. compasses: the measuring and drawing instrument used in geometry. (Notice that this figure of speech is carried through the remaining stanzas.)

And though it in the center sit,
    Yet when the other far doth roam,   30
It leans and hearkens after it,
    And grows erect as that comes home.

Such wilt thou be to me, who must,
    Like th' other foot, obliquely run;
Thy firmness makes my circle just,°   35
    And makes me end where I begun.

35. just: exact.

from *Holy Sonnets*

At the Round Earth's Imagined Corners

At the round earth's imagined corners,° blow
Your trumpets, angels; and arise, arise
From death, you numberless infinities
Of souls, and to your scattered bodies go;
All whom the flood did, and fire shall o'erthrow,   5
All whom war, dearth, age, agues, tyrannies,
Despair, law, chance hath slain, and you whose eyes
Shall behold God and never taste death's woe.°
But let them sleep, Lord, and me mourn a space,
For if above all these my sins abound,   10
'Tis late to ask abundance of thy grace
When we are there; here on this lowly ground
Teach me how to repent; for that's as good
As if thou'hadst° sealed my pardon with thy blood.

1. **imagined corners:** the Bible (Revelations 7), describing the Last Judgment, speaks of "four angels standing on the four corners of the earth, holding the four winds . . ."   7–8. **you . . . woe:** all those who are still living at the Last Judgment, and who are free from sin. (See Revelations 21:3–4.)   14. **thou'hadst:** Donne uses the apostrophe here to indicate that the two words should be run together in pronunciation.

Death, Be Not Proud

Death, be not proud, though some have callèd thee
Mighty and dreadful, for thou art not so;
For those whom thou think'st thou dost overthrow
Die not, poor Death; nor yet canst thou kill me.
From rest and sleep, which but thy pictures° be,   5
Much pleasure; then from thee much more must flow;
And soonest our best men with thee do go—
Rest of their bones and souls' delivery!
Thou'rt slave to fate, chance, kings, and desperate men,
And dost with poison, war, and sickness dwell;   10
And poppy or charms can make us sleep as well
And better than thy stroke. Why swell'st° thou then?
One short sleep past, we wake eternally,
And Death shall be no more: Death, thou shalt die.

5. **pictures**: images, imitations.   12. **swell'st**: become "puffed up" with importance, behave proudly or arrogantly.

Questions

1. What is the tone of "Woman's Constancy"—bitter, playful, or what? How is the tone created? Where does an example of irony occur?
2. Compare "The Message" to "Woman's Constancy." How do the two poems differ? What is primarily responsible for the difference: tone? organization? theme? something else? What do the poems have in common?
3. Explain in your own words the meaning of the first stanza of "Song." What is the paradox of the final lines of the poem? Does "Song" contain any other paradoxes? What are they?
4. In "A Valediction: Forbidding Mourning" what two kinds of love are contrasted? Explain lines 7 and 8: what is the specific meaning of "profanation" and "laity"? Analyze and discuss the metaphor of the last three stanzas.
5. What is the relationship between the octave and the sestet of "At the Round Earth's Imagined Corners"? What is the "lowly ground" of line 12? What is the effect of the list in lines 6 and 7?
6. What is the paradox on which "Death, Be Not Proud" is based? Consider especially lines 5–6 and 13–14. What is the effect of the caesura in line 14?

THE KING JAMES BIBLE

Before the King James, or Authorized Version of the Bible, there
were several other translations into English of both the Old and
New Testaments; and since the King James Bible there have been
still others. The King James Bible is, however, the best known and
probably the most widely used version, and in literary value no
other English translation can compare with it. It remains perhaps
the greatest work of prose or prose-poetry in the language, and
echoes of the King James Bible can be found in countless writers
from the seventeenth century to the present day.

The King James translation was the work of fifty-four scholars
from Oxford, Cambridge, and Westminster, appointed by King
James I in 1604. The complete translation was published in 1611.

The Psalms

The earliest of the Psalms go back to the time of David, but
most of them were written between 400 and 100 B.C. The
Greek word *psalmos* means the playing of a stringed instrument—undoubtedly, many of the Psalms were composed as
hymns to be sung in the service of the Temple.

Hebrew poetry had neither rhyme nor meter, and the English translators also avoided the devices. The Psalms are, however, intensely rhythmical. Notice lines 1 and 2 of Psalm
Nineteen, in which the second line repeats in different words
the idea of the first, and lines 13 and 14 of Psalm Ninety, in
which the second line says the opposite of the first. This use
of parallelism and contrast is characteristic of Hebrew poetry,
and it is one of the ways in which the Psalms develop their
strong rhythms.

Psalm Nineteen

The heavens declare the glory of God;
And the firmament showeth his handiwork.
Day unto day uttereth speech,

And night unto night showeth knowledge.
There is no speech nor language,   5
Where their voice is not heard.
Their line is gone out through all the earth.
And their words to the end of the world.
In them hath he set a tabernacle for the sun,
Which is as a bridegroom coming out of his chamber,   10
And rejoiceth as a strong man to run a race.
His going forth is from the end of the heaven,
And his circuit unto the ends of it:
And there is nothing hid from the heat thereof.
The law of the Lord is perfect, converting the soul: 15
The testimony of the Lord is sure, making wise the simple.
The statutes of the Lord are right, rejoicing the heart:
The commandment of the Lord is pure, enlightening the eyes.
The fear of the Lord is clean, enduring for ever:
The judgments of the Lord are true and righteous altogether.   20
More to be desired are they than gold, yea, than much fine gold;
Sweeter also than honey and the honeycomb.
Moreover by them is thy servant warned;
In keeping of them there is great reward.
Who can understand his errors?   25
Cleanse thou me from secret faults.
Keep back thy servant also from presumptuous sins;
Let them not have dominion over me: then shall I be upright,
And I shall be innocent from the great transgression.
Let the words of my mouth, and the meditation of my heart, be ac-
    ceptable in thy sight,   30
O Lord, my strength, and my redeemer.

Psalm Ninety

Lord, thou hast been our dwelling place
In all generations.
Before the mountains were brought forth,
Or ever thou hadst formed the earth and the world,

Even from everlasting to everlasting, thou art God.   5
Thou turnest man to destruction;
And sayest, "Return, ye children of men."
For a thousand years in thy sight
Are but as yesterday when it is past,
And as a watch in the night.   10
Thou carriest them away as with a flood; they are as asleep:
In the morning they are like grass which groweth up.
In the morning it flourisheth, and groweth up;
In the evening it is cut down, and withereth.
For we are consumed by thine anger,   15
And by thy wrath are we troubled.
Thou hast set our iniquities before thee,
Our secret sins in the light of thy countenance.
For all our days are passed away in thy wrath:
We spend our years as a tale that is told.   20
The days of our years are threescore years and ten;
And if by reason of strength they be fourscore years,
Yet is their strength labor and sorrow;
For it is soon cut off, and we fly away.
Who knoweth the power of thine anger?   25
Even according to thy fear, so is thy wrath.
So teach us to number our days,
That we may apply our hearts unto wisdom.
Return, O Lord, how long?
And let it repent thee concerning thy servants.   30
O satisfy us early with thy mercy;
That we may rejoice and be glad all our days.
Make us glad according to the days wherein thou hast afflicted us,
And the years wherein we have seen evil.
Let thy work appear unto thy servants,   35
And thy glory unto their children.
And let the beauty of the Lord our God be upon us:
And establish thou the work of our hands upon us;
Yea, the work of our hands establish thou it.

from *Ecclesiastes, or The Preacher*

The book of Ecclesiastes was written around 200 B.C. by a
man who identifies himself only as "Koheleth," the Hebrew
word for preacher. The following poem, a lyric on old age, is
part of the conclusion of the book.

Remember now thy Creator in the days of thy youth,
While the evil days come not,
Nor the years draw nigh, when thou shalt say,
I have no pleasure in them;
While the sun, or the light,   5
Or the moon, or the stars, be not darkened,
Nor the clouds return after the rain:
In the day when the keepers of the house shall tremble,
And the strong men shall bow themselves,
And the grinders cease because they are few,   10
And those that look out of the windows be darkened,
And the doors shall be shut in the streets,
When the sound of the grinding is low,
And he shall rise up at the voice of the bird,
And all the daughters of music shall be brought low: 15
Also when they shall be afraid of that which is high,
And fears shall be in the way,
And the almond tree shall flourish,
And the grasshopper shall be a burden,
And desire shall fail: 20
Because man goeth to his long home,
And the mourners go about the streets:
Or ever the silver cord be loosed,
Or the golden bowl be broken,
Or the pitcher be broken at the fountain,   25
Or the wheel broken at the cistern.
Then shall the dust return to the earth as it was:
And the spirit shall return unto God who gave it.

Questions

1. What examples of parallelism can you find in Psalm Nineteen? Of figurative language? Look closely at lines 15–20. How would you describe the rhythm of these lines? How is the rhythm created?
2. What is the theme of Psalm Ninety? How is the poem organized? Could the order of the lines be rearranged without creating any basic change in the psalm's effect? Why, or why not?
3. The lines from Ecclesiastes are richly symbolic. Beginning with line 13 they describe the physical weaknesses of old age. The "keepers of the house" are aged hands, the "grinders" are teeth. Try to explain the symbolism of some of the other images. What is the poet's attitude toward old age? In other words, what is the tone of his poem?

ROBERT HERRICK

1591–1674

Herrick attended Cambridge and after graduation spent most of his time in London as one of the "sons of Ben" (Jonson). He soon earned a reputation as a poet, but a short time later he entered the Anglican clergy and was sent to Devonshire. Here he became interested in the rustic, semi-pagan customs of his parishioners—the seasonal festivals, the dancing, and the color and charm of country life. At times, however, Herrick seems to have become discontented with Devonshire, although he made only one trip to London in fifteen or more years. In 1647 he was ejected from his post by the Puritans. He returned to London and published a volume of poetry—the work of over twenty-five years. The volume was not a failure, but fashions had changed in the years that Herrick had been away from London, and his poetry did not earn the popularity it might have if it had been published ten or fifteen years earlier.

After the restoration of the monarchy, Herrick was returned to his vicarage in Devonshire in 1662. He remained there until his death.

Herrick wrote in the tradition of Ben Jonson, although with a somewhat lighter, more graceful style. His poems are reminiscent of classical Latin lyrics in their clarity, simplicity, and light, mischievous tone.

The Argument of His Book

I sing of brooks, of blossoms, birds, and bowers:
Of April, May, of June and July flowers.
I sing of maypoles, hock carts,° wassails,° wakes,°
Of bridegrooms, brides, and of their bridal cakes.
I write of youth, of love, and have access   5
By these, to sing of cleanly wantonness.°
I sing of dews, of rains, and piece by piece
Of balm, of oil, of spice, and ambergris.°
I sing of times trans-shifting; and I write
How roses first came red, and lilies white.   10
I write of groves, of twilights, and I sing
The court of Mab,° and of the Fairy King.
I write of Hell; I sing (and ever shall)
Of Heaven, and hope to have it after all.

3. **hock carts:** the cart which carried the last load of a harvest. **wassails:**
Christmas festivities. (A bowl of wassail, a spiced ale, was passed around during Christmas parties and everyone drank a toast from it.) **wakes:** country
festivals in honor of the patron saint of the local church. 6. **wantonness:**
sportiveness, fancifulness. 8. **ambergris:** an oily substance, secreted by the
sperm whale, used in making perfume. 12. **Mab:** the queen of the fairies.

Delight in Disorder

A sweet disorder in the dress
Kindles in clothes a wantonness:
A lawn° about the shoulders thrown
Into a fine distraction:
An erring lace, which here and there   5
Enthralls the crimson stomacher:°
A cuff neglectful, and thereby
Ribbons to flow confusedly:
A winning wave, deserving note,
In the tempestuous petticoat: 10

3. **lawn:** a piece of fine linen. 6. **stomacher:** an ornamental covering worn
in the front of the dress.

A careless shoestring, in whose tie
I see a wild civility:
Do more bewitch me than when art
Is too precise in every part.

To Daffodils

Fair daffodils, we weep to see
 You haste away so soon;
As yet the early rising sun
 Has not attained his noon.
  Stay, stay,   5
 Until the hasting day
  Has run
 But to the evensong;°
And, having prayed together, we
 Will go with you along.   10

We have short time to stay, as you
 We have as short a spring;
As quick a growth to meet decay
 As you, or anything.
  We die,   15
 As your hours do, and dry
  Away,
 Like to the summer's rain;
Or as the pearls of morning's dew,
 Ne'er to be found again.   20

8. **evensong:** the evening prayer service.

Corinna's Going A-Maying

Celebrations of May Day, as the beginning of spring, the
season of fertility, date from ancient pagan times. Such
festivals still took place in rural England during Herrick's

lifetime. Notice how, throughout this poem, Herrick deliberately mixes pagan and Christian elements (just as did the country festivals he observed).

Get up, get up for shame, the blooming morn
Upon her wings presents the god unshorn.°
  See how Aurora° throws her fair
  Fresh-quilted colors through the air!
  Get up, sweet slug-a-bed, and see   5
  The dew bespangling herb and tree.
Each flower has wept, and bowed toward the east,
Above an hour since; yet you no dressed,
  Nay! not so much as out of bed?
  When all the birds have matins° said,   10
  And sung their thankful hymns; 'tis sin,
  Nay, profanation to keep in,
Whenas a thousand virgins on this day
Spring, sooner than the lark, to fetch in May.°

Rise, and put on your foliage, and be seen   15
To come forth, like the spring-time, fresh and green
  And sweet as Flora.° Take no care
  For jewels for your gown and hair;
  Fear not, the leaves will strew
  Gems in abundance upon you;   20
Besides, the childhood of the day has kept,
Against° you come, some orient pearls° unwept;
  Come, and receive them while the light
  Hangs on the dew-locks of the night,
  And Titan° on the eastern hill   25
  Retires himself, or else stands still
Till you come forth. Wash, dress, be brief in praying:
Few beads° are best, when once we go a-Maying.

2. **god unshorn:** Apollo, the sun god, often pictured with long hair.
3. **Aurora:** the dawn. 10. **matins:** morning prayers. 14. **fetch in May:** the custom of bringing in flowers on May Day, particularly the white hawthorne or "whitethorn," which was often called simply "May." 17. **Flora:** the flower goddess. 22. **Against:** for the time when. **orient pearls:** i.e., dewdrops. (*Orient* pearls were pearls of the highest luster and brilliance.) 25. **Titan:** another sun god. 28. **beads:** of the rosary; hence, prayers.

Come, my Corinna, come; and coming mark°
How each field turns a street, each street a park°   30
   Made green, and trimmed with trees; see how
   Devotion gives each house a bough
   Or branch; each porch, each door, ere this
   An ark, a tabernacle is,°
Made up of whitethorn neatly interwove,   35
As if here were those cooler shades of love.
   Can such delights be in the street
   And open fields, and we not see't?
   Come, we'll abroad, and let's obey
   The proclamation made for May,   40
And sin no more, as we have done, by staying;
But, my Corinna, come, let's go a-Maying.

There's not a budding boy or girl, this day,
But is got up and gone to bring in May.
   A deal of youth, ere this, is come   45
   Back, and with whitethorn laden home.
   Some have dispatched their cakes and cream,
   Before that we have left to dream;°
And some have wept, and wooed, and plighted troth,
And chose their priest, ere we can cast off sloth.   50
   Many a green gown has been given;
   Many a kiss, both odd and even;
   Many a glance too has been sent
   From out the eye, love's firmament;
Many a jest told of the key's betraying   55
This night, and locks picked, yet w'are not a-Maying.

Come, let us go, while we are in our prime,
And take the harmless folly of the time.
   We shall grow old apace° and die
   Before we know our liberty.   60

29. **mark:** observe. 30. **field . . . park:** town and country are now the
same. 33–34. **each . . . is:** each porch and door is now a place of worship,
like the Biblical ark and tabernacle. 48. **left to dream:** "left off," stopped,
dreaming. 59. **apace:** swiftly.

Our life is short, and our days run
As fast away as does the sun,
And as a vapor, or a drop of rain,
Once lost can ne'er be found again;
So when or you or I are made   65
A fable, song, or fleeting shade,°
All love, all liking, all delight,
Lies drowned with us in endless night.
Then while time serves,° and we are but decaying;
Come, my Corinna, come, let's go a-Maying.   70

66. **shade:** ghost, spirit.   69. **serves:** allows, provides the opportunity.

Questions

1. In "The Argument of His Book," what could Herrick mean by "I write of Hell; I sing . . . / Of Heaven"? What does he mean by "after all" in the last line?
2. Is "Delight in Disorder" merely about disorder of clothes, or does it have other implications? In particular consider the last two lines of the poem.
3. In "To Daffodils," what analogy does Herrick make between daffodils and man? What is the poem really about?
4. What are some of the pagan elements in "Corinna's Going a-Maying"? The Christian elements? How are the two combined? What are the results of this combination? Is Herrick merely confusing two different systems of belief? Or do you think he may have some other purpose in mind?
5. Herrick is being playful and humorous throughout much of "Corinna's Going a-Maying"—he does not take seriously many of his own comments (see ll. 10–12, 27–28, 33–34, and 41 especially). Is the poem entirely light in tone then? If not, could it be serious and playful at the same time? What about the last stanza: does the tone change at this point? In what way?

GEORGE HERBERT

1593–1633

Herbert attended Cambridge and while still an undergraduate began writing verse. After graduation, he thought for a time of entering government service, but after a few years chose to become an Anglican clergyman. He lived a quiet life as Rector of Bemerton, devoting himself to his parish duties, to music, and to religious poetry. His poems were published the year after his death.

After John Donne, Herbert is perhaps the finest of the metaphysical poets. In the eighteenth century, Samuel Johnson, in describing the metaphysical school of poetry, found its chief characteristic to be wit, or the combining "of dissimilar images, or discovery of occult resemblances in things apparently unlike." Herbert's poetry, devout as it is, is also frequently playful, serious emotion being mixed with whimsical ideas. He delighted to experiment with odd patterns and structures (see "The Altar") and with wordplay, as had his great predecessor, Donne.

The Altar

A broken altar, Lord, thy servant rears,
Made of a heart and cémented with tears;
Whose parts are as thy hand did frame;
No workman's tool hath touched the same.
A heart alone   5
Is such a stone
As nothing but
Thy power doth cut.
Wherefore each part
Of my hard heart   10
Meets in this frame
To praise thy name;
That if I chance to hold my peace,
These stones to praise thee may not cease.
Oh, let thy blessed sacrifice be mine,   15
And sanctify this altar to be thine.

The Pulley

When God at first made man,
Having a glass of blessings standing by—
"Let us," said he, "pour on him all we can;
Let the world's riches, which dispersed lie,
Contract into a span."°   5

So strength first made a way,
Then beauty flowed, then wisdom, honor, pleasure:
When almost all was out, God made a stay,
Perceiving that, alone of all his treasure,
Rest in the bottom lay.   10

"For if I should," said he,
"Bestow this jewel also on my creature,
He would adore my gifts instead of me,
And rest in nature, not the God of nature:
So both should losers be.   15

"Yet let him keep the rest,
But keep them with repining restlessness;
Let him be rich and weary, that at least,
If goodness lead him not, yet weariness
May toss him to my breast."°   20

5. **span:** a small space. **19–20. If . . . breast:** the final lines explain the
title: either goodness or weariness will act as a pulley, drawing man up to God.

Jordan* I

Who says that fictions only and false hair
Become a verse? Is there in truth no beauty?
Is all good structure in a winding stair?
May no lines pass except they do their duty
Not to a true, but painted chair?   5

* **Jordan:** the River Jordan in Palestine winds and twists a great deal—
Herbert apparently chose the title of this and the following poem to symbolize
the twisting, meandering poetry he describes.

George Herbert   **221**

Is it no verse except enchanted groves
And sudden arbors shadow coarse-spun lines?
Must purling streams refresh a lover's loves?
Must all be veiled, while he that reads, divines,°
 Catching the sense at two removes?°   10

Shepherds are honest people; let them sing.
Riddle who list° for me, and pull for prime;°
I envy no man's nightingale or spring,
Nor let them punish me with loss of rhyme,
 Who plainly say, My God, my King.   15

9. **divines:** guesses. 10. **Catching . . . removes:** discovering the meaning after further steps of interpretation. 12. **list:** desire, wish. **pull for prime:** draw for the winning hand in a card game.

Jordan II

When first my lines of heav'nly joys made mention,
Such was their luster, they did so excel,
That I sought out quaint words and trim invention;°
My thoughts began to burnish, sprout, and swell,
Curling with metaphors a plain intention,   5
Decking° the sense as if it were to sell.

Thousands of notions in my brain did run,
Off'ring their service, if I were not sped.
I often blotted what I had begun:
This was not quick° enough, and that was dead.   10
Nothing could seem too rich to clothe the sun,
Much less those joys which trample on his head.

As flames do work and wind when they ascend,
So did I weave myself into the sense.

3. **trim invention:** elegant ideas, elaborate subjects. 6. **Decking:** decorating. 10. **quick:** alive.

But while I bustled, I might hear a friend   15
Whisper, How wide° is all this long pretense!
There is in love a sweetness ready penned,
Copy out only that, and save expense.

16. **wide:** wide of the mark, futile.

Questions

1. In "The Altar" what does Herbert mean by "my hard heart" (l. 10)?
   Would you call the structure of this poem significant or merely clever?
   Why?
2. According to "The Pulley," why does God refuse to bestow rest on
   man? What is the pun in line 16?
3. What do Jordan I and II have to say about poetry? What kinds of
   poems are criticized? What kinds are praised? In "Jordan I," what do
   lines 4 and 5 mean? In "Jordan II," who might be the "friend" of
   line 15?

CAVALIER AND METAPHYSICAL POETS

The two main currents of poetry in the seventeenth century are
generally labeled "Cavalier" and "Metaphysical." The Cavaliers were
similar to Ben Jonson in their wish for clarity and simplicity. The
tone of much of their verse is light and occasionally rather cynical.
The Metaphysical poets carried on in the tradition started by Donne
—their work is devout, intellectual, and often complex in imagery.

EDMUND WALLER (1606–1687) is usually called a Cavalier poet,
though only a few of his brief lyrics reveal characteristics of that
school. SIR JOHN SUCKLING (1609–1642) was perhaps the typical
courtier and Cavalier poet—his work witty, cynical, and sometimes
superficial. He wrote a number of plays during his brief life, but
most of them are ignored today in favor of his shorter poems.
RICHARD LOVELACE (1618–1658) was a serious Cavalier poet, noted
for his personal honor and for his conscientious support of the
monarchy.

In his poetry RICHARD CRASHAW (1613?–1649) reveals both the

faults and virtues of the Metaphysical style: his images sometimes seem artificial, but all of his work reveals an intellectual vigor and a religious fervor. HENRY VAUGHAN (1622–1695), who called himself a disciple of George Herbert, lacked the skill in varying forms and rhythms that Herbert possessed, but in turn was able to reach a mystical profundity that Herbert rarely attained. THOMAS TRAHERNE (1637?–1674), one of the most original of the Metaphysical poets, was unknown until the beginning of this century. Manuscripts of his poetry and prose were discovered in the late 1890's and first published in 1903.

Old Age

EDMUND WALLER

The seas are quiet when the winds give o'er;
So calm are we when passions are no more.
For then we know how vain it was to boast
Of fleeting things, so certain to be lost.
Clouds of affection from our younger eyes   5
Conceal that emptiness which age descries.

The soul's dark cottage, battered and decayed,
Lets in new light through chinks that time hath made:
Stronger by weakness, wiser men become
As they draw near to their eternal home.   10
Leaving the old, both worlds at once they view
That stand upon the threshold of the new.

The Constant Lover

JOHN SUCKLING

Out upon it, I have loved
Three whole days together!

And am like to love three more,
    If it prove fair weather.

Time shall molt away his wings   5
    Ere he shall discover
In the whole wide world again
    Such a constant lover.

But the spite on't is, no praise
    Is due at all to me;   10
Love with me had made no stays,
    Had it any been but she.

Had it any been but she,
    And that very face,
There had been at least ere this   15
    A dozen dozen in her place.

To Lucasta, on Going to the Wars

RICHARD LOVELACE

Tell me not, Sweet, I am unkind,
    That from the nunnery
Of thy chaste breast and quiet mind
    To war and arms I fly.

True, a new mistress now I chase,   5
    The first foe in the field;
And with a stronger faith embrace
    A sword, a horse, a shield.

Yet this inconstancy is such
    As thou too shalt adore;   10
I could not love thee, Dear, so much,
    Loved I not honor more.

To Pontius Washing His Hands

RICHARD CRASHAW

Thy hands are washed, but oh, the water's spilt
That labored to have washed thy guilt;
The flood, if any can, that can suffice
Must have its fountain in thine eyes.

A Song

RICHARD CRASHAW

Lord, when the sense of thy sweet grace
Sends up my soul to seek thy face,
Thy blessed eyes breed such desire
I die in love's delicious fire.
    O love, I am thy sacrifice.   5
Be still triumphant, blessed eyes;
Still shine on me, fair suns! that I
Still may behold, though still I die.

Though still I die, I live again,
Still longing so to be still slain;   10
So gainful is such loss of breath,
I die even in desire of death.
    Still live in me this loving strife
Of living death and dying life;
For while thou sweetly slayest me,   15
Dead to myself, I live in thee.

The Retreat

HENRY VAUGHAN

Happy those early days when I
Shined in my angel-infancy!

Before I understood this place
Appointed for my second race,
Or taught my soul to fancy aught   5
But a white celestial thought;
When yet I had not walked above
A mile or two from my first love,
And looking back at that short space,
Could see a glimpse of his bright face;   10
When on some gilded cloud or flower
My gazing soul would dwell an hour,
And in those weaker glories spy
Some shadows of eternity;
Before I taught my tongue to wound   15
My conscience with a sinful sound,
Or had the black art° to dispense
A several° sin to every sense;
But felt through all this fleshly dress
Bright shoots° of everlastingness.   20

   Oh, how I long to travel back
And tread again that ancient track!
That I might once more reach that plain
Where first I left my glorious train,°
From whence th' enlightened spirit sees   25
That shady city of palm trees.°
But, ah, my soul with too much stay
Is drunk, and staggers in the way.
Some men a forward motion love,
But I by backward steps would move,   30
And when this dust falls to the urn,
In that state I came, return.°

---

17. **black art:** witchcraft, evil.   18. **several:** different.   20. **shoots:** buds, growths.   24. **train:** procession (of angels).   26. **city . . . trees:** "the promised land" (Deuteronomy 34:1–4).   31–32. **when . . . return:** when my remains ("this dust") are placed in the grave (or burial urn), I would return to Heaven in the same state of innocence in which I came to earth.

The Revival

HENRY VAUGHAN

Unfold, unfold! take in his light,
Who makes thy cares more short than night.
The joys, which with his Day star rise,
He deals to all, but drowsy eyes:°
And what the men of this world miss,   5
Some drops and dews of future bliss.
Hark! how his winds have changed their note,
And with warm whispers call thee out.
The frosts are past, the storms are gone:
And backward life° at last comes on.   10
The lofty groves in express° joys
Reply unto the turtle's° voice,
And here in dust and dirt, O here
The lilies of his love appear!

4. **drowsy eyes:** the eyes of worldly men, "blind" to the future (see ll. 5–6).
10. **backward life:** see "The Retreat," lines 21–30.   11. **express:** explicit, unmistakable.   12. **turtle's:** turtledove's.

Felicity

THOMAS TRAHERNE

Prompted to seek my bliss above the skies,
    How often did I lift mine eyes
        Beyond the spheres!°
Dame Nature told me there was endless space
Within my soul; I spied its very face.   5
        Sure it not for nought appears;
    What is there which a man may see
        Beyond the spheres?
        Felicity.

3. **spheres:** the nine crystal spheres which were thought to hold the sun, moon, stars, and planets. Heaven was believed to lie beyond the last sphere. (See ll. 8–9.)

There in the mind of God, that sphere of love,   10
    In nature, height, extent, above
        All other spheres,
A man may see himself, the world, the bride
Of God, his church, which as they there are eyed,
    Strangely exalted each appears;   15
    His mind is higher than the space
        Above the spheres,
        Surmounts all place.

No empty space—it is all full of sight,
    All soul and life, an eye most bright,   20
        All light and love,
Which doth at once all things possess and give,
Heaven and earth, with all that therein live;
    It rests at quiet, and doth move;
    Eternal is, yet time includes;   25
        A scene above
        All interludes.°

27. **interludes:** Technically, an interlude was a brief pantomime, or dramatic or musical presentation, introduced between the acts of a long play.

Questions

1. Explain the metaphor in lines 7 and 8 of "Old Age." What is the poet's attitude toward old age? toward youth?
2. What emotion does the speaker pretend to express in the first two lines of "The Constant Lover"? Is the tone of the poem serious, playful, or merely cynical? How is the tone created?
3. In "To Lucasta . . ." is the last stanza a compliment to the lady? Why, or why not? Does the poem contain a paradox? If so, what is it?
4. Explain the last four lines of Crashaw's "A Song." What do you think is meant by "living death and dying life"?
5. "The Retreat" presents a contrast between the life of childhood and the life of adulthood. What is the contrast? What is the "second race" (l. 4)? What would the first race be? the third? (See ll. 31–32.) How would you explain the metaphor in lines 19–20? How is "The Revival" related to "The Retreat"? Compare the two poems in as many ways as you can. Consider especially line 10 of "The Revival."

6. What is the main thought of "Felicity"? How are lines 4–5 related to the rest of the poem?

JOHN MILTON
1608–1674

During his years at Cambridge, Milton was respected by his classmates for his strong religious beliefs and also for his scholarly abilities. After graduation, he retired to his father's country home, where he spent five years of further study in European and classical literature. During these years he wrote some of his finest early poems, including "Lycidas," perhaps the most famous elegy in English.

Milton was a Puritan by background and training, and when the Civil War broke out while he was traveling in Europe, he rushed home to champion the Puritan cause. Perhaps more than any other writer before or since, Milton involved himself in the affairs of his time—and his time was a stormy one. Having written various attacks on the Anglican Church and the monarchy, and various defenses of the Puritans, he was appointed Latin Secretary to the Commonwealth in 1649. Until the restoration of the monarchy in 1660, he devoted himself entirely to political writing. During this period his eyesight began to fail; he was totally blind by 1652.

On the accession of Charles II, Milton was arrested but released with a fine. His books, however, were burned by the public hangman. In an age which represented everything he had fought against, and in difficult circumstances (including poverty and blindness), Milton now wrote his major works: *Paradise Lost*, the greatest epic in English; its sequel, *Paradise Regained;* and *Samson Agonistes,* a dramatic poem about another blind man persecuted for his beliefs but triumphant over his persecutors.

In his personal relationships Milton was often harsh and difficult, but he lived a heroic life, devoting the best part of it to fighting for his religious and political beliefs. And his best poetry is in the heroic style: solemn, majestic, moving, and full of the intense zeal of his faith.

On the Late Massacre at Piedmont

In 1655, The Waldenses, a Protestant sect living in the Piedmont area of northwestern Italy, were massacred on the orders of the Duke of Savoy, under whose protection they had been living (and who had promised them freedom of worship).

Avenge, O Lord, Thy slaughtered saints, whose bones
Lie scattered on the Alpine mountains cold;
Even them who kept Thy truth so pure of old,
When all our fathers worshiped stocks and stones,°
Forget not: in Thy book record their groans   5
Who were Thy sheep, and in their ancient fold
Slain by the bloody Piedmontese, that rolled
Mother with infant down the rocks. Their moans
The vales redoubled to the hills, and they
To Heaven. Their martyred blood and ashes sow   10
O'er all the Italian fields, where still doth sway
The triple tyrant;° that from these may grow
A hundredfold, who, having learnt Thy way,
Early may fly the Babylonian woe.°

3-4. Even . . . stones: the Waldenses had broken from the Church of Rome in the twelfth century, four hundred years before the Puritans had broken with the Anglican Church. Both sects had revolted in part because they objected to the worship of images and statues ("stocks and stones"). **12. triple tyrant:** the Pope, who Milton felt could have prevented the massacre. **14. Babylonian woe:** the destruction predicted for Babylon in Revelations 18.

On His Blindness

When I consider how my light is spent
Ere half my days°in this dark world and wide,
And that one talent° which is death to hide

2. half my days: Milton was 44 when he became totally blind. **3. one talent:** the Bible speaks of the man who hid his one talent and was therefore cast into outer darkness (see Matthew 25:24–30).

Lodged with me useless, though my soul more bent
To serve therewith my Maker, and present   5
My true account, lest He returning chide;
"Doth God exact day-labor, light denied?"
I fondly° ask. But Patience, to prevent
That murmur, soon replies, "God doth not need
Either man's work or his own gifts. Who best   10
Bear his mild yoke, they serve him best. His state
Is kingly: thousands at his bidding speed,
And post o'er land and ocean without rest;
They also serve who only stand and wait."

8. **fondly:** foolishly.

from *Paradise Lost*

Paradise Lost is an epic poem in twelve books in which Milton
set out to "justify the ways of God to men." The poem begins
with Satan's revolt against God and the fall of Satan and his
followers to Hell. Milton then describes the creation of Adam
and Eve in the Garden of Eden. After Satan's temptation,
both Adam and Eve sin by eating the fruit of the forbidden
tree of knowledge. The epic ends with the expulsion of Adam
and Eve from the Garden; before they leave, however, they
are granted a vision of the future, and are told of a redeemer
to come.

Invocation

from BOOK 1

Like the classical Greek and Roman epics, *Paradise Lost* opens
with an *invocation,* a plea for divine assistance in the creation
of the work. Milton's invocation, however, is addressed not
to Homer's muses but to God.

Of Man's first disobedience, and the fruit
Of that forbidden tree, whose mortal taste
Brought death into the world, and all our woe,

With loss of Eden, till one greater Man°
Restore us, and regain the blissful seat,   5
Sing, heavenly Muse, that on the secret top
Of Oreb, or of Sinai,° did'st inspire
That shepherd° who first taught the chosen seed,
In the beginning how the heavens and earth
Rose out of chaos: or, if Sion hill°   10
Delight thee more, and Siloa's° brook that flowed
Fast by the oracle of God, I thence
Invoke thy aid to my adventurous song,
That with no middle flight intends to soar
Above the Aonian mount,° while it pursues   15
Things unattempted yet in prose or rime.
And chiefly Thou, O Spirit,° That dost prefer
Before all temples the upright heart and pure,
Instruct me, for Thou know'st; Thou from the first
Wast present, and, with mighty wings outspread,   20
Dove-like, sat'st brooding on the vast abyss,
And mad'st it pregnant: what in me is dark,
Illumine; what is low, raise and support;
That to the height of this great argument
I may assert eternal Providence,   25
And justify the ways of God to men.
    Say first—for heaven hides nothing from Thy view,
Nor the deep tract of hell—say first, what cause
Moved our grand parents, in that happy state,
Favored of heaven so highly, to fall off   30
From their Creator, and transgress his will,
For° one restraint, lords of the world besides.
Who first seduced them to that foul revolt?
    The infernal Serpent; he it was, whose guile,

4. Man: Christ. 7. Oreb (or Horeb) and Sinai: mountains where God
spoke directly to Moses. 8. shepherd: Moses (often thought to be the author
of Genesis). 10. Sion hill: Mount Zion, the site of Jerusalem. 11. Siloa (or
Shiloah): a stream in Jerusalem. 15. Aonian mount: Mount Helicon in
Greece, sacred to the muses. Milton states that he will surpass the classical
works inspired by the muses, because his poem deals with a subject so profound
that it has never been attempted before. 17. Spirit: the Holy Ghost. 32. For:
except for.

John Milton   233

Stirred up with envy and revenge, deceived   35
The mother° of mankind; what time his pride
Had cast him out from heaven, with all his host
Of rebel angels; by whose aid, aspiring
To set himself in glory above his peers,
He trusted to have equaled the Most High,   40
If he opposed; and, with ambitious aim
Against the throne and monarchy of God,
Raised impious war in heaven, and battle proud,
With vain attempt. Him the Almighty Power
Hurled headlong flaming from the ethereal sky,   45
With hideous ruin and combustion, down
To bottomless perdition; there to dwell
In adamantine° chains and penal fire,
Who durst defy the Omnipotent to arms.

36. mother: Eve.   48. adamantine: unbreakable.

Satan's Defiance

from BOOK 1

After a tremendous battle in Heaven, Satan and his followers
are thrust into Hell. When they realize their fate, the fallen
angels begin to despair, but with the following speech Satan
urges them on to eternal warfare with God.

"Is this the region, this the soil, the clime,"
Said then the lost archangel,° "this the seat
That we must change for heaven; this mournful gloom
For that celestial light? Be it so, since He,
Who now is Sovereign, can dispose and bid   5
What shall be right: farthest from Him is best,
Whom reason hath equaled, force hath made supreme
Above His equals.° Farewell, happy fields,

2. archangel: Satan.   7-8. Whom . . . equals: Satan's sin was pride, and
he remains proud even in defeat. He argues here that he and his followers
were God's equals, and were defeated only by greater numbers.

Where joy for ever dwells! Hail, horrors! hail
Infernal world! and thou profoundest hell,   10
Receive thy new possessor—one who brings
A mind not to be changed by place or time:
The mind is its own place, and in itself
Can make a heaven of hell, a hell of heaven.
What matter where, if I be still the same,   15
And what I should be; all but less than He
Whom thunder hath made greater? Here at least
We shall be free: the Almighty hath not built
Here for His envy, will not drive us hence:
Here we may reign secure, and, in my choice,   20
To reign is worth ambition, though in hell;
Better to reign in hell, than serve in heaven."

Temptation and Fall

from BOOK 9

As the following passage begins, Satan, disguised as a serpent,
is speaking to Eve, tempting her to eat the fruit of the tree
of knowledge.

"And what are gods that man may not become
As they, participating° godlike food?
The gods are first, and that advantage use
On our belief, that all from them proceeds;
I question it, for this fair earth I see,   5
Warmed by the sun, producing every kind,
Them nothing. If they all things,° who enclosed
Knowledge of good and evil in this tree,
That whoso eats thereof, forthwith° attains
Wisdom without their leave? and wherein lies   10

2. participating: sharing. 7. Them . . . things: read the line as though
the verbs "producing" and "produced" appeared after "Them" and "they."
9. forthwith: immediately.

The offence, that man should thus attain to know?
What can your knowledge hurt Him, or this tree
Impart against His will, if all be His?
Or is it envy, and can envy dwell
In heavenly breasts? These, these and many more   15
Causes import your need of this fair fruit.
Goddess humane, reach then, and freely taste!"
    He ended, and his words replete with guile°
Into her heart too easy entrance won.
Fixed on the fruit she gazed, which to behold   20
Might tempt alone, and in her ears the sound
Yet rung of his persuasive words, impregned°
With reason, to her seeming,° and with truth . . .
Pausing a while, thus to herself she mused:
    "Great are thy virtues, doubtless, best of fruits,   25
Though kept from man, and worthy to be admired,
Whose taste, too long forborne, at first assay
Gave elocution to the mute, and taught
The tongue not made for speech to speak thy praise . . .°
Here grows the cure of all, this fruit divine,   30
Fair to the eye, inviting to the taste,
Of virtue to make wise; what hinders then
To reach,° and feed at once both body and mind?"
    So saying, her rash hand in evil hour
Forth reaching to the fruit, she plucked, she eat.°   35
Earth felt the wound, and nature from her seat
Sighing through all her works gave signs of woe,
That all was lost. Back to the thicket slunk
The guilty serpent, and well might, for Eve
Intent now wholly on her taste, nought else   40
Regarded; such delight till then, as seemed,
In fruit she never tasted, whether true
Or fancied so, through expectation high

---

18. **replete with guile:** full of deception.   22. **impregned:** filled with.
23. **to her seeming:** in her opinion.   28–29. **Gave . . . praise:** Satan, as the
serpent, had told Eve that eating the fruit had given him the power of speech.
32–33. **what . . . reach:** what prevents (me) from reaching.   35. **eat (ĕt):** an
older past tense of the word.

Of knowledge, nor was Godhead from her thought.°
Greedily she engorged without restraint,   45
And knew not eating death.°

44. **nor . . . thought:** she did not forget the possibility of becoming Godlike (through eating the fruit). 46. **And . . . death:** and did not realize she
was eating death.

The Departure from Eden

from BOOK 12

Before Adam and Eve are forced to leave Eden, the Archangel
Michael is sent to tell Adam of the future of man. That future
is not always a happy one, but Adam is encouraged by the
promise that a redeemer will come who will die in order that
man may once again gain eternal life. The following lines con-
clude the entire poem. As the passage begins, Adam is thank-
ing Michael for his revelations.

"Greatly instructed I shall hence depart,
  Greatly in peace of thought, and have my fill
  Of knowledge, what this vessel can contain;
  Beyond which was my folly to aspire.
  Henceforth I learn that to obey is best,   5
  And love with fear the only God, to walk
  As in His presence, ever to observe
  His providence, and on Him sole depend,
  Merciful over all His works, with good
  Still overcoming evil, and by small   10
  Accomplishing great things—by things deemed weak
  Subverting worldly strong, and worldly wise
  By simply meek; that suffering for truth's sake
  Is fortitude to highest victory,
  And to the faithful, death the gate of life—   15
  Taught this by His example whom I now
  Acknowledge my Redeemer ever blest."

John Milton   237

To whom thus also the Angel° last replied:
"This having learned, thou hast attained the sum
Of wisdom; hope no higher, though all the stars   20
Thou knew'st by name, and all the ethereal powers,
All secrets of the deep, all nature's works,
Or works of God in heaven, air, earth, or sea,
And all the riches of this world enjoy'dst,
And all the rule, one empire. Only add   25
Deeds to thy knowledge answerable; add faith;
Add virtue, patience, temperance; add love,
By name to come called charity, the soul
Of all the rest: then wilt thou not be loth°
To leave this paradise, but shalt possess   30
A paradise within thee, happier far.
Let us descend° now, therefore, from this top
Of speculation; for the hour precise
Exacts our parting hence; and, see! the guards,
By me encamped on yonder hill, expect   35
Their motion,° at whose front a flaming sword,
In signal of remove, waves fiercely round.
We may no longer stay. Go, waken Eve;
Her also I with gentle dreams have calmed,
Portending° good, and all her spirits composed   40
To meek submission: thou, at season fit,°
Let her with thee partake what thou hast heard—
Chiefly what may concern her faith to know,
The great deliverance by her seed to come
(For by the Woman's Seed°) on all mankind   45
That ye may live, which will be many days,
Both in one faith unanimous; though sad
With cause for evils past, yet much more cheered
With meditation on the happy end."
    He ended, and they both descend the hill.   50
Descended, Adam to the bower where Eve

18. **Angel:** Michael.   29. **loth:** reluctant.   32. **descend:** Michael had led
Adam to a high hill before making his revelations.   35–36. **expect their motion:** require their departure.   40. **portending:** foretelling.   41. **at season fit:**
at the proper time.   45. **Woman's Seed:** Christ.

Lay sleeping ran before, but found her waked;
And thus with words not sad she him received:
   "Whence thou return'st and whither went'st I know;
For God is also in sleep, and dreams advise,   55
Which He hath sent propitious,° some great good
Presaging,° since, with sorrow and heart's distress
Wearied, I fell asleep: but now lead on;
In me is no delay; with thee to go
Is to stay here; without thee here to stay   60
Is to go hence unwilling; thou to me
Art all things under Heaven, all places thou,
Who for my wilful crime art banished hence.
This further consolation yet secure
I carry hence: though all by me is lost,   65
Such favor I unworthy am vouchsafed,
By me the Promised Seed shall all restore."
   So spake our mother Eve; and Adam heard
Well pleased, but answered not; for now too nigh
The Archangel stood, and from the other hill   70
To their fixed station, all in bright array
The Cherubim descended, on the ground
Gliding meteorous,° as evening mist,
Risen from a river, o'er the marish° glides,
And gathers ground fast at the laborer's heel   75
Homeward returning. High in front advanced,
The brandished sword of God before them blazed
Fierce as a comet, which with torrid heat,
And vapor as the Libyan air adust,°
Began to parch that temperate clime; whereat   80
In either hand the hast'ning Angel caught
Our lingering parents, and to the eastern gate
Led them direct, and down the cliff as fast
To the subjected° plain; then disappeared.
They, looking back, all the eastern side beheld   85
Of paradise, so late their happy seat,

_____

56. **propitious:** favorable. 57. **Presaging:** predicting. 73. **meteorous:** in
mid air. 74. **marish:** marsh. 79. **adust:** parched, dry. 84. **subjected:** underlying.

Waved over by that flaming brand, the gate
With dreadful faces thronged and fiery arms:
Some natural tears they dropped, but wiped them soon;
The world was all before them, where to choose   90
Their place of rest, and Providence their guide:
They, hand in hand, with wandering steps and slow,
Through Eden took their solitary way.

Questions

Sonnets

1. Discuss in detail the sound effects employed in "On the Late Massacre in Piedmont:" its use of rhyme, rhythm, assonance, alliteration, caesura, etc. How do the sound effects help create the tone of the poem? What is the tone?
2. In "On His Blindness" what is the "one talent" mentioned in line 3? Who answers the speaker's questions? What is the answer?

FROM *Paradise Lost*

1. The poem opens, as do most epics, with an invocation and a description of the subject of the whole poem. At what point does the invocation end and the narrative begin? To whom is the invocation addressed? What is the effect of such an invocation? To put it another way, how would the poem have been affected if Milton had plunged immediately into the narrative without any introduction?
2. In his speech to the other fallen angels, how does Satan explain his fall from Heaven? What is Satan's state of mind—repentant, rebellious, despairing, or what? How does his state of mind affect your attitudes toward him?
3. In "Temptation and Fall" what arguments does Satan use to persuade Eve to eat the fruit of the tree of knowledge? How does Eve justify her eating the fruit? What might have been her real reason?
4. How has Adam reconciled himself to his expulsion from Eden? What about Eve? What consolation does she have? Is there a change of tone in the final lines of the poem? If so, what is the effect of the change?
5. Milton is said to have written in the "grand manner;" that is, in a dignified, elevated style. Would you agree with this description? If so, how is this style achieved? Milton and Shakespeare are the two greatest masters of English blank verse, yet each poet used the form in entirely different ways. How do their styles differ? (See pp. 193–94.)

ANDREW MARVELL

1621–1678

Marvell was educated at Cambridge and soon gained a reputation as a scholar, earning praise from as competent a judge as Milton. Marvell does not seem to have been involved in the religious and political controversies of his time, but after the establishment of the Commonwealth, he became assistant Latin secretary under Milton. He was elected to Parliament after the return of the king in 1660, and remained in government service until his death.

Marvell's finest poetry was written before he began his career in public service. His early poems are light, graceful lyrics which are often reminiscent of some of Donne's early poetry. In later years, Marvell turned to satirical poetry which seems to have been popular during his time, but which cannot compare in quality to his early work. Marvell's best poetry is in the metaphysical tradition—it is, in fact, the end of that tradition, for during his lifetime, and especially after his death, the poems written in that style often degenerated into mere mannerism. Marvell revived the style for a short time, recalling the skill and grace of Donne. Not surprisingly, his reputation, like Donne's, has enjoyed a revival in this century.

The Mower to the Glowworms

Ye living lamps, by whose dear light
The nightingale does sit so late,
And studying all the summer night,
Her matchless songs does meditate;

Ye county comets° that portend°   5
No war nor prince's funeral,
Shining unto no higher end
Than to presage the grass's fall;

---

5. **county comets:** a humorous analogy: glowworms are to a county as comets are to the universe. **portend:** comets were often thought to foreshadow disastrous events.

Ye glowworms, whose officious flame
To wand'ring mowers shows the way,   10
That in the night have lost their aim,
And after foolish fires do stray;

Your courteous lights in vain you waste,
Since Juliana° here is come,
For she my mind hath so displaced   15
That I shall never find my home.

14. **Juliana:** not a realistic character, but rather a stock figure of pastoral poetry, the typical shepherd's "loved one."

Bermudas

Where the remote Bermudas ride
In the ocean's bosom unespied,
From a small boat that rowed along,
The list'ning winds received this song:

What should we do but sing his praise   5
That led us through the wat'ry maze
Unto an isle so long unknown,
And yet far kinder than our own?
Where he the huge sea monsters wracks,
That lift the deep upon their backs,   10
He lands us on a grassy stage,
Safe from the storms and prelates'° rage.
He gave us this eternal spring
Which here enamels everything,
And sends the fowls to us in care,   15
On daily visits through the air.
He hangs in shades the orange bright,
Like golden lamps in a green night;

12. **prelate:** a bishop or archbishop; the power of the prelates was one of the issues that led to the Puritan revolt.

And does in the pomegranates close°
Jewels more rich than Ormus° shows.   20
He makes the figs our mouths to meet
And throws the melons at our feet,
But apples° plants of such a price,
No tree could ever bear them twice.
With cedars, chosen by his hand,   25
From Lebanon, he stores the land,
And makes the hollow seas that roar
Proclaim the ambergris on shore.
He cast, of which we rather boast,
The Gospel's pearl upon our coast,   30
And in these rocks for us did frame
A temple, where to sound his name.
Oh, let our voice his praise exalt,
Till it arrive at heaven's vault;
Which thence, perhaps, rebounding, may   35
Echo beyond the Mexic Bay.
    Thus sung they in the English boat
An holy and a cheerful note,
And all the way, to guide their chime,
With falling oars they kept the time.   40

19. **close:** enclose. 20. **Ormus** (or Ormuz): a Portuguese market near the
entrance of the Persian Gulf. It was often used as a symbol of great wealth.
23. **apples:** pineapples.

The Garden

How vainly men themselves amaze°
To win the palm, the oak, or bays,°
And their uncessant labors see
Crowned from some single herb or tree,
Whose short and narrow-vergèd° shade   5
Does prudently their toils upbraid;

1. **amaze:** bewilder, perplex. 2. **palm, oak, bays:** symbols of power or
achievement (compare the present-day military oak-leaf cluster). 5. **narrow-
vergèd:** tightly bordered, hence, small.

While all flowers and all trees do close
To weave the garlands of repose.

Fair quiet, have I found thee here,
And innocence, thy sister dear!   10
Mistaken long, I sought you then
In busy companies of men;
Your sacred plants, if here below,
Only among the plants will grow.
Society is all but rude,   15
To this delicious solitude.

No white nor red was ever seen
So am'rous as this lovely green.
Fond lovers, cruel as their flame,
Cut in these trees their mistress' name;   20
Little, alas, they know or heed
How far these beauties hers exceed!
Fair trees! wheres' e'er° your barks I wound,
No name shall but your own be found.

When we have run our passion's heat,   25
Love hither makes his best retreat.
The gods that mortal beauty chase,
Still in a tree did end their race:
Apollo hunted Daphne so,
Only that she might laurel grow;   30
And Pan did after Syrinx speed,
Not as a nymph, but for a reed.°

What wond'rous life in this I lead!
Ripe apples drop about my head;
The luscious clusters of the vine   35
Upon my mouth do crush their wine;

23. **wheres' e'er** wheresoever, wherever. **29–32. Apollo . . . reed:** as the
lines indicate, both Apollo and Pan pursued mortal maidens who were turned
into plants (Daphne into a laurel; Syrinx into a reed).

The nectarine and curious° peach
Into my hands themselves do reach;
Stumbling on melons as I pass,
Ensnared with flowers, I fall on grass.   40

Meanwhile the mind from pleasure less
Withdraws into its happiness;°
The mind, that ocean where each kind
Does straight its own resemblance find,
Yet it creates, transcending° these,   45
Far other worlds and other seas,
Annihilating all that's made
To a green thought in a green shade.°

Here at the fountain's sliding foot,
Or at some fruit tree's mossy root,   50
Casting the body's vest aside,
My soul into the boughs does glide;
There like a bird it sits and sings,
Then whets, then combs its silver wings;
And till prepared for longer flight,   55
Waves in its plumes the various light.

Such was that happy garden-state,
While man there walked without a mate;
After a place so pure and sweet,
What other help could yet be meet!°   60
But 'twas beyond a mortal's share
To wander solitary there;

37. **curious:** choice, excellent in flavor.   41–42. **Meanwhile . . . happiness:** the lines seem to mean that the mind withdraws from sensual pleasure into itself, its own happiness.   45. **transcending:** surpassing.   47–48. **Annihilating . . . shade:** either, 1. ⁻ducing everything to a green thought, or 2. replacing everything by a green thought. The ambiguity is probably deliberate. This entire stanza is difficult, but it is the key stanza of the poem, and its general meaning is clear: The mind rejects the pleasures of the senses, and also rejects everything artificial ("all that's made"), in favor of the only true realities, contemplation ("a green thought") and nature ("a green shade").   60. **meet:** suitable.

Two paradises 'twere, in one,
To live in paradise alone.

How well the skillful gard'ner drew   65
Of flowers and herbs this dial new,
Where, from above, the milder sun
Does through a fragrant zodiac run;°
And as it works, th' industrious bee
Computes its time as well as we.   70
How could such sweet and wholesome hours
Be reckoned but with herbs and flowers?

68. **Does . . . run:** during the year the sun progresses through the twelve
signs of the Zodiac ("Virgo," "Gemini," etc.).

Questions

1. What do the second and third stanzas of "The Mower to the Glowworms" imply about the nature of the speaker's love for Juliana? Does
   the poem create an effect of deep emotion? If not, what effect does it
   create?
2. Describe the structure of "Bermudas." The poem mentions a number
   of benefits to be enjoyed: do those benefits occur in any significant
   order? If so, what is the order and what is its significance?
3. In "The Garden" what two things are contrasted in the first stanza?
   What is the significance, if any, of the mythological references in
   Stanza 4? To what does Stanza 8 refer?
4. "The Garden" is a pastoral poem, perhaps the greatest in the English
   language. What is its theme? How is it similar to the other pastoral
   poems you have read (see pp. 182–83 and Glossary)? Can the
   poem be considered typical of pastoral poetry? Consider especially
   the ways in which it treats innocence vs. experience, society vs. solitude, city live vs. life in natural surroundings. What is "real" in the
   poem? What is false or artificial?

JOHN DRYDEN
1631-1700

Dryden's life seems typical of the changing nature of England in the late seventeenth century. His Puritan background led him to praise Cromwell in his early poems. With the Restoration he welcomed the return of Charles II, became an Anglican, and was made the first official Poet Laureate. When James II, a Catholic, became king in 1687, Dryden was converted to Catholicism and wrote a poem, *The Hind and the Panther*, defending the Catholic church. A year later James II was deposed, and Dryden's favor at court came to an end with the accession of William III, to whom he refused allegiance. He died in poverty in London. Dryden has often been criticized for his shifts in allegiance, but many other Englishmen acted as he did during these years, and it seems likely, from his writings, that his beliefs would have changed as they did regardless of the specific religious and political situation of his time.

Dryden's work exerted a very strong influence on the poets who followed him. Most of the poetry written during the hundred years after his death follows the style he began. Toward the close of the seventeenth century the Elizabethan and early seventeenth century lyric tradition—Metaphysical or Cavalier—was becoming stale, and England was ready for a new style that could better express the nation's growing preoccupation with reason, order, and decorum. In both his prose and poetry, Dryden's style is clear, precise, balanced, and polished. His verse lacks the heroic and tragic qualities of Milton's or Shakespeare's, but he was a master of the kinds of poetry he chose to write.

Song to a Fair, Young Lady,
Going Out of the Town in the Spring

Ask not the cause, why sullen spring
So long delays her flowers to bear;
Why warbling birds forget to sing,
And winter storms invert the year.

Chloris° is gone; and fate provides   5
To make it spring, where she resides.

Chloris is gone, the cruel fair;
   She cast not back a pitying eye:
But left her lover in despair;
   To sigh, to languish, and to die.   10
Ah, how can those fair eyes endure
To give the wounds they will not cure!

Great God of Love, why hast thou made
   A face that can all hearts command,
That all religions can invade,   15
   And change the laws of every land?
Where thou hadst placed such pow'r before,
Thou shouldst have made her mercy more.

When Chloris to the temple comes,
   Adoring crowds before her fall;   20
She can restore the dead from tombs,
   And every life but mine recall.
I only am by love designed
To be the victim for mankind.

5. **Chloris:** another stock character of the pastoral. Note, however, how the tradition is beginning to change in Dryden's time: the same attitudes and characters of pastoral poetry are present, but the setting is now the city, not the country.

Ah How Sweet It Is to Love

Ah how sweet it is to love,
Ah how gay is young desire!
And what pleasing pains we prove
When we first approach love's fire!
   Pains of love be sweeter far   5
   Than all other pleasures are.

Sighs which are from lovers blown,
Do but gently heave the heart:
Ev'n the tears they shed alone
Cure, like trickling balm their smart.   10
 Lovers when they lose their breath,
 Bleed away in easy death.

Love and time with reverence use,
Treat them like a parting friend:
Nor the golden gifts refuse   15
Which in youth sincere they send:
 For each year their price is more,
 And they less simple than before.

Love, like spring-tides full and high,
Swells in every youthful vein: 20
But each tide does less supply,
Till they quite shrink in again:
 If a flow in age appear,
 'Tis but rain, and runs not clear.

Ah Fading Joy, How Quickly Art Thou Past!

Ah fading joy, how quickly art thou past!
 Yet we thy ruin haste:
As if the cares of human life were few
 We seek out new:
And follow fate that does too fast pursue.   5

See how on every bough the birds express
 In their sweet notes their happiness.
 They all enjoy, and nothing spare;
But on their Mother Nature lay their care:
Why then should man, the lord of all below   10
 Such troubles choose to know
As none of all his subjects undergo?

Hark, hark, the waters fall, fall, fall;
And with a murmuring sound
Dash, dash, upon the ground,   15
To gentle slumbers call.

Alexander's Feast; or, the Power of Music

An Ode in Honor of St. Cecilia's Day

St. Cecilia was a Christian martyr who died in Rome during
the third century. She became the patron saint of music and
was, according to legend, the inventress of the organ. Dryden's tribute to her is probably his best-known poem.

1

'Twas at the royal feast, for Persia won
    By Philip's warlike son:°
    Aloft in awful state
    The godlike hero sate
        On his imperial throne: 5
    His valiant peers were placed around;
Their brows with roses and with myrtles bound
    (So should desert in arms be crowned).
The lovely Thaïs,° by his side,
Sate like a blooming Eastern bride   10
In flower of youth and beauty's pride.
    Happy, happy, happy pair!
        None but the brave,
        None but the brave,
    None but the brave deserves the fair.   15

CHORUS

    Happy, happy, happy pair!
        None but the brave,
        None but the brave,
    None but the brave deserves the fair.

    2. Philip's . . . son: Alexander the Great (356–323 B.C.), the son of Philip
of Macedon. Alexander, the conqueror of the world, is celebrating his defeat
of Persia.   9. Thaïs (thā´ĭs).

Timotheus,° placed on high 20
    Amid the tuneful choir,
With flying fingers touched the lyre:
    The trembling notes ascend the sky,
        And heavenly joys inspire.
    The song began from Jove, 25
    Who left his blissful seats above
    (Such is the power of mighty love).
A dragon's fiery form belied the god:°
Sublime on radiant spires he rode,
When he to fair Olympia° pressed; 30
And while he sought her snowy breast:
Then, round her slender waist he curled,
And stamped an image of himself, a sovereign of the world.
The listening crowd admire the lofty sound;
"A present deity," they shout around;
"A present deity," the vaulted roofs rebound: 35
        With ravished ears
        The monarch hears,
        Assumes the god,
        Affects to nod,
And seems to shake the spheres.° 40

CHORUS

        With ravished ears
        The monarch hears,
        Assumes the god,
        Affects to nod,
And seems to shake the spheres. 45

3

The praise of Bacchus° then the sweet musician sung,
    Of Bacchus ever fair and ever young:

20. **Timotheus** (tĭ·mŏth′ē·ŭs).   28. **A dragon's . . . god:** that is, Jove assumed the form of a dragon.   30. **Olympia:** Alexander's mother; Jove, as the legend goes, was his father.   41. **spheres:** see page 228.   47. **Bacchus** (băk′- ŭs): the god of wine.

The jolly god in triumph comes;
Sound the trumpets; beat the drums;   50
    Flushed with a purple grace
    He shows his honest face:
Now give the hautboys° breath; he comes, he comes.
    Bacchus, ever fair and young,
        Drinking joys did first ordain;   55
    Bacchus' blessings are a treasure,
    Drinking is the soldier's pleasure:
        Rich the treasure,
        Sweet the pleasure,
        Sweet is pleasure after pain.   60

    Bacchus' blessings are a treasure,
    Drinking is the soldier's pleasure;
        Rich the treasure,
        Sweet the pleasure,
        Sweet is pleasure after pain.   65

                4

Soothed with the sound, the king grew vain;
    Fought all his battles o'er again;
And thrice he routed all his foes; and thrice he slew the slain.
    The master° saw the madness rise;
        His glowing cheeks, his ardent eyes;   70
    And, while he heaven and earth defied,
    Changed his hand, and checked his pride
        He chose a mournful Muse,
        Soft pity to infuse:
    He sung Darius° great and good,   75
        By too severe a fate,
    Fallen, fallen, fallen, fallen,
        Fallen from his high estate,
    And weltering in his blood;
    Deserted, at his utmost need,   80

53. **hautboys** (hō'boiz): oboes.   69. **The master:** Timotheus.   75. **Da-**
rius: the Persian king whom Alexander had defeated.

By those his former bounty fed;
On the bare earth exposed he lies,
With not a friend to close his eyes.
With downcast looks the joyless victor sate,
    Revolving in his altered soul   85
        The various turns of chance below;
    And, now and then, a sigh he stole;
    And tears began to flow.

CHORUS

Revolving in his altered soul
    The various turns of chance below;   90
And, now and then, a sigh he stole;
And tears began to flow.

5

The mighty master smiled to see
That love was in the next degree:
'Twas but a kindred sound to move,   95
For pity melts the mind to love.
    Softly sweet, in Lydian° measures,
    Soon he soothed his soul to pleasures.
"War," he sung, "is toil and trouble;
Honor, but an empty bubble;   100
    Never ending, still beginning,
Fighting still, and still destroying:
    If the world be worth thy winning,
    Think, O think it worth enjoying;
    Lovely Thaïs sits beside thee,   105
    Take the good the gods provide thee."
The many rend the skies with loud applause;
So Love was crowned, but Music won the cause.
    The prince, unable to conceal his pain,
        Gazed on the fair   110
        Who caused his care,

---

97. **Lydian:** one of the scales in which Greek music was composed. The Lydian scale was noted for its lightness and delicacy.

And sighed and looked, sighed and looked,
Sighed and looked, and sighed again:
At length, with love and wine at once oppressed,
The vanquished victor sunk upon her breast.   115

CHORUS

The prince, unable to conceal his pain,
    Gazed on the fair
    Who caused his care,
And sighed and looked, sighed and looked,
Sighed and looked, and sighed again: 120
At length, with love and wine at once oppressed,
The vanquished victor sunk upon her breast.

6

Now strike the golden lyre again:
A louder yet, and yet a louder strain.
Break his bands of sleep asunder,   125
And rouse him, like a rattling peal of thunder.
    Hark, hark, the horrid sound
        Has raised up his head:
        As awaked from the dead,
    And amazed, he stares around.   130
"Revenge, revenge!" Timotheus cries,
    "See the Furies° arise!
    See the snakes that they rear,
    How they hiss in their hair,
And the sparkles that flash from their eyes!   135
    Behold a ghastly band,
    Each a torch in his hand!
Those are Grecian ghosts, that in battle were slain,
        And unburied remain°
        Inglorious on the plain: 140
        Give the vengeance due
        To the valiant crew.

132. **Furies**: the avenging spirits of Greek myth. 139. **unburied remain**:
the Greeks believed that the soul of an unburied person could not enter the
realm of the dead, but must wander aimlessly until the body was buried.

Behold how they toss their torches on high,
   How they point to the Persian abodes,
And glittering temples of their hostile gods!"   145
The princes applaud, with a furious joy;
And the king seized a flambeau° with zeal to destroy;
     Thaïs led the way,
     To light him to his prey,
And, like another Helen, fired another Troy.   150

CHORUS

And the king seized a flambeau with zeal to destroy;
     Thaïs led the way,
     To light him to his prey,
And, like another Helen, fired another Troy.°

7

     Thus, long ago,   155
  Ere heaving bellows learned to blow,
    While organs yet were mute;
    Timotheus, to his breathing flute,
     And sounding lyre,
Could swell the soul to rage, or kindle soft desire.   160
  At last, divine Cecilia came,
  Inventress of the vocal frame;°
The sweet enthusiast, from her sacred store,
  Enlarged the former narrow bounds,
  And added length to solemn sounds,   165
With nature's mother wit, and arts unknown before.
    Let old Timotheus yield the prize,
     Or both divide the crown;
    He raised a mortal to the skies;
    She drew an angel down.   170

GRAND CHORUS

  At last, divine Cecilia came,
  Inventress of the vocal frame;°

147. **flambeau:** a flaming torch.   149. **Helen . . . Troy:** see page 179.
162. **vocal frame:** the organ.

The sweet enthusiast, from her sacred store,
  Enlarged the former narrow bounds,
  And added length to solemn sounds,   175
With nature's mother wit, and arts unknown before.
  Let old Timotheus yield the prize,
    Or both divide the crown;
  He raised a mortal to the skies;
    She drew an angel down.   180

To the Memory of Mr. Oldham

John Oldham (1653–1683) was a poet whose best work was
satirical. Though generally considered unpolished and even
clumsy, his poetry was often powerful. Dryden shared Oldham's interest in satire, although he far surpassed the younger
man in technical mastery.

Farewell, too little and too lately known,
Whom I began to think and call my own:
For sure our souls were near allied, and thine
Cast in the same poetic mold with mine.
One common note on either lyre did strike,   5
And knaves and fools we both abhorred alike.
To the same goal did both our studies drive:
The last set out the soonest did arrive.
Thus Nisus fell upon the slippery place,
Whilst his young friend performed and won the race.°   10
O early ripe! to thy abundant store
What could advancing age have added more?
It might (what nature never gives the young)
Have taught the numbers° of thy native tongue.
But satire needs not those, and wit will shine   15
Through the harsh cadence of a rugged° line.
A noble error, and but seldom made,

9–10. **Thus Nisus . . . race:** Virgil, in the *Aeneid,* tells of a footrace between the Sicilians and Trojans. Nisus slipped and fell near the end, but
tripped the leading Sicilian so that a fellow-Trojan might win. 14. **numbers:**
meter (i.e., numbered, counted, syllables). 16. **rugged:** unmetrical.

When poets are by too much force betrayed.
Thy generous fruits, though gathered ere their prime,
Still showed a quickness; and maturing time   20
But mellows what we write to the dull sweets of rhyme.
Once more, hail, and farewell! farewell, thou young,
But ah! too short, Marcellus° of our tongue!
Thy brows with ivy and with laurels bound;
But Fate and gloomy night encompass thee around.   25

23. **Marcellus:** the son of the Roman emperor Augustus. Like Oldham,
he gave promise of great ability but died young.

Lines Printed Under the Engraved
Portrait of Milton, 1688

Three poets,° in three distant ages born,
Greece, Italy, and England did adorn.
The first in loftiness of thought surpassed,
The next in majesty, in both the last.
The force of Nature could no farther go;   5
To make a third she joined the former two.

1. **Three poets:** Homer, Virgil, Milton.

Questions

1. Does the style of "Song to a Fair, Young Lady" fit the short description
   of Dryden's style (p. 247)?
2. What is the theme of "Ah How Sweet It Is to Love"? of "Ah Fading
   Joy"? Do Dryden's songs share any characteristics of some of the
   Elizabethan songs you have read? If so, what are those characteristics?
3. In "Alexander's Feast" what moods does the music inspire in Alexander? What is Dryden saying about the power of music? How does
   "Alexander's Feast" become a compliment to St. Cecilia?
4. "Alexander's Feast" has been called one of the most musical of English
   poems. How are the musical effects created? In this respect, compare
   this poem to "The Bells" on page 119.
5. Explain lines 7–10 of "To the Memory of Mr. Oldham." What is Dryden's attitude toward Oldham's poetry?

THE EIGHTEENTH CENTURY

England's eighteenth century is often called the Age of Reason, and to some degree the poetry of this period reflects the qualities indicated by this name. Typical eighteenth-century verse is polished, sophisticated in tone, and often witty. In general, the writers of this time reveal greater interest in man's intellect than in his emotions —their poetry is often concerned with philosophical problems, with satire, and with the culture of city life. Most of these characteristics can be seen at their best in the work of Alexander Pope, who continued and refined the styles developed by Dryden in the previous century, and who dominated the poetry of the first half of the eighteenth century. Toward the end of the century, a number of younger poets, particularly Cowper, Burns, and Blake, broke away from the tradition of Dryden and Pope and began writing lyrics that concentrated less on intellect, wit, and satire and gave more emphasis to the poet's personal emotions.

MATTHEW PRIOR

1664–1721

Prior was educated at Cambridge. After graduation he took a post as secretary to the English Ambassador to The Netherlands, and this became the beginning of a long career in the diplomatic service. For Prior, poetry was something reserved for his leisure hours; in fact, he liked to speak of himself as "only a poet by accident." Although he wrote a number of serious works, his reputation rests on his lighter poems, somewhat reminiscent of the earlier Cavalier poets, particularly Suckling.

To Cloe Jealous, a Better Answer

Prior's "Cloe" is another conventional figure of pastoral verse.
A "Cloe" appears in some of the poems of Horace (see l. 26
and note).

Dear Cloe, how blubbered is that pretty face;
   Thy cheek all on fire, and thy hair all uncurled:
Prythee quit this caprice; and (as old Falstaff° says)
   Let us e'en talk a little like folks of this world.°

How canst thou presume, thou hast leave to destroy   5
   The beauties, which Venus but lent to thy keeping?
Those looks were designed to inspire love and joy:
   More ord'nary eyes may serve people for weeping.

To be vexed at a trifle or two that I writ,
   Your judgment at once, and my passion you wrong: 10
You take that for fact, which will scarce be found wit:
   Odds life!° must one swear to the truth of a song?

What I speak, my fair Cloe, and what I write, shows
   The difference there is betwixt nature and art:
I court others in verse; but I love thee in prose: 15
   And they have my whimsies, but thou hast my heart.

The god of us verse-men (you know, child) the sun,°
   How after his journeys he sets up his rest:
If at morning o'er earth 'tis his fancy to run;
   At night he declines on his Thetis's° breast.   20

So when I am wearied with wandering all day,
   To thee, my delight, in the evening I come:

---

3. **Falstaff:** a comic character who appears in a number of Shakespeare's
plays.   4. **Let . . . world:** in other words, "let's be realistic."   12. **Odds life!:**
an oath, a corruption of "God's life."   17. **god . . . sun:** Apollo, the sun-god,
was also known as the teacher of the muses, and thus became identified as the
god of poetry.   20. **Thetis:** a sea nymph.

No matter what beauties I saw in my way;
    They were all but my visits, but thou art my home.

Then finish, dear Cloe, this pastoral war;   25
    And let us, like Horace and Lydia,° agree:
For thou art a girl as much brighter than her,
    As he was a poet sublimer than me.

26. **Horace and Lydia:** Horace, the Roman poet, wrote a number of pastoral poems in which a Lydia appeared or was addressed.

Questions

1. What is Prior implying about the function of poetry, particularly in stanzas 3 and 4?
2. Describe the tone of the poem. How does the last stanza affect the tone?

ALEXANDER POPE

1688–1744

Pope dominated the first half of the eighteenth century, and the poetic styles he set remained influential for many years after his death. His poetry is witty, smooth, and restrained; and these are the qualities that his age respected. Pope took the heroic couplet that had been developed earlier by Dryden and mastered it as a vehicle for expressing ideas lucidly and forcefully.

Pope was the son of a prosperous London merchant. Because he was Catholic, he was denied admittance to Oxford and Cambridge, but he was able to gain a good education through private tutoring and his own reading. Left a cripple and a hunchback by childhood illness, he spent much of his early life in seclusion, devoting himself to studies and to writing. His *Pastorals,* which had been written some years earlier, were published in 1709, when Pope was twenty-one. Two years later appeared his first major poem, *An Essay on Criticism.* By the time he was twenty-five he was recognized as the most important poet of his day. Like Jonson and Dryden before him, Pope became something of a literary "dictator," gaining a large following and shaping the taste of his period.

Pope's best-known works, besides *An Essay on Criticism*, include *The Rape of the Lock*, a mock epic social satire; *The Dunciad*, a mock epic attacking corruptions of taste and literary judgment; and *An Essay on Man*, a long philosophical poem. Pope also made translations of Homer's *Iliad* and *Odyssey* and edited the works of Shakespeare.

Pope is rightfully famous for his "true ease in writing," the clarity and polish of his verse. Occasionally, however, as in the conclusion to *The Dunciad*, he reached an intellectual and emotional depth that is characteristic of only the greatest English poetry.

Ode on Solitude

Happy the man, whose wish and care
    A few paternal° acres bound,
Content to breathe his native air
        In his own ground.

Whose herds with milk, whose fields with bread,   5
    Whose flocks supply him with attire;
Whose trees in summer yield him shade,
        In winter fire.

Blest, who can unconcern'dly find
    Hours, days, and years slide soft away   10
In health of body, peace of mind,
        Quiet by day,

Sound sleep by night; study and ease
    Together mixed; sweet recreation,
And innocence, which most does please,   15
        With meditation.

2. **paternal:** belonging to the father; in other words, the land is kept within the family and passed from generation to generation.

Thus let me live, unseen, unknown;
Thus unlamented let me die;
Steal from the world, and not a stone
Tell where I lie.   20

from *An Essay on Man*

An Essay on Man was Pope's most ambitious work. In it, he
attempted to survey man completely: his virtues and defects,
his limitations and capabilities. The following excerpts from
the poem illustrate many of Pope's major themes. The poem
is an essay in verse, as the title indicates, and it reveals one
of Pope's greatest accomplishments: the rendering of English
verse into a vehicle for serious intellectual discussion.

Know then thyself, presume not God to scan;°
The proper study of mankind is man.
Placed on this isthmus of a middle state,°
A being darkly wise, and rudely great:
With too much knowledge for the skeptic° side,   5
With too much weakness for the stoic's pride,°
He hangs between; in doubt to act, or rest;
In doubt to deem himself a god, or beast;
In doubt his mind or body to prefer;
Born but to die, and reasoning but to err;   10
Alike in ignorance, his reason such,
Whether he thinks too little, or too much:
Chaos of thought and passion,° all confused;
Still by himself abused, or disabused;
Created half to rise, and half to fall;   15
Great lord of all things, yet a prey to all;
Sole judge of truth, in endless error hurled:
The glory, jest, and riddle of the world!
Go, wondrous creature! mount where science guides,

1. **scan:** examine, measure.   3. **middle state:** the condition of man, mid-
way between the angels and the beasts.   5. **skeptic:** one who doubts funda-
mental religious beliefs.   6. **stoic's pride:** The Stoic philosophers of Greece
were noted for their calm indifference to pleasure or pain.   13. **passion:** emotion.

Go, measure earth, weigh air, and state the tides;　　　20
Instruct the planets in what orbs to run,
Correct old time, and regulate the sun;
Go, soar with Plato to th' empyreal sphere,°
To the first good, first perfect, and first fair;
Or tread the mazy round his followers trod,　　　25
And quitting sense call imitating God;
As Eastern priests in giddy circles run,
And turn their heads to imitate the sun.
Go, teach Eternal Wisdom how to rule—
Then drop into thyself, and be a fool!　　　30
　Superior beings, when of late they saw
A mortal man unfold all Nature's law,
Admired such wisdom in an earthly shape,
And showed a Newton as we show an ape.
　Could he, whose rules the rapid comet bind,　　　35
Describe or fix one movement of his mind?
Who saw its fires here rise, and there descend,
Explain his own beginning, or his end?
Alas what wonder! man's superior part
Unchecked may rise, and climb from art to art;　　　40
But when his own great work is but begun,
What reason weaves, by passion is undone.
　Trace science then, with modesty thy guide;
First strip off all her equipage of pride;
Deduct what is but vanity, or dress,　　　45
Or learning's luxury, or idleness;
Or tricks to show the stretch of human brain,
Mere curious pleasure, or ingenious pain;
Expunge° the whole, or lop th' excrescent° parts
Of all our vices have created arts;　　　50
Then see how little the remaining sum,
Which served the past, and must the times to come!

● ● ●

24. empyreal (ĕm·pĭr'ē·ăl) sphere: the highest heaven; the source, according
to the Greek philosopher Plato, of the perfect ideas which are imitated by imperfect forms on earth.　49. expunge (ĕks·pŭnj'): erase. excrescent (ĕks·krĕs'-
ĕnt): excessive, useless.

Passions, like elements, though born to fight,
Yet, mixed and softened, in his work unite:
These 'tis enough to temper and employ;   55
But what composes man, can man destroy?
Suffice that reason keep to Nature's road,
Subject, compound them, follow her° and God.
Love, hope, and joy, fair pleasure's smiling train,
Hate, fear, and grief, the family of pain,   60
These mixed with art, and to due bounds confined,
Make and maintain the balance of the mind:
The lights and shades, whose well accorded strife
Gives all the strength and color of our life.
Pleasures are ever in our hands or eyes;   65
And when in act they cease, in prospect rise;
Present to grasp, and future still to find,
The whole employ of body and of mind.
All spread their charms, but charm not all alike;
On different senses different objects strike;   70
Hence different passions more or less inflame,
As strong or weak, the organs of the frame;
And hence one master passion in the breast,
Like Aaron's serpent,° swallows up the rest.

                    •   •   •

Extremes in Nature equal ends produce;   75
In man they join to some mysterious use;
Though each by turns the other's bound° invade,
As, in some well-wrought picture, light and shade,
And oft so mix, the difference is too nice°
Where ends the virtue, or begins the vice.   80
Fools! who from hence into the notion fall,
That vice or virtue there is none at all.
If white and black blend, soften, and unite

58. her: nature.   74. Aaron's serpent: in Egypt, Aaron, Moses' brother, cast
a rod before the Pharaoh and it became a serpent. The Pharaoh's sorcerers then
turned their rods to serpents, but Aaron's devoured all the others. (See Exodus
7:10–12.)   77. bound: boundary.   79. nice: subtle, hard to distinguish.

A thousand ways, is there no black or white?
Ask your own heart, and nothing is so plain;   85
'Tis to mistake them, costs the time and pain.

from *The Dunciad*

The Dunciad, as it was first published, was a brief satire on a
number of contemporary poets. A few years later Pope published a greatly expanded version of the poem which dealt
with a broader subject. He felt that the public's failure to
distinguish good poetry from bad implied a failure of judgment in all fields. Once man's reason and judgment had been
abandoned, chaos would come. Thus the final version of *The
Dunciad* begins as a criticism of inferior taste in literature
and ends with a vision of the end of the world. The following
passage is the conclusion to the poem.

O Muse!° (relate for you can tell alone;
Wits have short memories, and dunces none)
Relate, who first, who last resigned to rest,
Whose heads she° partly, whose completely, blest;
What charms could faction, what ambition lull,   5
The venal quiet, and entrance the dull;°
Till drowned was sense, and shame, and right, and wrong—
O sing, and hush the nations with thy song!

In vain, in vain—the all-composing hour
Resistless falls: the Muse obeys the power.   10
She° comes! she comes! the sable throne behold
Of night primeval and of chaos old!
Before her, fancy's gilded clouds decay,
And all its varying rainbows die away.
Wit shoots in vain its momentary fires,   15
The meteor drops, and in a flash expires.

1. **Muse:** Pope, in classical fashion, invokes the muse at the beginning of
this final section of the poem.   4. **she:** the Goddess of Dullness.   5–6. **What
. . . dull:** What charms could lull political controversy (*faction*) and ambition, quiet the corrupt (*venal*), and enchant the dull.   11. **She:** the Goddess
of Dullness.

As one by one, at dread Medea's strain,°
The sickening stars fade off th' ethereal plain;
As Argus' eyes, by Hermes' wand oppressed,°
Closed one by one to everlasting rest: 20
Thus at her felt approach, and secret might,
Art after art goes out, and all is night.
See skulking truth to her old cavern fled,
Mountains of casuistry° heaped o'er her head!
Philosophy,° that leaned on Heaven before,   25
Shrinks to her second cause,° and is no more.
Physic° of metaphysic° begs defense,
And metaphysic calls for aid on sense!
See mystery to mathematics fly!
In vain! they gaze, turn giddy, rave, and die.   30
Religion blushing veils her sacred fires,
And unawares morality expires.
Nor public flame, nor private, dares to shine;
Nor human spark is left, nor glimpse divine!
Lo! thy dread empire, chaos! is restored;   35
Light dies before thy uncreating word:°
Thy hand, great anarch!° lets the curtain fall;
And universal darkness buries all.

17. **Medea's strain:** in Greek myth, the sorceress Medea was said to be able
to darken the moon and the stars.   19. **Argus' . . . oppressed:** in Greek myth,
Argus was a hundred-eyed monster. Hermes used a magic wand to make all
the eyes close at once.   24. **casuistry** (kăzh'û·ĭs·trĭ): false reasoning or misleading arguments, especially regarding ethics and morals.   25. **Philosophy:**
"natural philosophy"; that is, science.   26. **second cause:** God was considered
the first cause of all events in nature; gravity was the second cause.   27. **Physic:**
medical science. **metaphysic:** theoretical philosophy, speculation.   36. **Light
. . . word:** compare Genesis 1:3: "And God said, let there be light: and there
was light."   37. **anarch:** one who creates or rules over anarchy, a state of complete disorder or chaos.

Engraved on the Collar of a Dog, Which I Gave
to His Royal Highness

I am his Highness' dog at Kew;
Pray tell me, sir, whose dog are you?

Epitaph

Intended for Sir Isaac Newton

Nature, and Nature's laws, lay hid in night,
God said, *Let Newton be!* And all was light.

Questions

Ode on Solitude

Compare the "Ode on Solitude" and "Sweet Are the Thoughts" (p. 175). What do the poems have in common? How do they differ?

FROM *An Essay on Man*

1. State in your own words the thought of each of the three passages from *An Essay on Man*. In general, what is Pope's attitude toward man? What does he think man is capable of? incapable of? What is Pope's view of man's reasoning abilities? of man's emotions?
2. What has Pope gained by putting this philosophical essay into verse form?

FROM *The Dunciad*

1. Compare the first eight lines with the opening of Milton's *Paradise Lost* (p. 232). In what ways do Pope's lines remind you of Milton's? How do they differ?
2. *The Dunciad* and *An Essay on Man* are both written in heroic couplets: are the two poems identical in rhythm? If not, how do they differ and what is responsible for the difference?

Epitaph Intended for Sir Isaac Newton

What are the various connotations of *night* and *light?* What is the Biblical allusion in these lines?

JAMES THOMSON

1700–1748

Thomson was born in Scotland and was a student for a short time at Edinburgh University. He had planned to enter the church, but instead decided on writing as a career, and he went to London in 1725 to try his luck. He established his reputation in the next year with the publication of *Winter*. The success of this poem encouraged Thomson to write *Spring, Summer,* and *Autumn,* and to publish the four poems together as *The Seasons* in 1730. Though uneven in quality, *The Seasons* is perhaps his finest work. To most Englishmen, however, Thomson is best known as the author of the patriotic song, "Rule, Britannia."

from *The Seasons*

The Coming of the Rain

At first a dusky wreath they° seem to rise,
Scare staining ether;° but by fast degrees,
In heaps on heaps, the doubling vapor° sails
Along the loaded sky, and mingling deep,
Sits on the horizon round, a settled gloom: 5
Not such as wintry storms on mortals shed,
Oppressing life; but lovely, gentle, kind,
And full of every hope and every joy,
The wish of Nature. Gradual sinks the breeze
Into a perfect calm; that not a breath   10
Is heard to quiver through the closing woods,
Or rustling turn the many twinkling leaves
Of aspen tall. The uncurling floods, diffused
In glassy breadth, seem through delusive lapse
Forgetful of their course.° 'Tis silence all,   15
And pleasing expectation. Herds and flocks

1. they: see line 3. 2. ether: the sky. 3. vapor: clouds. 13–15. The uncurling . . . course: with no wind, the streams ("floods") are smooth as glass, and seem, in this deceiving ("delusive") calm, to have forgotten to flow at all.

Drop the dry sprig, and mute-imploring, eye
The fallen verdure.° Hushed in short suspense
The plumy people° streak their wings with oil,
To throw the lucid moisture trickling off;   20
And wait the approaching sign to strike, at once,
Into the general choir. Even mountains, vales,
And forests seem, impatient, to demand
The promised sweetness. Man superior walks
Amid the glad creation, musing praise,   25
And looking lively gratitude. At last,
The clouds consign their treasures to the fields;
And, softly shaking on the dimpled pool
Prelusive° drops, let all their moisture flow,
In large effusion, o'er the freshened world.   30

18. verdure (vûr′dûr): vegetation. 19. plumy people: birds. (In many spe-
cies of birds, an oily substance is discharged through the wings to cover the
feathers and protect them against moisture.) 29. Prelusive: introductory.

Rule, Britannia

When Britain first at Heaven's command
  Arose from out the azure main,°
This was the charter of the land,
  And guardian angels sung this strain:
Rule, Britannia! rule the waves!   5
  Britons never will be slaves.

The nations not so blest as thee
  Must in their turns to tyrants fall,
While thou shalt flourish great and free,
  The dread and envy of them all.   10

Still more majestic shalt thou rise,
  More dreadful from each foreign stroke;
As the loud blast that tears the skies
  Serves but to root thy native oak.

2. azure main: blue sea.

Thee haughty tyrants ne'er shall tame;   15
   All their attempts to bend thee down
Will but arouse thy generous flame,
   But work their woe and thy renown.

To thee belongs the rural reign;
   Thy cities shall with commerce shine;   20
All thine shall be the subject main,
   And every shore it circles thine!

The Muses, still with freedom found,
   Shall to thy happy coast repair;
Blest isle, with matchless beauty crown'd,   25
   And manly hearts to guard the fair—
Rule, Britannia! rule the waves!
   Britons never will be slaves!

Questions

1. Are the lines from *The Seasons* effective as descriptive poetry? That
   is, do they create in you, the reader, a feeling of a coming spring
   storm? If so, how do the lines create this effect? How is imagery used
   in this passage? What kinds of images appear?
2. The language of the lines from *The Seasons* could be criticized to some
   extent. (For instance, consider "plumy people" for "birds" in line 19.
   Other examples could be cited.) Do these defects damage the poem
   badly? Or is the poem good enough in other respects to cause you to
   overlook its defects? Explain your answer.
3. In "Rule, Britannia" explain the simile of the third stanza. What makes
   this poem an effective patriotic song? What qualities does it share
   with, for instance, "The Star-Spangled Banner" or "America"?

THOMAS GRAY
1716–1771

Gray was born in London and educated at Eton and Cambridge. He left college without taking a degree to make a tour of France and Italy. On his return, he re-entered Cambridge to continue his studies, and he eventually became Professor of History and Modern Languages at the university.

Gray was one of the most popular poets of his age, even though the volume of his work was quite small. He spent years polishing and refining each of his poems; it is said that his most famous work, *Elegy Written in a Country Churchyard*, took seven years to write, yet the complete poem is only a little over a hundred lines long. Gray's reputation is no longer as high as it once was, perhaps because poets and readers eventually reacted against the high polish and elegant diction of his verse. At his best, however, as in the *Elegy*, Gray is a skillful and sometimes moving poet. His other poem included here, "On a Favorite Cat, Drowned in a Tub of Goldfishes," shows his skill in light verse.

On a Favorite Cat,
Drowned in a Tub of Goldfishes

'Twas on a lofty vase's side,
Where China's gayest art had dyed
   The azure flowers that blow;
Demurest of the tabby kind,
The pensive Selima reclined,   5
   Gazed on the lake below.

Her conscious tail her joy declared;
The fair round face, the snowy beard,
   The velvet of her paws,
Her coat, that with the tortoise vies,   10
Her ears of jet, and emerald eyes,
   She saw; and purred applause.

Still had she gazed; but 'midst the tide
Two angel forms were seen to glide,
   The genii° of the stream: 15
Their scaly armour's Tyrian° hue
Thro' richest purple to the view
   Betrayed a golden gleam.

The hapless nymph with wonder saw:
A whisker first and then a claw,   20
   With many an ardent wish,
She stretched in vain to reach the prize.
What female heart can gold despise?
   What cat's averse to fish?

Presumptuous maid! with looks intent   25
Again she stretched, again she bent,
   Nor knew the gulf between.
(Malignant fate sat by, and smiled.)
The slipp'ry verge her feet beguiled,
   She tumbled headlong in.   30

Eight times emerging from the flood
She mewed to ev'ry wat'ry god,
   Some speedy aid to send.
No dolphin came, no Nereid° stirr'd:
Nor cruel Tom, nor Susan heard.   35
   A fav'rite has no friend!

From hence, ye beauties undeceived,
Know, one false step is ne'er retrieved,
   And be with caution bold.
Not all that tempts your wand'ring eyes   40
And heedless hearts, is lawful prize;
   Nor all that glisters, gold.

15. **genii** (plural of *genius*): the spirits that reside in some place and give it its particular character. 16. **Tyrian:** purple. 34. **Nereid** (nĕr'ê·ĭd): in Greek mythology, a sea nymph.

Elegy Written in a Country Churchyard

The curfew tolls the knell of parting day,
The lowing herd wind slowly o'er the lea,°
The ploughman homeward plods his weary way,
And leaves the world to darkness, and to me.

Now fades the glimmering landscape on the sight,　　5
And all the air a solemn stillness holds,
Save where the beetle wheels his droning flight,
And drowsy tinklings lull the distant folds:°

Save that from yonder ivy-mantled tower
The moping owl does to the moon complain　　10
Of such as, wandering near her secret bower,
Molest her ancient solitary reign.

Beneath those rugged elms, that yew tree's shade,
Where heaves the turf in many a moldering heap,
Each in his narrow cell for ever laid,　　15
The rude forefathers of the hamlet sleep.

The breezy call of incense-breathing morn,
The swallow twitt'ring from the straw-built shed,
The cock's shrill clarion, or the echoing horn,
No more shall rouse them from their lowly bed.　　20

For them no more the blazing hearth shall burn,
Or busy housewife ply her evening care:
No children run to lisp their sire's return,
Or climb his knees the envied kiss to share.

Oft did the harvest to their sickle yield,　　25
Their furrow oft the stubborn glebe° has broke:
How jocund did they drive their team afield!
How bowed the woods beneath their sturdy stroke!

2. lea: meadow.　8. folds: sheep pens.　26. glebe: soil.

Let not ambition mock their useful toil,
  Their homely joys, and destiny obscure;   30
Nor grandeur hear with a disdainful smile
  The short and simple annals of the poor.

The boast of heraldry,° the pomp of pow'r,
  And all that beauty, all that wealth e'er gave,
Awaits alike th' inevitable hour: 35
  The paths of glory lead but to the grave.

Nor you, ye proud, impute to these the fault,
  If memory o'er that tomb no trophies raise,
Where through the long-drawn aisle and fretted vault°
  The pealing anthem swells the note of praise.   40

Can storied urn° or animated bust
  Back to its mansion call the fleeting breath?
Can honor's voice provoke the silent dust,
  Or flatt'ry soothe the dull cold ear of death?

Perhaps in this neglected spot is laid   45
  Some heart once pregnant with celestial fire;
Hands, that the rod of empire might have swayed,
  Or waked to ecstasy the living lyre.

But knowledge to their eyes her ample page
  Rich with the spoils of time did ne'er unroll;   50
Chill penury° repressed their noble rage,
  And froze the genial current of the soul.

Full many a gem of purest ray serene
  The dark unfathomed caves of ocean bear:
Full many a flower is born to blush unseen,   55
  And waste its sweetness on the desert air.

33. **heraldry:** the science or art of recording family trees; here, a symbol of
family pride.   39. **fretted vault:** domed ceilings decorated with carved patterns ("fretwork").   41. **storied urn:** probably an urn decorated, like many
Greek urns, with a scroll that indicated a story of some sort. (See p. 139.)
51. **penury:** poverty.

Some village Hampden° that with dauntless breast
  The little tyrant of his fields withstood,
Some mute inglorious Milton, here may rest,
  Some Cromwell° guiltless of his country's blood.   60

Th' applause of list'ning senates to command,
  The threats of pain and ruin to despise,
To scatter plenty o'er a smiling land,
  And read their history in a nation's eyes,

Their lot forbade: nor circumscribed° alone   65
  Their growing virtues, but their crimes confined;
Forbade to wade through slaughter to a throne,
  And shut the gates of mercy on mankind,

The struggling pangs of conscious truth to hide,
  To quench the blushes of ingenuous° shame,   70
Or heap the shrine of luxury and pride
  With incense kindled at the Muse's flame.

Far from the madding crowd's ignoble strife
  Their sober wishes never learned to stray;
Along the cool sequestered vale of life   75
  They kept the noiseless tenor° of their way.

Yet ev'n these bones from insult to protect
  Some frail memorial still erected nigh,
With uncouth rhymes and shapeless sculpture decked,
  Implores the passing tribute of a sigh   80

Their name, their years, spelt by th' unlettered muse,
  The place of fame and elegy supply:
And many a holy text around she strews,
  That teach the rustic moralist to die.

57. Hampden: John Hampden (1594–1643) resisted unjust taxes imposed
by King Charles I. 60. Cromwell: see page 202. 65. circumscribed: here,
kept within narrow limits. 70. ingenuous (ĭn·jĕn'ū·ŭs): innocent, unsophisti-
cated. 76. tenor: course, trend.

For who, to dumb forgetfulness a prey,   85
   This pleasing anxious being° e'er resigned,
Left the warm precincts° of the cheerful day,
   Nor cast one longing ling'ring look behind?

On some fond breast the parting soul relies,
   Some pious drops the closing eye requires;   90
E'en from the tomb the voice of nature cries,
   E'en in our ashes live their wonted fires.

For thee,° who, mindful of th' unhonored dead,
   Dost in these lines their artless tale relate;
If chance, by lonely contemplation led,   95
   Some kindred spirit shall inquire thy fate,

Haply some hoary-headed° swain may say,
   "Oft have we seen him at the peep of dawn
Brushing with hasty steps the dews away,
   To meet the sun upon the upland lawn;   100

"There at the foot of yonder nodding beech
   That wreathes its old fantastic roots so high.
His listless length at noontide would he stretch,
   And pore upon the brook that babbles by.

"Hard by yon wood, now smiling as in scorn,   105
   Muttering his wayward fancies he would rove;
Now drooping, woeful wan, like one forlorn,
   Or crazed with care, or crossed in hopeless love.

"One morn I missed him on the customed hill,
   Along the heath, and near his favorite tree;   110
Another came; nor yet beside the rill,°
   Nor up the lawn, nor at the wood was.he;

---

86. **being:** existence, life.   87. **precincts:** surroundings.   94. **thee:** the
speaker (note that the poem begins with the speaker addressing the reader
directly—see line 4—but now someone else seems to be addressing the original
speaker).   97. **hoary-headed:** white-haired.   111. **rill:** a small brook.

"The next with dirges due in sad array
  Slow through the church-way path we saw him borne—
Approach and read (for thou canst read) the lay   115
  Graved on the stone beneath yon aged thorn."

Here rests his head upon the lap of Earth
A youth, to fortune and to fame unknown;
Fair science frowned not on his humble birth,
And melancholy marked him for her own.   120

Large was his bounty, and his soul sincere;
* Heaven did a recompense as largely send:*
He gave to misery all he had, a tear,
* He gained from Heaven, 'twas all he wished, a friend.*

No farther seek his merits to disclose,   125
* Or draw his frailties from their dread abode,*
(There they alike in trembling hope repose,)
* The bosom of his Father and his God.*

Questions

On a Favorite Cat, Drowned in a Tub of Goldfishes

What is the tone of this poem? How is the tone achieved? How serious is the moral in the last stanza?

Elegy Written in a Country Churchyard

1. This poem was perhaps the most popular of its time, even with readers who generally cared little for poetry. This is still true to some extent today. What do you think accounts for the poem's popularity? What is its "message"?
2. The *Elegy* seems to be a poem that states simple, common ideas in a straightforward way. Is it merely that? For instance, the poem apparently begins with a speaker directly addressing the reader (see l. 4), but near the end (l. 93) the speaker is addressing someone else, or someone else is now addressing him. Who actually speaks lines 93–97? Can we tell? For whom is this elegy intended—those in the churchyard? the poet? both?

3. What is the relationship of The Epitaph to the rest of the poem? Does it seem to be merely tacked on at the end, or does it grow logically out of what has gone before?

OLIVER GOLDSMITH

1728–1774

Oliver Goldsmith was born in Ireland and educated at Trinity College, Dublin. Following his graduation, he thought for a time of entering the ministry, tried teaching, studied law, and finally decided to become a doctor. He seemed to be successful at nothing. After years of poverty, he turned to journalism and began writing articles for a London magazine.

He drifted into writing almost by accident, but he became one of the most versatile writers of his time. His work ranged from the essay to the novel to poetry to drama, and in each form he showed great skill and originality. Samuel Johnson's epitaph for him was appropriate: "He touched nothing that he did not adorn."

Goldsmith's reputation rests on his longer works, but the witty qualities that run through most of his writing can also be seen in his "Elegy on the Death of a Mad Dog."

Elegy on the Death of a Mad Dog

Good people all, of every sort,
  Give ear unto my song;
And if you find it wondrous short—
  It cannot hold you long.

In Islington there was a man,   5
  Of whom the world might say,
That still a godly race he ran—
  Whene'er he went to pray.

A kind and gentle heart he had,
   To comfort friends and foes;   10
The naked every day he clad—
   When he put on his clothes.

And in that town a dog was found,
   As many dogs there be,
Both mongrel, puppy, whelp, and hound,   15
   And cur of low degree.

This dog and man at first were friends;
   But when a pique° began,
The dog, to gain some private ends,
   Went mad, and bit the man.   20

Around from all the neighboring streets,
   The wondering neighbors ran,
And swore the dog had lost his wits,
   To bite so good a man.

The wound it seemed both sore and sad   25
   To every Christian eye;
And while they swore the dog was mad,
   They swore the man would die.

But soon a wonder came to light,
   That showed the rogues they lied;   30
The man recovered of the bite,
   The dog it was that died.

18. pique (pēk): here, disagreement.

Questions

Compare this poem to Gray's "On a Favorite Cat, Drowned in a Tub of Goldfishes." How does each poem create its humor? Which poem seems to you to be the more humorous? Why?

WILLIAM COWPER

1731–1800

Cowper * attended Westminster School and then studied law. After passing the bar examination, he entered government service and held a number of minor positions. At thirty, under pressure while trying to pass an examination for a higher post, Cowper suffered a mental collapse. For the rest of his life he was subject to extreme depression and remained under constant care, at times confined to an asylum.

Cowper's best-known work is *The Task*, a long poem in blank verse which anticipates in some ways the nature poetry of Wordsworth. "The Castaway," written a year before Cowper's death, is not typical of his nature poetry, but it foreshadows the way in which symbolism and personal emotion were to appear in the work of the Romantic poets who followed him.

The Castaway

Obscurest night involved the sky,
    Th' Atlantic billows roared,
When such a destined wretch as I,
    Washed headlong from on board,
Of friends, of hope, of all bereft,   5
His floating home for ever left.

No braver chief could Albion° boast
    Than he with whom we went.
Nor ever ship left Albion's coast,
    With warmer wishes sent.   10
He loved them both, but both in vain,
Nor him beheld, nor her again.

Not long beneath the whelming brine,
    Expert to swim, he lay;

* **Cowper** (kōō′pĕr). 7. **Albion:** England.

Nor soon he felt his strength decline,   15
 Or courage die away;
But waged with death a lasting strife,
Supported by despair of life.

He shouted: nor his friends had failed
 To check the vessel's course,   20
But so the furious blast prevailed,
 That, pitiless perforce,
They left their outcast mate behind,
And scudded° still before the wind.

Some succor yet they could afford;   25
 And, such as storms allow,
The cask, the coop, the floated cord,
 Delayed not to bestow.
But he (they knew) nor ship, nor shore,
Whate'er they gave, should visit more.   30

Nor, cruel as it seemed, could he
 Their haste himself condemn,
Aware that flight, in such a sea,
 Alone could rescue them;
Yet bitter felt it still to die   ·   35
Deserted, and his friends so nigh.

He long survives, who lives an hour
 In ocean, self-upheld;
And so long he, with unspent power,
 His destiny repelled;   40
And ever, as the minutes flew,
Entreated help, or cried—Adieu!

At length, his transient respite past,
 His comrades, who before

24. **scudded:** ran, were driven swiftly.

Had heard his voice in every blast,   45
    Could catch the sound no more.
For then, by toil subdued, he drank
    The stifling wave, and then he sank.

No poet wept him: but the page°
    Of narrative sincere,   50
That tells his name, his worth, his age,
    Is wet with Anson's° tear.
And tears by bards or heroes shed
Alike immortalize the dead.

I therefore purpose not, or dream,   55
    Descanting° on his fate,
To give the melancholy theme
    A more enduring date:
But misery still delights to trace
Its semblance in another's case.   60

No voice divine the storm allayed,
    No light propitious shone;
When, snatched from all effectual aid,
    We perished, each alone:
But I beneath a rougher sea,   65
Am whelmed in deeper gulfs than he.

49. **page:** of the ship's log. 52. **Anson's:** Baron George Anson (1697–
1762), was a well-known English admiral. 56. **Descanting:** discoursing, speaking at length.

Questions

1. In the last stanza Cowper makes an analogy between himself and the
   drowned man. Is Cowper anticipating his own death? Or, when he
   speaks of his "deeper gulfs," is he referring to something other than
   his death?
2. What do lines 61–62 mean? Do they mean the same thing to both the
   drowning man and the poet?

WILLIAM BLAKE

1757–1827

Blake spent almost his entire life in revolt against the period in which he lived. In an age which valued restraint, he praised excess and enthusiasm; at a time when most poets aimed for clarity, he wrote works of obscure symbolism and mysticism; living in the Age of Reason, Blake called reason evil.

He was the son of a London merchant who was interested in mysticism. Blake himself claimed that he began having visions at the age of four. By the time he was twelve he was drawing and writing poems to express his visions. At an early age he was apprenticed to an engraver, and he continued throughout his life to paint and engrave as well as write poetry.

His early volume of poetry, *Songs of Innocence*, expresses his belief that man is most happy in the simple state of childhood, before being corrupted by society or experience. A later collection, *Songs of Experience*, presents the contrast to this primitive state, showing the complex world of experience in which good and evil are mingled. In both of these books the poems are outwardly simple. His later works became increasingly complex, but even the most difficult of them contain passages of clear lyric beauty.

Blake was well-known as an artist during his lifetime, but it was only in our century that he became acknowledged as a great poet.

Love's Secret

Never seek to tell thy love,
    Love that never told can be;
For the gentle wind doth move
    Silently, invisibly.

I told my love, I told my love,   5
    I told her all my heart,
Trembling, cold, in ghastly fears.
    Ah! she did depart!

Soon after she was gone from me,
A traveler came by,   10
Silently, invisibly;
He took her with a sigh.

The Chimney Sweeper

from Songs of Innocence

When my mother died I was very young,
And my father sold me while yet my tongue
Could scarcely cry " 'weep! 'weep! 'weep! 'weep!"
So your chimneys I sweep, and in soot I sleep.

There's little Tom Dacre, who cried when his head,   5
That curled like a lamb's back, was shaved; so I said,
"Hush, Tom! never mind it, for, when your head's bare,
You know that the soot cannot spoil your white hair."

And so he was quiet, and that very night,
As Tom was asleeping, he had such a sight!   10
That thousands of sweepers, Dick, Joe, Ned, and Jack,
Were all of them locked up in coffins of black.

And by came an Angel who had a bright key,
And he opened the coffins and set them all free;
Then down a green plain leaping, laughing, they run,   15
And wash in a river, and shine in the sun.

Then naked and white, all their bags left behind,
They rise upon clouds and sport in the wind;
And the Angel told Tom, if he'd be a good boy,
He'd have God for his father, and never want joy.   20

And so Tom awoke, and we rose in the dark,
And got with our bags and our brushes to work.
Though the morning was cold, Tom was happy and warm;
So if all do their duty they need not fear harm.

Night

from *Songs of Innocence*

The sun descending in the west,
The evening star does shine;
The birds are silent in their nest,
And I must seek for mine.
The moon like a flower,   5
In heaven's high bower,
With silent delight
Sits and smiles on the night.

Farewell green fields and happy groves,
Where flocks have took delight: 10
Where lambs have nibbled, silent moves
The feet of angels bright:
Unseen they pour blessing,
And joy without ceasing,
On each bud and blossom,   15
And each sleeping bosom.

They look in every thoughtless nest,
Where birds are covered warm:
They visit caves of every beast,
To keep them all from harm.   20
If they see any weeping
That should have been sleeping,
They pour sleep on their head
And sit down by their bed.

When wolves and tigers howl for prey,   25
They pitying stand and weep,
Seeking to drive their thirst away,
And keep them from the sheep.
But if they rush dreadful,
The angels, most heedful,   30
Receive each mild spirit,
New worlds to inherit.

William Blake   285

And there the lion's ruddy eyes
Shall flow with tears of gold,
And pitying the tender cries,   35
And walking round the fold,
Saying "Wrath, by his° meekness,
And, by his health, sickness
Is driven away
From our immortal day.   40

"And now beside thee, bleating lamb,
I can lie down and sleep;
Or think on him who bore thy name,°
Graze after thee and weep.
For, wash'd in life's river,   45
My bright mane for ever
Shall shine like the gold
As I guard o'er the fold."

37. his: Christ's.   43. him . . . name: Christ, the "lamb of the world."

A Poison Tree

from Songs of Experience

I was angry with my friend:
I told my wrath, my wrath did end.
I was angry with my foe:
I told it not, my wrath did grow.

And I watered it in fears,   5
Night and morning with my tears;
And I sunnèd it with smiles,
And with soft deceitful wiles.

And it grew both day and night,
Till it bore an apple bright;   10
And my foe beheld it shine,
And he knew that it was mine,

And into my garden stole
When the night had veiled the pole:
In the morning glad I see   15
My foe outstretched beneath the tree.

Preface to *Milton*

And did those feet° in ancient time
Walk upon England's mountains green?
And was the Holy Lamb of God
On England's pleasant pastures seen?

And did the countenance divine   5
Shine forth upon our clouded hills?
And was Jerusalem builded here
Among these dark satanic mills?

Bring me my bow of burning gold!
Bring me my arrows of desire!   10
Bring me my spear! O clouds, unfold!
Bring me my chariot of fire!

I will not cease from mental fight,
Nor shall my sword sleep in my hand,
Till we have built Jerusalem   15
In England's green and pleasant land.

1. **those feet:** Christ's.

Questions

1. In "Love's Secret," why does Blake compare love to the wind? Why is the word *sigh* especially appropriate in the last line? Who might the "traveler" (l. 10) be?
2. What is the symbolism of the dream in "The Chimney Sweeper"? In this poem, how does the speaker's attitude differ from the poet's? In line 3, for instance, what does the speaker mean by " 'weep! 'weep!

'weep! 'weep!"? What does the poet mean? Does the speaker mean
the last line to be ironic? Does the poet?
3. Like "The Chimney Sweeper," "Night" is from *Songs of Innocence.*
In what ways—if any—are the two poems related? What can angels do?
What are they unable to do?
4. "A Poison Tree" is from *Songs of Experience.* How does the speaker
in this poem differ from the speaker in "The Chimney Sweeper"? In
what other ways can you compare and contrast these two poems?
5. What is the relationship between the first and second stanzas of the
"Preface to *Milton*"? What are "dark satanic mills"? How is the poem
organized? Does it build to a climax? If so, how?

ROBERT BURNS

1759–1796

Burns and Blake share some similarities: both men tended to reject
the attitudes of their time, and both brought back some of the wit
and melody of Elizabethan songs to English poetry. Beyond this,
they have little in common. Blake was unknown as a poet during
his lifetime, but Burns became extremely popular, and he exerted
some influence on the poets who followed him. In Burns' poetry
there is little symbolism or mysticism; his work is concerned with
the emotions rather than religious or philosophical ideas.

He was born in the southwestern part of Scotland, the son of a
poor farmer. He managed to receive only about three years of formal
schooling, but he read a great deal as a child and began writing some
poetry before he was sixteen. During these early years, he also became interested in Scottish folk songs, and this interest was later
reflected in all of his finest poetry. When he published his first
volume, he was immediately acclaimed as an untaught, "natural"
poet, though in Burns' case this was not entirely accurate. Just as in
the old folk songs, Burns' apparently simple poems concealed a great
deal of craftsmanship.

Burns tried his hand at poetry in standard English, but the results
were almost always poor. His best poems are those in Scottish di-
alect. They express no profound vision or complex ideas, but their
simplicity and sincerity have made them memorable.

My Luve

O my luve is like a red, red rose,
    That's newly sprung in June:
O my luve is like the melodie,
    That's sweetly played in tune.

As fair art thou, my bonnie lass,   5
    So deep in luve am I;
And I will luve thee still, my dear,
    Till a' the seas gang° dry:

Till a' the seas gang dry, my dear,
    And the rocks melt wi' the sun;   10
And I will luve thee still, my dear,
    While the sands o' life shall run.

And fare-thee-weel, my only luve!
    And fare-thee-weel a while!
And I will come again, my luve,   15
    Tho' it were ten thousand mile.

8. **gang:** go.

The Banks o' Doon

Ye banks and braes° o' bonnie Doon°
    How can ye blume sae fair!
How can ye chant, ye little birds,
    And I sae fu' o' care!

Thou'lt break my heart, thou bonnie bird   5
    That sings upon the bough;
Thou minds me o' the happy days
    When my fause luve was true.

1. **braes** (brāz): slopes. **Doon** (or **Don**): a river in northeast Scotland.

Thou'lt break my heart, thou bonnie bird
   That sings beside thy mate;   10
For sae I sat, and sae I sang,
   And wist na'° o' my fate.

Aft hae I roved by bonnie Doon
   To see the woodbine twine,
And ilka° bird sang o' its luve;   15
   And sae did I o' mine.

Wi' lightsome heart I pu'd a rose,
   Frae aff its thorny tree;
And my fause luver staw° the rose,
   But left the thorn wi' me.   20

12. **wist na':** knew not.   15. **ilka:** every.   19. **staw:** stole.

Bruce's March to Bannockburn

Robert Bruce (1274–1329) defeated the British at Bannockburn (in central Scotland) in 1314. He later became King
Robert I. This poem is supposed to be his address to his
troops before the battle.

Scots, wha hae wi' Wallace° bled,
Scots, wham Bruce has aften led,
Welcome to your gory bed,
   Or to victorie!

Now's the day, and now's the hour;   5
See the front° o' battle lour;°
See approach proud Edward's° power—
   Chains and slaverie!

1. **Wallace:** Sir William Wallace (1272?–1305) defeated the British in 1297.
6. **front:** face. **lour:** frown.   7. **Edward's:** probably referring to both Edward I
(King of England from 1272–1307) and Edward II (reigned 1307–1327).

Wha will be a traitor knave?
Wha can fill a coward's grave?   10
Wha sae base as be a slave?
        Let him turn and flee!

Wha, for Scotland's king and law,
Freedom's sword will strongly draw,
Free-man stand, or free-man fa',   15
        Let him follow me!

By oppression's woes and pains!
By your sons in servile chains!
We will drain our dearest veins,
        But they shall be free!   20

Lay the proud usurpers low!
Tyrants fall in every foe!
Liberty's in every blow!
        Let us do or die!

Questions

1. In "My Luve," what is the effect of the exaggerated figures of speech, especially in the third stanza? Do they make the poem seem insincere, or do they have some other effect?
2. What is the tone of "The Banks o' Doon"? Is there any symbolism in this simple lyric? If so, where does it occur?
3. How is "Bruce's March to Bannockburn" similar to Thomson's "Rule, Britannia" on page 269?

THE ROMANTIC POETS

The Romantic period in English poetry was brief. It is generally considered to have begun in 1798, when Wordsworth and Coleridge published their *Lyrical Ballads*. The period was over by 1832, the year that Tennyson published his first poem. Actually, most of the Romantic poets had completed their major work before this time. Within these few years, however, England experienced an outpouring of poetry second only to the Elizabethan age.

Like the Elizabethan age, the Romantic period was a time of great social change. Two revolutions had occurred just before the period began—in America and France. Most of the poets of this time were aware of the political issues of the day, and they also shared a concern over the lot of the common man. Beyond this, there were few similarities. Some poets showed a deep interest in nature; others were absorbed in philosophical ideas. A few returned to the Medieval period for inspiration, while others viewed classical Greece and Rome as models. Most poets were fascinated by the past, by remote lands, and by mystery of various kinds, but many dealt directly with the problems of their day. All in all, this was a remarkably varied and productive period in English poetry.

WILLIAM WORDSWORTH

1770–1850

Wordsworth was born in the Lake District of Northern England. Both of his parents died while he was still young, but his uncles supported him while he attended Cambridge. In 1791, after receiving his degree from Cambridge, Wordsworth visited France. He found himself in the midst of the French Revolution and immediately became sympathetic with the democratic principles of the revolutionaries. His interest in the common man remained with him all his life, even though he later rejected many of his youthful beliefs and many of the principles for which the French Revolution was fought.

After his return from France, Wordsworth led a quiet life. An inheritance in 1795 enabled him and his sister Dorothy to retire to the country, where they became neighbors and close friends of Samuel Taylor Coleridge. The two poets decided to collaborate, and in 1798 published a volume entitled *Lyrical Ballads.* The book is generally said to mark the beginning of Romantic poetry. In 1800, for a second edition of the work, Wordsworth wrote a preface in which he described his idea of poetry as the "spontaneous overflow of powerful feelings" and as "emotion recollected in tranquillity." He also emphasized the importance of using realistic language in poetry, as opposed to the artificial diction of some later eighteenth-century poets.

The first decade of the nineteenth century was a productive period for Wordsworth, but in later years his poetic powers declined. He was named poet laureate in 1843, but by this time his career was virtually over and so was the Romantic period. When he died in 1850, the other major Romantic poets—Coleridge, Byron, Shelley, and Keats—had been dead for many years.

Lines Composed a Few Miles above Tintern Abbey*

Five years have past; five summers, with the length
Of five long winters! and again I hear
These waters, rolling from their mountain springs
With a soft inland murmur. Once again
Do I behold these steep and lofty cliffs,   5
That on a wild secluded scene impress
Thoughts of more deep seclusion; and connect
The landscape with the quiet of the sky.
The day is come when I again repose
Here, under this dark sycamore, and view   10

* **Tintern Abbey:** the ruins of an ancient monastery on the banks of the Wye River, in Wales.

These plots of cottage ground, these orchard tufts,
Which at this season, with their unripe fruits,
Are clad in one green hue, and lose themselves
'Mid groves and copses.° Once again I see
These hedgerows, hardly hedgerows, little lines   15
Of sportive wood run wild: these pastoral farms,
Green to the very door; and wreaths of smoke
Sent up, in silence, from among the trees!
With some uncertain notice, as might seem
Of vagrant dwellers in the houseless woods,   20
Or of some hermit's cave, where by his fire
The hermit sits alone.
                            These beauteous forms,
Through a long absence, have not been to me
As is a landscape to a blind man's eye:
But oft, in lonely rooms, and 'mid the din   25
Of towns and cities, I have owed to them
In hours of weariness, sensations sweet,
Felt in the blood, and felt along the heart;
And passing even into my purer mind,
With tranquil restoration: feelings too   30
Of unremembered pleasure: such, perhaps,
As have no slight or trivial influence
On that best portion of a good man's life,
His little, nameless, unremembered acts
Of kindness and of love. Nor less, I trust,   35
To them I may have owed another gift,
Of aspect more sublime; that blessed mood,
In which the burthen of the mystery,
In which the heavy and the weary weight
Of all this unintelligible world,   40
Is lightened: that serene and blessed mood,
In which the affections gently lead us on,
Until, the breath of this corporeal frame°
And even the motion of our human blood
Almost suspended, we are laid asleep   45

14. **copses:** thickets.   43. **corporeal** (kôr·pō′rĕ·ăl) **frame:** the body.

In body, and become a living soul:
While with an eye made quiet by the power
Of harmony, and the deep power of joy,
We see into the life of things.
                              If this
Be but a vain belief, yet, oh! how oft—   50
In darkness and amid the many shapes
Of joyless daylight; when the fretful stir
Unprofitable, and the fever of the world,
Have hung upon the beatings of my heart—
How oft, in spirit, have I turned to thee,   55
O sylvan° Wye! thou wanderer through the woods,
How often has my spirit turned to thee!

  And now, with gleams of half-extinguished thought,
With many recognitions dim and faint,
And somewhat of a sad perplexity,   60
The picture of the mind revives again:
While here I stand, not only with the sense
Of present pleasure, but with pleasing thoughts
That in this moment there is life and food
For future years. And so I dare to hope,   65
Though changed, no doubt, from what I was when first
I came among these hills; when like a roe°
I bounded o'er the mountains, by the sides
Of the deep rivers, and the lonely streams,
Wherever nature led: more like a man   70
Flying from something that he dreads, than one
Who sought the thing he loved. For nature then
(The coarser pleasures of my boyish days,
And their glad animal movements all gone by)
To me was all in all. I cannot paint   75
What then I was. The sounding cataract°
Haunted me like a passion: the tall rock
The mountain, and the deep and gloomy wood,
Their colors and their forms, were then to me

  56. sylvan: wooded. 67. roe: deer. 76. cataract: waterfall.

An appetite; a feeling and a love,   80
That had no need of a remoter charm,
By thought supplied, nor any interest
Unborrowed from the eye. That time is past,
And all its aching joys are now no more,
And all its dizzy raptures. Not for this   85
Faint I, nor mourn nor murmur; other gifts
Have followed; for such loss, I would believe,
Abundant recompense. For I have learned
To look on nature, not as in the hour
Of thoughtless youth; but hearing oftentimes   90
The still, sad music of humanity,
Nor harsh nor grating, though of ample power
To chasten and subdue. And I have felt
A presence that disturbs me with the joy
Of elevated thoughts; a sense sublime   95
Of something far more deeply interfused,
Whose dwelling is the light of setting suns,
And the round ocean, and the living air,
And the blue sky, and in the mind of man;
A motion and a spirit, that impels   100
All thinking things, all objects of all thought,
And rolls through all things. Therefore am I still
A lover of the meadows and the woods,
And mountains; and of all that we behold
From this green earth; of all the mighty world   105
Of eye, and ear—both what they half create,
And what perceive;° well pleased to recognize
In nature and the language of the sense,
The anchor of my purest thoughts, the nurse,
The guide, the guardian of my heart, and soul   110
Of all my moral being.
                           Nor perchance,
If I were not thus taught, should I the more

106–107. Of eye . . . perceive: in Wordworth's time (and in fact during
the preceding century), many philosophers had argued that the senses distorted reality. That is, the eyes, for instance, "created" part of the image they
sent to the brain.

Suffer my genial° spirits to decay:
For thou art with me here upon the banks
Of this fair river; thou my dearest friend,   115
My dear, dear friend; and in thy voice I catch
The language of my former heart, and read
My former pleasures in the shooting lights
Of thy wild eyes. Oh! yet a little while
May I behold in thee what I was once,   120
My dear, dear sister! and this prayer I make,
Knowing that Nature never did betray
The heart that loved her; 'tis her privilege,
Through all the years of this our life, to lead
From joy to joy: for she can so inform   125
The mind that is within us, so impress
With quietness and beauty, and so feed
With lofty thoughts, that neither evil tongues,
Rash judgments, nor the sneers of selfish men,
Nor greetings where no kindness is, nor all   130
The dreary intercourse of daily life,
Shall e'er prevail against us, or disturb
Our cheerful faith, that all which we behold
Is full of blessings. Therefore let the moon
Shine on thee in thy solitary walk;   135
And let the misty mountain winds be free
To blow against thee: and, in after years,
When these wild ectasies shall be matured
Into a sober pleasure; when thy mind
Shall be a mansion for all lovely forms,   140
Thy memory be as a dwelling place
For all sweet sounds and harmonies; oh! then,
If solitude, or fear, or pain, or grief,
Should be thy portion, with what healing thoughts
Of tender joy wilt thou remember me,   145
And these my exhortations! Nor, perchance—
If I should be where I no more can hear
Thy voice, nor catch from thy wild eyes these gleams
Of past existence—wilt thou then forget

113. genial: here, inborn.

That on the banks of this delightful stream 150
We stood together; and that I, so long
A worshipper of Nature, hither came
Unwearied in that service: rather say
With warmer love—oh! with far deeper zeal
Of holier love. Nor wilt thou then forget, 155
That after many wanderings, many years
Of absence, these steep woods and lofty cliffs,
And this green pastoral landscape, were to me
More dear, both for themselves and for thy sake!

It Is a Beauteous Evening

It is a beauteous evening, calm and free;
The holy time is quiet as a nun
Breathless with adoration; the broad sun
Is sinking down in its tranquillity;
The gentleness of heaven is on the sea: 5
Listen! the mighty Being is awake,
And doth with his eternal motion make
A sound like thunder—everlastingly.
Dear child! dear girl! that walkest with me here,
If thou appear untouched by solemn thought, 10
Thy nature is not therefore less divine:
Thou liest in Abraham's bosom all the year;
And worship'st at the Temple's inner shrine,
God being with thee when we know it not.

Composed upon Westminster Bridge

Earth has not anything to show more fair:
Dull would he be of soul who could pass by
A sight so touching in its majesty:
This city now doth, like a garment, wear
The beauty of the morning; silent, bare, 5
Ships, towers, domes, theaters, and temples lie
Open unto the fields, and to the sky;

All bright and glittering in the smokeless air.
Never did sun more beautifully steep
In his first splendor, valley, rock, or hill;   10
Ne'er saw I, never felt, a calm so deep!
The river glideth at his own sweet will:
Dear God! the very houses seem asleep;
And all that mighty heart is lying still!

The World Is Too Much with Us

The world is too much with us; late and soon,
Getting and spending, we lay waste our powers:
Little we see in Nature that is ours;
We have given our hearts away, a sordid boon!°
The sea that bares her bosom to the moon;   5
The winds that will be howling at all hours,
And are up-gathered now like sleeping flowers;
For this, for everything, we are out of tune;
It moves us not. Great God! I'd rather be
A pagan suckled in a creed outworn.   10
So might I standing on this pleasant lea,
Have glimpses that would make me less forlorn;
Have sight of Proteus° rising from the sea;
Or hear old Triton° blow his wreathed horn.

4. **boon:** here, an unpaid service or favor.   13. **Proteus** (prō'tūs): a sea
god in Greek mythology.   14. **Triton** (trī'tŏn): another Greek sea god. He
was often pictured carrying a trumpet made of a spiral sea shell.

Questions

Lines Composed a Few Miles Above Tintern Abbey

1. This famous poem expresses clearly Wordsworth's concept of nature
   as "the nurse, the guide, the guardian . . . and soul" of his moral and
   spiritual being. Point out lines that deal specifically with nature and
   nature's influence over man.
2. The poem presents a contrast between childhood and adulthood. What
   has the poet gained with age? What has he lost? How does Words-

worth's view of childhood compare with Blake's in "The Chimney Sweeper" and "Night" (pp. 284–85)?

Sonnets

1. "It Is a Beauteous Evening" contrasts two types of religious devotion. What are they? (See l. 2 especially.) What is the theme of this poem?
2. What discovery about London does Wordsworth describe in "Composed upon Westminster Bridge"? Much of the power of this poem depends on a paradox. What is the paradox? (Note particularly the last two lines.)
3. In "The World Is Too Much with Us," what does the poet mean by the "world"? What comparison between modern and ancient times is expressed in the sestet? How is this poem similar to "The Oxen," page 137?

SIR WALTER SCOTT

1771–1832

Scott was born in Edinburgh and educated in the law. He became a practicing lawyer, and eventually held a governmental position, but his deepest interest was poetry, particularly early Scottish folk ballads. His first book was a collection of such ballads. A few years later he published his first original poem and met with immediate success. He remained the most popular English poet for quite a few years and then turned to the historical novel, achieving equal eminence in that field. In his own day, Scott's long narrative poems were his best-known works, but today's readers generally prefer his shorter lyrics, many of which were scattered throughout his novels. "Proud Maisie" is from *The Heart of Midlothian*.

Proud Maisie

Proud Maisie is in the wood,
    Walking so early;
Sweet Robin sits on the bush,
    Singing so rarely.

"Tell me, thou bonny bird,   5
    When shall I marry me?"
"When six braw° gentlemen
    Kirkward° shall carry ye."

"Who makes the bridal bed,
    Birdie say truly?"   10
"The gray-headed sexton
    That delves° the grave duly.°

"The glowworm o'er grave and stone
    Shall light thee steady;
The owl from the steeple sing   15
    Welcome, proud lady."

7. **braw:** well-dressed. 8. **Kirkward:** to the church. 12. **delves:** digs. **duly:** properly.

Questions

1. What characteristics of the typical ballad form are apparent in this poem?
2. What is the tone of the poem? What particular details make the poem effective?

SAMUEL TAYLOR COLERIDGE

1772–1834

Coleridge was a precocious child, reading the Bible by the time he was three. His father died when the boy was ten, and Coleridge was then sent to a charity school in London. A few years later he was accepted, again on a charity basis, at Cambridge. His first volume of poetry appeared in 1796. The next year he met Wordsworth and collaborated with him on the *Lyrical Ballads*. Coleridge's major contribution to the volume was *The Rime of the Ancient Mariner*, his greatest poem. Within the next two years he wrote some other excellent poems, including "Kubla Khan," but by 1800 his career as a poet was virtually over.

With the exception of a handful of minor poems and one major work, "Dejection" (1802), Coleridge devoted the rest of his life to prose—including criticism, philosophy, and political essays. He claimed that his work in philosophy had turned him from poetry, but his association with Wordsworth may also have been a factor. Wordsworth was a severe critic, and Coleridge seems to have needed a great deal of encouragement to go on with his imaginative work. In any case, though he stopped creating poetry, Coleridge turned out some significant prose, and today he is ranked as one of the greatest English critics.

His best-known poems represent quite a different aspect of Romanticism from Wordsworth's philosophic nature poems. As a child, one of Coleridge's favorite books was the *Arabian Nights*, and from those dream-world tales he seems to have developed his taste for mystery and the supernatural. Many other poets have dealt with such themes, but few have possessed Coleridge's power of making the supernatural seem real.

The Rime of the Ancient Mariner

This poem puzzled its readers and critics when it first appeared in 1798. Since then it has become perhaps the best loved narrative poem in English literature, and, especially in recent years, the subject of much critical analysis. Some of the speculation may be far-fetched, but it is clear that the poem exists on at least two levels of meaning. First, it is an exciting tale of the sea and an engrossing character sketch. Second, the poem goes beyond the surface narrative to become a symbolic study of the Christian tradition of sin, repentance, and redemption. In addition to these two main threads, the poem has suggested further symbolic meanings to many modern readers.

The prose commentary was not part of the original version of the poem, but was added by Coleridge to a later edition.

How a ship having passed the Line* was driven by storms to the cold country toward
the South Pole, and how from thence she made her course to the tropical latitude of the
great Pacific Ocean; and of the strange things that befell; and in what manner the
ancient Mariner came back to his own country.

PART I

*An ancient
Mariner
meeteth three
Gallants
bidden to a
wedding-
feast, and
detaineth one.*

It is an ancient Mariner,
And he stoppeth one of three.
"By thy long gray beard and glittering eye,
Now wherefore stopp'st thou me?

The Bridegroom's doors are opened wide,　　　　5
And I am next of kin;
The guests are met, the feast is set:
May'st hear the merry din."

He holds him with his skinny hand,
"There was a ship," quoth he.　　　　10
"Hold off! unhand me, gray-beard loon!"
Eftsoons° his hand dropt he.

*The Wedding-
Guest is spell-
bound by the
eye of the old
seafaring
man, and con-
strained to
hear his tale.*

He holds him with his glittering eye—
The Wedding-Guest stood still,
And listens like a three years' child:　　　　15
The Mariner hath his will.

The Wedding-Guest sat on a stone:
He cannot choose but hear;
And thus spake on that ancient man,
The bright-eyed Mariner.　　　　20

"The ship was cheered, the harbor cleared,
Merrily did we drop
Below the kirk,° below the hill,
Below the lighthouse top.

* **Line:** equator.　12. **Eftsoons:** soon afterward.　23. **kirk:** church.

Samuel Taylor Coleridge　303

The sun came up upon the left,   25
Out of the sea came he!
And he shone bright, and on the right
Went down into the sea.

Higher and higher every day,
Till over the mast at noon—"   30
The Wedding-Guest here beat his breast,
For he heard the loud bassoon.

The bride hath paced into the hall,
Red as a rose is she;
Nodding their heads before her goes   35
The merry minstrelsy.

The Wedding-Guest he beat his breast,
Yet he cannot choose but hear;
And thus spake on that ancient man,
The bright-eyed Mariner.   40

"And now the storm-blast came, and he
Was tyrannous and strong:
He struck with his o'ertaking wings,
And chased us south along.

With sloping masts and dipping prow,   45
As who pursued with yell and blow
Still treads the shadow of his foe,
And forward bends his head,
The ship drove fast, loud roared the blast,
And southward aye we fled.   50

And now there came both mist and snow,
And it grew wondrous cold:
And ice, mast-high, came floating by,
As green as emerald.

The land of
ice, and of
fearful sounds
where no
living thing
was to be
seen.

And through the drifts the snowy clifts   55
Did send a dismal sheen:
Nor shapes of men nor beasts we ken°—
The ice was all between.

The ice was here, the ice was there,
The ice was all around: 60
It cracked and growled, and roared and howled,
Like noises in a swound!°

Till a great
sea-bird,
called the
Albatross,
came through
the snow-fog,
and was
received with
great joy and
hospitality.

At length did cross an Albatross,
Thorough the fog it came;
As if it had been a Christian soul,   65
We hailed it in God's name.

It ate the food it ne'er had eat,°
And round and round it flew.
The ice did split with a thunder-fit;
The helmsman steered us through!   70

And lo! the
Albatross
proveth a
bird of good
omen, and
followeth the
ship as it
returned
northward
through fog
and floating
ice.

And a good south wind sprung up behind;
The Albatross did follow,
And every day, for food or play,
Came to the mariners' hollo!

In mist or cloud, on mast or shroud,°   75
It perched for vespers° nine;
Whiles all the night, through fog-smoke white,
Glimmered the white moon-shine."

The ancient
Mariner
inhospitably
killeth the
pious bird of
good omen.

"God save thee, ancient Mariner!
From the fiends, that plague thee thus!—   80
Why look'st thou so?"—"With my cross-bow
I shot the Albatross.

57. **ken:** here, saw. 62. **swound:** swoon, fainting spell. 67. **eat** (ĕt): eaten (an old form). 75. **shroud:** a line supporting the mast. 76. **vespers:** evening prayers.

Samuel Taylor Coleridge   305

"The Sun now rose upon the right:
Out of the sea came he,
Still hid in mist, and on the left   85
Went down into the sea.

And the good south wind still blew behind,
But no sweet bird did follow,
Nor any day for food or play
Came to the mariners' hollo!   90

And I had done a hellish thing,
And it would work 'em woe:
For all averred, I had killed the bird
That made the breeze to blow.
'Ah wretch!' said they, 'the bird to slay,   95
That made the breeze to blow!'

Nor dim nor red, like God's own head,
The glorious Sun uprist:
Then all averred, I had killed the bird
That brought the fog and mist.   100
' 'Twas right,' said they, 'such birds to slay,
That bring the fog and mist.'

The fair breeze blew, the white foam flew,
The furrow followed free;
We were the first that ever burst   105
Into that silent sea.

Down dropped the breeze, the sails dropped down,
'Twas sad as sad could be;
And we did speak only to break
The silence of the sea!   110

All in a hot and copper sky,
The bloody Sun, at noon,
Right up above the mast did stand,
No bigger than the Moon.

His shipmates cry out against the ancient Mariner, for killing the bird of good luck.

But when the fog cleared off, they justify the same, and thus make themselves accomplices in the crime.

The fair breeze continues; the ship enters the Pacific Ocean, and sails northward, even till it reaches the Line.

The ship hath been suddenly becalmed.

Day after day, day after day,   115
We stuck, nor breath nor motion;
As idle as a painted ship
Upon a painted ocean.

Water, water, everywhere,
And all the boards did shrink;   120
Water, water, everywhere
Nor any drop to drink.

The very deep did rot: O Christ!
That ever this should be!
Yea, slimy things did crawl with legs   125
Upon the slimy sea.

About, about, in reel and rout
The death-fires danced at night;
The water, like a witch's oils,
Burnt green, and blue, and white.   130

And some in dreams assured were
Of the Spirit that plagued us so:
Nine fathom deep he had followed us
From the land of mist and snow.

And every tongue, through utter drought,   135
Was withered at the root;
We could not speak, no more than if
We had been choked with soot.

Ah! well a-day! what evil looks
Had I from old and young!   140
Instead of the cross, the Albatross
About my neck was hung.

* **Josephus . . . Psellus:** Josephus Flavius (37?–100) and Michael Psellus
(sĕl'ŭs) (11th century) were historians.

PART III

"There passed a weary time. Each throat
Was parched, and glazed each eye.
A weary time! a weary time!   145
How glazed each weary eye,
When looking westward, I beheld
A something in the sky.

*The ancient
Mariner
beholdeth a
sign in the
element
afar off.*

At first it seemed a little speck,
And then it seemed a mist;   150
It moved and moved, and took at last
A certain shape, I wist.°

A speck, a mist, a shape, I wist!
And still it neared and neared:
As if it dodged a water-sprite,   155
It plunged and tacked and veered.

*At its nearer
approach, it
seemeth him
to be a ship;
and at a dear
ransom he
freeth his
speech from
the bonds of
thirst.*

With throats unslaked, with black lips baked,
We could nor laugh nor wail;
Through utter drought all dumb we stood!
I bit my arm, I sucked the blood,   160
And cried, 'A sail! a sail!'

With throats unslaked, with black lips baked,
Agape they heard me call;

A flash of joy;

Gramercy!° they for joy did grin,
And all at once their breath drew in,   165
As they were drinking all.

*And horror
follows. For
can it be a
ship that
comes onward
without wind
or tide?*

'See! see! (I cried) she tacks° no more!
Hither to work us weal;°
Without a breeze, without a tide,
She steadies with upright keel!'   170

---

152. **wist:** knew.   164. **Gramercy:** an exclamation of thankfulness.
167. **tacks:** turns.   168. **weal:** benefit.

The western wave was all a-flame;
The day was well nigh done!
Almost upon the western wave
Rested the broad bright Sun;
When that strange shape drove suddenly   175
Betwixt us and the Sun.

And straight the Sun was flecked with bars,
(Heaven's Mother send us grace!)
As if through a dungeon-grate he peered
With broad and burning face.   180

Alas! (thought I, and my heart beat loud)
How fast she nears and nears!
Are those her sails that glance in the Sun,
Like restless gossameres?°

Are those her ribs through which the Sun   185
Did peer, as through a grate?
And is that Woman all her crew?
Is that a Death? and are there two?
Is Death that woman's mate?

Her lips were red, her looks were free,°   190
Her locks were yellow as gold:
Her skin was as white as leprosy,
The nightmare Life-in-Death was she,
Who thicks man's blood with cold.

The naked hulk alongside came,   195
And the twain were casting dice;
'The game is done! I've won! I've won!'
Quoth she, and whistles thrice.

The Sun's rim dips; the stars rush out;
At one stride comes the dark;   200
With far-heard whisper, o'er the sea,
Off shot the specter-bark.

184. **gossameres:** a film of cobwebs.   190. **free:** wild.

Samuel Taylor Coleridge   309

We listened and looked sideways up!
Fear at my heart, as at a cup,
My life-blood seemed to sip!   205
The stars were dim, and thick the night,
The steersman's face by his lamp gleamed white;
From the sails the dew did drip—
At the rising   Till clomb° above the eastern bar
of the Moon,
The hornèd Moon, with one bright star   210
Within the nether° tip.

One after   One after one, by the star-dogged Moon,
another,
Too quick for groan or sigh,
Each turned his face with a ghastly pang,
And cursed me with his eye.   215

Four times fifty living men,
His shipmates   (And I heard nor sigh nor groan)
drop down
dead.   With heavy thump, a lifeless lump,
They dropped down one by one.

But Life-in-   The souls did from their bodies fly—   220
Death begins
her work on   They fled to bliss or woe!
the ancient
Mariner.   And every soul, it passed me by,
Like the whizz of my cross-bow!

PART IV

The Wedding-   "I fear thee, ancient Mariner!
Guest feareth
that a Spirit   I fear thy skinny hand!   225
is talking
to him;   And thou art long, and lank, and brown,
As is the ribbed sea-sand.

I fear thee and thy glittering eye,
But the   And thy skinny hand, so brown."
ancient
Mariner   "Fear not, fear not, thou Wedding-Guest!   230
assureth him   This body dropped not down.

209. **clomb:** climbed.   211. **nether:** lower.

of his bodily
life, and
proceedeth to
relate his
horrible
penance.
Alone, alone, all, all alone,
Alone on a wide, wide sea!
And never a saint took pity on
My soul in agony.   235

The many men, so beautiful!
And they all dead did lie:
And a thousand thousand slimy things
Lived on; and so did I.

I looked upon the rotting sea,   240
And drew my eyes away;
I looked upon the rotting deck,
And there the dead men lay.

I looked to heaven, and tried to pray;
But or° ever a prayer had gushed,   245
A wicked whisper came, and made
My heart as dry as dust.

I closed my lids, and kept them close,
And the balls like pulses beat;
For the sky and the sea, and the sea and the sky
Lay like a load on my weary eye,   251
And the dead were at my feet.

But the curse
liveth for him
in the eye of
the dead men.
The cold sweat melted from their limbs,
Nor rot nor reek did they:
The look with which they looked on me   255
Had never passed away.

In his
loneliness and
fixedness he
yearneth
toward the
journeying
Moon, and
An orphan's curse would drag to hell
A spirit from on high;
But oh! more horrible than that
Is the curse in a dead man's eye!   260

245. or: before.

Samuel Taylor Coleridge   311

the stars that
still sojourn,
yet still move
onward; and
everywhere
the blue sky
belongs to
them, and is
their
appointed
rest, and their
native country
and their own
natural
homes, which
they enter
unannounced,
as lords that
are certainly
expected and
yet there is a
silent joy at
their arrival.

Seven days, seven nights, I saw that curse,
And yet I could not die.

The moving Moon went up the sky,
And nowhere did abide:
Softly she was going up,   265
And a star or two beside—

Her beams bemocked° the sultry main,
Like April hoar-frost spread;
But where the ship's huge shadow lay,
The charmèd water burnt alway   270
A still and awful red.

By the light
of the Moon
he beholdeth
God's crea-
tures of the
great calm.

Beyond the shadow of the ship,
I watched the water-snakes:
They moved in tracks of shining white,
And when they reared, the elfish light   275
Fell off in hoary° flakes.

Within the shadow of the ship
I watched their rich attire:
Blue, glossy green, and velvet black,
They coiled and swam; and every track   280
Was a flash of golden fire.

Their beauty
and their
happiness.
He blesseth
them in
his heart.

O happy living things! no tongue
Their beauty might declare:
A spring of love gushed from my heart,
And I blessed them unaware: 285
Sure my kind saint took pity on me,
And I blessed them unaware.

The selfsame moment I could pray;
The spell
begins
to break.
And from my neck so free
The Albatross fell off, and sank   290
Like lead into the sea.

267. bemocked: mocked at. 276. hoary: white.

PART V

"Oh sleep! it is a gentle thing,
Beloved from pole to pole!
To Mary Queen the praise be given!
She sent the gentle sleep from Heaven,   295
That slid into my soul.

By grace of the holy Mother, the ancient Mariner is refreshed with rain.

The silly° buckets on the deck,
That had so long remained,
I dreamt that they were filled with dew;
And when I awoke, it rained.   300

My lips were wet, my throat was cold,
My garments all were dank;
Sure I had drunken in my dreams,
And still my body drank.

I moved, and could not feel my limbs;   305
I was so light—almost
I thought that I had died in sleep,
And was a blessed ghost.

He heareth sounds and seeth strange sights and commotions in the sky and the element.

And soon I heard a roaring wind:
It did not come anear;   310
But with its sound it shook the sails,
That were so thin and sere.°

The upper air burst into life!
And a hundred fire-flags sheen,°
To and fro they were hurried about!   315
And to and fro, and in and out,
The wan stars danced between.

And the coming wind did roar more loud,
And the sails did sigh like sedge!°

297. silly: empty.   312. sere: worn.   314. fire-flags sheen: bright flashes of lightning.   319. sedge: a coarse, grassy plant.

Samuel Taylor Coleridge   313

And the rain poured down from one black cloud   320
The Moon was at its edge.

The thick black cloud was cleft, and still
The Moon was at its side:
Like waters shot from some high crag,
The lightning fell with never a jag,   325
A river steep and wide.

The loud wind never reached the ship,
Yet now the ship moved on!

The bodies of
the ship's
crew are   Beneath the lightning and the Moon
inspired, and   The dead men gave a groan.   330
the ship
moves on;

They groaned, they stirred, they all uprose,
Nor spake, nor moved their eyes;
It had been strange, even in a dream,
To have seen those dead men rise.

The helmsman steered, the ship moved on;   335
Yet never a breeze up blew;
The mariners all 'gan work the ropes,
Where they were wont to do;
They raised their limbs like lifeless tools—
We were a ghastly crew.   340

The body of my brother's son
Stood by me, knee to knee:
The body and I pulled at one rope
But he said nought to me."

But not by
the souls of
the men, nor   "I fear thee, ancient Mariner!"   345
by daemons   "Be calm, thou Wedding-Guest!
of earth or
middle air,   'Twas not those souls that fled in pain,
but by a   Which to their corses came again,
blessed troop
of angelic   But a troop of spirits blest:

For when it dawned—they dropped their arms,
And clustered round the mast;   351
Sweet sounds rose slowly through their mouths,
And from their bodies passed.

Around, around, flew each sweet sound,
Then darted to the Sun;   355
Slowly the sounds came back again,
Now mixed, now one by one.

Sometimes a-dropping from the sky
I heard the skylark sing;
Sometimes all little birds that are,   360
How they seemed to fill the sea and air
With their sweet jargoning!

And now 'twas like all instruments,
Now like a lonely flute;
And now it is an angel's song,   365
That makes the heavens be mute.

It ceased; yet still the sails made on
A pleasant noise till noon,
A noise like of a hidden brook
In the leafy month of June,   370
That to the sleeping woods all night
Singeth a quiet tune.

Till noon we quietly sailed on,
Yet never a breeze did breathe:
Slowly and smoothly went the ship,   375
Moved onward from beneath.

The lonesome
Spirit from
the South Pole
carries on the
ship as far as
the Line, in
obedience to
the angelic
troop, but still
requireth
vengeance.
Under the keel nine fathom deep,
From the land of mist and snow,
The Spirit slid: and it was he
That made the ship to go.   380
The sails at noon left off their tune,
And the ship stood still also.

Samuel Taylor Coleridge   315

The Sun, right up above the mast,
Had fixed her to the ocean:
But in a minute she 'gan stir,   385
With a short uneasy motion—
Backwards and forwards half her length
With a short uneasy motion.

Then like a pawing horse let go,
She made a sudden bound: 390
It flung the blood into my head,
And I fell down in a swound.

*The Polar
Spirit's
fellow-
daemons, the
invisible
inhabitants of
the element,
take part in
his wrong;
and two of
them relate,
one to the
other, that
penance long
and heavy for
the ancient
Mariner hath
been accorded
to the Polar
Spirit, who
returneth
southward.*
How long in that same fit I lay,
I have not to declare;°
But ere my living life returned,   395
I heard and in my soul discerned
Two voices in the air.

'Is it he?' quoth one, 'Is this the man?
By Him who died on cross,
With his cruel bow he laid full low   400
The harmless Albatross.

The Spirit who bideth by himself
In the land of mist and snow,
He loved the bird that loved the man
Who shot him with his bow.'   405

The other was a softer voice,
As soft as honey-dew:
Quoth he, 'The man hath penance done,
And penance more will do.'

PART VI

First Voice

" 'But tell me, tell me! speak again,   410
Thy soft response renewing—

394. I . . . declare: I cannot say.

What makes that ship drive on so fast?
What is the ocean doing?'

Second Voice

'Still as a slave before his lord,
The ocean hath no blast;   415
His great bright eye most silently
Up to the Moon is cast—

If he may know which way to go;
For she guides him smooth or grim.
See, brother, see! how graciously   420
She looketh down on him.'

First Voice

*The Mariner
hath been
cast into a
trance; for the
angelic power
causeth the
vessel to drive
northward
faster than
human life
could endure.*

'But why drives on that ship so fast,
Without or wave or wind?'

Second Voice

'The air is cut away before,
And closes from behind.   425

Fly brother, fly! more high, more high!
Or we shall be belated:
For slow and slow that ship will go,
When the Mariner's trance is abated.'

*The super-
natural
motion is
retarded; the
Mariner
awakes, and
his penance
begins anew.*

I woke, and we were sailing on   430
As in a gentle weather:
'Twas night, calm night, the moon was high,
The dead men stood together.

All stood together on the deck,
For a charnel-dungeon° fitter: 435
All fixed on me their stony eyes,
That in the Moon did glitter.

435. **charnel-dungeon:** tomb.

Samuel Taylor Coleridge   317

The pang, the curse, with which they died,
Had never passed away:
I could not draw my eyes from theirs,   440
Nor turn them up to pray.

And now this spell was snapped: once more
I viewed the ocean green,
And looked far forth, yet little saw
Of what had else been seen—   445

Like one, that on a lonesome road
Doth walk in fear and dread,
And having once turned round walks on,
And turns no more his head;
Because he knows a frightful fiend   450
Doth close behind him tread.

But soon there breathed a wind on me,
Nor sound nor motion made:
Its path was not upon the sea,
In ripple or in shade.   455

It raised my hair, it fanned my cheek
Like a meadow-gale of spring—
It mingled strangely with my fears,
Yet it felt like a welcoming.

Swiftly, swiftly flew the ship,   460
Yet she sailed softly too:
Sweetly, sweetly blew the breeze—
On me alone it blew.

Oh! dream of joy! is this indeed
The lighthouse top I see?   465
Is this the hill? is this the kirk?
Is this mine own countree?

We drifted o'er the harbor-bar,
And I with sobs did pray—
O let me be awake, my God!   470
Or let me sleep alway.

The harbor-bay was clear as glass,
So smoothly it was strewn!
And on the bay the moonlight lay,
And the shadow of the Moon.   475

The rock shone bright, the kirk no less,
That stands above the rock:
The moonlight steeped in silentness
The steady weathercock.

The angelic
spirits leave
the dead
bodies,

And the bay was white with silent light   480
Till rising from the same,
Full many shapes, that shadows were,
In crimson colors came.

A little distance from the prow
Those crimson shadows were: 485
I turned my eyes upon the deck—
Oh, Christ! what saw I there!

Each corse lay flat, lifeless and flat,
And, by the holy rood!°
A man all light, a seraph-man,   490

And appear
in their own
forms of light.

On every corse there stood.

This seraph-band, each waved his hand;
It was a heavenly sight!
They stood as signals to the land,
Each one a lovely light;   495

This seraph-band, each waved his hand,
No voice did they impart—

489. **holy rood:** the cross.

No voice; but oh! the silence sank
Like music on my heart.

But soon I heard the dash of oars,   500
I heard the Pilot's cheer;
My head was turned perforce away,
And I saw a boat appear.

The Pilot and the Pilot's boy,
I heard them coming fast: 505
Dear Lord in Heaven! it was a joy
The dead men could not blast.

I saw a third—I heard his voice:
It is the Hermit good!
He singeth loud his godly hymns   510
That he makes in the wood.
He'll shrieve° my soul; he'll wash away
The Albatross's blood.

PART VII

The Hermit
of the Wood

"This Hermit good lives in that wood
Which slopes down to the sea.   515
How loudly his sweet voice he rears!
He loves to talk with marineres°
That come from a far countree.

He kneels at morn, and noon, and eve—
He hath a cushion plump: 520
It is the moss that wholly hides
The rotted old oak-stump.

The skiff-boat neared: I heard them talk,
'Why, this is strange, I trow!°
Where are those lights so many and fair,   525
That signal made but now?'

512. shrieve: absolve, relieve of a burden.   517. marineres: The spelling
indicates the pronunciation.   524. trow: think.

'Strange, by my faith!' the Hermit said—
'And they answered not our cheer!
The planks look warped! and see those sails,
How thin they are and sere!   530
I never saw aught like to them,
Unless perchance it were

Brown skeletons of leaves that lag
My forest-brook along;
When the ivy-tod° is heavy with snow,   535
And the owlet whoops to the wolf below,
That eats the she-wolf's young.'

'Dear Lord! it hath a fiendish look—
(The Pilot made reply)
I am a-feared.' 'Push on, push on!'   540
Said the Hermit cheerily.

The boat came closer to the ship,
But I nor spake nor stirred;
The boat came close beneath the ship,
And straight a sound was heard.   545

Under the water it rumbled on,
Still louder and more dread:
It reached the ship, it split the bay;
The ship went down like lead.

The ancient
Mariner is
saved in the
Pilot's boat.

Stunned by that loud and dreadful sound,   550
Which sky and ocean smote,
Like one that hath been seven days drowned
My body lay afloat;
But swift as dreams, myself I found
Within the Pilot's boat.   555

535. **ivy-tod:** ivy-bush.

Samuel Taylor Coleridge   321

Upon the whirl, where sank the ship,
The boat spun round and round;
And all was still, save that the hill
Was telling of the sound.

I moved my lips—the Pilot shrieked   560
And fell down in a fit;
The holy Hermit raised his eyes,
And prayed where he did sit.

I took the oars: the Pilot's boy,
Who now doth crazy go,   565
Laughed loud and long, and all the while
His eyes went to and fro.
'Ha! ha!' quoth he, 'full plain I see,
The Devil knows how to row.'

And now, all in my own countree,   570
I stood on the firm land!
The Hermit stepped forth from the boat,
And scarcely he could stand.

The ancient Mariner earnestly entreateth the Hermit to shrieve him; and the penance of life falls on him.

'O shrieve me, shrieve me, holy man!'
The Hermit crossed his brow.   575
'Say quick,' quoth he, 'I bid thee say—
What manner of man art thou?'

Forthwith this frame of mine was wrenched
With a woeful agony,
Which forced me to begin my tale;   580
And then it left me free.

And ever and anon throughout his future life an agony constraineth him to travel from land to land,

Since then, at an uncertain hour,
That agony returns:
And till my ghastly tale is told,
This heart within me burns.   585

I pass, like night, from land to land;
I have strange power of speech;
That moment that his face I see,
I know the man that must hear me:
To him my tale I teach. 590

What loud uproar bursts from that door!
The wedding-guests are there:
But in the garden-bower the bride
And bridemaids singing are:
And hark the little vesper bell 595
Which biddeth me to prayer!

O Wedding-Guest! this soul hath been
Alone on a wide, wide sea;
So lonely 'twas, that God himself
Scarce seemèd there to be. 600

O sweeter than the marriage-feast,
'Tis sweeter far to me,
To walk together to the kirk
With a goodly company!

To walk together to the kirk, 605
And all together pray,
While each to his great Father bends,
Old men, and babes, and loving friends,
And youths and maidens gay!

And to teach,
by his own
example, love
and reverence
to all things
that God
made and
loveth.
Farewell, farewell! but this I tell 610
To thee, thou Wedding-Guest!
He prayeth well, who loveth well
Both man and bird and beast.

He prayeth best, who loveth best
All things both great and small; 615
For the dear God who loveth us,
He made and loveth all."

Samuel Taylor Coleridge 323

The Mariner, whose eye is bright,
Whose beard with age is hoar,
Is gone: and now the Wedding-Guest   620
Turned from the Bridegroom's door.

He went like one that hath been stunned,
And is of sense forlorn:
A sadder and a wiser man,
He rose the morrow morn.   625

Kubla Khan

Or, A Vision in a Dream

"Kubla Khan" was quite literally a "vision in a dream."
Coleridge's own account of its composition tells us that he fell
asleep while reading the *Pilgrimage*, the colorful travel accounts of the sixteenth-century writer, Samuel Purchas. While
he was asleep, Coleridge dreamed two or three hundred lines
of a poem inspired by Purchas' description of Kubla Khan's
palace. When he awoke, he began to write down the poem.
He was unfortunately interrupted before he could finish, and
when he returned to the poem, he found that he could recall
no more of the dream.

In Xanadu did Kubla Khan
    A stately pleasure-dome decree:
Where Alph, the sacred river, ran
Through caverns measureless to man
    Down to a sunless sea.   5
So twice five miles of fertile ground
With walls and towers were girdled round:
And here were gardens bright with sinuous rills
Where blossomed many an incense-bearing tree,
And here were forests ancient as the hills,   10
Enfolding sunny spots of greenery.

But oh! that deep romantic chasm which slanted
Down the green hill athwart a cedarn cover!

A savage place! as holy and enchanted
As e'er beneath a waning moon was haunted   15
By woman wailing for her demon-lover!
And from this chasm, with ceaseless turmoil seething,
As if this earth in fast thick pants were breathing,
A mighty fountain momently° was forced,
Amid whose swift half-intermitted burst   20
Huge fragments vaulted like rebounding hail,
Or chaffy grain beneath the thresher's flail:°
And 'mid these dancing rocks at once and ever
It flung up momently the sacred river.
Five miles meandering with a mazy motion   25
Through wood and dale the sacred river ran,
Then reached the caverns measureless to man,
And sank in tumult to a lifeless ocean:
And 'mid this tumult Kubla heard from far
Ancestral voices prophesying war!   30

    The shadow of the dome of pleasure
    Floated midway on the waves;
    Where was heard the mingled measure
    From the fountain and the caves.
It was a miracle of rare device,   35
A sunny pleasure-dome with caves of ice!
    A damsel with a dulcimer°
    In a vision once I saw:
    It was an Abyssinian maid,
    And on her dulcimer she played,   40
    Singing of Mount Abora.
    Could I revive within me
    Her symphony and song,
    To such a deep delight 'twould win me,
That with music loud and long,   45
I would build that dome in air,

19. **momently:** at every moment. 22. **flail:** an instrument for threshing
grain by hand. The grain is beaten with the flail until the chaff (the husks) is
separated. 37. **dulcimer:** a stringed instrument, played with light hammers.

Samuel Taylor Coleridge   325

That sunny dome! those caves of ice!
And all who heard should see them there,
And all should cry, Beware! Beware!
His flashing eyes, his floating hair!   50
Weave a circle round him thrice,
And close your eyes with holy dread,
For he on honey-dew hath fed,
And drunk the milk of Paradise.

Questions

The Rime of the Ancient Mariner

1. Re-read lines 614–617. Is this whole poem a statement of specifically Christian theology? For instance, is the mariner's punishment justified by his crime? What about the fate of the rest of the crew?
2. The incredible events of the story are merely presented, never explained or justified. What effect does this have on our understanding and acceptance of the poem?
3. Do the stanzas become monotonous? If not, why not? What are some of the variations that Coleridge has introduced into the ballad stanza?
4. Notice that each of the first six parts ends with a reference to the albatross. What is the effect of this device?

Kubla Khan

This poem is usually praised primarily for its rich imagery and music. Although it is apparently only a fragment, is it merely a vivid description or does it have some kind of meaning? Consider the following questions in reaching your decision.

1. The first thirty-six lines describe the palace and its setting. The final section introduces the "damsel with a dulcimer" and also the speaker of the poem—the "I." What connection (if any) has the damsel with the preceding lines? with the whole poem?
2. Notice the contrasts in the first section: the "sunny pleasure-dome" and the "caves of ice"; the "tumultuous river" and the "lifeless ocean." Are there any other contrasts? Is there anything in contrast to the "ancestral voices prophesying war"?
3. What is the significance of the last six lines? of lines 42–47? In what sense could "Kubla Khan" be called a poem *about* poetry? *about* the poetic imagination?

WALTER SAVAGE LANDOR

1775–1864

Though Landor lived through the entire Romantic period, and in fact well past the end of it, his poetry often seems to be closer to the eighteenth century in spirit. He shared many of the political ideas that were current in his time, but in his writings he revealed his love of the classical ideals of order and restraint. One of his last works was a translation into English of a number of poems that he had originally written in Latin. Besides his poetry, Landor is also known for *Imaginary Dialogues,* a series of fictional prose dialogues between famous historical figures.

One Year Ago

One year ago my path was green,
My footstep light, my brow serene;
Alas! and could it have been so
    One year ago?

There is a love that is to last   5
When the hot days of youth are past:
Such love did a sweet maid bestow
    One year ago.

I took a leaflet from her braid
And gave it to another maid.   10
Love! broken should have been thy bow
    One year ago.

Past Ruin'd Ilion *

Past ruin'd Ilion Helen° lives,
    Alcestis° rises from the shades;
Verse calls them forth; 'tis verse that gives
    Immortal youth to mortal maids.

* **Ilion:** Troy.   1. **Helen:** see. p. 179.   2. **Alcestis** (ăl·sĕs′tĭs): in Greek legend, a bride who volunteered to die in place of her husband.

Soon shall oblivion's deepening veil   5
Hide all the peopled hills you see,
The gay, the proud, while lovers hail
These many summers you and me.

Questions

1. What is the tone of "One Year Ago"? What is the effect of the brief refrain?
2. Have you read any other poems in this book that have a theme similar to "Past Ruin'd Ilion"? What are they? What do you think the last stanza means?

GEORGE GORDON, LORD BYRON

1788–1824

At Cambridge, where he became notorious for his reckless living, Byron published his first volume of poems, *Hours of Idleness*. The book was criticized severely (with some reason) by the *Edinburgh Review*, and Byron, in reply, wrote his first major poem, "English Bards and Scotch Reviewers," a biting satire on the critics and on some contemporary poets.

After some years of travel through Europe and Asia Minor, he returned to England and published the first portions of a long narrative poem, *Childe Harold's Pilgrimage*. The poem caused a sensation. Byron himself said, "I awoke one morning and found myself famous." *Childe Harold's Pilgrimage* was followed by several similar narratives about lonely and romantic young men—a type that has come to be known as the "Byronic hero."

Byron left England in 1816 to live in Switzerland and Italy. In 1819 he began *Don Juan*, a long narrative combining the heroic and the satiric, perhaps his most characteristic work. He was the only Romantic poet who was successful at satire, and it is not surprising that Pope was one of his favorite poets. He was working on the seventeenth book of *Don Juan* at the time of his death.

Byron was deeply interested in the cause of individual freedom, and when Greece, which was dominated at that time by Turkey, began to fight for independence, Byron determined to contribute to the fight. He joined the Greek army but died of fever before he could get into action.

from *Childe Harold's Pilgrimage*

There is a pleasure in the pathless woods,
There is rapture on the lonely shore,
There is society, where none intrudes,
By the deep sea, and music in its roar:
I love not man the less, but nature more,   5
From these our interviews, in which I steal
From all I may be, or have been before,
To mingle with the universe, and feel
What I can ne'er express, yet can not all conceal.

Roll on, thou deep and dark blue ocean—roll!   10
Ten thousand fleets sweep over thee in vain;
Man marks the earth with ruin—his control
Stops with the shore; upon the watery plain
The wrecks are all thy deed, nor doth remain
A shadow of man's ravage, save his own,°   15
When, for a moment, like a drop of rain,
He sinks into thy depths with bubbling groan,
Without a grave, unknelled, uncoffined, and unknown.

His steps are not upon thy paths—thy fields
Are not a spoil for him—thou dost arise   20
And shake him from thee; the vile strength he wields
For earth's destruction thou dost all despise,
Spurning him from thy bosom to the skies,
And send'st him, shivering in thy playful spray
And howling, to his gods, where haply lies   25
His petty hope in some near port or bay,
And dashest him again to earth: there let him lay.

15. **save his own:** except his own (destruction).

George Gordon, Lord Byron   329

from *Don Juan*

In *Don Juan* (Byron pronounced it jōō'·än), the poet traces
the romantic adventures of the legendary Spanish lover. But
Byron constantly interrupts the narrative to engage in satire,
parody, or plain comedy. The following passages illustrate
some of the characteristics of this rambling mock epic.

> My poem's epic, and is meant to be
>   Divided in twelve books; each book containing,
> With love, and war, a heavy gale at sea,
>   A list of ships, and captains, and kings reigning,
> New characters; the episodes are three: 5
>   A panoramic view of Hell's in training,
> After the style of Virgil and of Homer,
> So that my name of epic's no misnomer.
>
> All these things will be specified in time,
>   With strict regard to Aristotle's rules,°   10
> The *Vade Mecum*° of the true sublime,
>   Which makes so many poets, and some fools:
> Prose poets like blank verse, I'm fond of rhyme,
>   Good workmen never quarrel with their tools;
> I've got new mythological machinery,   15
> And very handsome supernatural scenery.
>
> There's only one slight difference between
>   Me and my epic brethren gone before,
> And here the advantage is my own, I ween
>   (Not that I have not several merits more,   20
> But this will more peculiarly be seen);
>   They so embellish, that 'tis quite a bore
> Their labyrinth of fables to thread through,
> Whereas this story's actually true.

10. **Aristotle's rules:** in his *Poetics* the Greek philosopher had described the
successful practices of the poets and dramatists of his time. These descriptive
statements eventually came to be taken as "rules" for the composition of imaginative works.   11. *Vade Mecum* (vä'dĕ mē'kŭm): handbook (Latin, literally "go with me").

If any person doubt it, I appeal   25
    To history, tradition, and to facts,
To newspapers, whose truth all know and feel,
    To plays in five, and operas in three acts;
All these confirm my statement a good deal,
    But that which more completely faith exacts   30
Is, that myself, and several now in Seville,
Saw Juan's last elopement with the devil.

                    •   •   •

But for the present, gentle reader! and
    Still gentler purchaser! the bard—that's I—
Must, with permission, shake you by the hand,   35
    And so your humble servant, and good-by!
We meet again, if we should understand
    Each other; and if not, I shall not try
Your patience further than by this short sample—
'Twere well if others followed my example.   40

"Go, little book, from this my solitude!
    I cast thee on the waters—go thy ways!
And if, as I believe, thy vein be good,
    The world will find thee after many days."
When Southey's° read, and Wordsworth understood,   45
    I can't help putting in my claim to praise—
The four first rhymes are Southey's, every line:
For God's sake, reader! take them not for mine!

45. **Southey:** Robert Southey (1774–1843), a mediocre poet of the time.

She Walks in Beauty

She walks in beauty, like the night
    Of cloudless climes and starry skies,
And all that's best of dark and bright
    Meet in her aspect and her eyes,
Thus mellowed to that tender light   5
    Which heaven to gaudy day denies.

One shade the more, one ray the less,
　　Had half impaired the nameless grace
Which waves in every raven tress,
　　Or softly lightens o'er her face,　　　　　　　　　10
Where thoughts serenely sweet express
　　How pure, how dear their dwelling place.

And on that cheek and o'er that brow
　　So soft, so calm, yet eloquent,
The smiles that win, the tints that glow,　　　　　15
　　But tell of days in goodness spent,
A mind at peace with all below,
　　A heart whose love is innocent.

So, We'll Go No More A-Roving

So, we'll go no more a-roving
　　So late into the night,
Though the heart be still as loving,
　　And the moon be still as bright.

For the sword outwears its sheath,　　　　　　　5
　　And the soul wears out the breast,
And the heart must pause to breathe,
　　And love itself have rest.

Though the night was made for loving,
　　And the day returns too soon,　　　　　　　　10
Yet we'll go no more a-roving
　　By the light of the moon.

Questions

1. Compare Byron's view of nature in the stanzas from *Childe Harold's
   Pilgrimage* to Wordsworth's view in "Tintern Abbey." What about the
   two poets' views of man? How do they differ?

2. Byron wrote that *Don Juan* was "meant to be a little quietly facetious upon everything." What humorous devices has Byron used in these lines? How does the form of the poem (specifically, its rhyme scheme) contribute to its humor? Would the poem be as effective in blank verse? in heroic couplets? Why, or why not?
3. Compare "She Walks in Beauty" and "So, We'll Go No More A-Roving." Which poem do you prefer? Why? How do these two lyrics compare with some of the Elizabethan songs you have read? Explain your answer.

PERCY BYSSHE SHELLEY

1792–1822

Shelley's father was a conservative, practical man who never understood his somewhat eccentric son. The difficulties between the two increased through the years. To Shelley, his father eventually came to stand for everything he disliked, and much of his poetry is concerned with his revolt against the conservative, conventional standards his father had accepted.

Shelley entered Oxford in 1810 but was expelled a year later after he published a pamphlet called *On the Necessity of Atheism.* A short time later, when only nineteen, he married the sixteen-year-old Harriet Westbrook. The two then went to Ireland, where they distributed radical political pamphlets. Shelley returned to London and remained for a few years, but after Harriet's death he married again and went to live in Italy. It was in that country that he met Byron. The two men, unlike in most ways, shared many of the same political ideas, and they became close friends. A month before his thirtieth birthday, Shelley was sailing in the Gulf of Leghorn when a squall struck his boat and capsized it. Ten days later his body was washed ashore. He was cremated and his ashes were buried in Rome, next to the grave of Keats.

Two themes recur in Shelley's poetry: the possibility of a perfect society and the power of ideal love. Probably the most visionary of the Romantics, at his best he is a poet of great power.

Ode to the West Wind

I

O wild West Wind, thou breath of autumn's being,
Thou, from whose unseen presence the leaves dead
Are driven, like ghosts from an enchanter fleeing,

Yellow, and black, and pale, and hectic red,
Pestilence-stricken multitudes: O thou,   5
Who chariotest to their dark wintry bed

The wingèd seeds, where they lie cold and low,
Each like a corpse within its grave, until
Thine azure sister of the spring° shall blow

Her clarion° o'er the dreaming earth, and fill   10
(Driving sweet buds like flocks to feed in air)
With living hues and odors plain and hill:

Wild Spirit, which art moving everywhere;
Destroyer and preserver; hear, oh, hear!

II

Thou on whose stream, mid the steep sky's commotion,   15
Loose clouds like earth's decaying leaves are shed,
Shook from the tangled boughs of heaven and ocean,

Angels° of rain and lightning: there are spread
On the blue surface of thine aëry surge,
Like the bright hair uplifted from the head   20

Of some fierce Maenad,° even from the dim verge
Of the horizon to the zenith's° height,
The locks of the approaching storm. Thou dirge

9. **sister of the spring:** the south wind. 10. **clarion:** a trumpet with a high, clear tone. 18. **Angels:** here, messengers. 21. **Maenad** (me'năd): In ancient Greek religion Maenads were priestesses of the god Dionysus. 22. **zenith:** the point in the heavens directly overhead.

Of the dying year, to which this closing night
Will be the dome of a vast sepulcher,   25
Vaulted with all thy congregated might

Of vapors, from whose solid atmosphere
Black rain, and fire, and hail will burst: oh, hear!

III

Thou who didst waken from his summer dreams
The blue Mediterranean, where he lay,   30
Lulled by the coil of his crystálline streams,

Beside a pumice° isle in Baiae's° bay,
And saw in sleep old palaces and towers
Quivering within the wave's intenser day,

All overgrown with azure moss and flowers   35
So sweet, the sense faints picturing them! Thou
For whose path the Atlantic's level powers

Cleave themselves into chasms, while far below
The sea-blooms and the oozy woods which wear
The sapless foliage of the ocean, know   40

Thy voice, and suddenly grow gray with fear,
And tremble and despoil themselves: oh, hear!

IV

If I were a dead leaf thou mightest bear;
If I were a swift cloud to fly with thee;
A wave to pant beneath thy power, and share   45

The impulse of thy strength, only less free
Than thou, O uncontrollable! If even
I were as in my boyhood, and could be

32. **pumice:** formed from lava. **Baiae's** (bä'yäs) **bay:** a bay near Naples.

Percy Bysshe Shelley   335

The comrade of thy wanderings over heaven,
As then, when to outstrip thy skiey speed   50
Scarce seemed a vision;° I would ne'er have striven

As thus with thee in prayer in my sore need.
Oh, lift me as a wave, a leaf, a cloud!
I fall upon the thorns of life! I bleed!

A heavy weight of hours has chained and bowed   55
One too like thee: tameless, and swift, and proud.

V

Make me thy lyre, even as the forest is:
What if my leaves are falling like its own!
The tumult of thy mighty harmonies

Will take from both a deep, autumnal tone,   60
Sweet though in sadness. Be thou, Spirit fierce,
My spirit! Be thou me, impetuous one!

Drive my dead thoughts over the universe
Like withered leaves to quicken a new birth!
And, by the incantation of this verse,   65

Scatter, as from an unextinguished hearth
Ashes and sparks, my words among mankind!
Be through my lips to unawakened earth

The trumpet of a prophecy! O, wind,
If winter comes, can spring be far behind?   70

51. **vision:** that is, something unattainable.

To a Skylark

Hail to thee, blithe spirit!
Bird thou never wert,
That from heaven, or near it,
Pourest thy full heart
In profuse strains of unpremeditated art.   5

Higher still and higher
From the earth thou springest
Like a cloud of fire;
The blue deep thou wingest,
And singing still dost soar, and soaring ever singest.   10

In the golden lightning
Of the sunken sun,
O'er which clouds are bright'ning,
Thou dost float and run;
Like an unbodied joy whose race is just begun.   15

The pale purple even°
Melts around thy flight;
Like a star of heaven
In the broad daylight
Thou art unseen, but yet I hear thy shrill delight,   20

Keen as are the arrows
Of that silver sphere,°
Whose intense lamp narrows
In the white dawn clear,
Until we hardly see, we know that it is there.   25

All the earth and air
With thy voice is loud,
As, when night is bare,
From one lonely cloud
The moon rains out her beams, and heaven is overflowed.   30

What thou art we know not;
What is most like thee?
From rainbow clouds there flow not
Drops so bright to see
As from thy presence showers a rain of melody.   35

16. **even:** evening.   22. **silver sphere:** the morning star.

Percy Bysshe Shelley   337

Like a poet hidden
   In the light of thought,
Singing hymns unbidden,
   Till the world is wrought
To sympathy with hopes and fears it heeded not: 40

Like a high-born maiden
   In a palace tower,
Soothing her love-laden
   Soul in secret hour
With music sweet as love, which overflows her bower: 45

Like a glowworm golden
   In a dell of dew,
Scattering unbeholden
   Its aërial hue
Among the flowers and grass which screen it from the view: 50

Like a rose embowered
   In its own green leaves,
By warm winds deflowered,
   Till the scent it gives
Makes faint with too much sweet these heavy-wingèd thieves: 55

Sound of vernal° showers
   On the twinkling grass,
Rain-awakened flowers,
   All that ever was
Joyous, and clear, and fresh, thy music doth surpass.   60

Teach us, sprite or bird,
   What sweet thoughts are thine;
I have never heard
   Praise of love or wine
That panted forth a flood of rapture so divine: 65

56. **vernal:** spring.

Chorus Hymeneal,°
Or triumphal chaunt,
Matched with thine, would be all
But an empty vaunt,°
A thing wherein we feel there is hidden want.   70

What objects are the fountains°
Of thy happy strain?
What fields, or waves, or mountains?
What shapes of sky or plain?
What love of thine own kind? what ignorance of pain?   75

With thy clear keen joyance
Languor cannot be—
Shadow of annoyance
Never came near thee:
Thou lovest—but ne'er knew love's sad satiety.   80

Waking or asleep,
Thou of death must deem°
Things more true and deep
Than we mortals dream,
Or how could thy notes flow in such a crystal stream?   85

We look before and after
And pine for what is not:
Our sincerest laughter
With some pain is fraught;
Our sweetest songs are those that tell of saddest thought.   90

Yet if we could scorn
Hate, and pride, and fear;
If we were things born
Not to shed a tear,
I know not how thy joy we ever should come near.   95

66. **Chorus Hymeneal** (hĭ′mĕ·nē′ăl): marriage chant. (Hymen was the
Greek god of marriage.) 69. **vaunt:** boast. 71. **fountains:** sources (of inspiration). 82. **deem:** know.

Better than all measures
Of delightful sound—
Better than all treasures
That in books are found—
Thy skill to poet were,° thou scorner of the ground!   100

Teach me half the gladness
That thy brain must know,
Such harmonious madness
From my lips would flow,
The world should listen then—as I am listening now.   105

100. **were:** would be.

A Widow Bird

A widow bird sate mourning for her love
    Upon a wintry bough;
The frozen wind crept on above,
    The freezing stream below.

There was no leaf upon the forest bare,   5
    No flower upon the ground,
And little motion in the air
    Except the mill-wheel's sound.

Sonnet: England in 1819

An old, mad, blind, despised, and dying king°—
Princes, the dregs of their dull race, who flow
Through public scorn—mud from a muddy spring—
Rulers who neither see, nor feel, nor know,
But leech-like to their fainting country cling,   5

1. **An old . . . king:** George III had been insane since 1810. He died in 1820.

Till they drop, blind in blood, without a blow—
A people starved and stabbed in the untilled field—
An army, which liberticide° and prey
Makes as a two-edged sword to all who wield—
Golden and sanguine° laws which tempt and slay;   10
Religion Christless, Godless—a book sealed;
A Senate—time's worst statute° unrepealed—
Are graves, from which a glorious phantom° may
Burst, to illumine our tempestuous day.

8. **liberticide:** killer of liberty. 10. **sanguine:** red like blood. 12. **statute:** probably the laws limiting the rights of Catholics. These, and a number of other repressive laws, were modified or repealed in 1829 and in the Reform Act of 1832. 13. **phantom:** freedom.

Questions

Ode to the West Wind

1. The first three sections each describe the effect of the wind on an aspect of nature. What do sections IV and V deal with? What does the west wind seem to symbolize? What is the significance of the question in the last line?
2. Analyze the fabric of this poem, including as many of the sound devices discussed in Chapter VIII (pp. 101–26) as you can find. What is the effect of the various devices?

To a Skylark

1. How is "To a Skylark" related in thought to "Ode to the West Wind"? How does it differ in structure? Why is the structure of each poem appropriate to its content and tone?
2. Compare "To a Skylark" to "Nightingales," by Robert Bridges (p. 52). How are the poems alike? How do they differ?

Shorter Poems

1. Discuss the function of the imagery in "A Widow Bird."
2. What is the tone of "England in 1819"? This sonnet is one long sentence. What is the effect of this unusual punctuation? How is the conclusion of this poem similar to the conclusion of "Ode to the West Wind"?

JOHN KEATS

1795–1821

Keats was the son of a London livery-stable keeper. At sixteen he was apprenticed to a surgeon. He continued in this profession for five years, but his interests were turning more and more toward poetry. His strongest early influence was the poetry of Spenser—in fact one of his earliest poems was entitled "Imitation of Spenser." When he was twenty-one he went to London to continue his medical studies in London hospitals. There he met Leigh Hunt, a well-known poet and journalist of the day, who printed Keats' "Sonnet to Solitude" in his weekly paper, *The Examiner*. Encouraged by the publication, Keats gave up medicine to devote himself completely to poetry. He published his first volume of poetry the next year and then began work on a long poem, *Endymion*. When it was published in 1818, *Endymion* was attacked by some reviewers, and Shelley later felt that the attack was the cause of Keats' early death. The fact is that Keats himself recognized the defects in the poem and set about to perfect his art. In the first six months of 1819 he turned out a series of masterpieces, including "The Eve of St. Agnes," "Ode on a Grecian Urn," and "Ode to a Nightingale." In less than half a year, he had produced enough to rank as a major poet.

In February, 1820, he began to show signs of tuberculosis, the disease that had taken the lives of his brother and mother. He journeyed to Rome in the hope of preserving his health, but he died in February of 1821, eight months before his twenty-sixth birthday.

On First Looking into Chapman's Homer

At twenty-one, just as Keats was beginning his poetic career, he came upon a translation of Homer by the Elizabethan poet and dramatist, George Chapman. Keats and a friend, Charles Clarke, stayed up all night reading the work; this sonnet, one of the poet's first mature poems, was written the next morning.

Much have I traveled in the realms of gold,
  And many goodly states and kingdoms seen;
  Round many western islands have I been
Which bards in fealty° to Apollo° hold.
Oft of one wide expanse° had I been told,   5
  That deep-browed Homer ruled as his demesne;°
  Yet did I never breathe its pure serene°
Till I heard Chapman speak out loud and bold:
Then felt I like some watcher of the skies
  When a new planet swims into his ken;   10
Or like stout Cortez° when with eagle eyes
  He stared at the Pacific—and all his men
Looked at each other with a wild surmise—
  Silent, upon a peak in Darien.°

4. **fealty:** faithfulness. **Apollo:** see page 259. 5. **wide expanse:** literally, the Mediterranean Sea, over which Odysseus roamed; figuratively, the "world" of epic poetry, which Homer dominated. 6. **demesne** (dê·mēn'): domain, realm. 7. **serene:** air. 11. **Cortez:** Hernando Cortez, the conqueror of Mexico; actually, it was Vasco Balboa who discovered the Pacific. 14. **Darien:** Panama.

La Belle Dame sans Merci

Keats' handling of the ballad form in this poem is notable for its economy and its skillful use of detail. Also notable is the way in which the narrative suggests a number of symbolic or allegorical meanings. (The title means "the beautiful lady without pity.")

"O what can ail thee, knight-at-arms,
  Alone and palely loitering?
The sedge° has withered from the lake,
  And no birds sing.

"O what can ail thee, knight-at-arms,   5
  So haggard and so woebegone?
The squirrel's granary is full,
  And the harvest's done.

3. **sedge:** grasslike plants.

"I see a lily on thy brow
 With anguish moist and fever dew,   10
And on thy cheeks a fading rose
 Fast withereth too."

"I met a lady in the meads,°
 Full beautiful—a fairy's child,
Her hair was long, her foot was light,   15
 And her eyes were wild.

"I made a garland for her head,
 And bracelets too, and fragrant zone;°
She looked at me as she did love,
 And made sweet moan.   20

"I set her on my pacing steed
 And nothing else saw all day long,
For sidelong would she bend, and sing
 A fairy's song.

"She found me roots of relish sweet,   25
 And honey wild and manna dew,°
And sure in language strange she said
 'I love the true.'

"She took me to her elfin grot,°
 And there she wept, and sighed full sore,   30
And there I shut her wild wild eyes
 With kisses four.

"And there she lullèd me asleep,
 And there I dreamed—Ah! woe betide!
The latest dream I ever dreamed   35
 On the cold hill side.

---

13. **meads:** meadows. 18. **zone:** belt. 26. **manna dew:** a miraculously supplied food (the term appears in this sense in the Bible); the word may also refer to some type of drug. 29. **grot:** cave.

"I saw pale kings and princes too,
    Pale warriors, death-pale were they all:
They cried—'La Belle Dame sans Merci
    Hath thee in thrall!'°   40

"I saw their starved lips in the gloam
    With horrid warning gapèd wide,
And I awoke, and found me here
    On the cold hill side.

"And this is why I sojourn here   45
    Alone and palely loitering,
Though the sedge is withered from the lake,
    And no birds sing."

40. thrall: slavery.

To Autumn

I

Season of mists and mellow fruitfulness,
    Close bosom-friend of the maturing sun;
Conspiring with him how to load and bless
    With fruit the vines that round the thatch-eaves run;
To bend with apples the mossed cottage-trees,   5
    And fill all fruit with ripeness to the core;
        To swell the gourd, and plump the hazel shells
    With a sweet kernel; to set budding more,
And still more, later flowers for the bees,
Until they think warm days will never cease,   10
        For summer has o'er-brimmed their clammy cells.

II

Who hath not seen thee oft amid thy store?
    Sometimes whoever seeks abroad may find
    Thee sitting careless on a granary floor,

Thy hair soft-lifted by the winnowing° wind;   15
Or on a half-reaped furrow sound asleep,
   Drowsed with the fume of poppies, while thy hook
   Spares the next swath and all its twinèd flowers:
And sometimes like a gleaner° thou dost keep
   Steady thy laden head across a brook;   20
   Or by a cider-press,° with patient look,
      Thou watchest the last oozings hours by hours.

                              III

Where are the songs of spring? Ay, where are they?
   Think not of them, thou hast thy music too,
While barrèd clouds bloom the soft-dying day,   25
   And touch the stubble-plains with rosy hue;
Then in a wailful choir the small gnats mourn
   Among the river sallows,° borne aloft
   Or sinking as the light wind lives or dies;
And full-grown lambs loud bleat from hilly bourn;°   30
   Hedge-crickets sing; and now with treble soft
   The red-breast whistles from a garden-croft;°
      And gathering swallows twitter in the skies.

15. **winnowing:** to "winnow" grain is to fan it or blow it to separate the
chaff. Thus the "winnowing wind" in this line is imagined as blowing softly
through the hair of autumn.   19. **gleaner:** one who goes through a field following the reapers and gathering the grain they have missed.   21. **cider-press:**
a device which squeezes the juice from apples.   28. **sallows:** willows.
30. **bourn:** here, region.   32. **garden-croft:** a small garden next to a cottage.

Questions

On First Looking into Chapman's Homer

In the octave of this sonnet Keats uses geographical imagery. What
do these images stand for? What does line four mean? What two
similes does Keats use in the sestet?

La Belle Dame sans Merci

Could this story have an allegorical or symbolic interpretation? If so,
what might it be? Is there enough evidence in the poem itself to allow

us to make a firm decision on what it suggests symbolically? Does it matter particularly, or does the poem profit by being vague in certain respects?

To Autumn

1. Is this a purely descriptive poem? Is there any passing of time during the poem? Is there any development of thought? Is there a theme?
2. Discuss in detail Keats' use of rhythm.
3. What are some of the particularly vivid images? Is there anything significant about the *kinds* of images Keats uses? (See the second stanza, for example.)

THE VICTORIAN POETS

During the reign of Queen Victoria (1837–1901), England developed an enormous colonial empire and became the dominant world power. It was a period of great industrial expansion and wealth for some, but also a period of great poverty for many others. It was a time of optimism and faith in progress, but toward the end of the century many writers criticized the early Victorians as materialistic and unconcerned with anything but their own welfare. It was an era of religious revival, but also an era that witnessed a great conflict between science and religion, much of it centering on Darwin's theory of evolution.

Early in the period, most of the poets continued in the Romantic tradition, with Shelley being perhaps the greatest influence. Later, there came to be less emphasis on ideal beauty and emotional fervor and a growing concern with domestic life and social problems. During the last twenty years of the century, a variety of new "schools" of poetry began to develop, most of them in revolt against the beliefs and practices of their predecessors.

ALFRED, LORD TENNYSON

1809–1892

Tennyson attended Cambridge and while still an undergraduate published *Poems, Chiefly Lyrical*. But perhaps the most significant event in his Cambridge career was his close friendship with Arthur Henry Hallam, whose strong religious faith helped resolve many of the doubts the young Tennyson was experiencing.

Poems by Alfred Tennyson, published in 1832, contained some of the poet's best work, but the book was severely attacked by many of the same critics who had attacked Keats. For ten years Tennyson published no new work. Part of the reason for the long silence was undoubtedly the critical attacks, but the major cause was the death, in 1833, of Arthur Hallam, an event that had a profound effect on Tennyson. *In Memoriam,* his elegy of Hallam, was composed over many years and finally published in 1850.

A few years before the publication of *In Memoriam,* Tennyson had published a two-volume collection of poetry which firmly established his reputation. Wordsworth, who was then poet laureate, called him "the first of our living poets." In 1850, after Wordsworth's death, Tennyson was named poet laureate.

In the reaction against Victorianism which began at the end of the century, Tennyson was the target of many bitter attacks. It is true that his poorer poems often reflect the sentimentality and shallow beliefs of the period, but this is not true of his greatest work. Furthermore, his craftsmanship—his control of rhythm, rhyme, melody, of all the resources of language—ranks him the equal of the greatest technical perfectionists in the language—Shakespeare, Spenser, Milton, and Keats. Our own century has seen him regain his place as a major poet.

Ulysses

In this dramatic monologue Ulysses (the Latin version of the Greek "Odysseus") is pictured years after the adventures Homer relates in the *Odyssey.*

<blockquote>
It little profits that an idle king,
By this still hearth, among these barren crags,
Matched with an aged wife, I mete and dole°
Unequal laws unto a savage race,
That hoard, and sleep, and feed, and know not me.   5
I cannot rest from travel: I will drink
Life to the lees:° all times I have enjoyed
Greatly, have suffered greatly, both with those
That loved me, and alone; on shore, and when
</blockquote>

3. **mete and dole:** measure and give out.   7. **lees:** dregs, that which settles to the bottom of a cup.

Through scudding drifts the rainy Hyades°
Vexed the dim sea. I am become a name;
For always roaming with a hungry heart
Much have I seen and known: cities of men
And manners, climates, councils, governments,
Myself not least, but honored of them all—   15
And drunk delight of battle with my peers,
Far on the ringing plains of windy Troy.
I am a part of all that I have met;
Yet all experience is an arch wherethrough
Gleams that untraveled world, whose margin fades   20
For ever and for ever when I move.
How dull it is to pause, to make an end,
To rust unburnished, not to shine in use!
As though to breathe were life. Life piled on life
Were all too little, and of one to me   25
Little remains: but every hour is saved
From that eternal silence, something more,
A bringer of new things; and vile it were
For some three suns to store and hoard myself,
And this gray spirit yearning in desire   30
To follow knowledge, like a sinking star,
Beyond the utmost bound of human thought.

    This is my son, mine own Telemachus,°
To whom I leave the scepter and the isle—°
Well-loved of me, discerning to fulfill   35
This labor, by slow prudence to make mild
A rugged people, and through soft degrees
Subdue them to the useful and the good.
Most blameless is he, centered in the sphere
Of common duties, decent not to fail   40
In offices of tenderness, and pay
Meet adoration to my household gods,
When I am gone. He works his work, I mine.
    There lies the port: the vessel puffs her sail:

---

10. Hyades (hī′á-dēz): stars in the constellation Tarus, supposed to bring
rain.   33. Telemachus (tê-lĕm′á-kŭs): Ulysses' son would now be of an age to
rule.   34. isle: Ithaca, off the west coast of Greece, was Ulysses' kingdom.

There gloom the dark broad seas. My mariners,   45
Souls that have toiled, and wrought, and thought with me—
That ever with a frolic welcome took
The thunder and the sunshine, and opposed
Free hearts, free foreheads—you and I are old;
Old age hath yet his honor and his toil;   50
Death closes all: but something ere the end,
Some work of noble note, may yet be done,
Not unbecoming men that strove with gods.
The lights begin to twinkle from the rocks:
The long day wanes: the slow moon climbs: the deep   55
Moans round with many voices. Come, my friends,
'Tis not too late to seek a newer world.
Push off, and sitting well in order smite
The sounding furrows; for my purpose holds
To sail beyond the sunset, and the baths   60
Of all the western stars, until I die.
It may be that the gulfs will wash us down:
It may be we shall touch the Happy Isles,°
And see the great Achilles,° whom we knew.
Though much is taken, much abides; and though   65
We are not now that strength which in old days
Moved earth and heaven, that which we are, we are—
One equal temper of heroic hearts,
Made weak by time and fate, but strong in will
To strive, to seek, to find, and not to yield.   70

63. **Happy Isles:** where heroes went after death (also called the Elysian Fields). 64. **Achilles** (*à·kĭl'ēz*): one of the Greek heroes of the Trojan War, in which Ulysses also fought.

The Lotos-Eaters *

This poem is based on a short passage in Homer's *Odyssey:*
". . . on the tenth day we made the country of the Lotus-eaters, a race that live on vegetable foods. We disembarked

* **Lotos-Eaters:** the word *lotos* (more commonly, *lotus*) now generally refers to the water-lily. In the *Odyssey*, however, the word apparently refers to a plant or fruit that yields some narcotic-like drug.

to draw water, and my crews quickly set to on their midday meal by the ships. But as soon as we had had a mouthful and a drink, I sent some of my followers inland to find out what sort of human beings might be there, detailing two men for the duty with a third as messenger. Off they went, and it was not long before they were in touch with the Lotus-eaters. Now it never entered the heads of these natives to kill my friends; what they did was to give them some lotus to taste, and as soon as each had eaten the honeyed fruit of the plant, all thoughts of reporting to us or escaping were banished from his mind. All they now wished for was to stay where they were with the Lotus-eaters, to browse on the lotus and to forget that they had a home to return to." *

The Choric Song beginning at line 46 is sung by the men who have eaten the lotus.

"Courage!" he° said, and pointed toward the land,
"This mounting wave will roll us shoreward soon."
In the afternoon they came unto a land
In which it seemed always afternoon.
All round the coast the languid air did swoon,   5
Breathing like one that hath a weary dream.
Full-faced above the valley stood the moon;
And like a downward smoke, the slender stream
Along the cliff to fall and pause and fall did seem.

A land of streams! some, like a downward smoke,   10
Slow-dropping veils of thinnest lawn,° did go;
And some through wavering lights and shadows broke,
Rolling a slumbrous sheet of foam below.
They saw the gleaming river seaward flow
From the inner land: far off, three mountain tops,   15
Three silent pinnacles of aged snow,
Stood sunset-flushed: and, dewed with showery drops,
Up-clomb the shadowy pine above the woven copse.°

1. **he:** Ulysses.   11. **lawn:** linen.   18. **copse:** a small wood or thicket.

* From *The Odyssey*, translated by E. V. Rieu. Reprinted by permission of Penguin Books Ltd.

The charmèd sunset lingered low adown
In the red West: through mountain clefts the dale   20
Was seen far inland, and the yellow down
Bordered with palm, and many a winding vale
And meadow, set with slender galingale;°
A land where all things always seemed the same!
And round about the keel with faces pale,   25
Dark faces pale against that rosy flame,
The mild-eyed melancholy Lotos-eaters came.

Branches they bore of that enchanted stem,
Laden with flower and fruit, whereof they gave
To each, but whoso did receive of them,   30
And taste, to him the gushing of the wave
Far far away did seem to mourn and rave
On alien shores; and if his fellow spake,
His voice was thin, as voices from the grave;
And deep-asleep he seemed, yet all awake,   35
And music in his ears his beating heart did make.

They sat them down upon the yellow sand,
Between the sun and moon upon the shore;
And sweet it was to dream of Fatherland,
Of child, and wife, and slave; but evermore   40
Most weary seemed the sea, weary the oar,
Weary the wandering fields of barren foam.
Then someone said, "We will return no more";
And all at once they sang, "Our island home°
Is far beyond the wave; we will no longer roam."   45

Choric Song

I

There is sweet music here that softer falls
Than petals from blown roses on the grass,
Or night-dews on still waters between walls
Of shadowy granite, in a gleaming pass;

23. galingale: grasslike plants.   44. island home: Ithaca.

Alfred, Lord Tennyson   353

Music that gentlier on the spirit lies,　　　　　50
Than tired eyelids upon tired eyes;
Music that brings sweet sleep down from the blissful skies.
Here are cool mosses deep,
And through the moss the ivies creep,
And in the stream the long-leaved flowers weep,　　　55
And from the craggy ledge the poppy hangs in sleep.

II

Why are we weighed upon with heaviness,
And utterly consumed with sharp distress,
While all things else have rest from weariness?
All things have rest: why should we toil alone,　　　60
We only toil, who are the first of things,
And make perpetual moan,
Still from one sorrow to another thrown:
Nor ever fold our wings,
And cease from wanderings,　　　65
Nor steep our brows in slumber's holy balm;
Nor hearken what the inner spirit sings,
"There is no joy but calm!"
Why should we only toil, the roof and crown of things?

III

Lo! in the middle of the wood,　　　70
The folded leaf is wooed from out the bud
With winds upon the branch, and there
Grows green and broad, and takes no care,
Sun-steeped at noon, and in the moon
Nightly dew-fed; and turning yellow　　　75
Falls, and floats adown the air.
Lo! sweetened with the summer light,
The full-juiced apple, waxing over-mellow,
Drops in a silent-autumn night.
All its allotted length of days,　　　80
The flower ripens in its place,
Ripens and fades, and falls, and hath no toil,
Fast-rooted in the fruitful soil.

Hateful is the dark blue sky,
Vaulted o'er the dark blue sea.   85
Death is the end of life; ah, why
Should life all labor be?
Let us alone. Time driveth onward fast,
And in a little while our lips are dumb.
Let us alone. What is it that will last?   90
All things are taken from us, and become
Portions and parcels of the dreadful past.
Let us alone. What pleasure can we have
To war with evil? Is there any peace
In ever climbing up the climbing wave?   95
All things have rest, and ripen toward the grave
In silence—ripen, fall and cease:
Give us long rest or death, dark death, or dreamful ease.

V

How sweet it were, hearing the downward stream,
With half-shut eyes ever to seem   100
Falling asleep in a half-dream!
To dream and dream, like yonder amber light,
Which will not leave the myrrh-bush° on the height;
To hear each other's whispered speech;
Eating the lotos day by day,   105
To watch the crisping ripples on the beach,
And tender curving lines of creamy spray;
To lend our hearts and spirits wholly
To the influence of mild-minded melancholy;
To muse and brood and live again in memory,   110
With those old faces of our infancy
Heaped over with a mound of grass,
Two handfuls of white dust, shut in an urn of brass!°

---

103. **myrrh** (mûr)-**bush:** a small tree or shrub that produces a gum used in perfumes or incense. 113. **shut . . . brass:** the ancient Greek manner of burial.

Alfred, Lord Tennyson   355

VI

Dear is the memory of our wedded lives,
And dear the last embraces of our wives   115
And their warm tears: but all hath suffered change;
For surely now our household hearths are cold:
Our sons inherit us: our looks are strange:
And we should come like ghosts to trouble joy.
Or else the island princes over-bold   120
Have eat° our substance, and the minstrel sings
Before them of the ten years' war in Troy,
And our great deeds, as half-forgotten things.
Is there confusion in the little isle?
Let what is broken so remain.   125
The gods are hard to reconcile:
'Tis hard to settle order once again.
There *is* confusion worse than death,
Trouble on trouble, pain on pain,
Long labor unto aged breath,   130
Sore task to hearts worn out with many wars
And eyes grown dim with gazing on the pilot-stars.

VII

But, propped on beds of amaranth° and moly,°
How sweet (while warm airs lull us, blowing lowly)
With half-dropped eyelid still,   135
Beneath a heaven dark and holy,
To watch the long bright river drawing slowly
His waters from the purple hill—
To hear the dewy echoes calling
From cave to cave through the thick-twinèd vine—   140
To watch the emerald-colored water falling
Through many a woven acanthus°-wreath divine!
Only to hear and see the far-off sparkling brine,
Only to hear were sweet, stretched out beneath the pine.

121. **eat** (ĕt): eaten. 133. **amaranth** (ăm′a̍·rănth): large purple or crimson flowers. **moly**: an herb of legendary supernatural powers. 142. **acanthus** (a̍·kăn′thŭs): an herb.

The lotos blooms below the barren peak: 145
The lotos blows by every winding creek:
All day the wind breathes low with mellower tone:
Through every hollow cave and alley lone
Round and round the spicy downs the yellow lotos dust is blown.
We have had enough of action, and of motion we,   150
Rolled to starboard, rolled to larboard, when the surge was seething
    free,
Where the wallowing monster spouted his foam-fountains in the sea.
Let us swear an oath, and keep it with an equal mind,
In the hollow Lotos-land to live and lie reclined
On the hills like gods together, careless of mankind.   155
For they lie beside their nectar, and the bolts are hurled
Far below them in the valleys, and the clouds are lightly curled
Round their golden houses, girdled with the gleaming world:
Where they smile in secret, looking over wasted lands,
Blight and famine, plague and earthquake, roaring deeps and fiery
    sands,   160
Clanging fights, and flaming towns, and sinking ships, and praying
    hands.
But they smile, they find a music centered in a doleful song
Steaming up, a lamentation and an ancient tale of wrong,
Like a tale of little meaning though the words are strong;
Chanted from an ill-used race of men that cleave the soil,   165
Sow the seed, and reap the harvest with enduring toil,
Storing yearly little dues of wheat, and wine and oil;
Till they perish and they suffer—some, 'tis whispered—down in hell
Suffer endless anguish, others in Elysian valleys dwell,
Resting weary limbs at last on beds of asphodel.°   170
Surely, surely, slumber is more sweet than toil, the shore
Than labor in the deep midocean, wind and wave and oar;
Oh, rest ye, brother mariners, we will not wander more.

   170. asphodel (ăs'fô·dĕl): one of the plants of the lily family; here, perhaps
the narcissus.

from *In Memoriam*

In Memoriam, Tennyson's long elegy for Arthur Hallam, is actually a series of loosely related brief lyrics. The separate sections are held together by the common theme of grief, but, more important, they combine to form a record of Tennyson's progress from profund religious doubt to a final renewal of belief. The following excerpts indicate to some extent the stages in that progress.

Old yew, which graspest at the stones
   That name the under-lying dead,
   Thy fibers net the dreamless head;
Thy roots are wrapped about the bones.

The seasons bring the flower again,   5
   And bring the firstling to the flock;
   And in the dusk of thee, the clock
Beats out the little lives of men.

O not for thee the glow, the bloom,
   Who changest not in any gale,   10
   Nor branding summer suns avail
To touch thy thousand years of gloom:

And gazing on thee, sullen tree,
   Sick for thy stubborn hardihood,
   I seem to fail from out my blood,   15
And grow incorporate° into thee.

       •   •   •

Dark house,° by which once more I stand
   Here in the long unlovely street,
   Doors, where my heart was used to beat
So quickly, waiting for a hand,   20

16. **incorporate:** united in one body.   17. **house:** Hallam's house in London.

A hand that can be clasped no more—
    Behold me, for I cannot sleep,
    And like a guilty thing I creep
At earliest morning to the door.

He is not here; but far away   25
    The noise of life begins again,
    And ghastly through the drizzling rain
On the bald street breaks the blank day.

•   •   •

Ring out, wild bells, to the wild sky,
    The flying cloud, the frosty light: 30
    The year is dying in the night;
Ring out, wild bells, and let him die.

Ring out the old, ring in the new,
    Ring, happy bells, across the snow;
    The year is going, let him go;   35
Ring out the false, ring in the true.

Ring out the grief that saps the mind,
    For those that here we see no more;
    Ring out the feud of rich and poor,
Ring in redress to all mankind.   40

Ring out a slowly dying cause,
    And ancient forms of party strife;
    Ring in the nobler modes of life,
With sweeter manners, purer laws.

Ring out the want, the care, the sin,   45
    The faithless coldness of the times;
    Ring out, ring out my mournful rhymes,
But ring the fuller minstrel in.

Ring out false pride in place and blood,
    The civic slander and the spite;   50
    Ring in the love of truth and right,
Ring in the common love of good.

Alfred, Lord Tennyson 359

Ring out old shapes of foul disease,
　　Ring out the narrowing lust of gold;
　　Ring out the thousand wars of old,　　　　　　55
Ring in the thousand years of peace.

Ring in the valiant man and free,
　　The larger heart, the kindlier hand;
　　Ring out the darkness of the land,
Ring in the Christ that is to be.　　　　　　　60

· · ·

Dear friend, far off, my lost desire,
　　So far, so near in woe and weal;
　　O loved the most, when most I feel
There is a lower and a higher;

Known and unknown, human, divine;　　　　　　65
　　Sweet human hand and lips and eye;
　　Dear heavenly friend that canst not die,
Mine, mine, for ever, ever mine;

Strange friend, past, present, and to be;
　　Loved deeplier, darklier understood;　　　　70
　　Behold, I dream a dream of good,
And mingle all the world with thee.

· · ·

Thy voice is on the rolling air;
　　I hear thee where the waters run;
　　Thou standest in the rising sun,　　　　　　75
And in the setting thou art fair.

What art thou then? I cannot guess;
　　But though I seem in star and flower
　　To feel thee some diffusive power,
I do not therefore love thee less:　　　　　　80

My love involves the love before;
  My love is vaster passion now;
  Though mixed with God and Nature thou,
I seem to love thee more and more.

Far off thou art, but ever nigh;   85
  I have thee still, and I rejoice;
  I prosper, circled with thy voice;
I shall not lose thee though I die.

Questions

Ulysses

1. How does Ulysses feel about his adventures? How does he feel about
   the future? Is his longing for further travel simply a desire for more
   adventures, or is it something deeper? What does Ulysses mean when
   he says: "I am a part of all that I have met; / Yet all experience is
   an arch wherethrough / Gleams that untraveled world . . ."?
2. Tennyson lived in an age which accepted the idea of progress—which
   felt that the acquisition of knowledge must lead necessarily to a better
   world. Point to at least two passages which suggest that Tennyson's
   Ulysses also believes this.

The Lotos-Eaters

1. This poem clearly indicates Tennyson's technical mastery of the language. How does the music of the Choric Song express the mood of
   the singers? Discuss the technical aspects of the poem, especially the
   Choric Song. Be sure to point out examples of Tennyson's use of the
   sound devices outlined in Chapter VIII (pp. 102–26): rhythm,
   rhyme, assonance, consonance, euphony, etc. What is the accumulated
   effect of these devices?
2. What has Tennyson added to Homer's brief account of the Lotus-
   eaters? What has he left out? What is the effect of these additions and
   deletions?

FROM *In Memoriam*

1. Trace the progress from grief and despair to serenity and faith as seen
   in these selections. What is the tone of each section? the central idea?
2. All the sections are written in the same basic rhyme and rhythm patterns. What variations in fabric does Tennyson introduce to create
   different effects in each section?

EDWARD FITZGERALD

1809–1883

Fitzgerald attended Cambridge and, while there, gathered a group of remarkable friends, including Tennyson, the novelist William Makepeace Thackeray, and the historian Thomas Carlyle. Another friendship, with the Oriental scholar E. B. Cowell, became even more significant. Cowell introduced Fitzgerald to Persian literature, and this introduction led directly to Fitzgerald's translation of the *Rubáiyát* of the Persian poet, Omar Khayyám.

Khayyám was an astronomer and mathematician of the twelfth century. His poem was really a series of loosely related quatrains (*rubia*, plural, *rubáiyát*) expressing a nostalgia for the past, a skeptical attitude toward the present and future, and a general philosophy urging the enjoyment of the present day. Fitzgerald's translation was in many respects an original poem, for he arranged Khayyám's material freely and even added much of his own to the poem.

from *The Rubáiyát of Omar Khayyám of Naishápúr*

Wake! For the sun who scattered into flight
The stars before him from the field of night,
    Drives night along with them from Heav'n, and strikes
The sultan's turret with a shift of light.

Before the phantom of false morning° died,   5
Methought a voice within the tavern cried,
    "When all the temple is prepared within,
Why nods the drowsy worshipper outside?"

And, as the cock crew, those who stood before
The tavern shouted—"Open then the door!   10
    You know how little while we have to stay,
And, once departed, may return no more."

5. **false morning:** a light often seen on the horizon just before dawn.

Now the New Year° reviving old desires,
The thoughtful soul to solitude retires,
    Where the white hand of Moses° on the bough   15
Puts out, and Jesus from the ground suspires.°

Iram° indeed is gone with all his° rose,
And Jamshyd's° sev'n-ringed cup where no one knows;
    But still a ruby kindles in the vine,
And many a garden by the water blows.   20

And David's lips are locked; but in divine
High-piping Pehleví,° with "Wine! Wine! Wine!
    Red wine!"—the nightingale cries to the rose
That sallow cheek of hers to incarnadine.°

Come, fill the cup, and in the fire of spring   25
Your winter-garment of repentance fling:
    The bird of time has but a little way
To flutter—and the bird is on the wing.

Whether at Naishápúr° or Babylon,
Whether the cup with sweet or bitter run,   30
    The wine of life keeps oozing drop by drop,
The leaves of life keep falling one by one.

•   •   •

Why, all the saints and sages who discussed
Of the two worlds so wisely—they are thrust
    Like foolish prophets forth; their words to scorn   35
Are scattered, and their mouths are stopped with dust.

13. **New Year:** The Persian New Year began in the spring. 15. **white . . .
Moses:** Exodus 4:6 tells of the hand of Moses miraculously turning white.
The metaphor refers to the first appearance of blossoms on the bough.
16. **suspires:** breathes. (It was once believed that Jesus healed by breathing
on the sick.) 17. **Iram:** an ancient garden. **his:** its. 18. **Jamshyd** (jăm-
shĕd'): in Persian mythology, a supernatural being who became king of Persia. 22. **Pehleví** (pā'lĕ·vē): the language of ancient Persia. 24. **incarnadine**
(ĭn·kär'nà·dĭn): make red. 29. **Naishápúr:** Omar Khayyám's native village,
contrasted with the great city of Babylon.

Myself when young did eagerly frequent
Doctor and saint, and heard great argument
    About it and about: but evermore
Came out by the same door where in I went.   40

With them the seed of wisdom did I sow,
And with mine own hand wrought to make it grow;
    And this was all the harvest that I reaped—
"I came like water, and like wind I go."

                    •   •   •

Would but the desert of the fountain yield   45
One glimpse—if dimly, yet indeed, revealed,
    To which the fainting traveler might spring,
As springs the trampled herbage of the field!

Would but some wingèd angel ere too late
Arrest the yet unfolded roll of fate,   50
    And make the stern recorder otherwise
Enregister, or quite obliterate!

Ah love! could you and I with him° conspire
To grasp this sorry scheme of things entire,
    Would not we shatter it to bits—and then   55
Remold it nearer to the heart's desire!

                53. him: the "recorder" of l. 51.

Questions

1. What is the central idea of lines 1–32? How are lines 33–34 related
   to the previous lines?
2. What is the meaning of the last three quatrains? What is their tone?

ELIZABETH BARRETT BROWNING

1806–1861

Elizabeth Barrett Browning is best known today as the wife of
Robert Browning, but prior to her marriage, and even for some time
after it, she was a better-known poet than her husband. She was an
invalid for most of her life, and for a number of years before meeting Robert Browning, she was a virtual prisoner of her father, who
kept her confined to her home in the belief that he was safeguarding
her health. The story of Elizabeth's secret courtship by Browning,
and their marriage, is a famous one. It is the subject of a modern
play, *The Barretts of Wimpole Street*. Elizabeth Barrett Browning is
best known today for her *Sonnets from the Portuguese*, a sequence
of love sonnets addressed to her husband. "If Thou Must Love Me"
is perhaps the most famous sonnet from that sequence.

If Thou Must Love Me

If thou must love me, let it be for naught
Except for love's sake only. Do not say,
"I love her for her smile—her look—her way
Of speaking gently—for a trick of thought
That falls in well with mine, and certes° brought   5
A sense of pleasant ease on such a day"—
For these things in themselves, Belovèd, may
Be changed, or change for thee—and love, so wrought,
May be unwrought so. Neither love me for
Thine own dear pity's wiping my cheeks dry—   10
A creature might forget to weep, who bore
Thy comfort long, and lose thy love thereby!
But love me for love's sake, that evermore
Thou mayst love on, through love's eternity.

5. **certes** (sûr′tĕz): certainly.

In as many ways as you can, compare this sonnet with Shakespeare's Sonnet 116 (p. 189). Are the themes similar? If so, in what ways?

ROBERT BROWNING

1812–1889

Because Browning's parents were dissenters from the established church, he was prevented from entering either Oxford or Cambridge. Nevertheless, he became one of the best educated poets of his day. From his father's enormous library he amassed a store of knowledge—of the classics, the Middle Ages, the Renaissance, music, art, history, and philosophy—that he could not have acquired elsewhere. This mass of unusual knowledge is sometimes responsible for the difficulty and obscurity of his longer poems.

The most important event in Browning's life was his marriage to Elizabeth Barrett. Her father had refused to consent to the marriage, believing that it would destroy his daughter's frail health, but Elizabeth lived for fifteen years after the marriage, enjoying greater health than she had known since childhood. The Brownings lived in Italy during their marriage, and the joy of the years they spent together there is reflected in Browning's robust and optimistic poetry.

After his wife's death, Browning returned to England and began to enjoy some of the recognition he had earned after many years of work. The publication of *The Ring and the Book* (1868–69), his longest and most ambitious work, made him a public figure and led to the founding of a number of Browning Societies in England and America. In his last years he returned to Italy. He died in Venice.

Although Browning wrote many excellent lyric poems, his genius was most at home in the dramatic monologue. In all of his work, however, and not only in the monologues, Browning reveals his preoccupation with character and with dramatic situation, his interest in people rather than in nature.

Love Among the Ruins

The scene of this highly rhythmic monologue is the Campagna (kǎm·pän'yǎ), the open country surrounding Rome. The speaker is a shepherd anticipating his return to his home and his wife.

Where the quiet-colored end of evening smiles
    Miles and miles
On the solitary pastures where our sheep
    Half-asleep
Tinkle homeward through the twilight, stray or stop   5
    As they crop—
Was the site once of a city great and gay
    (So they say),
Of our country's very capital, its prince
    Ages since   10
Held his court in, gathered councils, wielding far
    Peace or war.

Now—the country does not even boast a tree
    As you see,
To distinguish slopes of verdure,° certain rills   15
    From the hills
Intersect and give a name to (else they run
    Into one),
Where the domed and daring palace shot its spires
    Up like fires   20
O'er the hundred-gated circuit of a wall
    Bounding all,
Made of marble, men might march on nor be pressed,
    Twelve abreast.

And such plenty and perfection, see, of grass   25
    Never was!
Such a carpet as, this summertime, o'erspreads
    And embeds

15. **verdure:** vegetation.

Every vestige of the city, guessed alone,°
 Stock or stone—   30
Where a multitude of men breathed joy and woe
 Long ago;
Lust of glory pricked their hearts up, dread of shame
 Struck them tame;
And that glory and that shame alike, the gold   35
 Bought and sold.

Now—the single little turret that remains
 On the plains,
By the caper° overrooted, by the gourd
 Overscored,°   40
While the patching houseleek's° head of blossom winks
 Through the chinks—
Marks the basement whence a tower in ancient time
 Sprang sublime,
And a burning ring, all round, the chariots traced 45
 As they raced,
And the monarch and his minions° and his dames
 Viewed the games.

And I know—while thus the quiet-colored eve
 Smiles to leave   50
To their folding, all our many tinkling fleece
 In such peace,
And the slopes and rills in undistinguished gray
 Melt away—
That a girl with eager eyes and yellow hair   55
 Waits me there
In the turret whence the charioteers caught soul
 For the goal,
When the king looked, where she looks now, breathless, dumb
 Till I come.   60

29. **guessed alone:** the location of the city can only be guessed at now, since the site is covered with grass. 39. **caper:** a shrub. 39–40. **gourd overscored:** the tower is marked ("scored") by a running vine. 41. **houseleek:** a plant with thick leaves and purple or yellow flowers. 47. **minions:** attendants or favorites.

But he looked upon the city, every side,
 Far and wide,
All the mountains topped with temples, all the glades'
 Colonnades,°
All the causeys,° bridges, aqueducts—and then,   65
 All the men!
When I do come, she will speak not, she will stand,
 Either hand
On my shoulder, give her eyes the first embrace
 Of my face,   70
Ere we rush, ere we extinguish sight and speech
 Each on each.

In one year they sent a million fighters forth
 South and North,
And they built their gods a brazen pillar high   75
 As the sky,
Yet reserved a thousand chariots in full force—
 Gold, of course.
Oh heart! oh blood that freezes, blood that burns!
 Earth's returns   80
For whole centuries of folly, noise and sin!
 Shut them in,
With their triumphs and their glories and the rest!
 Love is best.

63–64. glades' Colonnades: the trees seem to form a series of columns ("colonnades") around the open spaces in a wood. 65. causeys: causeways, raised highways.

The Laboratory

(Ancien régime)

The French subtitle (pron. än'syăn' rȧ'zhēm') means "the old order." It refers specifically to the period before the French Revolution, but Browning is using the term to indicate a less definite period in the past, probably sometime during

the Italian Renaissance. It was claimed that there were many
unsolved cases of poisoning among the nobility during the
Renaissance. The speaker here is talking to a chemist who is
obviously skilled in the mixing of poisons.

Now that I, tying thy glass mask° tightly,
My gaze through these faint smokes curling whitely,
As thou plyest thy trade in this devil's smithy—
Which is the poison to poison her prithee?

He is with her; and they know that I know   5
Where they are, what they do: they believe my tears flow
While they laugh, laugh at me, at me fled to the drear
Empty church to pray God in, for them!—I am here.

Grind away, moisten and mash up thy paste,
Pound at thy powder—I am not in haste!   10
Better sit thus, and observe thy strange things,
Than go where men wait me and dance at the King's.

That, in the mortar—you call it a gum?
Ah, the brave tree whence such gold oozings come!
And yonder soft phial, the exquisite blue,   15
Sure to taste sweetly—is that poison too?

Had I but all of them, thee and thy treasures,
What a wild crowd of invisible pleasures!
To carry pure death in an earring, a casket,°
A signet,° a fan-mount, a filigree basket!   20

Soon, at the King's a mere lozenge° to give
And Pauline should have just thirty minutes to live!
But to light a pastille,° and Elise, with her head
And her breast and her arms and her hands, should drop dead!

1. **glass mask:** for protection against poisonous gases. 19. **casket:** jewel
box. 20. **signet:** signet ring, a ring containing a family seal. (Rings, earrings,
etc. were considered good hiding places for poison.) 21. **lozenge:** a small piece
of candy. 23. **pastille:** here, a paste, burned to create a pleasing odor in a
room.

Quick—is it finished? The color's too grim!   25
Why not soft like the phial's, enticing and dim?
Let it brighten her drink, let her turn it and stir,
And try it and taste, ere she fix and prefer!

What a drop! She's not little, no minion° like me—
That's why she ensnared him: this never will free   30
The soul from those masculine eyes—say "no!"
To that pulse's magnificent come-and-go.

For only last night, as they whispered, I brought
My own eyes to beat on her so, that I thought
Could I keep them one half minute fixed, she would fall,   35
Shriveled; she fell not; yet this does it all!

Not that I bid you spare her the pain!
Let death be felt and the proof remain;
Brand, burn up, bite into its grace—
He is sure to remember her dying face!   40

Is it done? Take my mask off! Nay, be not morose;
It kills her, and this prevents seeing it close:
The delicate droplet, my whole fortune's fee—
If it hurts her, beside, can it ever hurt me?

Now, take all my jewels, gorge gold to your fill,   45
You may kiss me, old man, on my mouth if you will!
But brush this dust off me, lest horror it brings
Ere I know it—next moment I dance at the King's!

29. **minion:** here, a delicate person.

Porphyria's Lover

The rain set early in tonight,
    The sullen wind was soon awake,
It tore the elm-tops down for spite,
    And did its worst to vex the lake:
    I listened with heart fit to break.   5

Robert Browning   371

When glided in Porphyria; straight
    She shut the cold out and the storm,
And kneeled and made the cheerless grate
    Blaze up, and all the cottage warm;
    Which done, she rose, and from her form   10
Withdrew the dripping cloak and shawl,
    And laid her soiled gloves by, untied
Her hat and let the damp hair fall,
    And, last, she sat down by my side
    And called me. When no voice replied,   15
She put my arm about her waist,
    And made her smooth white shoulder bare,
And all her yellow hair displaced,
    And, stooping, made my cheek lie there,
    And spread, o'er all, her yellow hair,   20
Murmuring how she loved me—she
    Too weak, for all her heart's endeavor,
To set its struggling passion free
    From pride, and vainer ties dissever,
    And give herself to me forever.   25
But passion sometimes would prevail,
    Nor could tonight's gay feast restrain
A sudden thought of one so pale
    For love of her, and all in vain:
    So, she was come through wind and rain.   30
Be sure I looked up at her eyes
    Happy and proud; at last I knew
Porphyria worshiped me; surprise
    Made my heart swell, and still it grew
    While I debated what to do.   35
That moment she was mine, mine, fair,
    Perfectly pure and good: I found
A thing to do, and all her hair
    In one long yellow string I wound
    Three times her little throat around,   40
And strangled her. No pain felt she;
    I am quite sure she felt no pain.
As a shut bud that holds a bee,

I warily op'ed her lids: again
Laughed the blue eyes without a stain.   45
And I untightened next the tress
About her neck; her cheek once more
Blushed bright beneath my burning kiss:
I propped her head up as before,
Only, this time my shoulder bore   50
Her head, which droops upon it still:
The smiling rosy little head,
So glad it has its utmost will,
That all it scorned at once is fled,
And I, its love, am gained instead!   55
Porphyria's love: she guessed not how
Her darling one wish would be heard.
And thus we sit together now,
And all night long we have not stirred,
And yet God has not said a word!   60

Prospice

"Prospice" (prō·spĭk'ĭ) was written a short time after the
death of Elizabeth Barrett Browning. The closing lines refer to
her. The Latin title can be translated "look forward."

Fear death?—to feel the fog in my throat,
    The mist in my face,
When the snows begin, and the blasts denote
    I am nearing the place,
The power of the night, the press of the storm,   5
    The post of the foe;
Where he stands, the Arch Fear in a visible form,
    Yet the strong man must go:
For the journey is done and the summit attained,
    And the barriers fall,   10
Though a battle's to fight ere the guerdon° be gained,
    The reward of it all.

11. guerdon: reward.

I was ever a fighter, so—one fight more,
    The best and the last!
I would hate that death bandaged my eyes, and forebore,°
    And bade me creep past.   16
No! let me taste the whole of it, fare like my peers
    The heroes of old,
Bear the brunt, in a minute pay glad life's arrears°
    Of pain, darkness and cold.   20
For sudden the worst turns the best to the brave,
    The black minute's at end,
And the elements' rage, the fiend-voices that rave,
    Shall dwindle, shall blend,
Shall change, shall become first a peace out of pain,   25
    Then a light, then thy breast,
O thou soul of my soul! I shall clasp thee again,
    And with God be the rest!

15. **forbore:** held back, refrained from doing injury.   19. **arrears:** debts.

Questions

Love Among the Ruins

1. How many contrasts are presented in this poem? How is the theme related to these contrasts?
2. What is the metrical scheme of the poem? Are there any irregularities in the first stanza? If so, what are they?

The Laboratory

Who is the speaker? What is she planning to do? What, specifically, do we learn about her? How?

Porphyria's Lover

1. Why did the speaker strangle Porphyria? Why did he choose this particular moment for the murder? What might the last line mean?
2. What kind of poem is this? How is it like "The Laboratory"? How is it different?

Prospice

What attitude toward death is implied by this poem? How is the attitude indicated?

MATTHEW ARNOLD

1822–1888

Arnold was the son of the famous headmaster of Rugby School, Thomas Arnold. Matthew attended school under his father and later entered Oxford. After taking his degree he taught for a short time, entered politics briefly, and then took a government appointment as Inspector of Schools, a position he was to hold for thirty-five years. For ten years of this time he was also Professor of Poetry at Oxford, where his duties were light enough to allow him to continue his work for the government.

Arnold published his first volume of poetry in 1849. He continued to write poetry almost to the end of his life, but most of his major work had been published before he was thirty-five. From that point on, Arnold devoted most of his energies to literary and social criticism. He became, in fact, one of the major critics in English literature; in all of the nineteenth century only Coleridge can be considered his equal.

Perhaps because the mood of Arnold's poetry is consistently somber, he did not attain the popularity of his more optimistic contemporaries, Tennyson and Browning. He is, however, one of the major poets of the Victorian age.

To Marguerite

Yes: in the sea of life enisled,°
With echoing straits between us thrown,
Dotting the shoreless watery wild,
We mortal millions live *alone*.
The islands feel the enclasping flow,   5
And then their endless bounds they know.

But when the moon their hollows lights
And they are swept by balms of spring,

1. **enisled** (ĕn·īl'd'): made as an island, isolated.

And in their glens, on starry nights
The nightingales divinely sing,   10
And lovely notes, from shore to shore,
Across the sounds and channels pour;

Oh then a longing like despair
Is to their farthest caverns sent;
For surely once, they feel, we were   15
Parts of a single continent.
Now round us spreads the watery plain—
Oh might our marges° meet again!

Who ordered, that their longing's fire
Should be, as soon as kindled, cooled?   20
Who renders vain their deep desire?
A god, a god their severance ruled;
And bade betwixt their shores to be
The unplumbed, salt, estranging° sea.

18. **marges:** borders, shores.   24. **estranging:** separating.

Shakespeare

Others abide our question. Thou art free.
We ask and ask: thou smilest and art still,
Out-topping knowledge. For the loftiest hill
That to the stars uncrowns his majesty,
Planting his steadfast footsteps in the sea,   5
Making the heaven of heavens his dwelling-place,
Spares but the cloudy border of his base
To the foiled searching of mortality:
And thou, who didst the stars and sunbeams know,
Self-schooled, self-scanned,° self-honored, self-secure,   10
Didst walk on earth unguessed at. Better so!
All pains the immortal spirit must endure,
All weakness that impairs, all griefs that bow,
Find their sole voice in that victorious brow.

10. **self-scanned:** self-examined (compare the Greek motto, "Know thyself").

The Last Word

Creep into thy narrow bed,
Creep, and let no more be said!
Vain thy onset! all stands fast.
Thou thyself must break at last.

Let the long contention cease!   5
Geese are swans, and swans are geese.
Let them have it how they will!
Thou art tired; best be still.

They out-talked thee, hissed thee, tore thee!
Better men fared thus before thee;   10
Fired their ringing shot and passed,
Hotly charged—and sank at last.

Charge once more, then, and be dumb!
Let the victors, when they come,
When the forts of folly fall,   15
Find thy body by the wall.

Questions

1. What is the underlying metaphor of "To Marguerite"? What are the "islands" of line 5? The "caverns" of line 15? What contrast is expressed in the third stanza?
2. What is the "question" in line 1 of "Shakespeare"? Why is Shakespeare "free"? What might Arnold mean by saying that Shakespeare "out-tops knowledge"?
3. What sort of conflict is implied by the imagery of "The Last Word"? What does line 6 mean? Which seems to be certain—defeat or victory? Perhaps both? Explain.

DANTE GABRIEL ROSSETTI

1828–1882

Rossetti was born in London of Italian parents, political refugees from their own country. The boy showed an early talent for painting and by the time he was eighteen he had entered the art school of the Royal Academy. Throughout his life painting remained his primary interest, with his poetry taking second place, but in time his poetry came to be recognized as his most important work.

Rossetti was one of the founders of the Pre-Raphaelite school of painters, a school that urged a return to the naturalness and sincerity that they felt had vanished from art just before, or during, the career of the fifteenth-century Italian painter, Raphael. In poetry, the Pre-Raphaelite ideal led Rossetti and some of his followers to avoid dealing with philosophical or social questions of the day; in this respect they were clearly set apart from Tennyson, Browning, and Arnold. The Pre-Raphaelites were often criticized for their apparent belief in "art for art's sake," and some of the criticism was justified. But they made some notable contributions to English poetry, particularly in their skillful use of sensory detail and symbolism.

The Sonnet

A sonnet is a moment's monument—
   Memorial from the soul's eternity
   To one dead deathless hour. Look that it be,
Whether for lustral rite° or dire portent,°
Of its own arduous fullness reverent.   5
   Carve it in ivory or in ebony,
   As day or night may rule; and let time see
Its flowering crest impearled and orient.°

A sonnet is a coin; its face reveals
   The soul—its converse, to what power 'tis due: 10

4. **lustral rite:** purification ceremony. **dire portent:** forewarning of evil.
8. **orient:** bright, lustrous.

Whether for tribute to the august appeals
Of life, or dower in love's high retinue,
It serve; or 'mid the dark wharf's cavernous breath,
In Charon's° palm it pay the toll to death.

14. **Charon** (kā'rŏn): in Greek myth, the ferryman who, on payment of a toll, rowed the dead across the River Styx into Hades.

Silent Noon

Your hands lie open in the long, fresh grass—
    The finger-points look through like rosy blooms:
    Your eyes smile peace. The pasture gleams and glooms
'Neath billowing skies that scatter and amass.
All round our nest, far as the eye can pass,   5
    Are golden kingcup-fields with silver edge
    Where the cow parsley skirts the hawthorn hedge.
'Tis visible silence, still as the hourglass.

Deep in the sun-searched growths the dragon-fly
Hangs like a blue thread loosened from the sky: 10
    So this winged hour is dropped to us from above.
Oh! clasp we to our hearts, for deathless dower,
This close-companioned inarticulate hour
    When twofold silence was the song of love.

Questions

1. Explain the two major metaphors of which "The Sonnet" consists. What do the last two lines mean? How can a "dead" hour be "deathless" (l. 3)? What different kinds of sonnets does Rossetti's poem speak of?
2. Does Rossetti carry out in "Silent Noon" the definition and advice given in "The Sonnet"? Why, or why not?

GEORGE MEREDITH

1828–1909

Strictly by his date of birth, Meredith is a Victorian writer, but his work makes him seem much more a man of our own century. Today, most readers know him as a novelist, though in many ways his novels are more typical of the Victorian age than are his poems, particularly his sonnet sequence, *Modern Love*.

Meredith was born in Portsmouth of Welsh and Irish parents. At fourteen he was sent to school in Germany. On his return he worked for a time in a law office in London and then, in 1851, published his first volume of poems. Four years later he completed his first novel. He remained a productive writer for the rest of his life, turning out a number of excellent novels and many collections of poetry.

Meredith was aware of many of the religious and philosophical controversies that beset the Victorian era, and he dealt with them in his work, but unlike some of his contemporaries he did not despair over the conflicts, nor did he try to flee from them into some earlier, less complex age. It is perhaps this quality that makes him seem especially appealing to modern readers.

Lucifer in Starlight

On a starred night Prince Lucifer° uprose.
Tired of his dark dominion swung the fiend
Above the rolling ball° in cloud part screened,
Where sinners hugged their specter of repose.
Poor prey to his hot fit of pride were those.   5
And now upon his western wing he leaned,
Now his huge bulk o'er Afric's sands careened,
Now the black planet° shadowed Arctic snows.
Soaring through wider zones that pricked his scars
With memory of the old revolt° from Awe,°   10

1. **Prince Lucifer:** Satan. 3. **rolling ball:** earth. 8. **planet:** here, wanderer (the original meaning of the word). 10. **old revolt:** Satan's war with God, for which he was cast into Hell. **Awe:** God (as the cause of wonder and fear).

He reached a middle height, and at the stars,
Which are the brain of heaven, he looked, and sank.
Around the ancient track marched rank on rank,
The army of unalterable law.

from *Modern Love*

Modern Love is a sequence of fifty sonnets that together tell
the story of a tragic marriage. In the sequence Meredith used
the sixteen-line sonnet form that is occasionally found in early
Italian poetry.

Sonnet 30

What are we first? First, animals; and next
Intelligences at a leap; on whom
Pale lies the distant shadow of the tomb,
And all that draweth on the tomb for text.
Into which state comes love, the crowning sun: 5
Beneath whose light the shadow loses form.
We are the lords of life, and life is warm.
Intelligence and instinct now are one.
But nature says: "My children most they seem
When they least know me: therefore I decree   10
That they shall suffer." Swift doth young love flee,
And we stand wakened, shivering from our dream.
Then if we study nature we are wise.
Thus do the few who live but with the day:
The scientific animals are they.   15
Lady, this is my sonnet to your eyes.

Sonnet 43

Mark where the pressing wind shoots javelin-like,
Its skeleton shadow on the broad-backed wave!
Here is a fitting spot to dig love's grave;
Here where the ponderous breakers plunge and strike,

And dart their hissing tongues high up the sand: 5
In hearing of the ocean, and in sight
Of those ribbed wind-streaks running into white.
If I the death of love had deeply planned,
I never could have made it half so sure,
As by the unblest kisses which upbraid   10
The full-waked sense; or failing that, degrade!
'Tis morning: but no morning can restore
What we have forfeited. I see no sin:
The wrong is mixed. In tragic life, God wot,°
No villain need be! Passions spin the plot: 15
We are betrayed by what is false within.

14. wot: knows.

Questions

1. In "Lucifer in Starlight" what did Lucifer try to do? Why? Why did
   he fail? What are some of the technical devices used in this sonnet?
   Notice particularly lines 12, 13, and 14.
2. The most famous literary treatment of the Satan theme is Milton's
   Paradise Lost (see p. 232). How does Milton's treatment compare to
   Meredith's in "Lucifer in Starlight"? What does Meredith's sonnet
   imply about the power and significance of Lucifer?
3. Trace the development of the thought in Sonnet 30 from *Modern Love*.
   Note particularly the last line. Is it related at all to the rest of the
   poem? If so, how?
4. What is the tone of Sonnet 43? What might lines 14–16 mean? Why
   are we "betrayed by what is false within"?

CHRISTINA ROSSETTI

1830–1894

Christina Rossetti was the sister of Dante Gabriel Rossetti. All her
life she had a great deal of respect for her brother and his poetry,
but her own writing is markedly different from his. Whereas his work
was generally highly emotional and sensuous, hers was restrained,
somber, and almost always religious in inspiration.

Her life, through her choice, was quiet and somewhat isolated. But if her life was outwardly uneventful, she nevertheless had the opportunity of meeting many of the most famous men of her day—her brother's friends—and in this company she was recognized as an extraordinarily talented poet.

A Birthday

My heart is like a singing bird
 Whose nest is in a watered shoot:°
My heart is like an apple tree
 Whose boughs are bent with thickset fruit;
My heart is like a rainbow shell°   5
 That paddles in a halcyon° sea;
My heart is gladder than all these
 Because my love is come to me.

Raise me a dais° of silk and down;
 Hang it with vair° and purple dyes;   10
Carve it in doves and pomegranates,°
 And peacocks with a hundred eyes;
Work it in gold and silver grapes,
 In leaves and silver fleur-de-lys;°
Because the birthday of my life   15
 Is come, my love is come to me.

2. **shoot:** a new growth. 5. **shell:** a small boat. 6. **halcyon** (hăl′sĭ·ŭn): calm. 9. **dais** (dā′ĭs): platform. 10. **vair:** expensive fur from a particular kind of squirrel. 11. **pomegranates** (pŏm′grăn′ĭts): a tropical fruit. 14. **fleur-de-lys** (flûr′dē·lēz′): irises (French, literally, flower of the lily).

Song

When I am dead, my dearest,
 Sing no sad songs for me;
Plant thou no roses at my head,
 Nor shady cypress tree:

Be the green grass above me   5
    With showers and dewdrops wet:
And if thou wilt, remember,
And if thou wilt, forget.

I shall not see the shadows,
    I shall not feel the rain;   10
I shall not hear the nightingale
    Sing on as if in pain:
And dreaming through the twilight
    That doth not rise nor set,
Haply° I may remember,   15
And haply may forget.

15. Haply: by chance.

Questions

1. Compare and contrast the two stanzas of "A Birthday." In what sense
   does Miss Rossetti use the word *birthday*?
2. What is the tone of "Song"? What is the effect of the last two lines?

WILLIAM MORRIS

1834–1896

Morris was one of the most versatile members of the Pre-Raphaelite
circle; indeed, he was one of the most versatile men of the nineteenth
century. In addition to being a skilled poet he was a painter, a designer of furniture, rugs, and stained glass, and a printer and book
designer of great originality. Even today, the Morris Chair is well-
known, and books from Morris's Kelmscott Press are now collector's
items.

Morris attended Oxford and while there came under the influence
of Dante Gabriel Rossetti. He studied painting under Rossetti and
then branched out into the variety of arts that he was to become ex-

pert in. With such a wide range of interests, he was never able to
concentrate enough on his poetry to become a major writer, but
much of his poetry is excellent. In addition to his original writings
he made a number of translations, including versions of the *Iliad* and
Odyssey and *Beowulf*. In later years he also wrote a great deal of
social criticism.

I Know a Little Garden-Close

I know a little garden-close,
Set thick with lily and red rose,
Where I would wander if I might
From dewy morn to dewy night,
And have one with me wandering.   5
  And though within it no birds sing,
And though no pillared house is there,
And though the apple boughs are bare
Of fruit and blossom, would to God,
Her feet upon the green grass trod,   10
And I beheld them as before.
  There comes a murmur from the shore,
And in the place two fair streams are,
Drawn from the purple hills afar,
Drawn down unto the restless sea: 15
Dark hills whose flowers ne'er feed the bee,
The shore no ship has ever seen,
Tormented by the billows green,
Whose murmur comes unceasingly
.Unto the place for which I cry.   20
  For which I cry both day and night,
For which I let slip all delight,
That maketh me both deaf and blind,
Careless to win, unskilled to find,
And quick to lose what all men seek.   25
  Yet tottering as I am weak,
Still have I left a little breath

To seek within the jaws of death
An entrance to that happy place,
To seek the unforgotten face,   30
Once seen, once kissed, once reft° from me
Anigh° the murmuring of the sea.

31. reft: torn.   32. Anigh: near.

Questions

Describe the structure of this poem. How are the various sections
related? (The indented lines indicate sections.) Does the poem lead
to a climax of some sort? What is the climax?

ALGERNON CHARLES SWINBURNE

1837–1909

Swinburne was born in London and educated at Eton School. He
entered Oxford, but his high-strung temperament made him anything but a model student, and he left without taking a degree. He
returned to London where he was associated for a time with Rossetti's circle. His first volume of poems, published in 1860, received
little notice. In 1865 appeared a poetic tragedy, *Atalanta in Calydon,*
which brought him his first acclaim. During the next fifteen years,
he published a number of major works, but at the same time his
conduct was becoming increasingly erratic. In 1879 he suffered a
severe mental and physical breakdown, and from that year to the
end of his life he was confined—virtually a prisoner—in the home of
a friend.

Swinburne's reputation has undergone a number of transforma-
tions. During his lifetime he was usually either dismissed as a completely immoral versifier or called one of the greatest poets of the
language. Today, many of the ideas he expressed in his work are seen
to derive from his wish to shock his age, but he is nevertheless recognized as one of the most technically skilled poets in English.

A Forsaken Garden

In a coign° of the cliff between lowland and highland,
  At the sea-down's edge between windward and lee,
Walled round with rocks as an inland island,
  The ghost of a garden fronts the sea.
A girdle of brushwood and thorn encloses   5
  The steep square slope of the blossomless bed
Where the weeds that grew green from the graves of its roses
  Now lie dead.

The fields fall southward, abrupt and broken,
  To the low last edge of the long lone land.   10
If a step should sound or a word be spoken,
  Would a ghost not rise at the strange guest's hand?
So long have the gray bare walks lain guestless,
  Through branches and briars if a man make way,
He shall find no life but the sea wind's restless   15
  Night and day.

The dense hard passage is blind and stifled
  That crawls by a track none turn to climb
To the strait° waste place that the years have rifled
  Of all but the thorns that are touched not of time.   20
The thorns he spares when the rose is taken;
  The rocks are left when he wastes the plain;
The wind that wanders, the weeds wind-shaken,
  These remain.

Not a flower to be pressed of the foot that falls not;   25
  As the heart of a dead man the seed plots are dry;
From the thicket of thorns whence the nightingale calls not,
  Could she call, there were never a rose to reply.
Over the meadows that blossom and wither,
  Rings but the note of a sea bird's song.   30
Only the sun and the rain come hither
  All year long.

1. coign (koin): corner. 19. strait: barren, distressful.

The sun burns sear,° and the rain dishevels
  One gaunt bleak blossom of scentless breath,
Only the wind here hovers and revels,   35
  In a round where life seems barren as death.
Here there was laughing of old, there was weeping,
  Haply, of lovers none ever will know,
Whose eyes went seaward a hundred sleeping
      Years ago.   40

Heart handfast in heart as they stood, "Look thither,"
  Did he whisper? "Look forth from the flowers to the sea;
For the foam-flowers endure when the rose blossoms wither,
  And men that love lightly may die—but we?"
And the same wind sang, and the same waves whitened,   45
  And or ever° the garden's last petals were shed,
In the lips that had whispered, the eyes that had lightened,
      Love was dead.

Or they loved their life through, and then went whither?
  And were one to the end—but what end who knows?   50
Love deep as the sea as a rose must wither,
  As the rose-red seaweed that mocks the rose.
Shall the dead take thought for the dead to love them?
  What love was ever as deep as a grave?
They are loveless now as the grass above them   55
      Or the wave.

All are at one now, roses and lovers,
  Not known of the cliffs and the fields and the sea.
Not a breath of the time that has been hovers
  In the air now soft with a summer to be.   60
Not a breath shall there sweeten the seasons hereafter
  Of the flowers or the lovers that laugh now or weep,
When as they that are free now of weeping and laughter
      We shall sleep.

33. **sear:** scorchingly.   46. **or ever:** before.

Here death may deal not again for ever;   65
  Here change may come not till all change end.
From the graves they have made they shall rise up never,
  Who have left naught living to ravage and rend.
Earth, stones, and thorns of the wild ground growing,
  While the sun and the rain live, these shall be;   70
Till a last wind's breath, upon all these blowing,
    Roll the sea.

Till the slow sea rise, and the sheer cliff crumble,
  Till terrace and meadow the deep gulfs drink,
Till the strength of the waves of the high tides humble   75
  The fields that lessen, the rocks that shrink,
Here now in his triumph where all things falter,
  Stretched out on the spoils that his own hand spread,
As a god self-slain on his own strange altar,
    Death lies dead.   80

Questions

Why is this poem an illustration of the statement that Swinburne is
known for his music rather than for his thought? What is the thought
of this poem? Analyze thoroughly the musical quality of the poem.
What poetic devices has Swinburne used with particular effectiveness?

NINETEENTH–CENTURY AMERICAN POETRY

There were a number of poets active in America throughout the seventeenth and eighteenth centuries. With only a few exceptions, however, the colonial poets were content to imitate the work of the popular English poets of their day. It was not until the nineteenth century that American poetry started to develop its own distinct characteristics. It is significant that toward the end of the century, American poets began, in turn, to exercise a strong influence on many of their English contemporaries.

During the first part of the nineteenth century, American poetry developed its own themes and subjects, but in general most poets did not experiment in poetic techniques. Toward the end of the century, however, a number of poets broke away from traditional styles. The work of these writers, particularly that of Walt Whitman, foreshadowed many of the characteristics of twentieth-century poetry.

WILLIAM CULLEN BRYANT

1794–1878

Born and educated in Massachusetts, Bryant left his native state to begin a newspaper career in New York City. A few years after he started as a journalist he became an editor with one of the most famous New York papers, the *Evening Post*. He remained with this paper for over fifty years, during most of that time as editor-in-chief and part owner. Apart from his fame as a poet, Bryant achieved a reputation as one of the major figures in American journalism.

Bryant was twenty-three when he gained his first fame with the publication of "Thanatopsis." Actually, the poem had been written when he was only sixteen. Greater poets than Bryant were to follow, but he deserves to be called the first major American poet. He was also the first American poet to gain an international reputation.

To the Fringed Gentian*

Thou blossom bright with autumn dew,
And colored with the heaven's own blue,
That openest when the quiet light
Succeeds the keen and frosty night:

Thou comest not when violets lean   5
O'er wandering brooks and springs unseen,
Or columbines, in purple dressed,
Nod o'er the ground-bird's hidden nest.

Thou waitest late and com'st alone,
When woods are bare and birds are flown,   10
And frosts and shortening days portend
The aged year is near his end.

Then doth thy sweet and quiet eye
Look through its fringes to the sky,
Blue—blue—as if that sky let fall   15
A flower from its cerulean° wall.

I would that thus, when I shall see
The hour of death draw near to me,
Hope, blossoming within my heart,
May look to heaven as I depart.   20

* **Fringed Gentian** (jĕn'shăn): a blue flower found in eastern North America.   16. **cerulean** (sĕ·rōō'lĕ·ăn): blue.

Questions

Does the thought grow out of the poem, or is it merely tacked on at the end? Compare and contrast this poem with "To a Waterfowl" (page 18).

RALPH WALDO EMERSON

1803–1882

Emerson was born in Boston and educated at Harvard University. He taught school for a short time after graduating, then became pastor of the Second Church of Boston in 1829. Two years later he resigned this position and began his career in literature. He traveled to Europe, spending most of his time in England and Italy. He met many of the major writers of his time; one of them, the Scottish historian Thomas Carlyle, was to remain a lifelong friend and an important influence on much of Emerson's work.

Emerson is best known as an essayist, social critic, and philosopher, but he also wrote a great deal of poetry. His work is highly individual, and often uneven in quality, but much of it is excellent. He once said,

> The poet knows that he speaks adequately . . . only when
> he speaks somewhat wildly . . .

and his poetry often displays this characteristic. In his own day, his poems were sometimes criticized for their apparent lack of form and polish, but today his harsh rhythms and striking images appeal to many readers.

Brahma

Brahma is the supreme God of Hinduism, a religion and a philosophy that Emerson often dealt with in his writings. Brahma is the unchanging, underlying source of all reality, and is contrasted to Maya, the ordinary world of changing appearances.

> If the red slayer think he slays,
>   Or if the slain think he is slain,
> They know not well the subtle ways
>   I keep, and pass, and turn again.

Far or forgot to me is near;   5
    Shadow and sunlight are the same;
The vanished gods to me appear;
    And one to me are shame and fame.

They reckon ill who leave me out;
    When me they fly, I am the wings;   10
I am the doubter and the doubt,
    And I the hymn the Brahmin° sings.

The strong gods pine for my abode,
    And pine in vain the sacred Seven;°
But thou, meek lover of the good!   15
    Find me, and turn thy back on heaven.

12. Brahmin: the highest-ranking worshiper of Brahma.   14. sacred Seven:
the greatest saints in Hinduism.

Hamatreya

"Hamatreya" is based on a passage in one of the Hindu scrip-
tures, in which a prophet warns of the folly of those men who
claim that the earth, or any part of it, is theirs. The title of
the poem is derived from the name of the young man to whom
the prophet speaks.

Minott, Lee, Willard, Hosmer, Meriam, Flint,°
Possessed the land which rendered to their toil
Hay, corn, roots, hemp, flax, apples, wool, and wood.
Each of these landlords walked amidst his farm,
Saying, " 'Tis mine, my children's, and my name's: 5
How sweet the west wind sounds in my own trees!
How graceful climb those shadows on my hill!
I fancy these pure waters and the flags°
Know me, as does my dog: we sympathize;
And, I affirm, my actions smack of the soil."   10

1. Minott . . . Flint: the first settlers of Concord, Massachusetts.   8. flags:
stones.

Where are these men? Asleep beneath their grounds;
And strangers, fond° as they, their furrows plow.
Earth laughs in flowers, to see her boastful boys
Earth-proud, proud of the earth which is not theirs;
Who steer the plow, but cannot steer their feet   15
Clear of the grave.

They added ridge to valley, brook to pond,
And sighed for all that abounded their domain.
"This suits me for a pasture; that's my park;
We must have clay, lime, gravel, granite-ledge,   20
And misty lowland, where to go for peat.
The land is well—lies fairly to the south.
'Tis good, when you have crossed the sea and back,
To find the sitfast° acres where you left them."
Ah! the hot owner sees not Death, who adds   25
Him to his land, a lump of mould the more.
Hear what the Earth says:

EARTH SONG

                    "Mine and yours;
                    Mine, not yours.
                    Earth endures;   30
                    Stars abide—
                    Shine down in the old sea;
                    Old are the shores;
                    But where are old men?
                    I who have seen much,   35
                    Such have I never seen.

                    "The lawyer's deed
                    Ran sure,
                    In tail,°
                    To them, and to their heirs   40
                    Who shall succeed,

12. **fond:** foolish.   24. **sitfast:** firm, fixed.   39. **in tail:** entail, referring to
the passing on of property to a number of succeeding generations.

Without fail,
Forevermore.

"Here is the land,
Shaggy with wood,   45
With its old valley,
Mound, and flood.
But the heritors?
Fled like the flood's foam—
The lawyer, and the laws,   50
And the kingdom,
Clean swept herefrom.

"They called me theirs,
Who so controlled me;
Yet every one   55
Wished to stay, and is gone.
How am I theirs,
If they cannot hold me,
But I hold them?"

When I heard the Earth song,   60
I was no longer brave;
My avarice cooled
Like lust in the chill of the grave.

Fable

The mountain and the squirrel
Had a quarrel;
And the former called the latter "Little Prig."
Bun replied,
"You are doubtless very big;   5
But all sorts of things and weather
Must be taken in together
To make up a year
And a sphere.

And I think it's no disgrace   10
To occupy my place.
If I'm not so large as you,
You are not so small as I,
And not half so spry.
I'll not deny you make   15
A very pretty squirrel track;
Talents differ: all is well and wisely put;
If I cannot carry forests on my back,
Neither can you crack a nut."

Questions

1. Can you resolve the paradoxes in "Brahma"? Or are they merely un-
   solvable contradictions? In the final stanza, why might the "meek
   lover of the good" find Brahma while the seven saints "pine in vain"?
   Can you explain the last line?
2. What is the theme of "Hamatreya"? Is it part of the dramatic structure
   of the poem?
3. Could the first half of "Hamatreya" be a poem by itself? If not, what
   detail would have to be changed? Analyze the treatment of rhythm
   and rhyme in the Earth Song. Compare the form of this section to
   the form of Skelton's "To Mistress Margaret Hussey," page 154.
4. Why is "Fable" called by that title? What is the "moral"?

JOHN GREENLEAF WHITTIER

1807–1892

Whittier was born in Haverhill, Massachusetts. As a young man, he
worked in Boston as a journalist for a few years, but he preferred the
life of a small town and eventually returned to his birthplace, where
he spent most of his life. Unlike many of the poets contemporary
with him, Whittier was largely self-educated.

A Quaker, deeply devout, Whittier detested slavery, and much of
his poetry was directed against that institution. In later years, he
sometimes said that he had sacrificed poetry to reform, but much of

his antislavery poetry is of excellent quality. His most popular poems, however, were and still are those that deal with simple, homely subjects—rural life and the old traditions and legends of New England. "Proem," which means "preface" or "introduction," was written to stand at the beginning of Whittier's collected poems, published in 1849. It gives us an excellent picture of Whittier as a man and a poet.

Proem

I love the old melodious lays
Which softly melt the ages through,
    The songs of Spenser's golden days,
    Arcadian Sidney's° silvery phrase,
Sprinkling our noon of time with freshest morning dew.   5

Yet, vainly in my quiet hours
To breathe their marvelous notes I try;
    I feel them, as the leaves and flowers
    In silence feel the dewy showers.
And drink with glad still lips the blessing of the sky.   10

The rigor of a frozen clime,
The harshness of an untaught ear,
    The jarring words of one whose rhyme
    Beat often labor's hurried time,
Or duty's rugged march through storm and strife, are here.   15

Of mystic beauty, dreamy grace,
No rounded art the lack supplies;
    Unskilled the subtle lines to trace
    Or softer shades of nature's face,
I view her common forms with unanointed eyes.   20

4. **Arcadian Sidney's:** Sidney wrote a prose romance called *Arcadia*, which also contained many lyric poems.

Nor mine the seer-like power to show
The secrets of the heart and mind;
   To drop the plummet line° below
   Our common world of joy and woe,
A more intense despair or brighter hope to find.   25

Yet here at least an earnest sense
Of human right and weal is shown;
   A hate of tyranny intense,
   And hearty in its vehemence,
As if my brother's pain and sorrow were my own.   30

O freedom! if to me belong
Nor mighty Milton's gift divine,
   Nor Marvell's wit and graceful song,
   Still with a love as deep and strong
As theirs, I lay, like them, my best gifts on thy shrine!   35

23. plummet line: a lead-weighted line used on board ship to determine the
depth of the water.

Questions

In this poem Whittier is talking about his own poetry. What does he
feel are the strong points of his work? What are its weak points? What
does Whittier imply about the function of poetry?

HENRY WADSWORTH LONGFELLOW

1807–1882

Longfellow was by far the most popular poet of the nineteenth century in America, and his reputation rivaled Tennyson's in England.
But at the beginning of this century, Longfellow's reputation suffered in much the same way that Tennyson's did. Fortunately, present-day critics are reaching a more balanced view. If Longfellow is

no longer automatically thought of as the greatest American poet, he is nevertheless recognized as a major figure in our literature.

He was educated at Bowdoin College in Maine. After graduation, he traveled widely in Europe, studying the languages and literatures of France, Spain, Italy, Germany, and the Scandinavian countries. He returned to America to become Professor of Modern Languages at Harvard. He taught with distinction for eighteen years, finally leaving Harvard in order to devote all of his time to poetry.

His best-known poems are probably his longer works—especially *Hiawatha, The Courtship of Miles Standish,* and *Evangeline.* But in many respects his shorter poems, especially his poems of the sea and his sonnets, represent a greater poetic accomplishment. Few poets since the Elizabethan age have surpassed Longfellow's mastery of the sonnet form.

The Tide Rises, the Tide Falls

The tide rises, the tide falls,
The twilight darkens, the curlew° calls;
Along the sea-sands damp and brown
The traveler hastens toward the town,
    And the tide rises, the tide falls.   5

Darkness settles on roofs and walls,
But the sea, the sea in the darkness calls;
The little waves, with their soft, white hands,
Efface the footprints in the sands,
    And the tide rises, the tide falls.   10

The morning breaks; the steeds in their stalls
Stamp and neigh, as the hostler calls;
The day returns, but nevermore
Returns the traveler to the shore,
    And the tide rises, the tide falls.   15

2. **curlew** (kûr′lū): a large North American and European bird.

Chaucer

An old man in a lodge within a park;
The chamber walls depicted all around
With portraitures of huntsmen, hawk, and hound,
And the hurt deer. He listeneth to the lark,
Whose song comes with the sunshine through the dark   5
Of painted glass in leaden lattice bound;
He listeneth and he laugheth at the sound,
Then writeth in a book like any clerk.
He is the poet of the dawn,° who wrote
The Canterbury Tales,° and his old age   10
Made beautiful with song;° and as I read
I hear the crowing cock, I hear the note
Of lark and linnet, and from every page
Rise odors of plowed field or flowery mead.

9. **dawn:** *i.e.,* the beginning of English poetry. There had been many poets
before Chaucer (1340?–1400), but he was the first major figure and as such is
often called the father of English poetry. 10. **Canterbury Tales:** Chaucer's
major work. 10–11. **old age . . . song:** in his last years, Chaucer wrote a
number of brief lyrics.

Divina Commedia

Longfellow wrote six sonnets to accompany his translation of
the great Italian epic, Dante's *Divine Comedy.* The two that
follow introduced the first part of the poem, the "Inferno."

I

Oft have I seen at some cathedral door
A laborer, pausing in the dust and heat,
Lay down his burden, and with reverent feet
Enter, and cross himself, and on the floor
Kneel to repeat his paternoster° o'er;   5
Far off the noises of the world retreat;
The loud vociferations of the street
Become an undistinguishable roar.

5. **paternoster:** the Lord's Prayer.

So, as I enter here from day to day,
    And leave my burden° at this minster° gate,   10
    Kneeling in prayer, and not ashamed to pray,
    The tumult of the time disconsolate°
    To inarticulate murmurs dies away,
    While the eternal ages watch and wait.

10. burden: Longfellow began the translation as a way of easing his grief over the death of his wife. minster: literally, cathedral; here used figuratively for Dante's poem. 12. time disconsolate: Longfellow worked on the translation during the years of the Civil War. (See also note to l. 10.)

II

How strange the sculptures that adorn these towers!
    This crowd of statues, in whose folded sleeves
    Birds build their nests; while canopied with leaves
    Parvis° and portal bloom like trellised bowers,
And the vast minster seems a cross of flowers!   5
    But fiends and dragons on the gargoyled° eaves
    Watch the dead Christ between the living thieves,
    And, underneath, the traitor Judas lowers!°
Ah! from what agonies of heart and brain,
    What exultations trampling on despair,   10
    What tenderness, what tears, what hate of wrong,
What passionate outcry of a soul in pain,
    Uprose this poem of the earth and air,
    This medieval miracle of song!

4. Parvis: a court or enclosed space before a church. 6. gargoyled: decorated with gargoyles, grotesque figures projecting from the roof. Figuratively, the lines also refer to the many grotesque and evil characters that exist in Dante's poem. 8. lowers (lou'érz): frowns threateningly.

Questions

1. In "The Tide Rises, the Tide Falls" what is Longfellow implying about human experience as opposed to the life of nature? What is the effect of the refrain?
2. What is the effect of the imagery in "Chaucer"? What is Longfellow's view of Chaucer as a poet?

3. In the first *Divina Commedia* sonnet, what is the relationship between the octave and the sestet? What is the relationship between the sestet of the first sonnet and the octave of the second? What might be the symbolic meaning of line 6 of the second sonnet?
4. In what sense could the two *Divina Commedia* sonnets be said to form one poem? Trace the development of the thought of both poems.

EDGAR ALLAN POE

1809–1849

Edgar Poe was born in Boston, the son of traveling actors. Within two years of his birth, both of his parents had died. The boy was taken into the home of John Allan, a merchant of Richmond, Virginia, whose name Poe later added to his own.

After brief periods at the University of Virginia and West Point, Poe took a job as a magazine editor. He became an excellent editor, despite a number of personal difficulties, caused partly by his own erratic temperament and by excessive drinking, but also by the chronic illness of his young wife. At the same time he was writing short stories, poetry, and criticism, and making original contributions in each field. His reputation spread quickly to Europe, particularly to France, but his work was neglected in America, and his life was a constant struggle with poverty. In 1845 his wife died of tuberculosis in their bare cottage in New York. Four years later, at forty, Poe himself was dead.

Poe is recognized as one of the originators of the short story. He was also the first important literary critic in America. In poetry, his major contribution was his use of symbolism, which influenced many of the poets who followed him.

The City in the Sea

This strange, visionary poem may be based on the old legend of Atlantis, the city that was believed to have sunk beneath the Atlantic Ocean.

Lo! Death has reared himself a throne
In a strange city lying alone
Far down within the dim West,
Where the good and the bad and the worst and the best
Have gone to their eternal rest.   5
There shrines and palaces and towers
(Time-eaten towers that tremble not!)
Resemble nothing that is ours.
Around, by lifting winds forgot,
Resignedly beneath the sky   10
The melancholy waters lie.

No rays from the holy heaven come down
On the long nighttime of that town;
But light from out the lurid sea
Streams up the turrets silently—   15
Gleams up the pinnacles far and free—
Up domes—up spires—up kingly halls—
Up fanes°—up Babylon-like walls—
Up shadowy long-forgotten bowers
Of sculptured ivy and stone flowers—   20
Up many and many a marvelous shrine
Whose wreathèd friezes° intertwine
The viol, the violet, and the vine.
Resignedly beneath the sky
The melancholy waters lie.   25
So blend the turrets and shadows there
That all seem pendulous in air,
While from a proud tower in the town
Death looks gigantically down.

There open fanes and gaping graves   30
Yawn level with the luminous waves
But not the riches there that lie
In each idol's diamond eye—
Not the gayly-jeweled dead
Tempt the waters from their bed;   35

18. **fanes:** temples.   22. **friezes** (frēz′ĕz): an ornamental band on a building.

For no ripples curl, alas!
Along the wilderness of glass—
No swellings tell that winds may be
Upon some far-off happier sea—
No heavings hint that winds have been   40
On seas less hideously serene.

But lo, a stir in the air!
The wave—there is a movement there!
As if the towers had thrust aside,
In slightly sinking, the dull tide—   45
As if their tops had feebly given
A void within the filmy heaven.
The waves have now a redder glow—
The hours are breathing faint and low—
And when, amid no earthly moans,   50
Down, down that town shall settle hence,
Hell, rising from a thousand thrones,
Shall do it reverence.

To Helen

Helen, thy beauty is to me
   Like those Nicéan° barks of yore,
That gently, o'er a perfumed sea,
   The weary, wayworn wanderer° bore
To his own native shore.   5

On desperate seas long wont to roam,
   Thy hyacinth° hair, thy classic face,
Thy naiad° airs, have brought me home
   To the glory that was Greece
And the grandeur that was Rome.   10

   2. **Nicean** (nĭ·sē'ăn): probably pertaining to Nicaea, an ancient town in
Asia Minor. 4. **wanderer:** perhaps Odysseus. 7. **hyacinth:** a Homeric adjective for hair was "hyacinthine," usually meaning curly. 8. **naiad** (nā'ăd): a
water nymph.

Lo! in yon brilliant window-niche
How statue-like I see thee stand,
The agate lamp within thy hand!
Ah, Psyche,° from the regions which
Are Holy Land!   15

14. **Psyche** (sī'kè): the Greek word for "soul" or "mind," derived from the
name of the maiden beloved by Cupid.

Sonnet to Science

Science! true daughter of Old Time thou art!
Who alterest all things with thy peering eyes.
Why preyest thou thus upon the poet's heart,
Vulture, whose wings are dull realities?
How should he love thee? or how deem thee wise,   5
Who wouldst not leave him in his wandering
To seek for treasure in the jeweled skies,
Albeit he soared with an undaunted wing?
Hast thou not dragged Diana° from her car,
And driven the hamadryad° from the wood   10
To seek a shelter in some happier star?
Hast thou not torn the naiad from her flood,
The elfin from the green grass, and from me
The summer dream beneath the tamarind tree?°

9. **Diana:** the Roman goddess of the wood. Later, she also became known
as the goddess of the hunt and was often pictured riding in a chariot ("car").
10. **hamadryad** (hăm'á·drī'ăd): wood nymph. 14. **tamarind tree:** a tropical
tree.

Questions

1. What are some of the musical devices used in "The City in the Sea"?
   What is the meter? Are there any metrical variations? If so, what is
   their effect? Compare and contrast this poem with Coleridge's "Kubla
   Khan," page 324.

2. What is the effect of the many classical allusions in "To Helen"? What is the tone of the poem?
3. In "Sonnet to Science," what is Poe's complaint against science? Is his argument justified? Why, or why not?

OLIVER WENDELL HOLMES

1809–1894

It would be hard to find anyone quite as versatile as Oliver Wendell Holmes. After graduation from Harvard, he studied medicine in Edinburgh and Paris, and then returned to this country to become a successful physician in Cambridge and Boston. After some years of private practice, he became professor of anatomy at Harvard and dean of the medical school.

In the midst of his demanding medical profession he somehow found time to be a steadily productive writer as well as a renowned conversationalist. His best prose and poetry somehow capture the whimsical effect that his casual conversation must have had. "The Height of the Ridiculous" is one of his finest pieces of light verse. Holmes's serious poetry has not survived as well as his humorous work, but "The Chambered Nautilus" is an exception. It remains perhaps his best-known poem.

The Height of the Ridiculous

I wrote some lies once on a time
    In wondrous merry mood,
And thought, as usual, men would say
    They were exceeding good.

They were so queer, so very queer,   5
    I laughed as I would die;
Albeit, in the general way,
    A sober man am I.

I called my servant, and he came;
　　How kind it was of him   10
To mind a slender man like me,
　　He of the mighty limb!

"These to the printer," I exclaimed,
　　And, in my humorous way,
I added, (as a trifling jest,)   15
　　"There'll be the devil° to pay."

He took the paper, and I watched,
　　And saw him peep within;
At the first line he read, his face
　　Was all upon the grin.   20

He read the next; the grin grew broad,
　　And shot from ear to ear;
He read the third; a chuckling noise
　　I now began to hear.

The fourth; he broke into a roar;   25
　　The fifth; his waistband split;
The sixth; he burst five buttons off,
　　And tumbled in a fit.

Ten days and nights, with sleepless eye,
　　I watched that wretched man,   30
And since, I never dare to write
　　As funny as I can.

16. **devil:** a pun; a "printer's devil" is an apprentice printer.

The Chambered Nautilus

The nautilus is a shellfish having a spiral-shaped, compart-
mented shell. Its name means "sailor" and derives from its
tentacles (the "webs of living gauze" of l. 8), which resemble
sails.

This is the ship of pearl, which, poets feign,
   Sails the unshadowed main—
   The venturous bark that flings
On the sweet summer wind its purpled wings
In gulfs enchanted, where the Siren° sings,   5
   And coral reefs lie bare,
Where the cold sea-maids rise to sun their streaming hair.

Its webs of living gauze no more unfurl;
   Wrecked is the ship of pearl!
   And every chambered cell,   10
Where its dim dreaming life was wont to dwell,
As the frail tenant shaped his growing shell,
   Before thee lies revealed—
Its irised ceiling rent, its sunless crypt unsealed!

Year after year beheld the silent toil   15
   That spread his lustrous coil;
   Still, as the spiral grew,
He left the past year's dwelling for the new,
Stole with soft step its shining archway through,
   Built up its idle door,   20
Stretched in his last-found home, and knew the old no more.

Thanks for the heavenly message brought by thee,
   Child of the wandering sea,
   Cast from her lap, forlorn!
From thy dead lips a clearer note is born   25
Than ever Triton° blew from wreathèd horn!
   While on mine ear it rings,
Through the deep caves of thought I hear a voice that sings:

Build thee more stately mansions, O my soul,
   As the swift seasons roll!   30

5. **Siren:** see page 19.   26. **Triton:** see page 299.

Leave thy low-vaulted past!
Let each new temple, nobler than the last,
Shut thee from heaven with a dome more vast,
  Till thou at length art free,
Leaving thine outgrown shell by life's unresting sea!   35

Questions

1. What humorous devices does Holmes use in "The Height of the Ridiculous"?
2. In "The Chambered Nautilus," trace the development of the thought, stanza by stanza. What does Holmes mean by "stately mansions" in line 29 and by "outgrown shell" in line 35?

JAMES RUSSELL LOWELL
1819–1891

Lowell, who succeeded Longfellow as Professor of Modern Languages at Harvard, was a man of many interests. Unlike Longfellow, Lowell was not willing to let poetry become his sole vocation. In fact, most of his poetry was written in the brief span from 1845 to 1850. After these years, Lowell turned to teaching, to criticism, and toward the end of his life, to a diplomatic career.

Although his output was small, Lowell left us a number of striking poems. "The Courtin'" and the "Harvard Commemoration Ode" (a tribute to Lincoln) are well known. Perhaps his finest work, however, is his criticism in verse, *A Fable for Critics*. In this long poem he discusses a number of the famous writers of his day, commenting accurately and humorously on their strengths and weaknesses. The poem was published anonymously, and Lowell included a passage on his own writing—even in this case the critical remarks were surprisingly objective. Including the self-criticism was also a method of concealing the poem's authorship. Lowell revealed that it was his work only when a number of others had claimed it as theirs.

from *A Fable for Critics*

There comes Emerson first, whose rich words, every one,
Are like gold nails in temples to hang trophies on,
Whose prose is grand verse, while his verse the Lord knows,
Is some of it pr— No, 'tis not even prose;
I'm speaking of meters; some poems have welled   5
From those rare depths of soul that have ne'er been excelled;
They're not epics, but that doesn't matter a pin,
In creating, the only hard thing's to begin;
A grass-blade's no easier to make than an oak,
If you've once found the way, you've achieved the grand stroke;   10
In the worst of his poems are mines of rich matter,
But thrown in a heap with a crash and a clatter. . . .

POE AND LONGFELLOW

There comes Poe, with his raven, like Barnaby Rudge,°
Three fifths of him genius and two fifths sheer fudge,
Who talks like a book of iambs and pentameters,   15
In a way to make people of common sense damn meters,
Who has written some things quite the best of their kind,
But the heart somehow seems all squeezed out by the mind,
Who—but hey-dey! What's this? Messieurs Mathews° and Poe,
You mustn't fling mud-balls at Longfellow° so,   20
Does it make a man worse that his character's such
As to make his friends love him (as you think) too much?
Why, there is not a bard at this moment alive
More willing than he that his fellows should thrive,
While you are abusing him thus, even now   25
He would help either one of you out of a slough;
You may say that he's smooth and all that till you're hoarse,

---

13. **Barnaby Rudge:** the title character of a novel by Charles Dickens in
which a raven plays an important part. Poe reviewed the novel when it first
appeared, and it apparently gave him some ideas for his poem "The Raven."
19. **Cornelius Mathews,** a New York author. 20. **You . . . Longfellow:** both
Mathews and Poe had created a stir by their severe criticisms of Longfellow's
poetry.

But remember that elegance also is force;
After polishing granite as much as you will,
The heart keeps its tough old persistency still. . . .   30

HOLMES

There's Holmes, who is matchless among you for wit,
A Leyden jar° always full charged, from which flit
The electrical tingles of hit after hit;
In long poems 'tis painful sometimes, and invites
A thought of the way the new telegraph writes,   35
Which pricks down its little sharp sentences spitefully,
As if you'd got more than you'd title to rightfully,
And you find yourself hoping its wild father lightning
Would flame in for a second and give you a fright'ning. . . .

LOWELL

There is Lowell, who's striving Parnassus° to climb   40
With a whole bale of *isms*° tied together with rhyme; . . .
His lyre has some chords that would ring pretty well,
But he'd rather by half make a drum of the shell,
And rattle away till he's old as Methusalem,°
At the head of a march to the last new Jerusalem.   45

32. **Leyden jar:** a type of electrical condenser. 40. **Parnassus** (pär·năs′ŭs):
a mountain in Greece, regarded as the home of the Muses. 41. *isms:* as a
young man, Lowell was quite active in politics. 44. **Methusalem:** Methusaleh,
the oldest man mentioned in the Bible (Genesis 5:27).

Questions

1. Explain in your own words Lowell's criticisms of the various poets he
   mentions. In general, what is the tone of the criticism?
2. Discuss Lowell's use of exaggerated rhyme. Point out some other humorous devices in the poem.

WALT WHITMAN

1819–1892

Walt Whitman's first volume of poetry was called *Leaves of Grass*. He retained this title for all succeeding editions even when the book had expanded from the original twelve poems to more than four hundred. On its first appearance, a few critics and poets, including Ralph Waldo Emerson, praised the book, but in general the public was baffled by it. They could not understand its exuberance, its often extravagant language, and its acceptance of all aspects of life as proper subjects for poetry—the ugly as well as the beautiful.

Whitman was born on Long Island and spent his early life in Brooklyn and New York City. As a young man he worked for a number of newspapers. While still working as a journalist, he began writing some poetry in traditional form, but later he discarded most of the common poetic devices of the time and wrote instead in a loose, rolling rhythm, with no rhymes. The new style was influenced to some extent by the poetry of the King James Bible, and there may have been other influences as well, but in effect Whitman had created a new kind of poetry.

For many years, Whitman was almost completely ignored in this country. He made his reputation first in England, where the Rossettis and Swinburne were among the first to recognize his genius. Although not the inventor of free verse, Whitman was the first to explore extensively its musical possibilities, and his pioneering efforts have had a profound influence on many modern poets.

A Noiseless Patient Spider

A noiseless patient spider,
I marked where on a little promontory it stood isolated,
Marked how to explore the vacant vast surrounding,
It launched forth filament, filament, filament, out of itself,
Ever unreeling them, ever tirelessly speeding them.   5

And you O my soul where you stand,
Surrounded, detached, in measureless oceans of space,

Ceaselessly musing, venturing, throwing, seeking the spheres to con-
nect them.
Till the bridge you will need be formed, till the ductile° anchor hold,
Till the gossamer thread you fling catch somewhere, O my soul.   10

9. **ductile** (dŭk'tĭl): capable of being drawn or hammered very thin.

When I Peruse the Conquered Fame

When I peruse the conquered fame of heroes and the victories of
    mighty generals, I do not envy the generals,
Nor the President in his Presidency, nor the rich in his great house,
But when I hear of the brotherhood of lovers, how it was with them,
How together through life, through dangers, odium,° unchanging,
    long and long,
Through youth and through middle and old age, how unfaltering,
    how affectionate and faithful they were,   5
Then I am pensive—I hastily walk away filled with the bitterest envy.

4. **odium:** disgrace.

Come Up from the Fields, Father

Come up from the fields, father, here's a letter from our Pete,
And come to the front door, mother, here's a letter from thy dear son.

Lo, 'tis autumn,
Lo, where the trees, deeper green, yellower and redder,
Cool and sweeten Ohio's villages with leaves fluttering in the moder-
    ate wind,   5
Where apples ripe in the orchards hang and grapes on the trellised
    vines,
(Smell you the smell of the grapes on the vines?
Smell you the buckwheat where the bees were lately buzzing?)
Above all, lo, the sky so calm, so transparent after the rain, and with
    wondrous clouds,
Below too, all calm, all vital and beautiful, and the farm prospers
    well.   10

Down in the fields all prospers well,
But now from the fields come, father, come at the daughter's call,
And come to the entry, mother, to the front door come right away.

Fast as she can she hurries, something ominous, her steps trembling,
She does not tarry to smooth her hair nor adjust her cap.   15

Open the envelope quickly,
O this is not our son's writing, yet his name is signed,
O a strange hand writes for our dear son, O stricken mother's soul!
All swims before her eyes, flashes with black, she catches the main
    words only,
Sentences broken, *gunshot wound in the breast, cavalry skirmish,
    taken to hospital,*   20
At present low, but will soon be better.

Ah, now the single figure to me,
Amid all teeming and wealthy Ohio with all its cities and farms,
Sickly white in the face and dull in the head, very faint,
By the jamb of a door leans.   25

Grieve not so, dear mother (the just-grown daughter speaks through
    her sobs,
The little sisters huddle around speechless and dismayed),
See, dearest mother, the letter says Pete will soon be better.

Alas, poor boy, he will never be better (nor maybe needs to be bet-
    ter, that brave and simple soul),
While they stand at home at the door he is dead already,   30
The only son is dead.

But the mother needs to be better,
She with thin form presently dressed in black,
By day her meals untouched, then at night fitfully sleeping, often
    waking,
In the midnight waking, weeping, longing with one deep longing,
O that she might withdraw unnoticed, silent from life escape and
    withdraw,   36
To follow, to seek; to be with her dear dead son.

On the Beach at Night

On the beach at night,
Stands a child with her father,
Watching the east, the autumn sky.

Up through the darkness,
While ravening clouds, the burial clouds, in black masses spreading,
Lower sullen and fast athwart° and down the sky,   6
Amid a transparent clear belt of ether° yet left in the east,
Ascends large and calm the lord-star Jupiter,
And nigh at hand, only a very little above,
Swim the delicate sisters the Pleiades.°   10

From the beach the child holding the hand of her father,
Those burial clouds that lower victorious soon to devour all,
Watching, silently weeps.

Weep not, child,
Weep not, my darling,   15
With these kisses let me remove your tears,
The ravening clouds shall not long be victorious;
They shall not long possess the sky, they devour the stars only in
    apparition,°
Jupiter shall emerge, be patient, watch again another night, the Ple-
    iades shall emerge,
They are immortal, all those stars both silvery and golden shall shine
    out again,   20
The great stars and the little ones shall shine out again, they endure,
The vast immortal suns and the long-enduring pensive moons shall
    again shine.

Then dearest child mournest thou only for Jupiter?
Considerest thou alone the burial of the stars?

6. **athwart:** across. 7. **ether:** here, air or space. 10. **Pleiades** (plē'yă-
dēz): a group of stars near the constellation Orion. In Greek mythology, the
Pleiades were seven daughters of Atlas who were transformed into stars.
18. **in apparition:** in appearance (not in reality).

Something there is,   25
(With my lips soothing thee, adding I whisper,
I give thee the first suggestion, the problem and indirection,)
Something there is more immortal even than the stars,
(Many the burials, many the days and nights, passing away,)
Something that shall endure longer even than lustrous Jupiter,   30
Longer than sun or any revolving satellite,
Or the radiant sisters the Pleiades.

The Last Invocation

At the last, tenderly,
From the walls of the powerful fortressed house,
From the clasp of the knitted locks, from the keep of the well-closed
        doors,
Let me be wafted.

Let me glide noiselessly forth;   5
With the key of softness unlock the locks—with a whisper,
Set ope the doors O soul.

Tenderly—be not impatient,
(Strong is your hold O mortal flesh,
Strong is your hold O love.)   10

Questions

1. What is the comparison in "A Noiseless, Patient Spider"? Explain the
   imagery of the second stanza. Compare Whitman's method in this poem
   with Holmes' method in "The Chambered Nautilus" (p. 407).
2. In "When I Peruse the Conquered Fame," what two kinds of experience are contrasted? Is this contrast in any way related to the contrast
   in "When I Heard the Learn'd Astronomer" (p. 49)?
3. Is "Come Up from the Fields, Father" a sentimental poem or is it
   emotionally restrained? Explain your answer. Is it a moving poem?
   What is the effect of the description in lines 3–10? What is the meaning of the parenthetical statement in line 29?

4. Why is the child sad in "On the Beach at Night"? How does the speaker comfort her? Discuss the symbolism of this poem. Note especially lines 12 and 17–18. Consider the final section, lines 25–32. What is "more immortal even than the stars"?
5. In "The Last Invocation" what does the house symbolize? How is the symbolism worked out in detail?
6. Select any one of the Whitman poems included here and analyze it from the standpoint of fabric. What musical effects does Whitman create in his poetry? Compare Whitman's free verse to Longfellow's more traditional forms (pp. 399–401). What has Whitman gained by using free verse? What has he lost? How does his free verse compare to the verse of the King James Bible (p. 210)?

HERMAN MELVILLE

1819–1891

Around 1920, some American and British literary critics rediscovered an almost forgotten book and suddenly became aware of a major American writer. The book was *Moby Dick* and the writer was Herman Melville. Since his rediscovery in this century, Melville's writings have attracted a large audience. Today, his reputation rests on his fiction, particularly *Moby Dick,* but his poetry also merits attention.

Melville was born in New York City. He received little formal education: he began working at fifteen, and at twenty he shipped as a cabin boy on a merchant vessel. Two years later he signed for a voyage on the whaler *Acushnet.* (He was later to say that a whaling ship was "my Yale College and my Harvard.") After a few years at sea, he returned to this country and began a career as a novelist. His first books were romantic tales drawn from his experiences in the south seas, and they proved to be popular successes. But when Melville turned to highly symbolic fiction, in *Moby Dick* and other novels, he lost his audience. In later years, particularly the 1860's and 70's, more and more of his creative energy was given to poetry.

The Berg

I saw a ship of martial build
(Her standards set, her brave apparel on)
Directed as by madness mere
Against a stolid iceberg steer,
Nor budge it, though the infatuate° ship went down.   5
The impact made huge ice cubes fall
Sullen, in tons that crashed the deck;
But that one avalanche was all—
No other movement save the foundering wreck.

Along the spurs of ridges pale,   10
Not any slenderest shaft and frail,
A prism over glass-green gorges lone,
Toppled; nor lace of traceries fine,
Nor pendant drops in grot° or mine
Were jarred, when the stunned ship went down.   15
Nor sole° the gulls in cloud that wheeled
Circling one snow-flanked peak afar,

But nearer fowl the floes° that skimmed
And crystal beaches, felt no jar.
No thrill transmitted stirred the lock°   20
Of jack-straw° needle-ice at base;
Towers undermined by waves—the block
Atilt impending—kept their place.
Seals, dozing sleek on sliddery° ledges
Slipped never, when loftier edges   25
Through very inertia overthrown,
The impetuous ship in bafflement went down.

---

5. **infatuate**: here, foolish.   14. **grot**: grotto, cave.   16. **Nor sole**: not only.
18. **floes**: low masses of floating ice.   20. **lock**: tuft (as in *lock* of hair).
21. **jack-straw**: small pieces of straw or strips of some hard material.   24. **sliddery**: slippery.

Hard berg (methought), so cold, so vast,
With mortal damps self-overcast;
Exhaling still thy dankish breath—   30
Adrift dissolving, bound for death;
Though lumpish thou, a lumbering one—
A lumbering lubbard, loitering slow—
Impingers° rue thee and go down,
Sounding thy precipice below,   35
Nor stir the slimy slug° that sprawls
Along thy dead indifference of walls.

34. **Impingers:** those who strike upon or collide with something. 36. **slug:** a type of snail.

Questions

1. Discuss the symbolism of this poem. Why is it significant that the ship is "of martial build / (Her standards set, her brave apparel on)"? Why is it significant that the ship appears to strike the iceberg deliberately? What does the ship do to the iceberg and the animals on or around it? What is the effect of the iceberg's being personified the way it is? What do you think the symbolism implies?
2. Analyze the fabric of the poem, particularly lines 10–15 and 30–37.

HENRY TIMROD

1828–1867

Timrod was born in Charleston, South Carolina, and educated at the University of Georgia. He studied law and then taught for a short time before beginning his writing career. In 1861 he enlisted in the Confederate army but was discharged less than a year later because of ill health. During the remainder of the war he worked as a war correspondent and a newspaper editor. The last few years of his life were a constant struggle against poverty and disease. He died at thirty-nine.

Timrod's early verses were imitative of some of the English Romantic poets, but his work soon became strongly individual. His characteristic strength lies in his combination of emotional warmth with classical restraint—a quality that is sometimes reminiscent of Landor, but which Timrod reached in his own way.

I Know Not Why, but All This Weary Day

I know not why, but all this weary day,
Suggested by no definite grief or pain,
Sad fancies have been flitting through my brain;
Now it has been a vessel losing way,
Rounding a stormy headland; now a gray   5
Dull waste of clouds above a wintry main;
And then, a banner, drooping in the rain,
And meadows beaten into bloody clay.
Strolling at random with this shadowy woe
At heart, I chanced to wander hither! Lo!   10
A league of desolate marsh-land, with its lush,
Hot grasses in a noisome,° tide-left bed,
And faint, warm airs that rustle in the hush,
Like whispers round the body of the dead.

12. **noisome:** offensive to the smell.

Ode

This tribute to the Confederate dead was sung on the occasion of decorating the Confederate graves at Magnolia Cemetery in Charleston, S.C.

Sleep sweetly in your humble graves,
    Sleep, martyrs of a fallen cause;
Though yet no marble column craves
    The pilgrim here to pause.

In seeds of laurel in the earth   5
    The blossom of your fame is blown,

And somewhere, waiting for its birth,
    The shaft is in the stone!

Meanwhile, behalf the tardy years
    Which keep in trust your storied tombs,   10
Behold! your sisters bring their tears,
    And these memorial blooms.

Small tributes! but your shades will smile
    More proudly on these wreaths today,
Than when some cannon-molded pile°   15
    Shall overlook this bay.

Stoop, angels, hither from the skies!
    There is no holier spot of ground
Than where defeated valor lies,
    By mourning beauty crowned!   20

15. **cannon-molded pile:** monuments to soldiers are often made of melted cannon.

Questions

1. What is the form of "I Know Not Why, but All This Weary Day"?
What is the tone? Would you call this a sentimental poem? Why, or why not?
2. In "Ode" why are the soldiers' graves described as "humble"? What do you think the second stanza means? What emotion (or emotions) do you find in the poem?

EMILY DICKINSON

1830–1886

Emily Dickinson and Walt Whitman are generally considered the greatest nineteenth-century American poets, but it would be hard to find two writers so completely dissimilar. Whitman is at his best when he is direct, expansive, open, and when he can embrace as much experience as possible within a poem. Emily Dickinson's poetry is subtle, ironic, and usually most effective when it is most condensed.

Emily Dickinson was born in Amherst, Massachusetts, and educated at Amherst Academy and Mount Holyoke College. She seems to have enjoyed a normal childhood, and as a girl and young woman she was known for her liveliness and sense of humor. But for reasons that have never been fully explained, in her early twenties she began to withdraw more and more from ordinary contacts with the world. For the remaining thirty years of her life she was rarely seen outside the Dickinson home.

Her solitary life was not an idle one. She occupied her long hours with extensive correspondence with several friends, and with the writing of a large number of remarkable poems, many of which were included in her letters. Only a few of her poems were published during her lifetime, none of them with her permission. Almost all of her poems—over 1,000 in all—were found in her rooms after her death. The first selection of her work was published in 1890, but not until 1955 did a presumably complete edition appear. Some of her verses are clearly fragments or jottings that were never finished. But the majority of the poems are of such excellence that Emily Dickinson's place as a major poet is firm.

I Taste a Liquor Never Brewed

I taste a liquor never brewed,
From tankards scooped in pearl;
Not all the vats upon the Rhine
Yield such an alcohol!

Inebriate of air am I, 5
And debauchee of dew,
Reeling, through endless summer days,
From inns of molten blue.

When landlords turn the drunken bee
Out of the foxglove's door,   10
When butterflies renounce their drams,
I shall but drink the more!

Till seraphs swing their snowy hats,
And saints to windows run,
To see the little tippler   15
Leaning against the sun!

I Like to See It Lap the Miles

Here, the poet pictures the essential qualities of a locomotive
entirely through metaphor, with no direct statement.

I like to see it lap the miles,
And lick the valleys up,
And stop to feed itself at tanks;
And then, prodigious, step

Around a pile of mountains,   5
And, supercilious, peer
In shanties by the sides of roads;
And then a quarry pare°

To fit its sides, and crawl between,
Complaining all the while   10
In horrid, hooting stanza;
Then chase itself down hill

And neigh like Boanerges;°
Then, punctual as a star,
Stop—docile and omnipotent—   15
At its own stable door.

8. **pare:** here, slice or split. 13. **Boanerges** (bō'á·nûr'jēz): a noisy orator.

There's a Certain Slant of Light

There's a certain slant of light,
On winter afternoons,
That oppresses, like the weight
Of cathedral tunes.

Heavenly hurt it gives us;   5
We can find no scar,
But internal difference
Where the meanings are.

None may teach it anything,
'Tis the seal, despair—   10
An imperial affliction
Sent us of° the air.

When it comes, the landscape listens,
Shadows hold their breath;
When it goes, 'tis like the distance   15
On the look of death.

12. of: from.

My Life Closed Twice

My life closed twice before its close;
It yet remains to see
If immortality unveil
A third event to me,

So huge, so hopeless to conceive,   5
As these that twice befell.
Parting is all we know of heaven,
And all we need of hell.

If I Should Die

If I should die,
And you should live,
And time should gurgle on,
And morn should beam,
And noon should burn,   5
As it has usual done:
If birds should build as early,
And bees as bustling go,
One might depart at option
From enterprise below!   10
'Tis sweet to know that stocks will stand
When we with daisies lie,
That commerce will continue,
And trades as briskly fly.
It makes the parting tranquil   15
And keeps the soul serene,
That gentlemen so sprightly
Conduct the pleasing scene!

The Hummingbird

A route of evanescence°
With a revolving wheel;
A resonance of emerald,
A rush of cochineal;°

And every blossom on the bush   5
Adjusts its tumbled head—
The mail from Tunis,° probably,
An easy morning's ride!

1. evanescence (ĕv′á·nĕs′ĕns): something vaporlike.   4. cochineal: (kŏch′ĭ-nēl′): a red or purple dye.   7. Tunis: a city in northeast Africa.

The Mountain

The mountain sat upon the plain
In his eternal chair,
His observation omnifold,°
His inquest everywhere.

The seasons prayed around his knees,   5
Like children round a sire:
Grandfather of the days is he,
Of dawn the ancestor.

3. **omnifold:** here, of all times, eternal.

After Great Pain a Formal Feeling Comes

After great pain a formal feeling comes—
The nerves sit ceremonious like tombs;
The stiff heart questions—was it He that bore?
And yesterday—or centuries before?

The feet mechanical go round   5
A wooden way,
Of ground or air of ought,
Regardless grown;
A quartz contentment like a stone.

This is the hour of lead   10
Remembered if outlived
As freezing persons recollect
The snow —
First chill, then stupor, then
The letting go.   15

Questions

1. What is the liquor in "I Taste a Liquor Never Brewed"? What is the tone of this poem?

2. What is the locomotive compared to in "I Like to See It Lap the Miles"? What is the paradox in line 15? What kind of rhyme (if any) does Emily Dickinson use in this poem? What other sound devices can you find in these lines?

3. In "There's a Certain Slant of Light" what might be meant by "Heavenly hurt"? How can "cathedral tunes" be said to have "weight"? What might lines 6–8 mean?

4. What paradox is suggested by the last two lines of "My Life Closed Twice"?

5. What is the effect of line 3 in "If I Should Die"? What is the tone of the poem?

6. Compare "The Mountain" and "The Hummingbird." How are they similar? different? What is the relationship of the last two lines of "The Hummingbird" to the rest of the poem?

7. In "After Great Pain a Formal Feeling Comes" what kind of experience is being described? What is the effect of such phrases as "quartz contentment" or "hour of lead"? Would you call such phrases images? Why, or why not?

SIDNEY LANIER

1842–1881

Lanier was born in Georgia and educated at Oglethorpe College in that state. At the outbreak of the War Between the States, he enlisted in the Confederate army. Near the end of the war he was captured and spent some months in a Federal prison. The imprisonment weakened his already frail health, and the rest of his life was a struggle against tuberculosis. He died at thirty-nine.

Lanier was a gifted musician as well as a brilliant poet. His musical background led to his experiments with new forms of verse and new sound effects in language. He attempted to draw the arts of music and poetry closer together by modeling the structure of some of his poems after the structure of musical compositions. His efforts were not always completely successful, but they were unquestionably interesting and illuminating, and they paved the way for many later experimental poets.

In addition to his poetry, Lanier wrote a novel, *Tiger Lilies*, and a critical work, *The Science of English Verse*, in which he outlined his theories of rhythm and meter.

Song of the Chattahoochee*

Out of the hills of Habersham,°
Down the valleys of Hall,°
I hurry amain° to reach the plain,
Run the rapid and leap the fall,
Split at the rock and together again,   5
Accept my bed, or narrow or wide,
And flee from folly on every side
With a lover's pain to attain the plain
    Far from the hills of Habersham,
    Far from the valleys of Hall.   10

All down the hills of Habersham,
All through the valleys of Hall,
The rushes cried, *Abide, abide,*
The willful waterweeds held me thrall,°
The laving laurel turned my tide,   15
The ferns and the fondling grass said *Stay,*
The dewberry dipped for to work delay,
And the little reeds sighed, *Abide, abide,*
    Here in the hills of Habersham,
    Here in the valleys of Hall.   20

High o'er the hills of Habersham,
Veiling the valleys of Hall,
The hickory told me manifold
Fair tales of shade, the poplar tall

* **Chattahoochee** (chăt′*á*·hōō′chê): a river flowing from north to southwest Georgia. 1–2. Habersham, Hall: counties in Georgia. 3. **amain:** at full speed. 14. **thrall:** enslaved.

Wrought me her shadowy self to hold,　　　　　　25
The chestnut, the oak, the walnut, the pine,
Overleaning, with flickering meaning and sign,
Said, *Pass not, so cold, these manifold*
　　Deep shades of the hills of Habersham,
　　These glades in the valleys of Hall.　　　　30

And oft in the hills of Habersham,
And oft in the valleys of Hall,
The white quartz shone, and the smooth brook-stone
Did bar me of passage with friendly brawl,
And many a luminous jewel lone　　　　　　35
—Crystals clear or a-cloud with mist,
Ruby, garnet, and amethyst—
Made lures with the lights of streaming stone
　　In the clefts of the hills of Habersham,
　　In the beds of the valleys of Hall.　　　　40

But oh, not the hills of Habersham,
　　And oh, not the valleys of Hall
Avail: I am fain for° to water the plain.
Downward the voices of Duty call—
Downward, to toil and be mixed with the main;°　　45
The dry fields burn, and the mills are to turn,
And a myriad flowers mortally yearn,
And the lordly main from beyond the plain
　　Calls o'er the hills of Habersham,
　　Calls through the valleys of Hall.　　　　50

43. I am fain for: I wish.　**45. main:** sea.

Questions

Lanier was a musician as well as a poet. What are some of the sound devices that he has used to make this poem musical? *Is* this poem truly musical? Explain your answer.

Sidney Lanier　429

STEPHEN CRANE

1871–1900

Stephen Crane is known primarily as a novelist and a short-story writer—his most famous work is his novel *The Red Badge of Courage* —but he was also an accomplished poet.

Crane was born in Newark, New Jersey. After two years at college, he left school to begin his writing career as a newspaper reporter in New York City. His first novel was unsuccessful, but *The Red Badge of Courage*, published when he was only twenty-four, made his reputation. During the remaining five years of his life he produced a number of excellent short stories and poems. While working as a war correspondent during the Spanish-American War in Cuba, Crane earned a reputation for bravery under fire. But the experience ruined his health, and he died five months before his twenty-ninth birthday.

His father was a minister, and perhaps the strongest influence on Crane's poetry was the religious background he knew as a child. Many readers have noted the parable-like quality of his finest poems.

I Saw a Man

I saw a man pursuing the horizon;
Round and round they sped.
I was disturbed at this;
I accosted the man.
"It is futile," I said,   5
"You can never—"
"You lie," he cried,
And ran on.

The Wayfarer

The wayfarer,
Perceiving the pathway to truth,
Was struck with astonishment.

It was thickly grown with weeds.
"Ha," he said,   5
"I see that no one has passed here
In a long time."
Later he saw that each weed
Was a singular knife.
"Well," he mumbled at last,   10
"Doubtless there are other roads."

Questions

1. What is Crane's attitude toward the wayfarer and toward the man pursuing the horizon?
2. Are these two selections really poems at all? Justify your answer.

MODERN BRITISH POETRY

The poetry of the last few years of the nineteenth century and the first half of our own century is difficult to sum up briefly. After the deaths of the great Victorians—Tennyson, Browning, and Arnold—the poetic tradition began to break up into a number of "schools," until eventually it seemed as though there were as many kinds of poetry as there were poets. Some general characteristics became apparent, however. Symbolism began to occupy a more prominent place in the work of modern poets. The language of poetry seemed to draw closer to contemporary speech. Irony and a strong sense of pessimism were increasingly apparent in twentieth-century poetry. Finally, modern poets showed an increasing interest in experimenting with both form and subject. Certainly all of these characteristics could be found in the poetry of any previous age, but the twentieth century carried them to a greater degree than before. In the end, however, modern poetry is best understood in terms of individual poets. And because much of what is considered typical of modern poetry first appeared in the work of Thomas Hardy, it is customary to begin collections of modern British poetry with a selection of his poems.

THOMAS HARDY

1840–1928

The son of a stonemason, Hardy was apprenticed to an architect at the age of sixteen. In 1862 he became assistant to a London architect. He won two prizes and was on his way to becoming a distinguished architect when he gave up that profession and turned to writing.

He began his career in literature as a novelist. After some early failures, he established his reputation with *Under the Greenwood Tree*. His other novels include *The Return of the Native*, *Tess of the D'Urbervilles*, and *Jude the Obscure*. These last two works were severely criticized: the attacks hurt Hardy so deeply that after the publication of *Jude the Obscure* in 1896, he determined to write no more novels. In 1898, at the age of almost sixty, he turned to poetry exclusively. Until his death at eighty-eight he produced a vast amount of excellent poetry, ranging from tender lyrics and colloquial dialogues to tragedy and epic. He wrote in almost every kind of meter, form, and style, and his last volume displays as much interest in original experiment as his first.

Hardy is clearly modern in his ceaseless questioning of convention, his deliberately harsh rhythms, and his ironic combinations of the trivial and the profound. He is often called a pessimist, but his themes were tragic rather than merely pessimistic. In man's struggles and failures Hardy saw meaning and nobility, and he expressed his vision in poetry that, if not consistently eloquent, was always forceful.

Neutral Tones

We stood by a pond that winter day,
And the sun was white, as though chidden of° God,
And a few leaves lay on the starving sod;
    They had fallen from an ash, and were gray.

Your eyes on me were as eyes that rove   5
Over tedious riddles solved years ago;
And some words played between us to and fro
    On which lost the more by our love.

The smile on your mouth was the deadest thing
Alive enough to have strength to die;   10
And a grin of bitterness swept thereby
    Like an ominous bird a-wing. . . .

2. **chidden of:** scolded by.

Since then, keen lessons that love deceives,
And wrings with wrong, have shaped to me
Your face, and the God-cursed sun, and a tree,   15
And a pond edged with grayish leaves.

At the Draper's*

"I stood at the back of the shop, my dear,
But you did not perceive me.
Well, when they deliver what you were shown
I shall know nothing of it, believe me!"

And he coughed and coughed as she paled and said,   5
"O, I didn't see you come in there—
Why couldn't you speak?"—"Well, I didn't. I left
That you should not notice I'd been there.

"You were viewing some lovely things. 'Soon required
For a widow, of latest fashion';   10
And I knew 'twould upset you to meet the man
Who had to be cold and ashen

"And screwed in a box before they could dress you
'In the last new note in mourning,'
As they defined it. So, not to distress you,   15
I left you to your adorning."

* **Draper's:** clothier's.

Rome

(*At the Pyramid of Cestius near the Graves of Shelley and Keats*)

Who, then was Cestius
And what is he to me?
Amid thick thoughts and memories multitudinous
One thought alone brings he.

I can recall no word   5
Of anything he did;
For me he is a man who died and was interred
To leave a pyramid

Whose purpose was expressed
Not with its first design,   10
Nor till, far down in time, beside it found their rest
Two countrymen of mine.

Cestius in life, maybe,
Slew, breathed out threatening;
I know not. This I know: in death all silently   15
He does a finer thing.

In beckoning pilgrim feet
With marble finger high
To where, by shadowy wall and history-haunted street,
Those matchless singers lie. . . .   20

—Say, then, he lived and died
That stones which bear his name
Should mark, through time, where two immortal shades abide;
It is an ample fame.

The Darkling* Thrush

I leant upon a coppice° gate
    When frost was specter-gray,
And winter's dregs made desolate
    The weakening eye of day.
The tangled bine-stems scored the sky   5
    Like strings of broken lyres,
And all mankind that haunted nigh
    Had sought their household fires.

___

* **Darkling:** at dark, in the night.   1. **coppice:** a small grove of trees.

The land's sharp features seemed to be
   The century's corpse outleant,   10
His crypt tĥe cloudy canopy,
   The wind his death-lament.
The ancient pulse of germ and birth
   Was shrunken hard and dry,
And every spirit upon earth   15
   Seemed fervorless as I.

At once a voice arose among
   The bleak twigs overhead
In a full-hearted evensong
   Of joy illimited;°   20
An aged thrush, frail, gaunt, and small,
   In blast°-beruffled plume,
Had chosen thus to fling his soul
   Upon the growing gloom.

So little cause for carolings   25
   Of such ecstatic sound
Was written on terrestrial things
   Afar or nigh around,
That I could think there trembled through
   His happy good-night air   30
Some blessèd hope, whereof he knew
   And I was unaware.

20. **illimited:** limitless.   22. **blast:** wind.

Questions

1. What is the meaning of the last stanza of "Neutral Tones"?
2. Who is the speaker in "At the Draper's"? What is the situation? What is the tone? What are some of the elements which help to create the tone?
3. What is the effect of the rather unusual stanza form of "Rome"?
4. Is "The Darkling Thrush" an optimistic or a pessimistic poem? Explain your answer. Analyze the fabric of the poem. What is the effect of the various sound devices?

ROBERT BRIDGES

1844–1930

Educated at Eton and Oxford, Robert Bridges started a career as a surgeon before he became a poet and critic. At thirty-eight he retired permanently from the medical profession to devote himself entirely to literature. Perhaps the strongest characteristics of his poetry are its classical restraint and subtle rhythms. His lyrics show him to be a master of metrical techniques. His work was officially honored when he was named poet laureate in 1913.

In addition to his own work, Bridges was known for his encouragement of many fellow poets. It was he who was primarily responsible for the publication of the poems of Gerard Manley Hopkins (see p. 438).

London Snow

When men were all asleep the snow came flying,
In large white flakes falling on the city brown,
Stealthily and perpetually settling and loosely lying,
    Hushing the latest traffic of the drowsy town;
Deadening, muffling, stifling its murmurs failing;   5
Lazily and incessantly floating down and down:
    Silently sifting and veiling road, roof, and railing;
Hiding difference, making unevenness even,
Into angles and crevices softly drifting and sailing.
    All night it fell, and when full inches seven   10
It lay in the depth of its uncompacted lightness,
The clouds blew off from a high and frosty heaven;
    And all woke earlier for the unaccustomed brightness
Of the winter dawning, the strange unheavenly glare:
The eye marveled—marveled at the dazzling whiteness;   15
    The ear hearkened to the stillness of the solemn air;
No sound of wheel rumbling nor of foot falling,
And the busy morning cries came thin and spare.
    Then boys I heard, as they went to school, calling,

They gathered up the crystal manna° to freeze   20
Their tongues with tasting, their hands with snowballing;
  Or rioted in a drift, plunging up to the knees;
Or peering up from under the white-mossed wonder,
"O look at the trees!" they cried, "O look at the trees!"
  With lessened load a few carts creak and blunder,   25
Following along the white deserted way,
A country company long dispersed asunder:
  When now already the sun, in pale display
Standing by Paul's° high dome, spread forth below
His sparkling beams, and awoke the stir of the day.   30
  For now doors open, and war is waged with the snow;
And trains of somber men, past tale of number,
Tread long brown paths, as toward their toil they go:
  But even for them awhile no cares encumber
Their minds diverted; the daily word is unspoken,   35
The daily thoughts of labor and sorrow slumber
At the sight of the beauty that greets them, for the charm they have
  broken.

20. manna: food miraculously supplied by heaven.   29. Paul's: St. Paul's
cathedral.

Questions

Is this more than a purely descriptive poem? Explain. Discuss the
rhythm of the poem. What is unusual about it?

GERARD MANLEY HOPKINS

1844–1889

While at Oxford Hopkins became a convert to Catholicism. A few
years later he became a Jesuit priest. He had been writing poetry for
a number of years, but when he entered the priesthood he resolved to
write no more, feeling that poetry was incompatible with the life he
had chosen. Later, however, he asked for, and was granted, permis-

sion to resume writing, and for the last fifteen years of his life he was a highly productive poet. But he was hardly known, for only a few of his poems were published during his lifetime. He might still be unknown today if it had not been for his friend Robert Bridges. After Hopkins' death, Bridges set about collecting all of his poems, and eventually, in 1918, published most of them. It was thirty years after his death that Hopkins finally found an audience for his work. Today he is regarded as one of the major English poets.

Besides being a scholar and poet, Hopkins was a talented painter and musician. His feeling for design and melody helped shape the pattern of his poems. He was one of the great technical innovators in English poetry, and his work is sometimes difficult because of his originality and because of his unusual word order, concentrated imagery, and elaborate metaphors.

Heaven-Haven

A Nun Takes the Veil

I have desired to go
  Where springs not fail,
To fields where flies no sharp and sided hail,
  And a few lilies blow.

And I have asked to be 5
  Where no storms come,
Where the green swell is in the havens dumb
  And out of the swing of the sea.

Spring and Fall: To a Young Child

In this poem, and in the two that follow, Hopkins used a metrical system that he called "sprung rhythm." Hopkins' theories were somewhat complicated, but in practice "sprung rhythm" has two obvious effects. First, it means that the length of the poetic line is determined by counting *only* accented syllables: thus, for example, lines of six and eight syllables are considered the same length if both contain three accented syllables. Second, "sprung rhythm" involves the consistent accenting of syllables which, in traditional metrical schemes, would be unaccented. To assist the reader, Hopkins sometimes indicates which syllables are to be accented.

> Márgarét, are you gríeving
> Over Goldengrove unleáving?°
> Leáves, líke the things of man, you
> With your fresh thoughts care for, can you?
> Ah! ás the heart grows older   5
> It will come to such sights colder
> By and by, nor spare a sigh
> Though worlds of wanwood° leafmeal° lie;
> And yet you wíll weep and know why.
> Now no matter, child, the name: 10
> Sórrow's spríngs° áre the same.
> Nor mouth had, no nor mind, expressed
> What heart heard of, ghost° guessed:
> It ís the blight man was born for,
> It is Margaret you mourn for.   15

2. Hopkins was fond of unusual word-combinations. **Goldengrove unleaving** refers to a grove in autumn when the golden leaves are beginning to fall from the trees. 8. **wanwood:** dark or bare wood. **leafmeal:** leaf by leaf (as in "piecemeal"). 11. **springs:** sources. 13. **ghost:** soul.

Pied* Beauty

> Glory be to God for dappled° things—
>   For skies of couple-color as a brinded° cow;
>   For rose-moles all in stipple upon trout that swim;
>   Fresh-firecoal chestnut-falls; finches' wings;
>   Landscape plotted and pieced—fold, fallow, and plow;   5
>   And áll trádes, their gear and tackle and trim.

* **Pied:** composed of various colors. 1. **dappled:** spotted. 2. **brinded:** spotted or streaked.

All things counter,° original, spare, strange;
　　Whatever is fickle, freckled (who knows how?)
　　　With swift, slow; sweet, sour; adazzle, dim;
He fathers-forth whose beauty is past change:　　　　　　10
　　　　　　Praise him.

7. **counter:** in contrast, opposed (to the usual).

God's Grandeur

The world is charged with the grandeur of God.
　　It will flame out, like shining from shook foil;
　　It gathers to a greatness, like the ooze of oil
Crushed. Why do men then now not reck his rod?
Generations have trod, have trod, have trod;　　　　　　5
　　And all is seared with trade; bleared, smeared with toil;
　　And wears man's smudge and shares man's smell: the soil
Is bare now, nor can foot feel, being shod.

And for all this, nature is never spent;
　　There lives the dearest freshness deep down things;　　　　10
And though the last lights off the black West went
　　Oh, morning, at the brown brink eastward, springs—
Because the Holy Ghost over the bent
　　World broods with warm breast and with ah! bright wings.

Questions

1. On what metaphor is "Heaven-Haven" based? What is the relationship between the two stanzas?
2. In "Spring and Fall: To a Young Child," why is Margaret grieving? What do the fallen leaves symbolize? What does the last line mean?
3. What is the theme of "Pied Beauty"? How is the poem organized?
4. Discuss the various figures of speech in "God's Grandeur." What is the effect of lines 2 and 3? of lines 13 and 14?
5. Compare the theme of "God's Grandeur" to that of Wordsworth's sonnet, "The World Is Too Much with Us" (p.299). How are the poems similar? How are they different?

A. E. HOUSMAN

1859–1936

A. E. (Alfred Edward) Housman was educated at Oxford. After graduation he worked for a few years in the British Patent Office. He left that position to become a teacher. From 1892 to 1911, he was Professor of Latin at University College, London, and after 1911 he taught at Cambridge. In addition to his work as a poet, he made himself one of the greatest classical scholars of his day.

Housman published only two thin volumes of poetry during his lifetime. *A Shropshire Lad* appeared in 1896 and *Last Poems* in 1922. *More Poems*, edited by his brother Laurence, appeared in 1936, a few months after the poet's death.

Housman is frequently compared to Hardy. Pessimism and irony colored the vision that both expressed in their work. Unlike Hardy, however, Housman experimented very little with verse forms. Almost all of his poems, whether pure lyrics like "White in the Moon" or miniature dramatic narratives like "Farewell to Barn and Stack and Tree" (p. 25) and "The Carpenter's Son," adopt a basic ballad structure. The classical ideals in poetry that he knew as a scholar, particularly the emotional restraint and clarity of the best Latin poets, are characteristic of his work. In their seemingly artless style, Housman's brief poems are incomparable.

The Carpenter's Son

"Here the hangman stops his cart:
Now the best of friends must part.
Fare you well, for ill fare I;
Live, lads, and I will die.

"Oh, at home had I but stayed   5
'Prenticed to my father's trade,
Had I stuck to plane° and adze,°
I had not been lost, my lads.

7. plane, adze: carpenter's tools.

"Then I might have built perhaps
Gallows-trees for other chaps,   10
Never dangled on my own,
Had I but left ill alone.

"Now, you see, they hang me high,
And the people passing by
Stop to shake their fists and curse;   15
So 'tis come from ill to worse.

"Here hang I, and right and left
Two poor fellows hang for theft:
All the same's the luck we prove,
Though the midmost hangs for love.   20

"Comrades all, that stand and gaze,
Walk henceforth in other ways;
See my neck and save your own:
Comrades all, leave ill alone.

"Make some day a decent end,   25
Shrewder fellows than your friend.
Fare you well, for ill fare I:
Live, lads, and I will die."

White in the Moon

White in the moon the long road lies,
    The moon stands blank above;
White in the moon the long road lies
    That leads me from my love.

Still hangs the hedge without a gust.   5
    Still, still the shadows stay:
My feet upon the moonlight dust
    Pursue the ceaseless way.

The world is round, so travelers tell,
    And straight though reach the track,   10
Trudge on, trudge on, 'twill all be well,
    The way will guide one back.

But ere the circle homeward hies
    Far, far it must remove:
White in the moon the long road lies   15
    That leads me from my love.

Questions

1. Who is the speaker in "The Carpenter's Son"? What advice does he give to his friends? Is the advice meant to be taken seriously, or is it ironic?
2. What is the effect of the imagery in "White in the Moon"? Consider especially the first two stanzas. How does the poem use repetition to help create its effect?

ARTHUR SYMONS

1865–1945

Arthur Symons was born in Wales and educated at private schools. He early became interested in the French Symbolist poets, particularly Paul Verlaine and Charles Baudelaire, and much of his early work reveals their influence. His first poems were also often imitative of Swinburne and the Pre-Raphaelites. His later work is less imitative and more restrained, simple, and precise.

In addition to his poetry, Symons also wrote a number of excellent essays and short stories.

Modern Beauty

I am the torch, she saith, and what to me
If the moth die of me? I am the flame
Of beauty, and I burn that all may see
Beauty, and I have neither joy nor shame,

But live with that clear light of perfect fire   5
Which is to men the death of their desire.

I am Yseult° and Helen. I have seen
Troy burn, and the most loving knight lie dead.
The world has been my mirror, time has been
My breath upon the glass; and men have said,   10
Age after age, in rapture and despair,
Love's poor few words before my image there.

I live, and am immortal; in my eyes
The sorrow of the world, and on my lips
The joy of life, mingle to make me wise;   15
Yet now the day is darkened with eclipse:
Who is there still lives for beauty? Still am I
The torch, but where's the moth that still dares die?

7. **Yseult** (ĭ·sōōlt′): In Medieval legend, Yseult (or *Isolde* or *Iseult*), is the
beautiful wife of King Mark of Cornwall. She falls in love with the knight
Tristan (or Tristram), who is later killed by Mark. (In another version, he dies
from a wound received in battle.)

Questions

Who is the speaker? What do you think is the meaning of the second
stanza? What is the poem criticizing?

RUDYARD KIPLING

1865–1936

It is easy to understand why Kipling was the most popular poet in
England at the turn of the century. By that time the British public
had grown tired of the Pre-Raphaelite school and the related movements of the time. Kipling's verse was everything that Pre-Raphaelite
poetry was not—hearty, robust, and colorful.

Born in Bombay, Kipling lived most of his early life in India.

After a few years at school in England, he returned to India and began working as a journalist. At twenty-one he published a volume of light verse and the following year his first collection of short stories appeared. His best-known volume of verse is *Barrack-Room Ballads*, published in 1892.

Kipling's best work is a mixture of romantic outlook, realistic detail, and masterful rhythmic technique. If his poetry lacks subtlety, it is, at its best, vigorous and dramatic. Such poems as "The Ballad of East and West" and "Danny Deever" will always be popular.

The Ballad of East and West

Oh, East is East, and West is West, and never the twain shall meet,
Till Earth and Sky stand presently at God's great Judgment Seat;
But there is neither East nor West, Border, nor Breed, nor Birth,
When two strong men stand face to face, though they come from the
ends of the earth!

Kamal° is out with twenty men to raise the Border side,   5
And he has lifted the Colonel's mare that is the Colonel's pride.
He has lifted her out of the stable-door between the dawn and the
    day,
And turned the calkins° upon her feet, and ridden her far away.
Then up and spoke the Colonel's son that led a troop of the Guides:°
"Is there never a man of all my men can say where Kamal hides?"
Then up and spoke Mohammed Khan, the son of the Ressaldar:°
"If ye know the track of the morning mist, ye know where his pick-
    ets° are.   12
At dusk he harries the Abazai°—at dawn he is into Bonair,°
But he must go by Fort Bukloh to his own place to fare.
So if ye gallop to Fort Bukloh as fast as a bird can fly,   15

5. **Kamal** (kä·màl): the leader of the Afghans.   8. **calkins** (kôk'ĭnz): the turned-down edges of a horseshoe.   9. **Guides**: native troops serving with the British.   11. **Ressaldar**: an Indian commander of a cavalry troop.   12. **pickets**: scouts.   13. **Abazai** (ä·bà·zī′), **Bonair**: frontier settlements about forty miles apart.

By the favor of God ye may cut him off ere he win to the Tongue of
Jagai.
But if he be past the Tongue of Jagai, right swiftly turn ye then,
For the length and the breadth of that grisly plain is sown with
Kamal's men.
There is rock to the left, and rock to the right, and low lean thorn
between,
And ye may hear a breech-bolt snick where never a man is seen."
The Colonel's son has taken horse, and a raw rough dun° was he,
With the mouth of a bell and the heart of Hell and the head of a
gallows-tree.   22
The Colonel's son to the Fort has won, they bid him stay to eat—
Who rides at the tail of a Border thief, he sits not long at his meat.
He's up and away from Fort Bukloh as fast as he can fly,   25
Till he was aware of his father's mare in the gut of the Tongue of
Jagai,
Till he was aware of his father's mare with Kamal upon her back,
And when he could spy the white of her eye, he made the pistol
crack.
He has fired once, he has fired twice, but the whistling ball went
wide.
"Ye shoot like a soldier," Kamal said. "Show now if ye can ride!"
It's up and over the Tongue of Jagai, as blown dust-devils go,   31
The dun he fled like a stag of ten, but the mare like a barren doe.
The dun he leaned against the bit and slugged his head above,
But the red mare played with the snaffle bars,° as a maiden plays
with a glove.
There was rock to the left and rock to the right, and low lean thorn
between,   35
And thrice he heard a breech-bolt snick tho' never a man was seen.
They have ridden the low moon out of the sky, their hoofs drum up
the dawn,
The dun he went like a wounded bull, but the mare like a new-
roused fawn.
The dun he fell at a watercourse—in a woeful heap fell he,
And Kamal has turned the red mare back, and pulled the rider free.

21. dun: grayish-brown.   34. snaffle bars: bridle-bits without curbs.

He has knocked the pistol out of his hand—small room was there to
    strive,   41
"'Twas only by favor of mine," quoth he, "ye rode so long alive:
There was not a rock for twenty mile, there was not a clump of tree,
But covered a man of my own men with his rifle cocked on his knee.
If I had raised my bridle hand, as I have held it low,   45
The little jackals that flee so fast were feasting all in a row.
If I had bowed my head on my breast, as I have held it high,
The kite° that whistles above us now were gorged till she could not
    fly."
Lightly answered the Colonel's son: "Do good to bird and beast,
But count who come for the broken meats before thou makest a
    feast.   50
If there should follow a thousand swords to carry my bones away,
Belike the price of a jackal's meal were more than a thief could pay.
They will feed their horse on the standing crop, their men on the
    garnered grain,
The thatch of the byres° will serve their fires when all the cattle are
    slain.
But if thou thinkest the price be fair—thy brethren wait to sup,   55
The hound is kin to the jackal-spawn—howl, dog, and call them up!
And if thou thinkest the price be high, in steer and gear and stack,
Give me my father's mare again, and I'll fight my own way back!"
Kamal has gripped him by the hand and set him upon his feet.
"No talk shall be of dogs," said he, "when wolf and gray wolf meet.
May I eat dirt if thou hast hurt of me in deed or breath;   61
What dam° of lances brought thee forth to jest at the dawn with
    Death?"
Lightly answered the Colonel's son: "I hold by the blood of my clan:
Take up the mare for my father's gift—by God, she has carried a
    man!"
The red mare ran to the Colonel's son, and nuzzled against his
    breast;   65
"We be two strong men," said Kamal then, "but she loveth the
    younger best.
So she shall go with a lifter's dower, my turquoise-studded rein,

48. kite: hawk.   54. byres: cow barns.   62. dam: mother.

My 'broidered saddle and saddlecloth, and silver stirrups twain."
The Colonel's son a pistol drew, and held it muzzle end,
"Ye have taken the one from a foe," said he. "Will ye take the mate
    from a friend?"   70
"A gift for a gift," said Kamal straight; "a limb for the risk of a limb.
Thy father has sent his son to me, I'll send my son to him!"
With that he whistled his only son, that dropped from a mountain
    crest—
He trod the ling° like a buck in spring, and he looked like a lance in
    rest.
"Now here is thy master," Kamal said, "who leads a troop of the
    Guides,   75
And thou must ride at his left side as shield on shoulder rides.
Till Death or I cut loose the tie, at camp and board and bed,
Thy life is his—thy fate it is to guard him with thy head.
So, thou must eat the White Queen's meat, and all her foes are thine,
And thou must harry thy father's hold for the peace of the Border-
    line.   80
And thou must make a trooper tough and hack thy way to power—
Belike they will raise thee to Ressaldar when I am hanged in Pesha-
    wur!"°

They have looked each other between the eyes, and there have found
    no fault.
They have taken the Oath of the Brother-in-Blood on leavened bread
    and salt;
They have taken the Oath of the Brother-in-Blood on fire and fresh-
    cut sod,   85
On the hilt and the shaft of the Khyber knife,° and the Wondrous
    Names of God.°
The Colonel's son he rides the mare and Kamal's boy the dun.
And two have come back to Fort Bukloh where there went forth but
    one.

    74. ling: heather.   82. Peshawur (pĕ·shä'wȧr): the British government
headquarters in Northwest Frontier Province.   86. Khyber (kī'bĕr) knife: a
knife used in the battle of Khyber Pass, a narrow road between India and Af-
ghanistan. Wondrous Names of God: the one hundred Mohammedan names
given to God.

And when they drew to the Quarter Guard,° full twenty swords flew
  clear—
There was not a man but carried his feud with the blood of the
  mountaineer.   90
"Ha' done! ha' done!" said the Colonel's son. "Put up the steel at your
  sides!
Last night ye had struck at a Border thief—tonight 'tis a man of the
  Guides!"

Oh, East is East, and West is West, and never the twain shall meet,
Till Earth and Sky stand presently at God's great Judgment Seat;
But there is neither East nor West, Border, nor Breed, nor Birth, 95
When two strong men stand face to face, though they come from the
  ends of the earth!

89. **Quarter Guard:** sentry post.

Danny Deever

"What are the bugles blowin' for?" said Files-on-Parade.°
"To turn you out, to turn you out," the Color Sergeant° said.
"What makes you look so white, so white?" said Files-on-Parade.
"I'm dreadin' what I've got to watch," the Color Sergeant said.
  For they're hangin' Danny Deever, you can 'ear the Dead March
    play,   5
  The regiment's in 'ollow square—they're hangin' him today;
  They've taken of his buttons off an' cut his stripes away,
  An' they're hangin' Danny Deever in the mornin'.

"What makes the rear-rank breathe so 'ard?" said Files-on-Parade.
"It's bitter cold, it's bitter cold," the Color Sergeant said.   10
"What makes that front-rank man fall down?" says Files-on-Parade.
"A touch of sun, a touch of sun," the Color Sergeant said.
  They are hangin' Danny Deever, they are marchin' of 'im round.

1. **Files-on-Parade:** the soldier who directs marching formations. 2. **Color
Sergeant:** the flag bearer.

They 'ave 'alted Danny Deever by 'is coffin on the ground:
An 'e'll swing in 'arf a minute for a sneakin' shootin' hound—   15
O they're hangin' Danny Deever in the mornin'!

" 'Is cot was right-'and cot to mine," said Files-on-Parade.
" 'E's sleepin' out an' far tonight," the Color Sergeant said.
"I've drunk 'is beer a score o' times," said Files-on-Parade.
" 'E's drinkin' bitter beer alone," the Color Sergeant said.   20
     They are hangin' Danny Deever, you must mark 'im to 'is place,
     For 'e shot a comrade sleepin'—you must look 'im in the face;
     Nine 'undred of 'is county° an' the regiment's disgrace,
     While they're hangin' Danny Deever in the mornin'.

"What's that so black agin the sun?" said Files-on-Parade.   25
"It's Danny fightin' 'ard for life," the Color Sergeant said.
"What's that that whimpers over'ead?" said Files-on-Parade.
"It's Danny's soul that's passin' now," the Color Sergeant said.
     For they're done with Danny Deever, you can 'ear the quickstep
          play,
     The regiment's in column, an' they're marchin' us away;   30
     Ho! the young recruits are shakin', an' they'll want their beer
          today,
     After hangin' Danny Deever in the mornin'.

     23. **county:** that is, soldiers from Danny Deever's county.

Questions

1. The first stanza of "The Ballad of East and West," repeated at the
   end, states the theme in general terms. The main body of the poem
   illustrates the theme. What is the theme and how, specifically, is it
   illustrated? Compare this poem to "The Highwayman," page 112.
   What do they have in common? How do they differ?
2. Why could "Danny Deever" be called a dramatic poem? What are
   some of its balladlike elements?

WILLIAM BUTLER YEATS

1865-1939

Yeats, the son of the Irish artist John B. Yeats, was born in Sandy-mount, Ireland, and educated in Dublin and London. He spent much of his childhood in the remote district of Sligo in Ireland, where the wild landscape and romantic atmosphere seems to have influenced much of his early poetry. He was a central, and highly active, figure in the so-called Irish Renaissance at the turn of the century. As a young man, his interest in the cause of Irish nationalism and the movement to revive the Irish language and the old Celtic traditions led him to help organize a national theater, for which he wrote a number of plays in both prose and verse. At the same time he was active as a folklorist, collecting and publishing many Celtic tales and legends. During much of his life he was also a pamphleteer, essayist, and editor. Finally, he was, for many years, active in public life; after Ireland gained its independence, he was elected a Senator of the Irish Free State.

Yeats began his poetic career as a romantic and ended as a modern. His earliest poems were delicately musical verses about the shadowy dreamworld of Celtic legend. But by the time of *The Green Helmet* in 1910 his art was undergoing a radical change. His rich imagery was becoming more economical and sharp, his tone more conversational, his themes more intellectual and realistic. These characteristics were even more apparent in the volumes that followed, particularly *The Tower* and *The Winding Stair*. As he grew older his poetic power increased—his last volumes are as original and experimental as his earliest. Many critics consider him the greatest poet of the English language in the twentieth century.

After Long Silence

Speech after long silence; it is right,
All other lovers being estranged or dead,
Unfriendly lamplight hid under its shade,
The curtains drawn upon unfriendly night,

That we descant° and yet again descant   5
Upon the supreme theme of art and song:
Bodily decrepitude is wisdom; young
We loved each other and were ignorant.

5. **descant:** speak at length.

An Irish Airman Foresees His Death

I know that I shall meet my fate
Somewhere among the clouds above;
Those that I fight I do not hate,
Those that I guard I do not love;°
My country is Kiltartan Cross,   5
My countrymen Kiltartan's poor,
No likely end could bring them loss
Or leave them happier than before.
Nor law, nor duty bade me fight,
Nor public men, nor cheering crowds,   10
A lonely impulse of delight
Drove to this tumult in the clouds;
I balanced all, brought all to mind,
The years to come seemed waste of breath,
A waste of breath the years behind   15
In balance with this life, this death.

4. **Those . . . love:** Although Ireland was neutral in World War I, many
Irishmen volunteered to serve with British forces. At times they must have felt,
as Yeats' airman does, that they were fighting *for* an enemy, since Ireland was
trying to gain its independence during these years.

Easter, 1916

The history of English rule in Ireland was marked by a series
of violent rebellions from the fifteenth century on. One of the
bloodiest was the so-called Rising of Easter Monday, 1916.
Two thousand Irish nationalists occupied many of the public

buildings in Dublin and managed to hold out for six days.
When the rebellion was finally crushed, fifteen of the Irish
leaders were executed. Yeats was not entirely in sympathy
with the Rising, and his poem reveals his complex attitudes
toward the Irish leaders.

I have met them at close of day
Coming with vivid faces
From counter or desk among gray
Eighteenth-century houses.
I have passed with a nod of the head   5
Or polite meaningless words,
Or have lingered awhile and said
Polite meaningless words,
And thought before I had done
Of a mocking tale or a gibe°   10
To please a companion
Around the fire at the club,
Being certain that they and I
But lived where motley° is worn:
All changed, changed utterly: 15
A terrible beauty is born.

That woman's° days were spent
In ignorant goodwill,
Her nights in argument
Until her voice grew shrill.   20
What voice more sweet than hers
When, young and beautiful,
She rode to harriers?
This man° had kept a school
And rode our wingèd horse;°   25

10. **gibe:** scoffing remark. 14. **motley:** the multi-colored garments of the
professional fool or jester. 17. **That woman:** a Countess Markiewicz, who
took part in the rebellion and was sentenced to life imprisonment. 24. **This
man:** Patrick Pearse, head of the rebellious forces. He was a leader in the
Gaelic language movement and also a poet. 25. **wingèd horse:** Pegasus, the
flying horse of Greek mythology, is often used as a symbol of poetic inspiration.

This other° his helper and friend
Was coming into his force;
He might have won fame in the end,
So sensitive his nature seemed,
So daring and sweet his thought.   30
This other man° I had dreamed
A drunken, vainglorious lout.
He had done most bitter wrong
To some who are near my heart,
Yet I number him in the song;   35
He, too, has resigned his part
In the casual comedy;
He, too, has been changed in his turn,
Transformed utterly:
A terrible beauty is born.   40

Hearts with one purpose alone
Through summer and winter seem
Enchanted to a stone
To trouble the living stream.
The horse that comes from the road,   45
The rider, the birds that range
From cloud to tumbling cloud,
Minute by minute they change;
A shadow of cloud on the stream
Changes minute by minute;   50
A horsehoof slides on the brim,
And a horse plashes within it;
The long-legged moorhens dive,
And hens to moorcocks call;
Minute by minute they live: 55
The stone's in the midst of all.

Too long a sacrifice
Can make a stone of the heart.
O when may it suffice?

26. **This other:** Thomas MacDonagh, a writer and a leader in the rebellion.
31. **This . . . man:** Major John MacBride, another Irish revolutionary.

That is heaven's part, our part   60
To murmur name upon name,
As a mother names her child
When sleep at last has come
On limbs that had run wild.
What is it but nightfall?   65
No, no, not night but death;
Was it needless death after all?
For England may keep faith°
For all that is done and said.
We know their dream; enough   70
To know they dreamed and are dead;
And what if excess of love
Bewildered them till they died?
I write it out in a verse—
MacDonaugh and MacBride   75
And Connolly° and Pearse
Now and in time to be,
Wherever green is worn,
Are changed, changed utterly:
A terrible beauty is born.   80

68. **England . . . faith:** plans for granting Ireland some measure of independence had begun early in the century, but were postponed at the outbreak of the war in 1914. Many Irishmen felt that England would grant independence once the war was over. 76. **Connolly:** John Connolly, Pearse's partner in the rebellion.

Sailing to Byzantium

Byzantium (later Constantinople) was the capital of Eastern Christendom until its destruction in the fifteenth century. To Yeats, however, the city became a symbol of an ideal world where art, religion, law—in short, all aspects of life—were unified. There the artist, according to Yeats, "spoke to the multitude and the few alike." There the soul left the world of nature and change, and entered an eternal, unchanging existence.

I

That is no country° for old men. The young
In one another's arms, birds in the trees
—Those dying generations—at their song,
The salmon-falls, the mackerel-crowded seas,
Fish, flesh, or fowl, commend all summer long   5
Whatever is begotten, born, and dies.
Caught in that sensual music all neglect
Monuments of unaging intellect.°

II

An aged man is but a paltry thing,
A tattered coat upon a stick, unless   10
Soul clap its hands and sing, and louder sing
For every tatter in its mortal dress,
Nor is there singing school but° studying
Monuments of its own magnificence;
And therefore I have sailed the seas and come   15
To the holy city of Byzantium.

III

O sages standing in God's holy fire
As in the gold mosaic of a wall,°
Come from the holy fire, perne in a gyre,°
And be the singing masters of my soul.   20
Consume my heart away; sick with desire
And fastened to a dying animal
It knows not what it is; and gather me
Into the artifice of eternity.°

1. **That . . . country:** literally, Ireland, but symbolically, the entire world of birth, death, constant change. 8. **Monuments . . . intellect:** the permanent objects or images created by art and the mind. 13. **but:** except (one that is). 17–18. **sages . . . wall:** The Church of Hagia Sophia ("Holy Wisdom"), Byzantium's greatest work of architecture, has figures of sages in mosaic on its walls. 19. **perne in a gyre:** descend in a spiral motion. 24. **artifice of eternity:** the artist's eternal creation (see l. 8).

Once out of nature° I shall never take   25
My bodily form from any natural thing,
But such a form as Grecian goldsmiths make°
Of hammered gold and gold enameling
To keep a drowsy emperor awake;
Or set upon a golden bough to sing   30
To lords and ladies of Byzantium
Of what is past, or passing, or to come.

25. **out of nature:** out of the world of sense, of birth, and of death (and into the unchanging world of intellect and art). 27. **such . . . make:** Byzantine art was a combination of Greek (that is, Western) influences and Eastern; it tended to be abstract and highly formal rather than realistic. In their art the "Grecian goldsmiths" would thus imitate the forms of their imagination, *not* natural things.

An Acre of Grass

Picture and book remain,
An acre of green grass
For air and exercise,
Now strength of body goes;
Midnight, an old house   5
Where nothing stirs but a mouse.

My temptation is quiet.
Here at life's end
Neither loose imagination,
Nor the mill of the mind   10
Consuming its rag and bone,°
Can make the truth known.

11. **rag and bone:** Yeats' symbol for an old man's memories of the past. Note the contrast with the "loose imagination" of line 9. Neither memory nor uncontrolled fancies can reach the truth. Only a passionate insight, the "old man's frenzy" of line 13, will achieve wisdom.

Grant me an old man's frenzy,
Myself must I remake
Till I am Timon and Lear°   15
Or that William Blake°
Who beat upon the wall
Till Truth obeyed his call;

A mind Michael Angelo° knew
That can pierce the clouds,   20
Or inspired by frenzy
Shake the dead in their shrouds;
Forgotten else by mankind,
An old man's eagle mind.

15. **Timon and Lear:** The title-characters of two Shakespearean plays. Both
were old men who struggled through near-madness to gain a measure of
wisdom about themselves and mankind.   16. **Blake:** see page 283.   19. **Michael Angelo:** Michelangelo, the great Italian artist of the sixteenth century.
Yeats has in mind Michelangelo's power of depicting the supernatural, particularly in his painting of *The Last Judgment.*

Questions

1. Who is the speaker in "After Long Silence"? What is the situation?
   What are some of the metrical irregularities? What is their effect? Do
   they imply that Yeats might be suggesting the opposite of what the
   speaker is saying? (Notice particularly the last line.)
2. In "An Irish Airman Foresees His Death" why has the speaker chosen
   to fight? What is his attitude toward his probable death?
3. What seems to be the theme of "Easter, 1916"? Discuss the symbolism
   of the poem. What is the symbolic meaning of a heart turning to
   stone? What is the meaning of "a terrible beauty is born"? Why "terrible"?
4. In "Sailing to Byzantium" why has the speaker come to Byzantium?
   What is the paradox on which the poem is based? Compare this poem
   to "The Garden," page 243. Each poem presents a sharp contrast. Is
   it the same? If so, what side of the contrast does each poem choose?
   Why?
5. What is the situation of the speaker in "An Acre of Grass"? What has
   he lost? What does he wish to gain? What is the significance of the
   contrast between lines 7 and 13? What is the significance of the title?

JOHN MASEFIELD

1878–

Born in Herefordshire, England, John Masefield went to sea at the age of fourteen as a cabin boy on a merchant ship. After some years of wandering he settled in New York and began working in a carpet factory in Yonkers. While in this country he began reading a number of English poets, particularly Chaucer, and when he returned to London in 1897 it was with the determination to become a poet himself. His first book, *Salt-Water Ballads* (1902), showed the influence of his nautical background and marked the beginning of a long career that was to lead eventually to the poet laureateship.

Masefield revived the art of long narrative poetry with such volumes as *The Everlasting Mercy* and *Dauber*. Another aspect of his art is seen in such shorter poems as "Sea-Fever" (p. 122) and "Night on the Downland," lyrics which show his mastery of subtle rhythms and effective imagery.

*Night on the Downland**

Night is on the downland, on the lonely moorland,
On the hills where the wind goes over sheep-bitten turf,
Where the bent grass beats upon the unplowed poorland
And the pine woods roar like the surf.

Here the Roman lived on the wind-barren lonely,   5
Dark now and haunted by the moorland fowl;
None comes here now but the peewit° only,
And mothlike death in the owl.

Beauty was here on this beetle-droning downland;
The thought of a Caesar in the purple came   10
From the palace by the Tiber in the Roman townland
To this wind-swept hill with no name.

* **Downland:** hilly pastures.   7. **peewit** (or **pewit**): a small gull.

Lonely beauty came here and was here in sadness,
Brave as a thought on the frontier of the mind,
In the camp of the wild upon the march of madness,   15
The bright-eyed Queen of the Blind.

Now where beauty was are the wind-withered gorses,°
Moaning like old men in the hill-wind's blast;
The flying sky is dark with running horses,
And the night is full of the past.   20

17. gorses: shrubs.

The West Wind

It's a warm wind, the west wind, full of birds' cries;
I never hear the west wind but tears are in my eyes.
For it comes from the west lands, the old brown hills,
And April's in the west wind, and daffodils.

It's a fine land, the west land, for hearts as tired as mine,   5
Apple orchards blossom there, and the air's like wine.
There is cool green grass there, where men may lie at rest,
And the thrushes are in song there, fluting from the nest.

"Will ye not come home, brother? ye have been long away,
It's April, and blossom time, and white is the may;   10
And bright is the sun, brother, and warm is the rain—
Will ye not come home, brother, home to us again?

"The young corn is green, brother, where the rabbits run,
It's blue sky, and white clouds, and warm rain and sun.
It's song to a man's soul, brother, fire to a man's brain,   15
To hear the wild bees and see the merry spring again.

"Larks are singing in the west, brother, above the green wheat,
So will ye not come home, brother, and rest your tired feet?
I've a balm for bruised hearts, brother, sleep for aching eyes,"
Says the warm wind, the west wind, full of birds' cries.   20

It's the white road westwards is the road I must tread
To the green grass, the cool grass, and rest for heart and head,
To the violets and the warm hearts and the thrushes' song,
In the fine land, the west land, the land where I belong.

Questions

1. Is "Night on the Downlands" more than purely descriptive? Why, or why not?
2. Analyze the rhythm of "The West Wind." What are some of the metrical irregularities? What are their effects? Would you call this a musical poem? Why, or why not?

JAMES STEPHENS

1882–1950

James Stephens was born in Dublin. He gained his first recognition with the publication of *The Crock of Gold* (1912), a novel blending fantasy and poetic imagery. Most of his verse also reveals an interest in the odd or fantastic, but at his best the fantasy is blended with irony, mysticism, and occasional profundity.

In addition to his poetry and the novel mentioned above, Stephens wrote a great deal of prose fiction, much of it re-creations of traditional Irish folktales.

The Shell

And then I pressed the shell
Close to my ear
And listened well,
And straightway like a bell
Came low and clear   5
The slow, sad murmur of the distant seas,
Whipped by an icy breeze
Upon a shore

Wind-swept and desolate.
It was a sunless strand° that never bore   10
The footprint of a man,
Nor felt the weight
Since time began
Of any human quality or stir
Save what the dreary winds and waves incur.   15
And in the hush of waters was the sound
Of pebbles rolling round,
Forever rolling with a hollow sound.
And bubbling seaweeds as the waters go,
Swish to and fro   20
Their long, cold tentacles of slimy gray.
There was no day,
Nor ever came a night
Setting the stars alight
To wonder at the moon: 25
Was twilight only and the frightened croon,°
Smitten to whimpers, of the dreary wind
And waves that journeyed blind—
And then I loosed my ear. . . . O, it was sweet
To hear a cart go jolting down the street.   30

10. **strand:** shore. 26. **croon:** groan.

Questions

Until the last two lines "The Shell" is virtually pure description. What
do the last two lines add?

SIEGFRIED SASSOON

1886–

Sassoon was educated at Cambridge and began writing poetry while
still an undergraduate. During World War I he was a captain in the
Royal Welsh Fusiliers. His earliest poems were, according to Sassoon, "mostly weak imitations of Tennyson, Swinburne, and Rossetti."

His experiences in battle shaped his vision and made him an original poet. Few poets have written of war with such anger and deep bitterness. Occasionally, however, Sassoon captures fleeting moments of poignancy, as in "Concert Party."

Concert Party

(Egyptian Base Camp)

They are gathering round . . .
Out of the twilight; over the gray-blue sand,
Shoals of low jargoning men drift inward to the sound—
The jangle and throb of a piano . . . tum-ti-tum . . .
Drawn by a lamp, they come   5
Out of the glimmering lines of their tents, over the shuffling sand.

O sing us the songs, the songs of our own land,
You warbling ladies in white.
Dimness conceals the hunger in our faces,
This wall of faces risen out of the night,   10
These eyes that keep their memories of the places
So long beyond their sight.

Jaded and gay, the ladies sing; and the chap in brown
Tilts his gray hat; jaunty and lean and pale,
He rattles the keys . . . some actor-bloke from town . . .   15
'God send you home'; and then 'A long, long trail';
'I hear you calling me'; and 'Dixieland' . . .

Sing slowly . . . now the chorus . . . one by one
We hear them, drink them; till the concert's done.
Silent, I watch the shadowy mass of soldiers stand.   20
Silent, they drift away, over the glimmering sand.

Questions

What is the tone of this poem? What is the effect of the pauses in the rhythm? What is the effect of the rhythm in general?

EDWARD THOMAS

1887–1917

Before 1912, Edward Thomas had written little but journalistic hack-work. In 1912 his friendship with Robert Frost, then living in England, turned him to poetry. His first volume of poems, dedicated to Frost, was published in 1917, the year that Thomas was killed in battle.

Calm and contemplative, Thomas's poems deal with ordinary life in the English countryside. His best work is notable for its accuracy of detail and its quiet sense of melancholy.

The New House

Now first, as I shut the door,
　I was alone
In the new house; and the wind
　Began to moan.

Old at once was the house,　　　　　　　　　　5
　And I was old;
My ears were teased with the dread
　Of what was foretold,

Nights of storm, days of mist, without end;
　Sad days when the sun　　　　　　　　　　10
Shone in vain: old griefs and griefs
　Not yet begun.

All was foretold me; naught
　Could I foresee;
But I learned how the wind would sound　　　15
　After these things should be.

Questions

What is the theme of this poem? How is the form appropriate to the theme?

T. S. ELIOT

1888–

One of the most influential of modern poets, Thomas Stearns Eliot was born in St. Louis, Missouri, and educated at Harvard. Later, he studied at Oxford and at the Sorbonne in Paris. In 1914 he settled permanently in London, where he became a teacher, editor, and publisher. In 1927 he was naturalized as a British subject.

The publication of his first volume, *Prufrock and Other Observations,* was greeted with both praise and jeers, but the book established Eliot as the spokesman for a generation of poets disillusioned with contemporary society. The title poem, "The Love Song of J. Alfred Prufrock," deals with one of Eliot's main themes—the spiritual vacuum, the boredom of the modern world. Eliot explored the theme again in *The Waste Land* and "The Hollow Men." After "The Hollow Men," Eliot's poetry became somewhat more hopeful and more explicitly religious. *Ash Wednesday* and *The Rock* express the theme of resignation, and *Four Quartets* points toward the hope of redemption.

Like William Butler Yeats, Eliot devoted many years to an attempt to revive poetic drama. Of his many plays, *Murder in the Cathedral, The Family Reunion,* and *The Cocktail Party* are perhaps the best known, although all of his works have appeared on the stage in England and the United States and most of them have been reasonably successful.

Eliot's critical writings have been as influential as his poetry: he deserves much of the credit for the revival of interest in Donne and the Metaphysical poets, and in many of the previously ignored Elizabethan dramatists.

The Love Song of J. Alfred Prufrock

The irony of Eliot's picture of modern man's frustrations begins with the title. The poem is called a "love song" but in fact it is a monologue dealing with the loss of love. The introductory quotation is from Dante's *Inferno;* Dante, visiting

Hell, asks the name of one of the condemned souls, whose reply can be translated as follows:

If I thought my answer were to one who could return to the world, I would not reply. But since no one ever returned alive from this depth, I can answer thee without fear of disgrace.

S'io credesse che mia risposta fosse
A persona che mai tornasse al mondo,
Questa fiamma staria senza piu scosse.
Ma perciocche giammai di questo fondo
Non torno vivo alcun, s'i'odo il vero,
Senza tema d'infamia ti rispondo.

Let us go then, you and I,
When the evening is spread out against the sky
Like a patient etherized upon a table;
Let us go, through certain half-deserted streets,
The muttering retreats   5
Of restless nights in one-night cheap hotels
And sawdust restaurants with oyster-shells:
Streets that follow like a tedious argument
Of insidious intent
To lead you to an overwhelming question. . . .   10
Oh, do not ask, "What is it?"
Let us go and make our visit.

In the room the women come and go
Talking of Michelangelo.

The yellow fog that rubs its back upon the windowpanes,   15
The yellow smoke that rubs its muzzle on the windowpanes,
Licked its tongue into the corners of the evening,
Lingered upon the pools that stand in drains,
Let fall upon its back the soot that falls from chimneys,
Slipped by the terrace, made a sudden leap,   20
And seeing that it was a soft October night,
Curled once about the house, and fell asleep.

T. S. Eliot   467

And indeed there will be time
For the yellow smoke that slides along the street,
Rubbing its back upon the windowpanes;   25
There will be time, there will be time
To prepare a face to meet the faces that you meet;
There will be time to murder and create,
And time for all the works and days of hands
That lift and drop a question on your plate;   30
Time for you and time for me,
And time yet for a hundred indecisions,
And for a hundred visions and revisions,
Before the taking of a toast and tea.

In the room the women come and go   35
Talking of Michelangelo.

And indeed there will be time
To wonder, "Do I dare?" and, "Do I dare?"
Time to turn back and descend the stair,
With a bald spot in the middle of my hair—   40
(They will say: "How his hair is growing thin!")
My morning coat, my collar mounting firmly to the chin,
My necktie rich and modest, but asserted by a simple pin—
(They will say: "But how his arms and legs are thin!")
Do I dare   45
Disturb the universe?
In a minute there is time
For decisions and revisions which a minute will reverse.

For I have known them all already, known them all:
Have known the evenings, mornings, afternoons,   50
I have measured out my life with coffee spoons;
I know the voices dying with a dying fall
Beneath the music from a farther room.
        So how should I presume?

And I have known the eyes already, known them all—   55
The eyes that fix you in a formulated phrase,

And when I am formulated, sprawling on a pin,
When I am pinned and wriggling on the wall,
Then how should I begin
To spit out all the butt ends of my days and ways?   60
    And how should I presume?

And I have known the arms already, known them all—
Arms that are braceleted and white and bare
(But in the lamplight, downed with light brown hair!)
Is it perfume from a dress   65
That makes me so digress?
Arms that lie along a table, or wrap about a shawl,
    And should I then presume?
    And how should I begin?

———

Shall I say, I have gone at dusk through narrow streets   70
And watched the smoke that rises from the pipes
Of lonely men in shirt-sleeves, leaning out of windows? . . .

I should have been a pair of ragged claws
Scuttling across the floors of silent seas.

———

And the afternoon, the evening, sleeps so peacefully!   75
Smoothed by long fingers,
Asleep . . . tired . . . or it malingers,
Stretched on the floor, here beside you and me.
Should I, after tea and cakes and ices,
Have the strength to force the moment to its crisis?   80
But though I have wept and fasted, wept and prayed,
Though I have seen my head (grown slightly bald) brought in upon
        a platter,°
I am no prophet—and here's no great matter;
I have seen the moment of my greatness flicker,

82. **head . . . platter:** an allusion to John the Baptist, who was beheaded
by Herod.

And I have seen the eternal Footman° hold my coat, and snicker,
And in short, I was afraid.   86

And would it have been worth it, after all,
After the cups, the marmalade, the tea,
Among the porcelain, among some talk of you and me,
Would it have been worthwhile,   90
To have bitten off the matter with a smile,
To have squeezed the universe into a ball
To roll it toward some overwhelming question,
To say: "I am Lazarus, come from the dead,
Come back to tell you all, I shall tell you all"—   95
If one, settling a pillow by her head,
        Should say: "That is not what I meant at all;
        That is not it, at all."

And would it have been worth it, after all,
Would it have been worthwhile,   100
After the sunsets and the dooryards and the sprinkled streets,
After the novels, after the teacups, after the skirts that trail along the
        floor—
And this, and so much more?—
It is impossible to say just what I mean!
But as if a magic lantern threw the nerves in patterns on a screen:
Would it have been worthwhile   106
If one, settling a pillow or throwing off a shawl,
And turning toward the window, should say:
        "That is not it at all,
        That is not what I meant, at all."   110

        ➤

No! I am not Prince Hamlet, nor was meant to be;
Am an attendant lord, one that will do
To swell a progress,° start a scene or two,
Advise the prince; no doubt, an easy tool,
Deferential, glad to be of use,   115

85. **eternal Footman:** death. Even Prufrock's end will be trivial, undignified.
113. **swell a progress:** help to fill out a procession.

Politic, cautious, and meticulous;
Full of high sentence,° but a bit obtuse;
At times, indeed, almost ridiculous—
Almost, at times, the Fool.°

I grow old. . . . I grow old. . . .   120
I shall wear the bottoms of my trousers rolled.°

Shall I part my hair behind? Do I dare to eat a peach?°
I shall wear white flannel trousers, and walk upon the beach.
I have heard the mermaids singing, each to each.

I do not think that they will sing to me.   125

I have seen them riding seaward on the waves
Combing the white hair of the waves blown back
When the wind blows the water white and black.

We have lingered in the chambers of the sea
By sea-girls wreathed with seaweed red and brown   130
Till human voices wake us, and we drown.

117. **high sentence:** eloquent sayings or proverbs.   119. **Fool:** a standard
character in many Shakespearean plays. Like Prufrock, the fool or jester talks a
great deal but performs no significant actions, and is generally an object of ridi-
cule.   121. **bottoms . . . rolled:** probably referring to the bell-bottom, un-
cuffed trousers that were in fashion at the time the poem was written. They
were worn by younger men; as Prufrock grows older he will have to wear pants
with cuffs ("rolled").   122. **dare . . . peach:** as an old man, Prufrock may
have to wear false teeth, and eating a peach will be difficult.

The Hollow Men

"The Hollow Men" continues the theme of "The Love Song of
J. Alfred Prufrock"—the spiritual vacuum, the barrenness of
modern life. In this poem, however, some other kind of existence is at least hinted at, although the "hollow men" reject it.

*Mistah Kurtz—he dead.**
                    A penny for the Old Guy.†

                              I

We are the hollow men
We are the stuffed men
Leaning together
Headpiece filled with straw. Alas!
Our dried voices, when   5
We whisper together
Are quiet and meaningless
As wind in dry grass
Or rats' feet over broken glass
In our dry cellar   10
Shape without form, shade without color,
Paralyzed force, gesture without motion;

Those who have crossed
With direct eyes, to death's other Kingdom°
Remember us—if at all—not as lost   15
Violent souls, but only
As the hollow men
The stuffed men.

---

* *Mistah Kurtz—he dead:* the line is from Joseph Conrad's story *Heart of Darkness.* Kurtz is a European trader and adventurer who journeys to the Congo with grand schemes of gaining wealth and civilizing the natives. Once there, however, he succumbs to savage rituals, eventually allowing himself to be worshiped as a god and leading rites which involve, among other things, cannibalism. The narrator of Conrad's story describes Kurtz as being "hollow at the core."   † *Old Guy:* in 1605, Guy Fawkes took part in a plot to blow up the House of Commons, but the plot failed and he was executed. Since then, straw dummies representing Fawkes have been paraded in England and burned on the anniversary of the plot (November 5). The "penny" cry is used on this day by children to obtain gifts, much as "trick or treat" is used on Halloween. 13–14. Those . . . Kingdom: those who have chosen deliberately ("with direct eyes") either Heaven or Hell. Fawkes and Kurtz were "lost, violent souls" but unlike the hollow men they at least *chose* their fate.

Eyes I dare not meet in dreams
In death's dream kingdom°   20
These do not appear:
There, the eyes are
Sunlight on a broken column
There, is a tree swinging
And voices are   25
In the wind's singing
More distant and more solemn
Than a fading star.

Let me be no nearer
In death's dream kingdom   30
Let me also wear
Such deliberate disguises
Rat's coat, crowskin, crossed staves
In a field
Behaving as the wind behaves   35
No nearer—

Not that final meeting
In the twilight kingdom°

III

This is the dead land
This is cactus land   40
Here the stone images
Are raised, here they receive
The supplication of a dead man's hand
Under the twinkle of a fading star.

---

20. **death's dream kingdom:** this life, which is a kind of death also, but does not have to be faced directly (as "death's other Kingdom" does).
38. **twilight kingdom:** a place between the "dream kingdom" of line 20 and the "other Kingdom" of line 14. In other words, a place of judgment, of "final meeting."

Is it like this   45
In death's other kingdom
Waking alone
At the hour when we are
Trembling with tenderness
Lips that would kiss   50
Form prayers to broken stone.

IV

The eyes are not here
There are no eyes here
In this valley of dying stars
In this hollow valley   55
This broken jaw of our lost kingdoms

In this last of meeting places
We grope together
And avoid speech
Gathered on this beach of the tumid river°   60

Sightless, unless
The eyes reappear
As the perpetual star
Multifoliate rose°
Of death's twilight kingdom   65
The hope only
Of empty men.

V

Here we go round the prickly pear°
Prickly pear prickly pear

60. **tumid:** swollen. **river:** the River Acheron, which in Dante's *Divine Comedy* (and Roman and Greek myth) divides this life from the next. 62–64. **eyes . . . rose:** the star and the rose are traditional emblems of Christ and the Virgin Mary. In the *Divine Comedy* they also appear as symbols of the Divine Presence and of Paradise. 68. **Here . . . pear:** the prickly pear is desert cactus and is thus an appropriate substitution, in this "cactus land," for the usual "mulberry bush."

Here we go round the prickly pear   70
At five o'clock in the morning.

Between the idea
And the reality
Between the motion
And the act   75
Falls the Shadow
          For Thine is the Kingdom°

Between the conception
And the creation
Between the emotion   80
And the response
Falls the Shadow
          Life is very long°

Between the desire
And the spasm   85
Between the potency
And the existence
Between the essence
And the descent
Falls the Shadow   90
          For Thine is the Kingdom

For Thine is
Life is
For Thine is the

This is the way the world ends   95
This is the way the world ends
This is the way the world ends
Not with a bang but a whimper.

77. *For . . . Kingdom:* from the Lord's Prayer. 83. *Life is very long:* from another Conrad novel, *An Outcast of the Islands.* The phrase is spoken to the central character, Peter Willems. He, like Kurtz, proves to be "hollow," betraying all those who had trusted him.

Journey of the Magi

The Magi were the wise men who journeyed to the Nativity
at Bethlehem, bringing various offerings. The first five lines of
the poem were adapted by Eliot from the Nativity Sermon
delivered by Bishop Lancelot Andrewes in 1622.

"A cold coming we had of it,
Just the worst time of the year
For a journey, and such a long journey:
The ways deep and the weather sharp,
The very dead of winter."   5
And the camels galled, sore-footed, refractory,°
Lying down in the melting snow,
There were times we regretted
The summer palaces on slopes, the terraces,
And the silken girls bringing sherbet.   10
Then the camel men cursing and grumbling
And running away, and wanting their liquor and women,
And the night fires going out, and the lack of shelters,
And the cities hostile and the towns unfriendly
And the villages dirty and charging high prices: 15
A hard time we had of it.

At the end we preferred to travel all night,
Sleeping in snatches,
With the voices singing in our ears, saying
That this was all folly.   20

Then at dawn we came down to a temperate valley,
Wet, below the snow line, smelling of vegetation;
With a running stream and a water mill beating the darkness,
And three trees on the low sky,
And an old white horse galloped away in the meadow.   25
Then we came to a tavern with vine leaves over the lintel,°

6. **refractory**: unmanageable.   26. **lintel**: the horizontal span over the doorway.

Six hands at an open door dicing for pieces of silver,
And feet kicking the empty wineskins.
But there was no information, and so we continued
And arrived at evening, not a moment too soon   30
Finding the place; it was (you may say) satisfactory.

All this was a long time ago, I remember,
And I would do it again, but set down
This set down
This: were we led all that way for   35
Birth or Death? There was a Birth, certainly,
We had evidence and no doubt. I had seen birth and death,
But had thought they were different; this Birth was
Hard and bitter agony for us, like Death, our death.
We returned to our places, these Kingdoms,   40
But no longer at ease here, in the old dispensation,
With an alien people clutching their gods.
I should be glad of another death.

Questions

The Love Song of J. Alfred Prufrock

1. The progression of thought in the poem is psychological rather than logical—a "stream of consciousness." Try to justify the abrupt transitions between lines 12 and 13, 14 and 15, and 72 and 73. What are some of the other abrupt transitions? What is their effect?
2. Like all dramatic monologues, Eliot's poem reveals the character of the speaker. Indeed, the poem is a kind of self-examination. What kind of a man is Prufrock? What does he reveal about himself? about his world?
3. What is the theme of the poem? Is it ever explicitly stated? If not, how is it expressed?

The Hollow Men

1. What does the poem say about the "hollow men"? about their world? In what ways is this poem related to "The Love Song of J. Alfred Prufrock"?
2. What is the effect of the final section? What specific devices are responsible for the effect?

1. This poem is spoken by one of the Magi years after the journey to the Nativity. What is the tone of the description of the journey? What is the speaker's attitude toward what he has seen?
2. Can you explain the "birth-death" paradox of lines 35–43? Why should the speaker "be glad of another death"?

WILFRED OWEN

1893–1918

Wilfred Owen was educated at London University. In spite of poor health he enlisted in the army in 1915. He was awarded the Military Cross for bravery in October, 1918, and was killed the next month, one week before the end of the war.

Owen was unknown as a poet until 1920, when his friend Siegfried Sassoon collected and published his work. Technically, Owen was a remarkably original poet—few mature writers have equalled his skill in the use of assonance, alliteration, consonance, and imperfect rhyme. But probably the most striking characteristic of his poetry is its bitterness against war and its deep compassion for those caught in it.

Anthem for Doomed Youth

What passing-bells for these who die as cattle?
Only the monstrous anger of the guns.
Only the stuttering rifles' rapid rattle
Can patter out their hasty orisons.°
No mockeries for them; no prayers nor bells,   5
Nor any voice of mourning save the choirs—
The shrill, demented choirs of wailing shells;
And bugles calling for them from sad shires.

What candles may be held to speed them all?
Not in the hands of boys, but in their eyes   10

4. **orisons:** prayers.

Shall shine the holy glimmers of good-bys.
The pallor of girls' brows shall be their pall;
Their flowers the tenderness of patient minds,
And each slow dusk a drawing-down of blinds.

Questions

What are some of the sound devices of this poem? Can you explain
the effectiveness of the image in the last line?

C. DAY LEWIS
1904–

C. (Cecil) Day Lewis was born in Ireland and educated at Oxford,
where he became associated with a group of post-war poets which
included W. H. Auden and Stephen Spender. These three were the
leaders of the new generation of writers that came into prominence
in the nineteen-thirties, as the influence of the older poets, particularly Eliot and Yeats, began to diminish.

Lewis' first volumes of poetry received little notice, but by the
early thirties his work was being given more and more praise. His
brief lyrics are generally felt to be his finest poems. He has also written some excellent criticism of modern poetry as well as several detective stories.

Consider These, for We Have Condemned Them

Consider these, for we have condemned them;
Leaders to no sure land, guides their bearings lost
Or in league with robbers have reversed the signposts,
Disrespectful to ancestors, irresponsible to heirs.
Born barren, a freak growth, root in rubble,   5
Fruitlessly blossoming, whose foliage suffocates,
Their sap is sluggish, they reject the sun.

The man with his tongue in his cheek, the woman
With her heart in the wrong place, unhandsome, unwholesome;
Have exposed the new-born to worse than weather,   10
Exiled the honest and sacked the seer.
These drowned the farms to form a pleasure-lake,
In time of drought they drain the reservoir
Through private pipes for baths and sprinklers.

Getters not begetters; gainers not beginners;   15
Whiners, no winners; no triers, betrayers;
Who steer by no star, whose moon means nothing.
Daily denying, unable to dig:
At bay in villas from blood relations,
Counters of spoons and content with cushions   20
They pray for peace, they hand down disaster.

They that take the bribe shall perish by the bribe,
Dying of dry rot, ending in asylums,
A curse to children, a charge on the state.
But still their fears and frenzies infect us;   25
Drug nor isolation will cure this cancer:
It is now or never, the hour of the knife,
The break with the past, the major operation.

Questions

Lewis is discussing the plight of contemporary civilization. What is it?
Who are the "these" of the title?

JOHN BETJEMAN
1906–

John Betjeman, educated at Marlborough School and at Oxford, is a
noted architectural authority as well as a poet. He has enjoyed considerable popular success as a poet—when he published his *Collected*

Poems, the book became a best-seller, a rare event for a book of poetry in this century. He is considered by many to be the most likely
successor to John Masefield as poet laureate. Betjeman's poetry is
generally satiric, polished, and witty, bordering on the line between
comedy and seriousness.

In Westminster Abbey

Let me take this other glove off
   As the *vox humana*° swells,
And the beauteous fields of Eden
   Bask beneath the Abbey bells.
Here, where England's statesmen lie,   5
Listen to a lady's cry.

Gracious Lord, oh bomb the Germans.
   Spare their women for Thy Sake,
And if that is not too easy
   We will pardon Thy Mistake.   10
But, gracious Lord, whate'er shall be,
Don't let anyone bomb me.

Keep our Empire undismembered,
   Guide our Forces by Thy Hand,
Gallant blacks from far Jamaica,   15
   Honduras and Togoland;
Protect them Lord in all their fights,
And, even more, protect the whites.

Think of what our Nation stands for,
   Books from Boots, and country lanes,   20
Free speech, free passes, class distinction,
   Democracy and proper drains.
Lord, put beneath Thy special care
One-eighty-nine Cadogan Square.

2. *vox humana:* an organ note that resembles the human voice.

Although dear Lord I am a sinner, 25
   I have done no major crime;
Now I'll come to Evening Service
   Whensoever I have time.
So, Lord, reserve for me a crown,
And do not let my shares go down. 30

I will labor for Thy Kingdom,
   Help our lads to win the war,
Send white feathers to the cowards,
   Join the Women's Army Corps,
Then wash the Steps around Thy Throne 35
In the Eternal Safety Zone.

Now I feel a little better,
   What a treat to hear Thy Word
Where the bones of leading statesmen
   Have so often been interred. 40
And now, dear Lord, I cannot wait
Because I have a luncheon date.

Questions

Of what is this poem a satire? Characterize the speaker.

LOUIS MacNEICE

1907–1963

Like C. Day Lewis, Louis MacNeice was educated at Oxford, where
he too became a member of the new poetic movement that started
in the late twenties and early thirties. He taught at the Universities of Birmingham and London, and also at Cornell University in
New York. Much of his poetry is concerned with the current political
and social issues of his time, though perhaps to a lesser extent than

the work of C. Day Lewis. MacNeice also wrote light verse, criticism, and a poetic drama, *Out of the Picture*.

The British Museum Reading Room

Under the hivelike dome the stooping haunted readers
Go up and down the alleys, tap the cells of knowledge—
    Honey and wax, the accumulation of years—
Some on commission, some for the love of learning,
Some because they have nothing better to do   5
Or because they hope these walls of books will deaden
    The drumming of the demon in their ears.

Cranks, hacks, poverty-stricken scholars,
In pince-nez,° period hats or romantic beards
    And cherishing their hobby or their doom.   10
Some are too much alive and some are asleep
Hanging like bats in a world of inverted values,
Folded up in themselves in a world which is safe and silent:
    This is the British Museum Reading Room.

Out on the steps in the sun the pigeons are courting,   15
Puffing their ruffs and sweeping their tails or taking
    A sunbath at their ease
And under the totem poles—the ancient terror—
Between the enormous fluted Ionic columns
There seeps from heavily jowled or hawklike foreign faces   20
    The guttural sorrow of the refugees.

9. **pince-nez** (păns'nā′): glasses which clip to the nose by a spring.

Questions

What three things are contrasted in this poem? (See ll. 18–19.) In what sense is the contrast ironic?

STEPHEN SPENDER

1909–

At eighteen, the year before he entered Oxford, Stephen Spender printed on his own press a volume of his poems. A second volume was published while he was still an undergraduate. His third book, *Poems* (1933), firmly established his reputation. Spender is one of the most lyrical and romantic of the poets who began their careers in the nineteen-thirties.

Perhaps more than anyone else, Spender has brought the machine into modern poetry. "The Express" is probably the finest example of the way he incorporates the modern industrial age into his work.

The Express

After the first powerful plain manifesto
The black statement of pistons, without more fuss
But gliding like a queen, she leaves the station.
Without bowing and with restrained unconcern
She passes the houses which humbly crowd outside,   5
The gasworks and at last the heavy page
Of death, printed by gravestones in the cemetery.
Beyond the town there lies the open country
Where, gathering speed, she acquires mystery,
The luminous self-possession of ships on ocean.   10
It is now she begins to sing—at first quite low
Then loud, and at last with a jazzy madness—
The song of her whistle screaming at curves,
Of deafening tunnels, brakes, innumerable bolts.
And always light, aerial, underneath   15
Goes the elate° meter of her wheels.
Steaming through metal landscape on her lines
She plunges new eras of wild happiness
Where speed throws up strange shapes, broad curves
And parallels clean like the steel of guns.   20

16. **elate:** elated, joyful.

At last, further than Edinburgh or Rome,
Beyond the crest of the world, she reaches night
Where only a low streamline brightness
Of phosphorus on the tossing hills is white.
Ah, like a comet through flames she moves entranced   25
Wrapped in her music no bird song, no, nor bough
Breaking with honey buds, shall ever equal.

Mask

The face of the landscape is a mask
Of bone and iron lines where time
Has plowed its character.
I look and look to read a sign,
Through errors of light and eyes of water   5
Beneath the land's will, of a fear
And the memory of a struggle,
As man behind his mask still wears a child.

Questions

1. What is the poet's attitude toward the train in "The Express"? At what
   point does the poem cease to be purely descriptive?
2. What is the tone of "Mask"? the theme?

DYLAN THOMAS

1914–1953

One of the most original poetic talents of our time was that of the
Welsh poet, Dylan Thomas. At first glance Thomas' poems often
seem to be obscure and undisciplined, but on examination the ob-

scurities disappear and a remarkably strict organization becomes apparent. But the most striking characteristic of Thomas' poetry is unquestionably his fresh and completely original use of words. Among modern poets, only Hopkins can equal his daring experiments with language and rhythms.

Thomas' formal education ended with his graduation from grammar school. For a time he was a newspaper reporter and later a writer of documentary film scripts. During World War II he served as an anti-aircraft gunner. He published his first volume of poems at twenty, and followed it with a number of other publications. He also wrote plays, a novel, and a number of short stories.

Thomas was perhaps the finest reader of poetry in our time. He made a number of reading tours in England and America, and also recorded a number of readings of his work. He was in New York to record his own and others' poetry when he died suddenly at the age of thirty-nine.

Was There a Time

Was there a time when dancers with their fiddles
In children's circuses could stay their troubles?
There was a time they could cry over books,
But time has set its maggot on their track.
Under the arc of the sky they are unsafe.   5
What's never known is safest in this life.
Under the skysigns they who have no arms
Have cleanest hands, and, as the heartless ghost
Alone's unhurt, so the blind man sees best.

Do Not Go Gentle into That Good Night

Thomas constantly experimented with new poetic patterns, but he could also handle traditional forms with great skill. Here he takes an old French form, the villanelle, and turns it into a moving elegy for his father.

Do not go gentle into that good night,
Old age should burn and rave at close of day;
Rage, rage against the dying of the light.

Though wise men at their end know dark is right,
Because their words had forked no lightning they
Do not go gentle into that good night.

Good men, the last wave by, crying how bright
Their frail deeds might have danced in a green bay,
Rage, rage against the dying of the light.

Wild men who caught and sang the sun in flight,
And learn, too late, they grieved it on its way,
Do not go gentle into that good night.

Grave men, near death, who see with blinding sight
Blind eyes could blaze like meteors and be gay,
Rage, rage against the dying of the light.

And you, my father, there on the sad height,
Curse, bless, me now with your fierce tears, I pray.
Do not go gentle into that good night.
Rage, rage against the dying of the light.

And Death Shall Have No Dominion

And death shall have no dominion.
Dead men naked they shall be one
With the man in the wind and the west moon;
When their bones are picked clean and the clean bones gone,
They shall have stars at elbow and foot;
Though they go mad they shall be sane,
Though they sink through the sea they shall rise again;
Though lovers be lost love shall not;
And death shall have no dominion.

Dylan Thomas   487

And death shall have no dominion.   10
Under the windings of the sea
They lying long shall not die windily;
Twisting on racks when sinews give way,
Strapped to a wheel, yet they shall not break;
Faith in their hands shall snap in two,   15
And the unicorn evils run them through;
Split all ends up they shan't crack;
And death shall have no dominion.

And death shall have no dominion.
No more may gulls cry at their ears   20
Or waves break loud on the seashores;
Where blew a flower may a flower no more
Lift its head to the blows of the rain;
Though they be mad and dead as nails,
Heads of the characters hammer through daisies;°   25
Break in the sun till the sun breaks down,
And death shall have no dominion.

25. **Heads . . . daisies:** The dead ("the characters") shall rise again (see l. 7). With "Heads" and "hammer," the line puns on the "nails" of the previous line: the shape of a daisy is also like that of a nail. There may also be a hint here of the doctrine of reincarnation, the belief that the dead return to life in other forms.

Questions

1. In "Was There a Time" how can "they who have no arms / Have cleanest hands"? What is the theme of this poem?
2. In "Do Not Go Gentle into That Good Night," what is the "good night"? Why should men—wise men, good men, wild men, and grave men—not go "gentle" into it? What should they "rage against"? Why? How can the speaker's father both curse and bless him?
3. Analyze the structure and fabric of "Do Not Go Gentle into That Good Night."
4. What is the effect of the repetition of the title line in "And Death Shall Have No Dominion"? What is the theme? Why will death have no dominion? Compare this poem to Donne's sonnet "Death Be Not Proud," page 209.

MODERN AMERICAN POETRY

Especially during the last half of the nineteenth century, American poets struck out on their own, drawing farther and farther away from the methods of their English contemporaries. This trend continued through the early years of the twentieth century, as many of the younger American poets followed the lines of development begun by Walt Whitman, Emily Dickinson, and Stephen Crane. After World War I, however, the poetry of England and America once more drew closer together, but this time it was often the American poets who set the styles and exerted the greater influence. (The loss of many young English poets in the war was very likely a factor in this change.)

One of the most significant events in both modern American and British poetry was the founding of *Poetry* magazine in Chicago in 1912. Many of the most original and influential poets of our time were first published in *Poetry*—without the magazine they might never have gained an audience.

In general, modern American poetry displays a wide range of subject matter, an interest in experimentation, and a frequent use of complex imagery and symbolism. In recent years, however, a number of poets have revived successfully some of the more traditional poetic forms and techniques.

EDGAR LEE MASTERS

1869–1950

Edgar Lee Masters was born in Kansas. His family moved to Illinois while he was still a small boy. After a few years of elementary schooling, he studied law with his father and then went to Chicago, where he eventually became a successful lawyer. His early volumes of verse were for the most part weak imitations of Poe, Shelley, Keats, and others, but in 1915 he published *Spoon River Anthology*, a series of monologues spoken from the grave by inhabitants of Masters' fictitious Middle Western town, Spoon River. In this volume Masters did what one of his own characters ("Petit, the Poet," page 59) failed to do—he dramatized the ordinary life of the village. An original, realistic, and thoroughly American work, *Spoon River Anthology* was an immediate success. Although Masters remained a productive writer throughout his life, producing nearly fifty volumes of prose and poetry, his reputation today rests on this one volume.

Lucinda Matlock

I went to the dances at Chandlerville,
And played snap-out at Winchester.
One time we changed partners
Driving home in the moonlight of middle June,
And then I found Davis.   5
We were married and lived together for seventy years,
Enjoying, working, raising the twelve children,
Eight of whom we lost
Ere I had reached the age of sixty.
I spun, I wove, I kept the house, I nursed the sick,   10
I made the garden, and for holiday
Rambled over the fields where sang the larks,
And by Spoon River gathering many a shell,
And many a flower and medicinal weed—
Shouting to the wooded hills, singing to the green valleys.   15
At ninety-six I had lived enough, that is all,
And passed to a sweet repose.
What is this I hear of sorrow and weariness,
Anger, discontent and drooping hopes?
Degenerate sons and daughters,   20
Life is too strong for you—
It takes life to love Life.

What does the last line mean? In what way does the entire poem explain the last line? Masters' poem is in free verse—does it employ any rhythmical devices at all? If so, what are they?

EDWIN ARLINGTON ROBINSON

1869–1935

Robinson was almost fifty years old before he began to be known to either the critics or the public, but once he gained the reputation he deserved, he held it firmly. During the last decade of his life he was generally recognized as one of America's two or three greatest living poets.

While Robinson was trying to earn a living in New York, after having published some unsuccessful volumes, President Theodore Roosevelt read one of his books, wrote a favorable review of it, and then gave Robinson a job in the New York Custom House. Robinson kept the job until 1910, thereafter living on a small legacy and on the increasing financial success of his books.

Gardiner, Maine, Robinson's home town, figures in many of his poems as "Tilbury Town," and some of his memorable character portraits are drawn from the life he knew in Gardiner. Robinson's distinction as a poet lies primarily in his ability to evoke the quality of New England life and to create memorable characters.

Robinson used the traditional forms—he was a master of the sonnet and of blank verse—but his style was thoroughly individual. His best work is a blend of penetrating character analysis, colloquial language, and an ironic tone.

New England

Here where the wind is always north-north-east
And children learn to walk on frozen toes,
Wonder begets an envy of all those

Who boil elsewhere with such a lyric yeast
Of love that you will hear them at a feast   5
Where demons would appeal for some repose,
Still clamoring where the chalice overflows
And crying wildest who have drunk the least.

Passion is here a soilure° of the wits,
We're told, and Love a cross for them to bear;   10
Joy shivers in the corner where she knits
And Conscience always has the rocking chair,
Cheerful as when she tortured into fits
The first cat that was ever killed by Care.

9. **soilure:** soiling.

Cliff Klingenhagen

Cliff Klingenhagen had me in to dine
With him one day; and after soup and meat,
And all the other things there were to eat,
Cliff took two glasses and filled one with wine
And one with wormwood.° Then, without a sign   5
For me to choose at all, he took the draught
Of bitterness himself, and lightly quaffed
It off, and said the other one was mine.

And when I asked him what the deuce he meant
By doing that, he only looked at me   10
And grinned, and said it was a way of his.
And though I know the fellow, I have spent
Long time a-wondering when I shall be
As happy as Cliff Klingenhagen is.

5. **wormwood:** a bitter liquid made from an herb.

George Crabbe

Crabbe (1754–1832) is not read much today, but he was noted in his time for his realistic poems about English village and country life. He and Robinson had much in common as poets: both were interested in individual psychology and in the effect of environment on character; in addition, both poets wrote realistically and sometimes bitterly about the life they knew.

Give him the darkest inch your shelf allows,
Hide him in lonely garrets, if you will—
But his hard, human pulse is throbbing still
With the sure strength that fearless truth endows.
In spite of all fine science disavows,   5
Of his plain excellence and stubborn skill
There yet remains what fashion cannot kill,
Though years have thinned the laurel from his brows.

Whether or not we read him, we can feel
From time to time the vigor of his name   10
Against us like a finger for the shame
And emptiness of what our souls reveal
In books that are as altars where we kneel
To consecrate the flicker, not the flame.

The Clerks

I did not think that I should find them there
When I came back again; but there they stood,
As in the days they dreamed of when young blood
Was in their cheeks and women called them fair.
Be sure they met me with an ancient air—   5
And yes, there was a shop-worn brotherhood
About them; but the men were just as good,
And just as human as they ever were.

Edwin Arlington Robinson   493

And you that ache so much to be sublime,
And you that feed yourselves with your descent,   10
What comes of all your visions and your fears?
Poets and kings are but the clerks of Time,
Tiering° the same dull webs of discontent
Clipping the same sad alnage° of the years.

13. **Tiering:** arranging in layers or tiers.   14. **alnage:** official measurement of woolen cloth.

Questions

1. "New England" is an extended metaphor or two closely related metaphors. Explain. What is the effect of the personifications in the sestet? According to Robinson, how does New England differ from "elsewhere"?
2. What is the similarity in thought between "Cliff Klingenhagen" and "Lucinda Matlock," page 490. Which poem expresses its meaning more directly? Explain.
3. Explain the metaphor of the last two lines of "George Crabbe."
4. What is the theme of "The Clerks"? What is Robinson's attitude toward the clerks? Toward kings and poets?

AMY LOWELL

1874–1925

Amy Lowell was born into a distinguished Boston family: James Russell Lowell was a cousin of her grandfather, one of her brothers was a famous astronomer, another brother was president of Harvard. Miss Lowell's first volume of poetry was imitative, but the second, *Sword Blades and Poppy Seed* (1914) marked her as one of the leaders of the Imagists, a group that was to have a strong influence on modern poetry. Among other ideals, the Imagists held that poetry should concentrate on using the "hard and clear image" and the "exact word." These were worthy aims, but in too many cases Imagist poetry became a mechanical exercise, lacking both emotion and thought. Miss Lowell's poetry does not always avoid these pitfalls, but at her best, in such poems as "Meeting-House Hill," her brilliant and dynamic images create a strong dramatic effect.

Meeting-House * Hill

I must be mad, or very tired,
When the curve of a blue bay beyond a railroad track
Is shrill and sweet to me like the sudden springing of a tune,
And the sight of a white church above thin trees in a city square
Amazes my eyes as though it were the Parthenon.°   5
Clear, reticent, superbly final,
With the pillars of its portico° refined to a cautious elegance,
It dominates the weak trees,
And the shot of its spire
Is cool and candid,   10
Rising into an unresisting sky.

Strange meeting house
Pausing a moment upon a squalid hilltop.
I watch the spire sweeping the sky,
I am dizzy with the movement of the sky;   15
I might be watching a mast
With its royals set full
Straining before a two-reef breeze.
I might be sighting a tea clipper,
Tacking into the blue bay,   20
Just back from Canton
With her hold full of green and blue porcelain
And a Chinese coolie leaning over the rail
Gazing at the white spire
With dull, sea-spent eyes.   25

* **Meeting-House:** some early New England sects preferred to use this term,
rather than "church" or "chapel." 5. **Parthenon:** the famous temple in Athens,
built in the fifth century B.C. 7. **portico:** porch.

Questions

1. What is the theme of this poem? What are some of the symbols which
   help to create the theme?
2. Consider the organization of the poem. What are the relationships, if
   any, between the two stanzas?

ROBERT FROST

1874–1963

Frost, known as one of the most accurate interpreters of New England life, was born in San Francisco. His parents were native New Englanders, however, and after the death of his father, Frost's mother brought the family back to New England. After being graduated from high school, Frost entered Dartmouth College but left after a few months to take work in a local mill. For a number of years, while continually writing, he struggled to support himself and his growing family on a small farm. Finally, after many years of near-poverty, he moved to England in 1912 with his family. With the publication of *A Boy's Will* in 1913 and *North of Boston* in 1914, Frost was recognized in England as an important new poet. He returned to the United States in 1915 to find himself famous.

After 1915 Frost published numerous volumes of poetry. His last book, *In the Clearing*, published in 1962—his eighty-eighth year—showed no decline in power.

Frost struggled for many years to reach any audience for his work, but he eventually became a highly popular poet. He wrote of ordinary country people and of ordinary occurrences in an unpretentious, colloquial style. These characteristics contribute to his popular appeal, but they have tended to hide some other important qualities of his work. Even a quick glance at such poems as "Neither Out Far Nor In Deep" or "Provide, Provide" will show that Frost could be passionate and bitter as well as calm and unassuming. Like Housman, Frost often hid irony and subtlety beneath a surface simplicity.

The Death of the Hired Man

Mary sat musing on the lamp flame at the table
Waiting for Warren. When she heard his step,
She ran on tip-toe down the darkened passage
To meet him in the doorway with the news
And put him on his guard. "Silas is back."   5

She pushed him outward with her through the door
And shut it after her. "Be kind," she said.
She took the market things from Warren's arms
And set them on the porch, then drew him down
To sit beside her on the wooden steps.   10
"When was I ever anything but kind to him?
But I'll not have the fellow back," he said.
"I told him so last haying, didn't I?
'If he left then,' I said, 'that ended it.'
What good is he? Who else will harbor him   15
At his age for the little he can do?
What help he is there's no depending on.
Off he goes always when I need him most.
'He thinks he ought to earn a little pay,
Enough at least to buy tobacco with,   20
So he won't have to beg and be beholden.'
'All right,' I say, 'I can't afford to pay
Any fixed wages, though I wish I could.'
'Someone else can.' 'Then someone else will have to.'
I shouldn't mind his bettering himself   25
If that was what it was. You can be certain,
When he begins like that, there's someone at him
Trying to coax him off with pocket money—
In haying time, when any help is scarce.
In winter he comes back to us. I'm done."   30

"Sh! not so loud: he'll hear you," Mary said.

"I want him to: he'll have to soon or late."

"He's worn out. He's asleep beside the stove.
When I came up from Rowe's I found him here,
Huddled against the barn door fast asleep,   35
A miserable sight, and frightening, too—
You needn't smile—I didn't recognize him—
I wasn't looking for him—and he's changed.
Wait till you see."

"Where did you say he'd been?"

"He didn't say. I dragged him to the house,   40
And gave him tea and tried to make him smoke.
I tried to make him talk about his travels,
Nothing would do: he just kept nodding off."

"What did he say? Did he say anything?"
"But little."

        "Anything? Mary, confess   45
He said he'd come to ditch the meadow for me."

"Warren!"

    "But did he? I just want to know."

"Of course he did. What would you have him say?
Surely you wouldn't grudge the poor old man
Some humble way to save his self-respect.   50
He added, if you really care to know,
He meant to clear the upper pasture, too.
That sounds like something you have heard before?
Warren, I wish you could have heard the way
He jumbled everything. I stopped to look   55
Two or three times—he made me feel so queer—
To see if he was talking in his sleep.
He ran on Harold Wilson—you remember—
The boy you had in haying four years since.
He's finished school, and teaching in his college.   60
Silas declares you'll have to get him back.
He says they two will make a team for work:
Between them they will lay this farm as smooth!
The way he mixed that in with other things.
He thinks young Wilson a likely lad, though daft   65
On education—you know how they fought
All through July under the blazing sun,
Silas up on the cart to build the load,
Harold along beside to pitch it on."

"Yes, I took care to keep well out of earshot."   70

"Well, those days trouble Silas like a dream.
You wouldn't think they would. How some things linger!
Harold's young college boy's assurance piqued him.
After so many years he still keeps finding
Good arguments he sees he might have used.   75
I sympathize. I know just how it feels
To think of the right thing to say too late.
Harold's associated in his mind with Latin.
He asked me what I thought of Harold's saying
He studied Latin like the violin   80
Because he liked it—that an argument!
He said he couldn't make the boy believe
He could find water with a hazel prong—°
Which showed how much good school had ever done him.
He wanted to go over that. But most of all   85
He thinks if he could have another chance
To teach him how to build a load of hay—"

"I know, that's Silas' one accomplishment.
He bundles every forkful in its place,
And tags and numbers it for future reference,   90
So he can find and easily dislodge it
In the unloading. Silas does that well.
He takes it out in bunches like birds' nests.
You never see him standing on the hay
He's trying to lift, straining to lift himself."   95

"He thinks if he could teach him that, he'd be
Some good perhaps to someone in the world.
He hates to see a boy the fool of books.
Poor Silas, so concerned for other folk,
And nothing to look backward to with pride,   100

83. find water . . . prong: referring to the belief that underground sources
of water can be found by holding a forked twig and walking back and forth
over the area in question. The twig is supposed to bend down when it is over
water.

And nothing to look forward to with hope,
So now and never any different."

Part of a moon was falling down the west,
Dragging the whole sky with it to the hills.
Its light poured softly in her lap. She saw   105
And spread her apron to it. She put out her hand
Among the harplike morning-glory strings,
Taut with the dew from garden bed to eaves,
As if she played unheard some tenderness
That wrought on him beside her in the night.   110
"Warren," she said, "he has come home to die:
You needn't be afraid he'll leave you this time."

"Home," he mocked gently.

                              "Yes, what else but home?
It all depends on what you mean by home.
Of course he's nothing to us, any more   115
Than was the hound that came a stranger to us
Out of the woods, worn out upon the trail."

"Home is the place where, when you have to go there,
They have to take you in."

                              "I should have called it
Something you somehow haven't to deserve."   120

Warren leaned out and took a step or two,
Picked up a little stick, and brought it back
And broke it in his hand and tossed it by.
"Silas has better claim on us, you think,
Than on his brother? Thirteen little miles   125
As the road winds would bring him to his door.
Silas has walked that far no doubt today.
Why didn't he go there? His brother's rich,
A somebody—director in the bank."

"He never told us that."

                "We know it though."   130

"I think his brother ought to help, of course.
I'll see to that if there is need. He ought of right
To take him in, and might be willing to—
He may be better than appearances.
But have some pity on Silas. Do you think   135
If he'd had any pride in claiming kin
Or anything he looked for from his brother,
He'd keep so still about him all this time?"

"I wonder what's between them."

                        "I can tell you.
Silas is what he is—we wouldn't mind him—   140
But just the kind that kinsfolk can't abide.
He never did a thing so very bad.
He don't know why he isn't quite as good
As anyone. Worthless though he is,
He won't be made ashamed to please his brother."   145

"I can't think Si ever hurt anyone."

"No, but he hurt my heart the way he lay
And rolled his old head on that sharp-edged chair back
He wouldn't let me put him on the lounge.
You must go in and see what you can do.   150
I made the bed up for him there tonight.
You'll be surprised at him—how much he's broken.
His working days are done; I'm sure of it."

"I'd not be in a hurry to say that."

"I haven't been. Go, look, see for yourself.   155
But, Warren, please remember how it is:
He's come to help you ditch the meadow.

He has a plan. You mustn't laugh at him.
He may not speak of it, and then he may.
I'll sit and see if that small sailing cloud   160
Will hit or miss the moon."

                    It hit the moon.
Then there were three there, making a dim row,
The moon, the little silver cloud, and she.

Warren returned—too soon, it seemed to her,
Slipped to her side, caught up her hand and waited.   165

"Warren?" she questioned.

                    "Dead," was all he answered.

A Leaf-Treader

I have been treading on leaves all day until I am autumn-tired.
God knows all the color and form of leaves I have trodden on and
    mired.
Perhaps I have put forth too much strength and been too fierce from
    fear.
I have safely trodden under foot the leaves of another year.

All summer long they were overhead more lifted up than I;   5
To come to their final place in earth they had to pass me by.
All summer long I thought I heard them threatening under their
    breath,
And when they came it seemed with a will to carry me with them to
    death.

They spoke to the fugitive in my heart as if it were leaves to leaf;
They tapped at my eyelids and touched my lips with an invitation to
    grief.   10
But it was no reason I had to go because they had to go.
Now up, my knee, to keep on top of another year of snow.

Departmental, or My Ant Jerry

An ant on the tablecloth
Ran into a dormant moth
Of many times her size.
He showed not the least surprise.
His business wasn't with such.   5
He gave it scarcely a touch,
And was off on his duty run.
Yet if he encountered one
Of the hive's enquiry squad
Whose work is to find out God   10
And the nature of time and space,
He would put him onto the case.
Ants are a curious race;
One crossing with hurried tread
The body of one of their dead   15
Isn't given a moment's arrest—
Seems not even impressed.
But he no doubt reports to any
With whom he crosses antennae,
And they no doubt report   20
To the higher up at court.
Then word goes forth in Formic:°
"Death's come to Jerry McCormic,
Our selfless forager Jerry.
Will the special Janizary°   25
Whose office it is to bury
The dead of the commissary
Go bring him home to his people.
Lay him in state on a sepal.°
Wrap him for shroud in a petal.   30
Embalm him with ichor° of nettle.°

---

22. **Formic:** here, ant language. (*Formic acid* is contained in a fluid secreted by ants.) 25. **Janizary:** a Turkish soldier. 29. **sepal:** leaf. 31. **ichor**
(ī′kôr): any thin fluid that is discharged from plants or animals. **nettle:** a
prickly plant.

This is the word of your Queen."
And presently on the scene
Appears a solemn mortician;
And taking formal position   35
With feelers calmly atwiddle,
Seizes the dead by the middle,
And heaving him high in air,
Carries him out of there.
No one stands round to stare.   40
It is nobody else's affair.

It couldn't be called ungentle.
But how thoroughly departmental.

Neither Out Far nor In Deep

The people along the sand
All turn and look one way.
They turn their back on the land.
They look at the sea all day.

As long as it takes to pass   5
A ship keeps raising its hull;
The wetter ground like glass
Reflects a standing gull.

The land may vary more;
But wherever the truth may be—   10
The water comes ashore,
And the people look at the sea.

They cannot look out far.
They cannot look in deep.
But when was that ever a bar   15
To any watch they keep?

Provide, Provide

The witch that came (the withered hag)
To wash the steps with pail and rag
Was once the beauty Abishag,°

The picture pride of Hollywood.
Too many fall from great and good   5
For you to doubt the likelihood.

Die early and avoid the fate.
Or if predestined to die late,
Make up your mind to die in state.

Make the whole stock exchange your own!   10
If need be occupy a throne,
Where nobody can call *you* crone.

Some have relied on what they knew;
Others on being simply true.
What worked for them might work for you.   15

No memory of having starred
Atones for later disregard
Or keeps the end from being hard.

Better to go down dignified
With boughten friendship at your side   20
Than none at all. Provide, provide!

3. **Abishag:** King David's beautiful young attendant in his old age. (See
I Kings 1:1–4.)

Questions

The Death of the Hired Man

1. All that we know of Silas we learn from Mary and Warren. Why does
Frost not show us Silas himself?

2. How does Warren's attitude toward Silas differ from Mary's? Why has Frost made his two characters disagree?
3. Discuss the description in lines 103–110. Why do you think Frost interrupted the dialogue with description at that particular point?

The Shorter Poems

1. In "A Leaf-Treader," how can the leaves speak to the "fugitive" in the speaker's heart? What is their "invitation to grief" (l. 10)? Analyze the fabric of the poem.
2. Of what is "Departmental" a satire? What is the effect of the form of the poem? Would the poem be complete without the last two lines? Explain your answer.
3. What does Frost imply about human nature in "Neither Out Far nor In Deep"?
4. What is the tone of "Provide, Provide"? Notice particularly the fifth stanza. What does that stanza have to do with the rest of the poem? Explain the irony of the last stanza.

CARL SANDBURG

1878–

Carl Sandburg was born in Galesburg, Illinois, and after a few years of schooling, went to work at thirteen as a helper on a milk wagon. During the next few years he worked at one time or another as a sceneshifter in a theater, as a trucker in a brickyard, as a railroad construction worker, and as a harvest hand in the wheatfields of the Middle West.

After serving in the Spanish-American war, Sandburg studied at Lombard College and then got a job as a newspaperman, meanwhile devoting most of his spare time to poetry. He published his first volume in 1904, but he remained unknown until *Poetry* magazine published a group of his poems in 1914. In 1916 *Chicago Poems* appeared and brought Sandburg both fame and notoriety. Many of the poems were criticized as coarse, ugly, unpoetic—criticisms that sounded much like the remarks made about Whitman's verse a half-century earlier. Sandburg's kinship to Whitman is apparent not only in the choice of "unpoetic" subjects, but also in Sandburg's glorifica-

tion of democracy and the common man, in his handling of free
verse, and in the optimism and tenderness that lies beneath the
surface harshness of his work.

Grass

Pile the bodies high at Austerlitz° and Waterloo.°
Shovel them under and let me work:
    I am the grass; I cover all.

And pile them high at Gettysburg,
And pile them high at Ypres° and Verdun.°   5
Shovel them under and let me work.
Two years, ten years, and passengers ask the conductor:
    What place is this?
    Where are we now?

    I am the grass.   10
    Let me work.

1. **Austerlitz, Waterloo:** battles of the Napoleonic Wars. 5. **Ypres** (ē′pr′,
but in English often wĭ′pērz) and **Verdun:** battles of World War I.

Wind Song

Long ago I learned how to sleep,
In an old apple orchard where the wind swept by counting its money
    and throwing it away,
In a wind-gaunt orchard where the limbs forked out and listened or
    never listened at all,
In a passel of trees where the branches trapped the wind into
    whistling, "Who, who are you?"
I slept with my head in an elbow on a summer afternoon and there
    I took a sleep lesson.   5
There I went away saying: I know why they sleep, I know how they
    trap the tricky winds.

Long ago I learned how to listen to the singing wind and how to
    forget and how to hear the deep whine,
Slapping and lapsing under the day blue and the night stars:
    Who, who are you?

    Who can ever forget   10
    listening to the wind go by
    counting its money
    and throwing it away?

Jazz Fantasia

Drum on your drums, batter on your banjos, sob on the long cool
    winding saxophones. Go to it, O jazzmen.

Sling your knuckles on the bottoms of the happy tin pans, let your
    trombones ooze, and go husha-husha-hush with the slippery
    sandpaper.

Moan like an autumn wind high in the lonesome treetops, moan soft
    like you wanted somebody terrible, cry like a racing car slipping
    away from a motorcycle cop, bang-bang! you jazzmen, bang
    altogether drums, traps, banjos, horns, tin cans—make two
    people fight on the top of a stairway and scratch each other's
    eyes in a clinch tumbling down the stairs.

Can the rough stuff . . . Now a Mississippi steamboat pushes up
    the night river with a hoo-hoo-hoo-oo . . . and the green lan-
    terns calling to the high soft stars . . . a red moon rides on
    the humps of the low river hills. . . . Go to it, O jazzmen.

Questions

1. Compare "Grass" and "The Shrine of Gettysburg," from *John Brown's
   Body*, by Stephen Vincent Benét (p. 83). How are the poems alike?
   How do they differ? Consider especially the use of irony.

2. What is the theme of "Wind Song"? What, for instance, is meant by "Who, who are you?" and by the wind "counting its money and throwing it away"?

3. What are some of the particularly effective sound devices in "Jazz Fantasia"?

WALLACE STEVENS

1879–1955

Wallace Stevens was born in Reading, Pennsylvania, and educated at Harvard University and New York Law School. After leaving school he practiced law in New York City until 1916, when he became associated with a Connecticut insurance company. He was named a vice-president of the company in 1934, a position he held until his death.

Although some of his poetry appeared in magazines as early as 1913, Stevens was so self-critical of his work that his first volume, *Harmonium,* did not appear until 1923. After twelve years of silence, Stevens published his second volume, *Ideas of Order.* Thereafter, he published with somewhat greater frequency. Among his other collections are *The Man with the Blue Guitar, Notes Toward a Supreme Fiction,* and his *Collected Poems,* published shortly before his death.

Much of Stevens' early poetry was ambiguous and elusive, concerned with a strange blending of fantasy and reality, and revealing a preoccupation with color and sound. His later work retained many of these characteristics, but added more human elements: an examination of order in man and society and a concern with man's bewilderment and doubt. In addition, much of his later work deals with the problems of the nature of poetry and the relationship between imagination and reality.

Bouquet of Belle Scavoir*

It is she alone that matters.
She made it. It is easy to say
The figures of speech, as why she chose
This dark, particular rose.

Everything in it is herself.   5
Yet the freshness of the leaves, the burn
Of the colors, are tinsel changes,
Out of the changes of both light and dew.

How often had he walked
Beneath summer and the sky   10
To receive her shadow° into his mind . . .
Miserable that it was not she.

The sky is too blue, the earth too wide.
The thought of her takes her away.
The form of her in something else   15
Is not enough.

The reflection of her here, and then there,
Is another shadow, another evasion,
Another denial. If she is everywhere,
She is nowhere, to him.   20

But this she has made. If it is
Another image, it is one she has made.
It is she that he wants, to look at directly,
Someone before him to see and to know.

* **Belle Scavoir** (så'vwår'): literally, pleasing knowledge (Old French).
A more colloquial rendering might be "beautiful imaginings" or "pleasant
thoughts"; the poem itself, however, acts as the most accurate explanation of
its title. 11. shadow: image.

Gallant Château*

Is it bad to have come here
And to have found the bed empty?

One might have found tragic hair,
Bitter eyes, hands hostile and cold.

There might have been a light on a book   5
Lighting a pitiless verse or two.

There might have been the immense solitude
Of the wind upon the curtains.

Pitiless verse? A few words tuned
And tuned and tuned and tuned.   10

It is good. The bed is empty,
The curtains are stiff and prim and still.

* **Gallant** (gȧ·lănt′) **Château** (shă·tō′): a *château* is a French castle or large country home; *gallant* may mean either "stately" or "amorous."

Of Modern Poetry

The poem of the mind in the act of finding
What will suffice. It has not always had
To find: the scene was set; it repeated what
Was in the script.
              Then the theater was changed
To something else. Its past was a souvenir.   5

It has to be living, to learn the speech of the place.
It has to face the men of the time and to meet
The women of the time. It has to think about war
And it has to find what will suffice. It has
To construct a new stage. It has to be on that stage   10
And, like an insatiable actor, slowly and
With meditation speak words that in the ear,

In the delicatest ear of the mind, repeat,
Exactly, that which it wants to hear, at the sound
Of which, an invisible audience listens,   15
Not to the play, but to itself, expressed
In an emotion as of two people, as of two
Emotions becoming one. The actor is
A metaphysician in the dark, twanging
An instrument, twanging a wiry string that gives   20
Sounds passing through sudden rightnesses, wholly
Containing the mind, below which it cannot descend,
Beyond which it has no will to rise.
                                        It must
Be the finding of a satisfaction, and may
Be of a man skating, a woman dancing, a woman   25
Combing. The poem of the act of the mind.

Questions

1. What is the significance of the title of "Bouquet of Belle Scavoir"?
   What is the theme? What might be the meaning of lines 19–20?
2. In "Gallant Château," why might it be "bad to have come here"? Why
   is it "good"? What is the tone of this question and answer? What does
   stanza 5 imply?
3. In "Of Modern Poetry," explain the metaphor in the first five lines.
   What is Stevens saying about older poetry? How must modern poetry
   be different? Why? What does Stevens mean by "what will suffice"?
   What is implied about poetry in lines 18–23?

WILLIAM CARLOS WILLIAMS

1883–1963

William Carlos Williams studied medicine at the University of
Pennsylvania. After two years of internship and a year of study in
Leipzig, Germany, he settled down to practice medicine in his birth-
place, Rutherford, New Jersey.

Williams' first two volumes of verse, published in 1909 and 1913, showed the influence of the Imagist group. His later volumes showed an increasing originality and vigor, while still revealing Williams' sharing of the Imagist's preference for sharp physical description, symbolism, and relatively simple language. His free verse, closer to traditional poetic rhythm than to the verse of Whitman or Sandburg, allowed Williams to create a conversational, colloquial tone and a rhythm that seems close to everyday speech. His poetry was continually concerned with the objects and details of everyday experience; he once wrote: "No ideas but in things."

Poem

By the road to the contagious hospital,
under the surge of the blue
mottled clouds driven from the
northeast—cold wind. Beyond, the
waste of broad, muddy fields,   5
brown with dried weeds, standing and fallen

patches of standing water,
the scattering of tall trees.

All along the road the reddish,
purplish, forked, upstanding, twiggy   10
stuff of brushes and small trees
with dead, brown leaves under them
leafless vines—

Lifeless in appearance, sluggish,
dazed spring approaches—   15

They enter the new world naked,
cold, uncertain of all
save that they enter. All about them
the cold, familiar wind—

Now the grass, tomorrow   20
the stiff curl of wild-carrot leaf.

William Carlos Williams   513

One by one objects are defined—
It quickens: clarity, outline of leaf,

But now the stark dignity of
entrance—still, the profound change   25
has come upon them; rooted, they
grip down and begin to awaken.

Questions

1. What time of year is being described?
2. Although the imagery is that of birth and growth in nature, what is this poem really about? Note particularly line 1 and lines 16–19.

EZRA POUND

1885–

Pound was born in Idaho and educated at the University of Pennsylvania and at Hamilton College in New York. He had entered college at fifteen; by the time he was twenty he had returned to the University of Pennsylvania as an instructor. He later taught for a few months at Wabash College in Indiana, and then left the country to live in England, France, and Italy. During World War II, Pound, who was living in Italy at the time, became an active supporter of Facism. At the end of the war, he was returned to America and charged with treason. He was never brought to trial: after examination by four psychiatrists he was declared insane and committed to a mental hospital. Years later he was released and returned to Italy.

Regardless of our judgment of Pound as a human being, it is impossible to deny his importance to modern poetry. He was one of the founders of the Imagist movement, he helped introduce many fine poets to the public, and he was a constant and highly skilled experimenter in new verse forms and rhythms. His work has had a great deal of influence on many poets, including such figures as Yeats, Eliot, William Carlos Williams, Hart Crane, and Archibald MacLeish.

Salutation

O Generation of the thoroughly smug
    and thoroughly uncomfortable,
I have seen fishermen picnicking in the sun,
I have seen them with untidy families,
I have seen their smiles full of teeth
    and heard ungainly laughter.
And I am happier than you are,   5
And they were happier than I am;
And the fish swim in the lake
    and do not even own clothing.

The River-Merchant's Wife: a Letter

(After Rihaku *)

While my hair was still cut straight across my forehead
I played about the front gate, pulling flowers.
You came by on bamboo stilts, playing horse,
You walked about my seat, playing with blue plums.
And we went on living in the village of Chokan: 5
Two small people, without dislike or suspicion.

At fourteen I married My Lord you.
I never laughed, being bashful.
Lowering my head, I looked at the wall.
Called to, a thousand times, I never looked back.   10

At fifteen I stopped scowling,
I desired my dust to be mingled with yours
Forever and forever and forever.
Why should I climb the lookout?

At sixteen you departed,   15
You went into far Ku-to-yen, by the river of swirling eddies,

* *After Rihaku:* see page 71.

Ezra Pound   515

And you have been gone five months.
The monkeys make sorrowful noise overhead.
You dragged your feet when you went out.
By the gate now, the moss is grown, the different mosses, 20
Too deep to clear them away!
The leaves fall early this autumn, in wind.
The paired butterflies are already yellow with August
Over the grass in the West garden;
They hurt me. I grow older. 25
If you are coming down through the narrows of the river Kiang,
Please let me know beforehand,
And I will come out to meet you
    As far as Cho-fu-sa.

Questions

1. In "Salutation" why is the speaker happier than the "generation of the thoroughly smug"? Why are the fishermen happier than he? What about the fish?
2. Restraint and understatement are often more moving than emotional statement. Why is "The River-Merchant's Wife: a Letter" an example of the poetry of understatement? What are some of the details which help to create the emotion? What *is* the emotion?

ROBINSON JEFFERS

1887–1962

Robinson Jeffers was born in Pittsburgh and received much of his early education in Europe. When he was fifteen his family moved to California. During the next few years he studied at a number of institutions, including the University of Southern California and Washington University. His first volumes of poetry were ignored, but the publication in 1925 of *Tamar and Other Poems* brought him his first recognition. His other works include *Cawdor* (1928) and *Selected Poetry* (1938).

In his characteristic work Jeffers was the most darkly pessimistic of modern poets. His poetry is often bitter and brutal in tone. But despite the pessimism of his ideas, the style of his verse is colorful and vigorous, full of elemental and explosive power.

Love the Wild Swan

"I hate my verses, every line, every word,
Oh pale and brittle pencils ever to try
One grass blade's curve, or the throat of one bird
That clings to twig, ruffled against white sky.
Oh cracked and twilight mirrors ever to catch   5
One color, one glinting flash, of the splendor of things.
Unlucky hunter, Oh bullets of wax,
The lion beauty, the wild-swan wings, the storm of the wings."
—This wild swan of a world is no hunter's game.
Better bullets than yours would miss the white breast,   10
Better mirrors than yours would crack in the flame.
Does it matter whether you hate your . . . self? At least
Love your eyes that can see, your mind that can
Hear the music, the thunder of the wings. Love the wild swan.

Questions

1. What is the "wild swan"? Why should it be loved? Who is the hunter?
2. What is the form of this poem? In what ways does it vary from more traditional treatments of this particular form?

MARIANNE MOORE

1887–

After her graduation from Bryn Mawr College in 1909, Miss Moore taught for four years at the United States Indian School at Carlisle, Pennsylvania, and later was an assistant in a branch of the New York Public Library. From 1925 until the magazine ceased publication in 1929, she was editor of *The Dial,* the outstanding literary review of its day.

Miss Moore is a highly original, and sometimes difficult, poet. Her best work is witty, ironic, and intellectual rather than emotional. At first glance, her poems may seem to lack musical qualities, but a subtle rhythm will often appear after further reading. "Poetry" is perhaps her best-known poem.

Poetry

I, too, dislike it: there are things that are important beyond all this
      fiddle.
  Reading it, however, with a perfect contempt for it, one
      discovers in
  it, after all, a place for the genuine.
    Hands that can grasp, eyes
    that can dilate, hair that can rise   5
      if it must, these things are important not because a

high-sounding interpretation can be put upon them but because they
      are
  useful. When they become so derivative as to become
      unintelligible,
  the same thing may be said for all of us, that we
    do not admire what   10
    we cannot understand: the bat
      holding on upside down or in quest of something to

eat, elephants pushing, a wild horse taking a roll, a tireless wolf under
  a tree, the immovable critic twitching his skin like a horse that
      feels a flea, the base-
ball fan, the statistician—   15
    nor is it valid
      to discriminate against 'business documents and

school books'; all these phenomena are important. One must make a
    distinction

however; when dragged into prominence by half poets, the result
    is not poetry,
nor till the poets among us can be   20
   'literalists of
    the imagination'—above
      insolence and triviality and can present

for inspection, imaginary gardens with real toads in them, shall we
    have
it. In the meantime, if you demand on the one hand,   25
the raw material of poetry in
   all its rawness and
    that which is on the other hand
      genuine, then you are interested in poetry.

Questions

1. Compare this statement about the nature of poetry to that in "Of
Modern Poetry" (p. 511). How is "a place for the genuine" related
to "what will suffice"? What are "imaginary gardens with real toads in
them"? Is this metaphor similar to Wallace Stevens' stage imagery?
2. Note the curious form of this poem. Does it seem appropriate or
merely mechanical? Consider also the language of the poem. In many
ways, it seems to be deliberately flat, commonplace, "unpoetic" (see
ll. 25–29). What is the effect of the language?

JOHN CROWE RANSOM

1888–

Born in Tennessee, John Crowe Ransom was educated at Vanderbilt University and at Oxford as a Rhodes scholar. He returned to
this country after completing his work at Oxford, and taught at
Vanderbilt from 1914 to 1937. He then transferred to Kenyon College in Ohio, where he founded the *Kenyon Review,* one of the finest
literary magazines of recent years.

Ransom's poetry often hides surprising emotion beneath a witty, mocking exterior. His work can shift quickly from whimsy to irony and then to sentiment, and still retain its distinctive tone. Though he has never gained a wide public following, Ransom holds a respected place among modern poets. He is also known as a fine critic.

Piazza* Piece

—I am a gentleman in a dustcoat trying
To make you hear. Your ears are soft and small
And listen to an old man not at all;
They want the young men's whispering and sighing.
But see the roses on your trellis dying   5
And hear the spectral singing of the moon—
For I must have my lovely lady soon.
I am a gentleman in a dustcoat trying.

—I am a lady young in beauty waiting
Until my truelove comes, and then we kiss.   10
But what gray man among the vines is this
Whose words are dry and faint as in a dream?
Back from my trellis, sir, before I scream!
I am a lady young in beauty waiting.

* Piazza (pĭ-ăz'à): here, a veranda, a porch.

Janet Waking

Beautifully Janet slept
Till it was deeply morning. She woke then
And thought about her dainty-feathered hen,
To see how it had kept.

One kiss she gave her mother,   5
Only a small one gave she to her daddy
Who would have kissed each curl of his shining baby;
No kiss at all for her brother.

"Old Chucky, Old Chucky!" she cried,
Running on little pink feet upon the grass   10
To Chucky's house, and listening. But alas,
Her Chucky had died.

It was a transmogrifying° bee
Came droning down on Chucky's old bald head
And sat and put the poison. It scarcely bled,   15
But how exceedingly

And purply did the knot
Swell with the venom and communicate
Its rigor! Now the poor comb stood up straight
But Chucky did not.   20

So there was Janet
Kneeling on the wet grass, crying her brown hen
(Translated far beyond the daughters of men)
To rise and walk upon it.

And weeping fast as she had breath   25
Janet implored us, "Wake her from her sleep!"
And would not be instructed in how deep
Was the forgetful kingdom of death.

13. **transmogrifying** (trăns·mŏg′rĭ·fī·ĭng): causing change or transformation, especially with an absurd or grotesque result.

Questions

1. What is the theme of "Piazza Piece"? Who is the gentleman? Why is he wearing a dustcoat? (See the passage from *Macbeth*, p. 69.) What is the significance of lines 5 and 6?
2. What is the tone of "Janet Waking"? Is it consistent throughout or are there sudden shifts in tone? If there are shifts, what are their effects?
3. Discuss in detail the various kinds of irony used in "Janet Waking." Note lines 13–14 and 19–20, among others. Is this a serious poem? Why, or why not?

CONRAD AIKEN

1889–

Conrad Aiken was born in Savannah, Georgia and educated at
Harvard. After graduation he traveled for a few years and then
settled in Massachusetts to devote all of his time to literature. For
much of his life he lived alternately in England and America, finally
settling permanently in this country.

Aiken's poetry is full of subtle overtones and implications—at its
best, it is also intensely lyrical. In addition to his poetry, Aiken has
written a number of short stories and novels.

Music I Heard

Music I heard with you was more than music,
And bread I broke with you was more than bread;
Now that I am without you, all is desolate;
All that was once so beautiful is dead.

Your hands once touched this table and this silver,   5
And I have seen your fingers hold this glass.
These things do not remember you, beloved,
And yet your touch upon them will not pass.

For it was in my heart you moved among them,
And blessed them with your hands and with your eyes;   10
And in my heart they will remember always—
They knew you once, O beautiful and wise.

Questions

The theme of this poem is a common one. What is it? How has Aiken
interpreted the theme freshly?

EDNA ST. VINCENT MILLAY

1892–1950

During her lifetime Miss Millay was one of the most popular of modern American poets. She published her first volume of poetry, *Renascence,* in 1917, the year of her graduation from Vassar College. The title poem, however, had been written a number of years earlier, when Miss Millay was barely nineteen. It is still probably her most popular poem.

Lacking the complexity and obscurity of many modern poets, Miss Millay's poetry reveals many ties to the nineteenth-century romantic tradition, with occasional overtones of Elizabethan diction. She wrote a great many sonnets, some of which are among the finest written in our century.

Wild Swans

I looked in my heart while the wild swans went over;
   And what did I see I had not seen before?
   Only a question less or a question more;
Nothing to match the flight of wild birds flying.
Tiresome heart, forever living and dying!   5
   House without air! I leave you and lock your door!
Wild swans, come over the town, come over
The town again, trailing your legs and crying!

I Shall Go Back

I shall go back again to the bleak shore
And build a little shanty on the sand
In such a way that the extremest band
Of brittle seaweed will escape my door
But by a yard or two, and nevermore   5
Shall I return to take you by the hand;

I shall be gone to what I understand
And happier than I ever was before.

The love that stood a moment in your eyes,
The words that lay a moment on your tongue,   10
Are one with all that in a moment dies,
A little undersaid and oversung;
But I shall find the sullen rocks and skies
Unchanged from what they were when I was young.

Questions

1. In line 3 of "Wild Swans," what is meant by "a question less or a question more"?
2. In "I Shall Go Back," what is the speaker returning to? Why? What contrast between nature and man is implied in these two poems?

ARCHIBALD MacLEISH

1892–

Archibald MacLeish was born in Illinois and educated at Yale and at Harvard Law School. After teaching briefly at Harvard, he practiced law in Boston for three years, and then turned to poetry. Even as a poet, however, he remained active in public life. From 1939 to 1944 he was Librarian of Congress, and from 1944 to 1945 Assistant Secretary of State. In 1949 he became Boylston Professor of Rhetoric and Oratory at Harvard, an appointment he held until 1962.

MacLeish's early work was strongly influenced by Pound, Eliot, and a number of French symbolist poets. His later poetry is increasingly original. One of his most ambitious works is *Conquistador*, a long poem on the Spanish conquest of Mexico. His other works include two verse plays: *The Fall of the City*, presented first on radio in 1937 and revived for television in 1962; and *J.B.*, a modern interpretation of the story of Job, which appeared successfully on Broadway in 1958–59.

Ars Poetica*

A poem should be palpable and mute
As a globed fruit

Dumb
As old medallions to the thumb

Silent as the sleeve-worn stone   5
Of casement ledges where the moss has grown—

A poem should be wordless
As the flight of birds

➤

A poem should be motionless in time
As the moon climbs   10

Leaving, as the moon releases
Twig by twig the night-entangled trees,

Leaving, as the moon behind the winter leaves,
Memory by memory the mind—

A poem should be motionless in time   15
As the moon climbs

➤

A poem should be equal to:
Not true

For all the history of grief
An empty doorway and a maple leaf   20

For love
The leaning grasses and two lights above the sea—

A poem should not mean
But be.

* **Ars Poetica**: The art of poetry (Latin).

Questions

1. Through a series of similes and metaphors "Ars Poetica" attempts to describe the nature of poetry. Try to explain as many of the similes and metaphors as you can. For instance, how can a poem be "dumb," "silent," and "wordless"? Explain the effectiveness of lines 9–14.
2. How can a poem be "equal to" but "not true"? What are some of the implications of the last two lines?

E. E. CUMMINGS

1894–1962

E. E. (Edward Estlin) Cummings was born in Cambridge, Massachusetts, and educated at Harvard, where his father taught English literature. In 1917 Cummings served as an ambulance driver in France, later becoming a private in the American army. After the war, he went to Paris, where he won recognition as a poet and a painter. Later he settled in New York City.

Cummings' poetry bewilders many readers, mainly through its unconventional appearance on the page. But his themes are generally not complex, and the spirit of his poetry is intensely lyrical. Whether he was writing bitter satire or a childlike lyric, Cummings was always witty and often surprisingly tender.

Sonnet

a wind has blown the rain away and blown
the sky away and all the leaves away,
and the trees stand. I think i too have known
autumn too long

           (and what have you to say,
wind wind wind—did you love somebody   5
And have you the petal of somewhere in your heart
pinched from dumb summer?

O crazy daddy
of death dance cruelly for us and start
the last leaf whirling in the final brain
of air!) Let us as we have seen see   10
doom's integration . . . a wind has blown the rain

away and the leaves and the sky and the
trees stand:
              the trees stand. The trees,
suddenly wait against the moon's face.

in Just-

        in Just-
        spring   when the world is mud-
        luscious the little
        lame balloonman

        whistles   far   and wee   5

        and eddieandbill come
        running from marbles and
        piracies and it's
        spring

        when the world is puddle-wonderful   10

        the queer
        old balloonman whistles
        far   and   wee
        and bettyandisbel come dancing

        from hop-scotch and jump-rope and   15

        it's
        spring
        and
            the

> balloonMan   whistles
> far
> and
> wee

20. **goat-footed:** in Greek mythology one of the symbols of spring was Pan, a creature with the upper body of a man and the legs and feet of a goat.

Questions

1. In "Sonnet" what might the trees symbolize? What is the tone of this poem?
2. Through whose eyes are we looking in "in Just-"? How can we tell? Can you justify the curious arrangement of the poem's lines? Is it appropriate to the theme? The speaker?

HAROLD LEWIS COOK

1897–

Harold Lewis Cook was educated at Union College in New York and at Cambridge. After completing his education he taught for a number of years at private schools and colleges in France and the United States. He was also active in industry as a management consultant. In recent years he has taught creative writing at the Instituto Allende in Mexico.

Cook's poetry is generally traditional in form. Within the older patterns, however, his strange, foreboding images raise many of the issues that concern modern man.

Warning

> You walk the hills, blind in your dreaming.
>   You pace the valleys, and hear no sound.
> A flower falls, a star falls,
>   But neither, falling, can astound

The hard, man-ridden mind that never—   5
    Save to the ways of man—will thrill.
No mountain frightens you, no ocean,
    And no rain-rotten daffodil.

The snake of silence soon will coil
    Around your narrow pulsing wrist,   10
His head lie pillowed in the palm
    Of that same hand your lover kissed.

You are the bread Time feeds upon,
    You are the sweet that tickles Death;
Between the bread and sweet there lies   15
    Only the little space of breath.

Your proud hair twisted in a root,
    You will, perhaps, remember Earth;
Your nail will learn the feel of stone,
    Your heel will measure a worm's girth.   20

Questions

To whom is the "warning" directed? Why? What exactly is the warning? What is the effect of the metaphors in Stanzas 3 and 4—the
"snake," the "bread," and the "sweet"? What about the images in the
last two lines?

HART CRANE

1899–1932

In his short life Hart Crane published only two volumes: *White
Buildings* in 1926 and *The Bridge* in 1930. He showed perhaps
greater promise than any other young poet of his time, but his life
was marked by emotional instability, and he never achieved the personal discipline that might have made him a great poet. In 1932,
during a voyage in the Caribbean, he committed suicide by leaping
from his ship.

The Bridge, Crane's most ambitious work, is an attempt at a modern epic. In its best passages the poem has energy and grandeur, but in many places it becomes obscure and disorganized. Crane's shorter poetry is generally clearer and more effective. Of the following poems, "At Melville's Tomb" is from *White Buildings;* "Fear" and "Postscript" are from the posthumous *Collected Poems* (1933).

Fear

The host, he says that all is well
And the firewood glow is bright;
The food has a warm and tempting smell—
But on the window licks the night.

Pile on the logs. . . . Give me your hands,   5
Friends! No—it is not fright. . . .
But hold me . . . somewhere I heard demands. . . .
And on the window licks the night.

Postscript

Though now but marble are the marble urns,
Though fountains droop in waning light, and pain
Glitters on the edges of wet ferns,
I should not dare to let you in again.

Mine is a world foregone though not yet ended—   5
An imagined garden gray with sundered boughs
And broken branches, wistful and unmended,
And mist that is more constant than your vows.

At Melville's Tomb

This is a difficult poem which can perhaps be understood only in a somewhat general way. It is included here as an example of Crane's later work.

Often beneath the wave, wide from this ledge
The dice of drowned men's bones he saw bequeath
An embassy. Their numbers as he watched,
Beat on the dusty shore and were obscured.

And wrecks passed without sound of bells,   5
The calyx° of death's bounty giving back
A scattered chapter, livid hieroglyph,°
The portent wound in corridors of shells.

Then in the circuit calm of one vast coil,
Its lashings charmed and malice reconciled,   10
Frosted eyes there were that lifted altars;
And silent answers crept across the stars.

Compass, quadrant and sextant contrive°
No farther tides . . . High in the azure steeps
Monody° shall not wake the mariner.   15
This fabulous shadow only the sea keeps.

6. calyx: the leafy part of a flower.   7. hieroglyph (hī′ĕr·ŏ·glĭf′): a character or symbol in ancient picture-writing.   13. contrive: here, probably, chart
or measure.   15. Monody: a dirge or lament sung by a single voice.

Questions

1. Of what is the night a symbol in "Fear"? What might the "demands"
   be in line 7?
2. What is the underlying metaphor of "Postscript"? What is the meaning
   of the image in lines 2 and 3: ". . . pain / Glitters on the edges of
   wet ferns"?
3. In "At Melville's Tomb," what might the last line mean? Try to work
   out some of the complex images in the poem.

KENNETH FEARING

1902–1961

Kenneth Fearing was born in Chicago and educated at the University of Wisconsin. After graduation he worked as a salesman, millhand, and newspaper reporter. His first volume of poetry, *Angel Arms*, appeared in 1929. His other collections of poetry include *Afternoon of a Pawnbroker* (1944) and *Stranger at Coney Island* (1948).

Fearing's fast-moving and exciting poems deal with a wide range of characters: from spies and gangsters to clubwomen and executives. His best work combines satire with an ominous vision of a feverish, high-powered civilization.

Confession Overheard in a Subway

You will ask how I came to be eavesdropping, in the first place.
The answer is, I was not.
The man who confessed to these several crimes (call him John
    Doe) spoke into my right ear on a crowded subway train, while
    the man whom he addressed (call him Richard Roe) stood at
    my left.
Thus, I stood between them, and they talked, or sometimes shouted,
    quite literally straight through me.
How could I help but overhear?   5
Perhaps I might have moved away to some other strap. But the aisles
    were full.
Besides, I felt, for some reason, curious.

"I do not deny my guilt," said John Doe. "My own, first, and after
    that my guilty knowledge of still further guilt.
I have counterfeited often, and successfully.
I have been guilty of ignorance, and talking with conviction. Of in-
    tolerable wisdom, and keeping silent.   10
Through carelessness, or cowardice, I have shortened the lives of
    better men. And the name for that is murder.
All my life I have been a receiver of stolen goods."

"Personally, I always mind my own business," said Richard Roe. "Sensible people don't get into those scrapes."

I was not the only one who overheard this confession.
Several businessmen, bound for home, and housewives and mechanics, were within easy earshot.   15
A policeman sitting in front of us did not lift his eyes, at the mention of murder, from his paper.
Why should I be the one to report these crimes?
You will understand why this letter to your paper is anonymous. I will sign it: Public Spirited Citizen, and hope that it cannot be traced.
But all the evidence, if there is any clamor for it, can be substantiated.
I have heard the same confession many times since, in different places.   20
And now that I think of it, I had heard it many times before.

"Guilt," said John, "is always and everywhere nothing less than guilt.
I have always, at all times, been a willing accomplice of the crass and the crude.
I have overheard, daily, the smallest details of conspiracies against the human race, vast in their ultimate scope, and conspired, daily, to launch my own.
You have heard of innocent men who died in the chair. It was my greed that threw the switch.   25
I helped, and I do not deny it, to nail that guy to the cross, and shall continue to help.
Look into my eyes, you can see the guilt.
Look at my face, my hair, my very clothing, you will see guilt written plainly everywhere.
Guilt of the flesh. Of the soul. Of laughing, when others do not. Of breathing and eating and sleeping.
I am guilty of what? Of guilt. Guilty of guilt, that is all, and enough."

Richard Roe looked at his wristwatch and said: "We'll be twenty minutes late.   31
After dinner we might take in a show."

Now, who will bring John Doe to justice for his measureless crimes?
I do not, personally, wish to be involved.
Such nakedness of the soul belongs in some other province, probably
    the executioner's.   35
And who will bring the blunt and upright Richard Roe to the ac-
    cuser's stand, where he belongs?
Or will he deny and deny his partnership?

I have done my duty, as a public spirited citizen, in any case.

Questions

The theme of this poem is guilt. The question is, Who is guilty of
what? John Doe says that he is "guilty of guilt." What about the other
two characters—Richard Roe, to whom the confession is addressed, and
the speaker, who is writing the poem as an anonymous letter to a newspaper? What are some of the implications of the poem? Discuss each
of the men. Who, for instance, seems the wisest of the three? The
guiltiest? The least guilty?

THEODORE SPENCER

1902–1949

A distinguished poet, critic, and teacher, Theodore Spencer was a
graduate of Princeton, Harvard, and Cambridge. He was a scholar
in Elizabethan literature and in the modern novel and drama. The
outbreak of World War II prevented him from assuming the position of permanent lecturer in English literature at Cambridge. After
the war he became Boylston Professor of Rhetoric and Oratory at
Harvard, but died less than three years after taking the post. The
first Theodore Spencer Memorial Lecture at Harvard was delivered
by T. S. Eliot.

Spencer's typical verse is melodic, lyrical, and generally whimsical on the surface. But beneath the surface often lies biting satire, all
the more biting because of its wit.

The Circus; or One View of It

Said the circus man, Oh what do you like
Best of all about my show—
The circular rings, three rings in a row,
With animals going around, around,
Tamed to go running round, around,   5
And around, round, around they go;
Or perhaps you like the merry-go-round,
Horses plunging sedately up,
Horses sedately plunging down,
Going around the merry-go-round;   10
Or perhaps you like the clown with a hoop,
Shouting, rolling the hoop around;
Or the elephants walking around in a ring
Each trunk looped to a tail's loop,
Loosely ambling around the ring;   15
How do you like this part of the show?
Everything's busy and on the go;
The peanut men cry out and sing,
The round fat clown rolls on the ground,
The trapeze ladies sway and swing,   20
The circus horses plunge around
The circular rings, three rings in a row;
Here they come, and here they go.
And here you sit, said the circus man,
Around in a circle to watch my show;   25
Which is show and which is you,
Now that we're here in this circus show,
Do I know? Do you know?
But hooray for the clowns and the merry-go-round,
The painted horses plunging round,   30
The live, proud horses stamping the ground,
And the clowns and the elephants swinging around;
Come to my show; hooray for the show,
Hooray for the circus all the way round!
Said the round exuberant circus man.   35
Hooray for the show! said the circus man.

Theodore Spencer   535

Questions

1. What is the tone of this poem? Is there a shift in tone anywhere in it?
2. Of what might the circus be a symbol? What is Spencer satirizing? What is the significance of lines 26–28? What is the effect of the many repetitions of certain key words? (See ll. 4–6, for instance.)

RICHARD EBERHART

1904–

Richard Eberhart was born in Minnesota and educated at the University of Minnesota, at Dartmouth College, at Harvard, and at Cambridge. During World War II he served in the Navy, rising to the rank of Lieutenant Commander. After the war he returned to enter business and eventually became vice-president of an industrial firm. In recent years he has lectured and taught at a number of universities.

Because of the simplicity and directness of his language and the homeliness of his imagery, Eberhart has often been compared to Robert Frost. His best work, however, is unquestionably individual.

If I Could Only Live at the Pitch
That Is Near Madness

If I could only live at the pitch that is near madness
When everything is as it was in my childhood
Violent, vivid, and of infinite possibility:
That the sun and the moon broke over my head.

Then I cast time out of the trees and fields,   5
Then I stood immaculate in the Ego;
Then I eyed the world with all delight,
Reality was the perfection of my sight.

And time had big handles on the hands,
Fields and trees a way of being themselves.   10
I saw battalions of the race of mankind
Standing stolid, demanding a moral answer.

I gave the moral answer and I died
And into a realm of complexity came
Where nothing is possible but necessity   15
And the truth wailing there like a red babe.

Questions

What basic contrasts are implied by this poem? Consider especially
lines 1–3 and 14–15. What might the "moral answer" be? What happens when it is given?

W. H. AUDEN

1907–

W. H. (Wystan Hugh) Auden was born in York, England, and educated at Oxford. After graduation he spent five years as a teacher in
a boys' school. In 1939 he came to the United States to lecture, and
he has lived in this country almost continuously since then. In 1946
he became an American citizen.

While still an undergraduate at Oxford, Auden became associated
with a group of young poets whose work was experimental in technique and distinguished by its note of protest against the social and
political conditions of the day. Stephen Spender, C. Day Lewis, and
Louis MacNeice were among the members of the group.

Auden's first volume, *Poems* (1930), was difficult and sometimes
hopelessly obscure. Echoes of Hopkins and Eliot were often apparent. But in a short time Auden had found his own style. Difficulties
still remained in his work, but they grew out of his dealing with difficult ideas. The language was clearer and more restrained; the imagery was no longer borrowed from other poets but was original and

effective. His works include *On This Island* (1937), *For the Time Being* (1944), and *The Age of Anxiety* (1947). Today, he is recognized as a major poet. His influence on many younger writers has been strong.

The Unknown Citizen

(To JS/07/M/378 This Marble Monument Is Erected by the State)

He was found by the Bureau of Statistics to be
One against whom there was no official complaint,
And all the reports on his conduct agree
That, in the modern sense of an old-fashioned word, he was a saint,
For in everything he did he served the Greater Community.   5
Except for the War till the day he retired
He worked in a factory and never got fired,
But satisfied his employers, Fudge Motors Inc.
Yet he wasn't a scab° or odd in his views,
For his Union reports that he paid his dues,   10
(Our report on his Union shows it was sound)
And our Social Psychology workers found
That he was popular with his mates and liked a drink.
The Press are convinced that he bought a paper every day
And that his reactions to advertisements were normal in every way.
Policies taken out in his name prove that he was fully insured,   16
And his Health card shows he was once in hospital but left it cured.
Both Producers Research and High-Grade Living declare
He was fully sensible to the advantages of the Installment Plan
And had everything necessary to the Modern Man,   20
A phonograph, a radio, a car, and a frigidaire.
Our researchers into Public Opinion are content
That he held the proper opinions for the time of year;
When there was peace, he was for peace; when there was war, he
    went.
He was married and added five children to the population,   25

9. **scab:** a nonunion worker hired to take the place of a striker.

Which our Eugenist° says was the right number for a parent of his
   generation,
And our teachers report that he never interfered with their educa-
   tion.
Was he free? Was he happy? The question is absurd:
Had anything been wrong, we should certainly have heard.

26. **Eugenist** (ū′jė·nĭst): one who studies human heredity and tries to im-
prove offspring.

Musée des Beaux Arts*

About suffering they were never wrong,
The Old Masters: how well they understood
Its human position; how it takes place
While someone else is eating or opening a window or just walking
   dully along;
How, when the aged are reverently, passionately waiting   5
For the miraculous birth, there always must be
Children who did not specially want it to happen, skating
On a pond at the edge of the wood:
They never forgot
That even the dreadful martyrdom must run its course   10
Anyhow in a corner, some untidy spot
Where the dogs go on with their doggy life and the torturer's horse
Scratches its innocent behind on a tree.

In Brueghel's *Icarus*,° for instance: how everything turns away
Quite leisurely from the disaster; the plowman may   15
Have heard the splash, the forsaken cry,
But for him it was not an important failure; the sun shone
As it had to on the white legs disappearing into the green

* **Musée des Beaux Arts** (mū′zā′ dĕ bō′zàr′): Museum of Fine Arts
(French). 14. **Breughel's** *Icarus:* a painting entitled *The Fall of Icarus* by
the sixteenth-century Flemish painter, Pieter Breughel (brŭ′gĕl). In Greek
myth, Icarus flew with wings made by his father, Dedalus. The wings were
fastened to his body with wax, and when the boy flew too near the sun the wax
melted, the wings dropped off, and he fell into the sea.

W. H. Auden   539

Water; and the expensive delicate ship that must have seen
Something amazing, a boy falling out of the sky,   20
Had somewhere to get to and sailed calmly on.

In Memory of W. B. Yeats

(d. Jan. 1939)

I

He disappeared in the dead of winter:
The brooks were frozen, the airports almost deserted,
And snow disfigured the public statues;
The mercury sank in the mouth of the dying day.
O all the instruments agree   5
The day of his death was a dark cold day.

Far from his illness
The wolves ran on through the evergreen forests,
The peasant river was untempted by the fashionable quays;°
By mourning tongues   10
The death of the poet was kept from his poems.

But for him it was his last afternoon as himself,
An afternoon of nurses and rumors;
The provinces of his body revolted,
The squares of his mind were empty,   15
Silence invaded the suburbs,
The current of his feeling failed: he became his admirers.°

Now he is scattered among a hundred cities
And wholly given over to unfamiliar affections;
To find his happiness in another kind of wood   20
And be punished under a foreign code of conscience.
The words of a dead man
Are modified in the guts of the living.

9. **quays** (kēz): landings, wharves. 17. **he . . . admirers:** dead, he lives
on only in his poems, and in the admirers of those poems.

But in the importance and noise of tomorrow
When the brokers are roaring like beasts on the floor of the Bourse,°
And the poor have the sufferings to which they are fairly accus-
      tomed,   26
And each in the cell of himself is almost convinced of his freedom;
A few thousand will think of this day
As one thinks of a day when one did something slightly unusual.

                O all the instruments agree   30
                The day of his death was a dark cold day.

                        II

You were silly like us: your gift survived it all;
The parish of rich women, physical decay,
Yourself: mad Ireland hurt you into poetry.
Now Ireland has her madness and her weather still,   35
For poetry makes nothing happen: it survives
In the valley of its saying where executives
Would never want to tamper; it flows south
From ranches of isolation and the busy griefs,
Raw towns that we believe and die in; it survives,   40
A way of happening, a mouth.

                        III

                Earth, receive an honored guest;
                William Yeats is laid to rest:
                Let the Irish vessel lie
                Emptied of its poetry.   45

                Time that is intolerant
                Of the brave and innocent,
                And indifferent in a week
                To a beautiful physique,

                Worships language and forgives   50
                Everyone by whom it lives;

25. **Bourse** (bŏŏrs): the Paris stock exchange.

Pardons cowardice, conceit,
Lays its honors at their feet.

Time that with this strange excuse
Pardoned Kipling and his views,   55
And will pardon Paul Claudel,
Pardons him for writing well.°

In the nightmare of the dark
All the dogs of Europe bark,
And the living nations wait,   60
Each sequestered in its hate;°

Intellectual disgrace
Stares from every human face,
And the seas of pity lie
Locked and frozen in each eye.   65

Follow, poet, follow right
To the bottom of the night,
With your unconstraining voice
Still persuade us to rejoice;

With the farming of a verse   70
Make a vineyard of the curse,°
Sing of human unsuccess
In a rapture of distress;

In the deserts of the heart
Let the healing fountain start,   75
In the prison of his days
Teach the free man how to praise.

55–57. **Pardoned . . . well:** Kipling was often criticized for his imperialistic views. Paul Claudel (1865–1955), a French poet, dramatist, and statesman, was accused of pro-fascist policies and it is said he advocated cooperation with the Germans when they occupied France. Yeats himself was somewhat antidemocratic in his political attitudes. 59–61. **All . . . hate:** the poem was written in 1940, after the war had broken out. 71. **Make . . . curse:** turn evil into good.

The Shorter Poems

1. What is the significance of the title of "The Unknown Citizen"? Why was the unknown citizen a "saint"? Why is he unknown? Discuss the tone of the poem. What details affect the tone most significantly? What is the effect of the opening "epitaph"? What is Auden satirizing in the poem?
2. What does "Musée des Beaux Arts" claim the Old Masters understood about suffering? What are some of the images which express this idea most clearly?

In Memory of W. B. Yeats

1. What has happened to Yeats' poetry after his death?
2. What is the effect of the repetition of lines 5 and 6 in lines 30 and 31? What might line 34 mean?
3. What view of poetry is expressed in lines 36–41? in lines 66–77? What can poetry do? What can't it do? Why is the poet's voice "unconstraining" (line 68)? How can it persuade us?
4. What is the relationship between the first and second sections? Between the second and third? What effects are created by the changes of form?

FREDERIC PROKOSCH

1908–

Frederic Prokosch was born in Wisconsin and educated at various schools in the United States and Europe. He is one of the most widely traveled of American poets. He studied at Yale and at Cambridge, and during World War II he worked for the United States Office of War Information in Stockholm. After the war he studied in Rome, and since then has lived and traveled in Europe and America.

Like many writers of his generation, Prokosch is concerned in his work with the intellectual and spiritual confusion of his day. His dreamlike and romantic poems picture a world in decay and their mood is one of deep gloom.

Song

When dusk caresses all our heads,
When all the curtains touch the sill,
When darkness cloaks the troubled beds
    And torches dot the hill,

When ships divide the intriguing night,   5
When lust new agonies explores,
When sailors watch the flickering light
    Along their luckless shores,

When all the impassioned lovers kiss,
When madmen count the stars anew,   10
When whales in their gigantic bliss
    Lie trembling two by two,

When drums cry out and trumpets blow,
And bombers split the town apart,
When exiles march to still their woe   15
    With bullets in the heart,

Slowly the cruel moon moves higher,
She gains her old ice-pitted throne!
And one whose beauty shone like fire
    Lies down to die alone.   20

Evening

Pears from the boughs hung golden,
The street lay still and cool,
Children with books and satchels
Came sauntering home from school;
The dusk fled softly inward   5
Across each darkening sill,
The whole sweet autumn slumbered,
The street lay cool and still:

The children moved through twilight,
The village steeple gleamed,   10
Pears from their boughs hung trembling,
And suddenly it seemed,
Shaken with such a wildness
Of terror and desire,
My heart burst into music   15
And my body into fire.

Questions

1. Of the first sixteen lines of "Song," eleven begin with *When*. What effect does this heavy repetition have on the last stanza? Why is the moon "cruel" and what do the last two lines mean?
2. Of what experience is "Evening" a description? Can you explain lines 13 and 14? Is there any thematic relationship between this poem and Eberhart's "If I Could Only Live at the Pitch That Is Near Madness" (p. 536)?

KARL SHAPIRO

1913–

Karl Shapiro was born in Baltimore and educated at the University of Virginia and at Johns Hopkins University. During World War II he served overseas; his first two volumes of poetry were published while he was stationed in the South Pacific from 1942 to 1945. In recent years he has edited magazines and taught and lectured at a number of universities.

In his poetry, Shapiro's typical tone is ironic and detached as he deals with the complex modern world.

Auto Wreck

Its quick soft silver bell beating, beating,
And down the dark one ruby flare
Pulsing out red light like an artery,

The ambulance at top speed floating down
Past beacons and illuminated clocks   5
Wings in a heavy curve, dips down,
And brakes speed, entering the crowd.
The doors leap open, emptying light;
Stretchers are laid out, the mangled lifted
And stowed into the little hospital.   10
Then the bell, breaking the hush, tolls once,
And the ambulance with its terrible cargo
Rocking, slightly rocking, moves away,
As the doors, an afterthought, are closed.

We are deranged, walking among the cops   15
Who sweep glass and are large and composed.
One is still making notes under the light.
One with a bucket douches ponds of blood
Into the street and gutter.
One hangs lanterns on the wrecks that cling,   20
Empty husks of locusts, to iron poles.

Our throats were tight as tourniquets,
Our feet were bound with splints, but now
Like convalescents intimate and gauche,
We speak through sickly smiles and warn   25
With the stubborn saw° of common sense,
The grim joke and the banal resolution.
The traffic moves around with care,
But we remain, touching a wound
That opens to our richest horror.   30

Already old, the question Who shall die?
Becomes unspoken Who is innocent?
For death in war is done by hands;
Suicide has cause and stillbirth, logic.
But this invites the occult mind,   35

26. saw: saying, proverb.

Cancels our physics with a sneer,
And spatters all we knew of dénouement°
Across the expedient and wicked stones.

37. dénouement (dā·nōō′mäN): French, literally, "untying." Used generally to mean the outcome of a plot, the solution of a complex situation.

Questions

At what point does this become something more than a descriptive poem? What issues are raised in the last stanza? Why does an ordinary auto accident raise these issues? How does the wreck "invite the occult mind" and "cancel our physics"?

PETER VIERECK

1916–

Peter Viereck was born in New York City and educated at Harvard and Oxford. After serving in Africa and Italy during World War II he returned to this country to become a teacher. His first book, published when he was twenty-five, was not a collection of poetry but a scholarly political study. His first volume of poetry, *Terror and Decorum,* published in 1948, won high praise, as did his later *Strike Through the Mask!* Viereck's work is experimental, vigorous, and exciting. Although he occasionally presents subtleties and complexities, his poetry is generally emotionally and intellectually direct.

Kilroy

During World War II, "Kilroy was here" was an expression written almost everywhere by American soldiers. No one knows how it started, but eventually the phrase came to symbolize the feeling that no place was too distant or dangerous —for "Kilroy" or for any other man who shared his spirit.

Also Ulysses° once—that other war.
　　　　(Is it because we find his scrawl
　　　　Today on every privy door
　　　　That we forget his ancient role?)
Also was there—he did it for the wages—　　　　　　　　5
When a Cathay-drunk Genoese° set sail.
Whenever "longen folk to goon on pilgrimages,"°
Kilroy is there;
　　　　　　　　　he tells The Miller's Tale.°

At times he seems a paranoic king
Who stamps his crest on walls and says "My Own!"　　10
But in the end he fades like a lost tune,
Tossed here and there, whom all the breezes sing.
"Kilroy was here"; these words sound wanly gay,
　　　　Haughty yet tired with long marching.
He is Orestes°—guilty of what crime?—　　　　　　　15
　　　　For whom the Furies° still are searching;
　　　　When they arrive, they find their prey
(Leaving his name to mock them) went away.
Sometimes he does not flee from them in time:
"Kilroy was—"
　　　　　　　　with his blood a dying man　　　　　20
　　　　Wrote half the phrase out in Bataan.°

Kilroy, beware. "HOME" is the final trap
That lurks for you in many a wily shape:
In pipe-and-slippers plus a Loyal Hound
　　　　Or fooling around, just fooling around.　　　　25
Kind to the old (their warm Penelope°)

---

　　1. Ulysses (or Odysseus): see page 349. 6. Cathay-drunk Genoese: Co-
lumbus set out to find a passage to the Orient. 7. "longen . . . pilgrimages:
a line from the "Prologue" to Chaucer's Canterbury Tales. 8. The Miller's
Tale: one of the Canterbury Tales, filled with bawdy humor. 15. Orestes: in
Greek myth, Orestes killed the murderer of his father and then became a
wanderer, pursued by the Furies (l. 16), the spirits of revenge. 21. Bataan:
a peninsula in the Philippines, captured by the Japanese after heavy fighting in
1942. 26. Penelope: the wife of Ulysses.

But fierce to boys,
            thus "home" becomes that sea,
Horribly disguised, where you were always drowned—
            (How could suburban Crete° condone
The yarns you would have V-mailed° from the sun?)—   30
And folksy fishes sip Icarian tea.

One stab of hopeless wings imprinted your
            Exultant Kilroy-signature
Upon sheer sky for all the world to stare:
            "I was there! I was there! I was there!"   ·35

God is like Kilroy. He, too, sees it all;
That's how He knows of every sparrow's fall;
That's why we prayed each time the tightropes cracked
On which our loveliest clowns contrived their act.
The G. I. Faustus° who was
                        everywhere   40
Strolled home again. "What was it like outside?"
Asked Can't, with his good neighbors Ought and But
And pale Perhaps and grave-eyed Better Not;
For "Kilroy" means: the world is very wide.
            He was there, he was there, he was there!   45

And in the suburbs Can't sat down and cried.

29. **Crete:** where Icarus flew from (see note to l. 14, p. 539). 30. **V-mailed:** V-mail was a special mail used by servicemen during the war. 40. **Faustus:** see page 184.

Questions

According to the poem, who was and is Kilroy? What does he signify? What is the effect of the many allusions in the poem—classical, medieval, and modern? What is the meaning of lines 42–43? Of the last line?

ROBERT LOWELL

1917–

Robert Lowell is the great grand-nephew of James Russell Lowell and a distant cousin of Amy Lowell. He was born in Boston and educated at Harvard, at Kenyon College (where he studied under John Crowe Ransom), and at Louisiana State University. He has lectured and taught at various colleges and at one time was Consultant in Poetry to the Library of Congress.

Lowell's poems are often as complex as any written in this century. In many respects his work is reminiscent of the metaphysical poets' or of Hart Crane's. But through the complexity and the occasional obscurity the reader can see a profoundly religious poet as well as one of the most powerful poetic talents of recent years.

The Holy Innocents

Listen, the hay-bells tinkle as the cart
Wavers on rubber tires along the tar
And cindered ice below the burlap mill
And ale-wife° run. The oxen drool and start
In wonder at the fenders of a car   5
And blunder hugely up St. Peter's hill.
These are the undefiled by woman—their
Sorrow is not the sorrow of this world:
King Herod shrieking vengeance at the curled-
Up knees of Jesus choking in the air,   10

A king of speechless clods and infants. Still
The world out-Herods Herod; and the year,
The nineteen-hundred forty-fifth of grace,
Lumbers with losses up the clinkered° hill
Of our purgation; and the oxen near   15
The worn foundations of their resting place,

4. ale-wife: herring.   14. clinkered: brick.

The holy manger where their bed is corn
And holly torn for Christmas. If they die,
As Jesus, in the harness, who will mourn?
Lamb of the shepherds, Child, how still you lie.　　　20

Questions

1. Discuss the symbolism of this poem. What do the oxen represent? Who
   is "a king of speechless clods and infants"? What might lines 19–20
   mean?
2. What does the poem imply about the modern world? What is meant
   by "the world out-Herods Herod"?

RICHARD WILBUR

1921–

Richard Wilbur was born in New York City and educated at Amherst College and Harvard. During World War II he served in Italy
and Germany. After the war he returned to Harvard for graduate
study and teaching. He has since taught at a number of colleges in
the East. He began writing verse at an early age, but it was not until
after the war that he started writing in earnest. His work has received a number of awards in recent years.

Wilbur is sometimes called one of the "New Formalists" because
of his attempt to revive the traditional patterns of rhythm and
rhyme. His poetry as a whole, however, is clearly individual and
clearly modern.

A Black November Turkey

Nine white chickens come
With haunchy walk and heads
Jabbing among the chips, the chaff, the stones
And the cornhusk-shreds,

And bit by bit infringe   5
A pond of dusty light,
Spectral in shadow until they bobbingly one
By one ignite.

Neither pale nor bright,
The turkey-cock parades   10
Through radiant squalors, darkly auspicious as
The ace of spades,

Himself his own cortège°
And puffed with the pomp of death,
Rehearsing over and over with strangled râle°   15
His latest breath.

The vast black body floats
Above the crossing knees
As a cloud over thrashed branches, a calm ship
Over choppy seas,   20

Shuddering its fan and feathers
In fine soft clashes
With the cold sound that the wind makes, fondling
Paper-ashes.

The pale-blue bony head   25
Set on its shepherd's crook°
Like a saint's death-mask, turns a vague, superb
And timeless look

Upon these clocking hens
And the cocks that one by one,   30
Dawn after mortal dawn, with vulgar joy
Acclaim the sun.

---

13. cortège (kôr·tĕzh′): funeral procession.   15. râle: an abnormal breathing sound.   26. shepherd's crook: a staff.

Questions

1. What are some of the details that make this description so vivid and real? What is the purpose of the first two stanzas?
2. Discuss the poem's irony. Consider the contrast between Stanza 4 and Stanzas 7 and 8. What is the effect of such terms as "vulgar joy" (l. 31) and the pun in line 29? How does the rather unusual structure reinforce the irony?

GLOSSARY

A

abstract. An abstract noun names a quality or an idea: *justice, love, solitude, sharpness,* etc. A concrete noun names a tangible object, something that can be visualized: *man, house, statue,* etc. An abstract statement considers an idea or a quality by itself, not as it relates to some object: "All is vanity." "When will return the glory of your prime?" Poetry frequently presents abstract ideas through concrete imagery. For example, the broken statue in "Ozymandias" (p. 8) is an image through which Shelley presents the abstract idea of the vanity of power and glory.

accent. In spoken language, an emphasis given to a word or a syllable within a word. Accented syllables are spoken at a somewhat higher pitch and with greater volume than unaccented syllables; there may be other distinguishing characteristics as well. *Stress* is often used as a synonym for *accent,* and the terms *light beat* and *heavy beat* are occasionally used to refer respectively to unaccented and accented syllables. See pages 101–07.

allegory. A literary device in which an entire series of actions are meant to symbolize other actions and imply other meanings. A typical example is the presentation of a man's life as a long and sometimes difficult journey.

alliteration. See page 108.

ambiguity. The suggestion of two or more possible meanings.

anapest. See page 102.

assonance. See page 108.

B

ballad. A narrative poem, generally simple in form and meant to be sung. The *folk ballad* is, as the name implies, of popular origin; most of the Scottish and English versions seem to have developed during the fourteenth to sixteenth centuries. The *literary ballad* is a modern imitation of the techniques of the folk ballad. See pages 21 and 149.

beat. See *accent.*

blank verse. Unrhymed iambic pentameter. See page 103.

C

cacophony. See page 108.

caesura. See page 109.

chorus. See *refrain.*

concrete. Tangible, capable of being perceived by the senses. See *abstract.*

connotation. The suggestion or implications of a word, beyond its literal meaning. See page 6.

consonance. See page 108.

couplet. Two consecutive rhyming lines.

D

dactyl. See page 102.

denotation. The literal meaning of a word. See page 6.

dimeter. See page 102.

double rhyme. See page 107.

dramatic. A term used generally to refer to the moving or emotionally exciting qualities in a work of art. More specifically, *dramatic* is used to describe a work of literature which presents characters and situations entirely through dialogue and action with no direct statement by the author. In this sense, *dramatic* is often used in contrast to *lyric* and *narrative* poetry.

dramatic monologue. A type of poem which presents the words of a particular character as he speaks to a silent listener. See page 60.

E

end-stopped. Referring to lines of poetry whose endings coincide with natural speech pauses—the opposite of *run-on* lines.

elegy. A lament for the dead. The elegy usually, but not always, expresses personal grief. See pages 273 and 358.

epic. A long narrative poem generally centering upon a representative hero who takes part in a series of significant adventures. Some of the most famous epics are the *Iliad* and the *Odyssey*, reputedly by the Greek poet Homer; the *Aeneid* by the Roman poet Virgil; *Beowulf*, an anonymous Anglo-Saxon epic; and *Paradise Lost* by John Milton.

euphony. See page 109.

F

fabric. A general term for all those aspects of a poem that have to do with sound. See pages 101–26.

feminine rhyme. See page 107.

figurative language. Language which employs figures of speech to express its meaning in the most vivid and precise way. Poetry depends almost exclusively on the use of figurative language. See pages 89–100.

figure of speech. A form of expression which is distinguished by an unusual use of language and which suggests more than it states directly. Most figures of speech are forms of comparison—metaphor, simile, personification—and the comparison is often between an abstract idea and a concrete object. Usually, but not

always, a figure of speech is also an image. See pages 89–100.

foot. The unit of measure in one system of scanning or analyzing English verse. See pages 101–07.

form. The structure of a poem, the manner in which all of its elements are organized. In ordinary usage, *form* is often spoken of as distinct from *content;* in other words, *what* a poem says is distinguished from *how* it says it. In a successful poem, however, form and content can never be separated without altering the meaning.

H

heptameter. See page 102.
hexameter. See page 102.

I

iamb. See page 102.

image. The representation in words of any sense experience. Images are commonly visual, but they may deal with the other senses as well. The creation of an image in poetry generally involves the use of figures of speech. Imagery in poetry is used to make the abstract and general become concrete, specific, and vivid. See pages 5–10 and 89–100.

imperfect rhyme. See page 108.
impersonal. See *objective.*
internal rhyme. See page 107.

irony. 1. *Verbal irony* occurs when a statement is made in which the intended meaning is the opposite of the literal meaning. *Sarcasm* is one form of verbal irony, *understatement* another. 2. *Dramatic irony* (or *irony of situation*) is common to all forms of literature. It occurs when an action produces a result opposite to what was expected. A good example of dramatic irony occurs in "Ozymandias" (p. 8), where the statue has come to symbolize the opposite of what it was intended to symbolize.

L

levels of meaning. See *shades of meaning*.

lyric. *Lyric poetry* is usually defined as poetry whose primary effect is the communication of emotion or mood. In this sense, it is often distinguished from narrative and dramatic poetry.

M

masculine rhyme. See page 107.

metaphor. See page 90.

meter. In English poetry, the systematic arrangement of accented and unaccented syllables in regular, repeated patterns. See pages 101–07.

mock epic (or mock heroic). A poem about trivial or humorous events written in the grand manner of a true epic. Two well-known examples of the type are Samuel Butler's *Hudibras* and Alexander Pope's *The Rape of the Lock*.

monometer. See page 102.

mood. The general emotional atmosphere of a poem.

moral (or moral lesson). A direct statement of the theme of a poem, made within the poem itself. Generally, the most effective poems are those that avoid any outright statement of theme and instead allow the reader to reach his own conclusions about deeper meanings, if any exist.

music. See *fabric*.

N

narrative. As the name implies, *narrative poetry* is poetry which is primarily concerned with telling a story. Most of the old folk ballads are narrative in nature, though like all narrative poems they also contain lyric and dramatic elements.

O

objective. When applied to a poem or a poet, involving as little personal feeling and interpretation as possible. Dramatic poetry is generally considered the most objective or impersonal type of poetry, lyric poetry the most personal or subjective. Clearly, however, these distinctions are matters of degree: some dramatic poetry can be subjective, some lyrics highly objective.

octameter. See page 102.

octave. The first eight lines of an Italian sonnet.

ode. The ode is a long lyric poem elevated in style and serious in theme. It is often addressed to a person, place, object, or abstract idea. In Greek poetry the ode was characterized by a particular form and meter; in English, however, there is no ode "form" as such, so this type of poem can be defined only in terms of tone and content.

onomatopoeia. See page 108.

organization. See *form*.

overtones. See *connotation*.

P

paradox. A statement that seems contradictory but contains some measure of truth or provides some insight into experience. The Bible uses paradox often: "He that findeth his life shall lose it: and he that loseth his life for my sake shall find it." (Matt. 10:39)

paraphrase. A prose statement of the general meaning of a poem. Most poetry is impossible to paraphrase with complete accuracy, since a poem's meaning is a result of form, imagery, and rhythm working together and any paraphrase must ignore these poetic elements. Paraphrase can be a useful technique, however, so long as its limitations are recognized.

pastoral poetry. In general, poetry dealing with simple characters (often shepherds and their loves) in an unspoiled country setting. The pastoral has often been used by

English poets to create a set of contrasts between a simple, "natural" life and a corrupt, "artificial" one, between what is real, valuable, and lasting and what is false, trivial, and temporary. See pages 182 and 243.

pathetic fallacy. Like personification, pathetic fallacy is the giving of human characteristics to nature or objects. More specifically, it is the device of reflecting one's own emotions in nature. A good example occurs in *Adonais*, where Shelley writes of the winds as though they felt the grief he feels: "And the wild winds flew round, sobbing in their dismay."

pentameter. See page 102.

personal. See *subjective*.

personification. See page 91.

pyrrhic. See page 105.

Q

quatrain. A four-line stanza, one of the most common forms in English poetry. Some typical rhyme schemes include: *abab, abcb, abba.* Quatrain can also refer to a group of four lines whose rhyme scheme is repeated within a larger scheme. A Shakespearean sonnet consists of three quatrains and a couplet: *abab cdcd efef gg.*

R

refrain. A line or group of lines repeated at various intervals throughout a poem. Most songs and ballads make use of a refrain.

rhetorical question. A question that implies its own answer or the answer to which is obvious to both the listener and speaker.

rhyme. The repetition in two words of the same concluding sound. The final sounds must be preceded by *different* sounds: *night-knight* is not rhyme but mere repetition, since the two words sound exactly

the same; *night-flight* is rhyme, since different sounds precede the identical concluding sounds. See pages 107–08.

rhyme scheme. The particular pattern made by the rhymes at the ends of the lines of a poem or a stanza. See page 108.

rhythm. In the English language, the more or less regular recurrence of accented syllables. All language is rhythmical to some extent: in even the most carelessly written prose, some rhythm is still present, though it is quite irregular. At the other extreme, as rhythm becomes more and more regular it approaches *meter*. Most English poetry is metrical; what is known as "free verse," however, is rhythmical but not metrical.

run-on. Referring to a line whose ending does not correspond to a natural speech pause. See *end-stopped*.

S

scansion. The analysis of a poem's metrical scheme.

secondary pauses. See page 109.

sestet. The last six lines of an Italian sonnet.

simile. See page 89.

shades of meaning. Because poetry creates its meaning in part through form, imagery, and connotation, a poem will often suggest meanings far beyond those that it states literally. Such varying shades of meaning are one of the most effective devices of poetry, for a poem gains power through its ability to suggest rather than state meanings. See pages 11–20.

soliloquy. In Elizabethan drama (and in a few modern plays), a speech that is supposed to represent the unspoken thoughts of a character. See page 193.

sonnet. A lyric poem of fourteen lines of iambic pentameter. There are two major types, classified by rhyme scheme. The *Italian* sonnet is composed of an octet rhyming *abba-abba*, followed by a sestet containing three new rhymes in any order: *cde cde* and *cd cd ee* are typical patterns. The division between the octave and sestet generally marks an abrupt change in thought or tone. The *Shakespearean* sonnet is composed of three quatrains and a couplet: *abab cdcd efef gg*. In this type, a change of thought or tone often occurs in the couplet. Most sonnets show characteristics of either the Italian or Shakespearean type, but there have been many variations of these rhyme schemes, and there have even been sixteen line sonnets (p. 381) and sonnets written in hexameters (p. 172).

spondee. See page 105.

stanza. A recurring group of lines combined according to a definite rhyme scheme or other distinguishing pattern.

stress. See *accent*.

structure. See *form*.

subjective. When applied to poetry, any work that expresses its author's own thoughts, attitudes, or emotions. All poetry is subjective to some extent, since all poetic expression involves organization, and organization in turn suggests an interpretation. See *objective*.

suggestion. See *connotation*.

symbol. See page 90.

T

tetrameter. See page 102.

tone. The attitude of the poet toward his theme or subject, as that attitude is revealed by his choice of form, words, images, rhythms, etc. See pages 72–88.

total effect. The result of all the elements of a poem working together. In a sense the total effect is also the *total meaning*, but to some readers "meaning" refers only to that part of a poem that can be paraphrased, disregarding all poetic devices. "Total effect" avoids this implication.

trimeter. See page 102.

triple rhyme. See page 107.

trochee. See page 102.

U

unaccented rhyme. See page 107.

understatement. Saying less than the situation seems to call for—a form of verbal irony. Understatement is often used as a comic device; it also can function effectively in a serious work, the poet's restraint acting in such a way as to cause a stronger emotional response in the reader.

W

weak rhyme. See page 107.

INDEX OF AUTHORS AND TITLES